Mass Media/Mass Culture

An Introduction

CULTURAL HISTORY OF THE MASS MEDIA THROUGH MEDIA PROGRESSION CYCLES

Books	Magazines	Newspapers	Motion Pictures	Radio	Television	Recorded Music		
E*							c. 2500 B.C.	Sumerian clay tablets.
E							c. 600 B.C.	Papyrus scrolls used in Egypt.
E							540 B.C.	First public library founded, in Athens.
E							1st century A.D.	Books regarded as household treasures by the elite.
E							5th century	Great Library of Alexandria, Egypt, destroyed.
E							5th–10th centuries	Books preserved in monasteries.
E							9th century	Chinese invent printing.
E							13th century	Rise of European universities.
E							1456	Gutenberg Bible printed from movable type.
E/P							16th century	Books become the first mass-produced and mass-distributed commodity.
E/P							16th century	Books help spread the ideas of the Protestant Reformation; authorities invoke censorship to control printers.
		E					17th century	Development of newspapers.
E		E					17th century	Printing comes to America.
	E	E					18th century	Development of magazines.
E	E	E					18th–19th centuries	Industrial Revolution.
E	E	E					1775–1783	American Revolution.
E	E	E					19th century	Rise of American novelists and publishing houses.
P	P	P					1833	*New York Sun* founded, first penny press.
P	P	P					1844	Samuel Morse invents telegraph.
P	P	P					1852	*Uncle Tom's Cabin* is published; sells 7 million copies, helps spark Civil War (1861–65).
P	P	P					1865–1900s	American industrial expansion; rapid growth of popular magazines.

CULTURAL HISTORY OF THE MASS MEDIA THROUGH MEDIA PROGRESSION CYCLES

Books	Magazines	Newspapers	Motion Pictures	Radio	Television	Recorded Music	Year	Event
P	P	P				E	1887	Thomas A. Edison invents the "talking machine," the phonograph.
P	P	P	E			E	1888	First motion-picture camera developed in Edison's laboratory.
P	P	P	P	E		E	1901	Guglielmo Marconi sends wireless sound across the Atlantic.
P	P	P	P	E		E	1906	Lee De Forest makes voice transmission by radio possible.
P	P	P	P	E		E	1917	U.S. enters World War I; U.S. Navy takes over broadcasting from American Marconi Co.
P	P	P	P	E		E	1920	KDKA (Pittsburgh) goes on the air for Westinghouse—first fully licensed station with continuous broadcasting.
P	P	P	P	E/P	E	P	1920s	Black music helps recording industry expand its sales; the Roaring '20s also known as the Jazz Age.
P	P	P	P	P	E	P	1930s	Radio soap operas offer escape from the Great Depression.
P	P	P	P	P	E	P	1941–45	U.S. fights in World War II.
P	P	P	P	P	E/P	P	1948	Television's breakthrough year; CBS and NBC begin offering regular news and entertainment on TV.
P	P	P	P	P	E/P	P	1951	Microwave relay system provides coast-to-coast television broadcasts.
S	P	P	S	S	P	S	1956	Television begins extensive coverage of presidential elections.
S	S	P	S	S	P	S	1960s	Computer age begins.
S	S	P	S	S	P/S	S	1970s	Commercial satellites are launched.
S	S	P	S	S	S	S	1980s	Cable television and VCRs change American viewing habits; network popularity begins to decline.
S	S	S	S	S	S	S	1980s–90s	Information age arrives.

*E—Elitist   P—Popular   S—Specialized

Mass Media/ Mass Culture

An Introduction

Stan Le Roy Wilson
College of the Desert

Random House

New York

To All My Children
(not the TV soap opera)

First Edition
987654321
Copyright © 1989 by Random House, Inc.

Library of Congress Cataloging-in-Publication Data
Wilson, Stan Le Roy.
  Mass media/mass culture.
  Bibliography: p.
  Includes index.
  1. Mass media—History.   2. Popular culture.
I. Title.
P90.W494 1988   001.51′09   88–31714
ISBN 0-394-36655-7

Manufactured in the United States of America

Cover photo and design: Marcia Salo

Chapter Opening Photo Credits
1: Baron Wolman/NFL Photos; 2: Reuters/Bettmann Newsphotos; 3: Mark Antman/The
Image Works; 4: Dion Ogust/The Image Works; 5: Arthur Glauberman/Photo Researchers;
6: Alan Carey/The Image Works; 7: Dennis Stock/Magnum Photos; 8: Bohdan Hrynewych/
Stock, Boston; 9: Joel Gordon; 10: Reuters/Bettmann Newsphotos; 11: Barbara Rios/Photo
Researchers; 12: Michael Grecco/Stock, Boston; 13: AP/Wide World Photos; 14: Mike
Mazzaschi/Stock, Boston; 15: Reuters/Bettmann Newsphotos

Preface

After 27 years of teaching journalism and mass communication at two- and four-year colleges and universities, I find that my introductory course in mass media has changed dramatically. No longer exclusively for journalism majors and others seeking careers in mass communication, it has become a general education course taken by all kinds of *consumers* of the mass media.

Students in the introductory course come into the class taking the mass media for granted. They know that their lives are surrounded by newspapers, magazines, books, records and tapes, radio, television, movies, advertising and public relations. Yet they have little understanding of how influential the media are in shaping their culture and their lives. Even the occasional cultists who enroll in the course—bikers, surf punks or whatever—have no idea that they are often not "doing their own thing" but are the products of a commercialized, mediated effort.

To explain the importance of the mass media for these students, I needed a textbook that covered the historical development and current operations of the media while focusing on their cultural impact. Unable to find what I was looking for, I ended up writing this book.

FEATURES OF THE BOOK

Mass Media/Mass Culture explains the relationship between mass media and mass culture in the first two chapters. It then examines the mass media chapter by chapter, connecting cultural issues to the history and current operations of each medium. The cultural emphasis does not come at the expense of the history of the media. Indeed, it adds to the historical perspective by showing how developments and changes in the media have played a role in altering our culture.

This book attempts to foster an awareness of how the media work, how they are changing, and how they affect us. It traces the role the mass media played during the Industrial Revolution in meeting cultural needs and suggests that they will play an even more profound role as we complete our move to the new "information age."

The discussions of the various media draw on a concept developed by media researchers John Merrill and Ralph Lowenstein. They have shown that the mass media go through three stages of evolution—elitist, popular and specialized—which they call the media progression cycle. Each media chapter examines the medium in terms of this cycle.

In this book, I also advance the theory that media industries may be more concerned with new technologies than with the content of the media. Satellite technology doesn't ensure accuracy in reporting; access to 36 channels doesn't guarantee that there is something worth watching on television. I suggest that there is a need to give equal attention to content in media if the quality of our civilization is to keep pace with technology.

If at times the tone of this book seems critical, it does not stem from an anti-media bias but rather from an effort to stimulate thinking by presenting the whole media picture—warts and all. The reader can be assured that I am not anti-media. Before becoming a student and teacher of mass communication, I spent a number of years working as a newspaper and radio journalist and as a public relations practitioner. As the son of a newspaperman, I have been associated with mass communication my entire life. I believe, however, that we can get a higher level of performance from the media if we want it and demand it.

Throughout the book I have tried to keep the discussions brief without omitting the details necessary to make the issues understandable. I have also used a conversational writing style to make the book more accessible to students. In addition, I have used many current examples and illustrations. However, this work is not intended to be the final word on mass communication. No textbook can be, because the field is changing daily. Instead, this book is designed to provide a background for classroom discussions and contemporary supplemental reading on current media issues.

ORGANIZATION OF THE BOOK

Mass Media/Mass Culture is organized into four sections: "Communication and Culture," "Development of Print Media," "Development of Electronic Media," and "Media Shapers and Cultural Effects."

Chapter 1, "Culture and Communication: Basic Concepts," defines and explains popular culture, the EPS (media progression) cycle, and the communication process. It includes discussions of such items as agenda setting, gatekeeping and information processing.

Chapter 2, "Culture and Mass Communication: How They Interact," reviews the impact of mass communication on our culture since the introduction of moveable type by Gutenberg in the fifteenth century. Rapid changes in mass culture since the Industrial Revolution are highlighted, as are modern-day cultural impacts.

Chapter 3, "Political Press Theories and Foreign Media," describes the four basic press theories in operation around the world today and provides an overview of how the mass media operate in several different countries.

Chapter 4, "Book Publishing: Past and Present," begins the chapter-by-chapter media analysis by exploring the development of books from early clay tablets to today's mass-market paperbacks and specialized publications. It focuses on the impact books have had on Western civilization, as well as on the historical evolution of censorship.

Chapter 5, "Magazines: The Specialized Medium," examines the evolution of magazine publishing and how magazines have found a niche in our culture by serving highly specialized interests. Various current trends in specialized magazines are also discussed.

Chapter 6, "Newspapers: Past, Present and Problems," first recounts the historical development of newspapers and then focuses on the tension between the need for newspapers to make money and their obligation to keep the public informed. It also discusses changing trends in newspapers and examines major news wire services.

Chapter 7, "Motion Pictures: Cultural Reflections," begins the examination of the electronic media by tracing the development of motion pictures from Edison's kinetoscope to the special-effects wizardry of George Lucas and Steven Spielberg. It shows how the movie industry changed the culture, and how the culture changed the industry.

Chapter 8, "Radio: A Wireless Wonder," describes the three very different roles radio has played in our society—a device for ship-to-shore communication, the primary home news and entertainment medium in the 1930s and 1940s, and a specialized medium of music, news and talk during the television era.

Chapter 9, "Television: From Soap to Satellites," explores the evolution and cultural impact of television on American popular culture. In particular, the chapter examines three major concerns about this pervasive medium: the excessive portrayal of violence, television's influence on children and the rise of televangelism.

Chapter 10, "Recorded Music: Powerful and Controversial," concludes the electronic media section with a discussion of the role of popular music and the controversies that have surrounded it since the jazz era of the 1920s. Readers are given a perspective on the current debate over rock lyrics as well as an insight into how culturally powerful popular music has become.

Chapter 11, "Advertising: Selling the Message," begins a discussion of how others use the mass media to influence the culture. This chapter examines various theories on advertising effectiveness and describes the many propaganda devices used to sell messages. The controversy surrounding subliminal imbedding is also examined.

Chapter 12, "Public Relations: Creating an Image," explores how public relations has evolved since the nineteenth century. Modern professional PR practices are described and contrasted with early-day press agentry.

Chapter 13, "The Selling of American Politics," looks at how the mass media are employed to sell candidates and issues. The role of political consultants and the use of vote videos, television and direct mail are examined. The chapter also discusses some of the controversies surrounding media coverage of American politics.

Chapter 14, "Changing Trends in Media Technology," provides an overview of the rapidly developing technology used in mass communications. It covers cable television, satellite communication, computers, home video equipment, videotext, teletext, fiber optics, digital sound, multichannel multipoint distribution service (MMDS), direct broadcast satellites (DBS), high-definition television (HDTV) and low-power television (LPTV). It concludes with a discussion of home information centers and telecommuting and their implications for the future.

Chapter 15, "Media Ethics: Regulations and Cultural Consequences," discusses the ethical issues facing the mass media, describes the types of regulations that control American mass media and suggests the cultural consequences if the content of the mass media fails to keep pace with the rapidly changing technologies.

RESOURCES FOR INSTRUCTORS

An Instructor's Manual has been prepared to assist instructors in their teaching. It provides sample syllabi and assignments, as well as other teaching materials. It is available for examination upon request.

ACKNOWLEDGMENTS

In writing this book, I have become indebted to many individuals. My sincere thanks go to the following people, who made valuable suggestions while reviewing all or part of the manuscript: John Bigby, Santa Rosa Junior College; Michael Cicero, Highline College; John DeMott, Memphis State University; Bob Gassaway, University of New Mexico; Earl Grow, University of Wisconsin–Milwaukee; Saundra Hybels, Lock Haven University; Robert J. Illidge, Wichita State University; Laurence Jankowski, Bowling Green State University; Joli Jensen, University of Texas–Austin; Val E. Limburg, Washington State University; Jim Martin, Scottsdale Community College; Alan Miller, University of Maine at Orono; Alston Morgan, Oral Roberts University; Ruth Ann Ragland, University of New Mexico; Regina G. Sherard, University of North Carolina; Edward J. Smith, Texas A & M University; Douglas P. Starr, Texas A & M University; Robert M. Steele, University of Maine at Orono; Karen M. Stoddard, College of Notre Dame of Maryland; Michael L. Turney, Northern Kentucky University; and James R. Wilson, California State University, Fresno.

Credit for any success this book may achieve must be shared with an outstanding team of professionals at Random House. I'd like to give special thanks to Roth Wilkofsky, who had faith in this project from its inception; Kathleen Domenig and Peter LaBella, who painstakingly guided the manuscript through its various stages and made numerous suggestions for its improvement; and Jennifer Sutherland, whose meticulous attention to detail put the polishing touches on the manuscript.

I also wish to thank my family for their patience and understanding while I worked on this project.

And lastly, special thanks must go to the many students who over the years have given me feedback and the impetus to compile this information. It is for them and those who follow that this book is written.

Contents

Preface   vii

Part 1   Culture and Communication   1

Chapter 1   Culture and Communication: Basic Concepts   3
Culture   4
The Development of Mass Media through Time: The EPS Cycle   5
The Communication Process   7
Information Processing by the Media   15
Information Processing by the Consumer   19
Summary   20

Chapter 2   Culture and Mass Communication: How They Interact   23
The Beginning of Mass Communication   24
The Protestant Reformation and Mass Communication   26
Development of the Novel   27
Industrialization   27
Mass Media in Mass Society   30
Mass Mediation of Leisure   31
Box 2.1   The Super Bowl: Exporting Popular Culture   32
Criticism of Mass Society   33
Box 2.2   Mass Culture Shapes the Mass Media   35
Commercialization of Culture   35
Cults in Popular Culture   37
Box 2.3   The Trekkies "Star Trek" through the Media   38
Summary   41

Chapter 3   Political Press Theories and Foreign Media   45
Authoritarian Theory   46
Libertarian Theory   48
The Soviet Communist Concept   50
The Social Responsibility Concept   51
Box 3.1   The Society of Professional Journalists, Sigma Delta Chi, Code of Ethics   52
The Press in Foreign Lands   54
Summary   63

Part 2   The Development of Print Media   65

Chapter 4   Book Publishing: Past and Present   67
Origins of Books   68
Early Books and the Elite   71
Stages of Book Publishing in the United States   72
Box 4.1   Facing the World or the Haps and Mishaps of Harry Vane, by Horatio
Alger, Jr.   76

Box 4.2   *Barbie: Her Life and Times* by BillyBoy   79
Box 4.3   Comic Books: International Classics   81
Box 4.4   The Diary of Anne Frank   86
Box 4.5   Keep Bookbusters Out of Our Libraries   88
Summary   89

Chapter 5   Magazines: The Specialized Medium   93

History of Magazines   96
Box 5.1   Magazines Reflect Cultural Changes   99
Decline of General-Interest Magazines   103
Types of Magazines   105
Box 5.2   Magazines of the 1980s   106
Box 5.3   The Teenzines   108
Specialization and Popular Culture   109
Summary   111

Chapter 6   Newspapers: Past, Present and Problems   115

Early Origins of Newspapers   116
The Colonial American Press (1690–1820s)   118
The Penny-Press Era (1833–1865)   123
Box 6.1   Police Office   124
The Yellow Journalism Era (1865–1900)   126
Box 6.2   Women in Journalism   129
The Twentieth Century Press   130
Box 6.3   Supermarket Journalism: Giving Us What Enquiring Minds Want to Know   132
Newspapers as Businesses   135
News Wire Services   137
Biases and Other Problems   138
Summary   140

Part 3   Development of Electronic Media   143

Chapter 7   Motion Pictures: Cultural Reflections   145

Early History   148
The Rise of Comedy   150
Box 7.1   *The Kid*, A Charlie Chaplin Classic   152
Sound Joins Motion   152
A Way of Life   155
The Giant Is Crippled   158
Youth, Sex, Violence and Special Effects   161
Current Trends   163
Box 7.2   The Business of Movies Today   164
Summary   168

Chapter 8   Radio: A Wireless Wonder   173

Harnessing Sound Waves   174
Box 8.1   Companion to "Prairie" Lovers Ends His Reign   176
Beginning of Radio as a Mass Medium   179

Development of Radio News   181
Box 8.2   Edward R. Murrow: A Tongue as Descriptive as a Paint Brush   184
Development of Radio Entertainment   184
Radio Loses Its Niche   188
Specialization Gives Radio a New Niche   189
Technology and Specialization   192
Public Radio   193
Summary   193

Chapter 9   Television: From Soaps to Satellites   197
How It Began   198
Evolution of Television Entertainment   200
Box 9.1   Requiem for a Heavyweight   202
Box 9.2   Fred Silverman: TV's Tarnished "Golden Boy"   205
Box 9.3   The Soap Operas of Television   206
Box 9.4   *Hill Street Blues:* A 1980s Trendsetter   208
Box 9.5   A Fourth Television Network in the 1990s?   210
Development of Television News   210
The Cultural Impact of Television   216
Box 9.6   Toy Makers Invade Europe via TV Satellites   222
Television Specializes   225
Summary   227

Chapter 10   Recorded Music: Powerful and Controversial   233
How It All Began   234
Recorded Music Enters the Popular Culture   236
Box 10.1   The Changing World of the Jukebox   239
Rock Music Changes   241
Box 10.2   Is Paul Dead? Some in the 1960s Thought So   246
Rock Specializes   247
Box 10.3   "Heavenly Metal Music"   248
Box 10.4   U2: From Punk Lyrics to Social Consciousness   249
The Music Video Phenomenon (MTV)   250
Box 10.5   The British Invasion Reversed   251
Controversies Surrounding Rock Music   252
Box 10.6   Rock against Drugs   255
Box 10.7   The Business of Music   256
Other Forms of Recorded Music   257
Summary   257

Part 4   Media Shapers and Cultural Effects   261

Chapter 11   Advertising: Selling the Message   263
How Advertising Developed   264
Theories on Advertising Effectiveness   266
Propaganda Devices   268
Controversies Surrounding Advertising   273
Television Advertising   274

Motivational Research   277
Box 11.1   VALS Research Leads to New Magazine Genre   283
Summary   283

Chapter 12   Public Relations: Creating an Image   287
What Is Public Relations?   288
The History of Public Relations   289
Duties of PR Practitioners   292
Examples of Public Relations Activities   293
Controversies Surrounding PR Practices   296
Box 12.1   Declaration of Principles of the Public Relations Society of America   298
Summary   298

Chapter 13   The Selling of American Politics   303
Opinion Leader Theory   304
The Rise of the Political Consultant   305
Box 13.1   Profile of a Political Consultant   306
The Rise of Political Ads and Media Influence   308
Box 13.2   Television Political Advertising, Reagan Style   314
Box 13.3   Democrats Put It Together for TV in 1988; Ratings Decline   315
Effective Political Media   317
Box 13.4   Pretesting Political Campaign Ads   318
News Coverage of Elections   320
Summary   322

Chapter 14   Changing Trends in Media Technology   327
Predicting the Future   327
Cable Television   329
Satellite Communication   331
Box 14.1   "People Meters": High-Tech Media Monitors   332
Computers   335
Home Video Equipment   337
Merging Print and Electronics   338
Other Technological Advances   341
Implications for the Future   344
Summary   345

Chapter 15   Media Ethics, Regulations and Cultural Consequences   349
News Media Ethics   350
Media Ethics and Economics   354
Media Ethics and Entertainment   356
Regulating the Mass Media   361
Cultural Consequences   369
Summary   371

Glossary   375
Index   381

Part 1

Culture
and
Communication

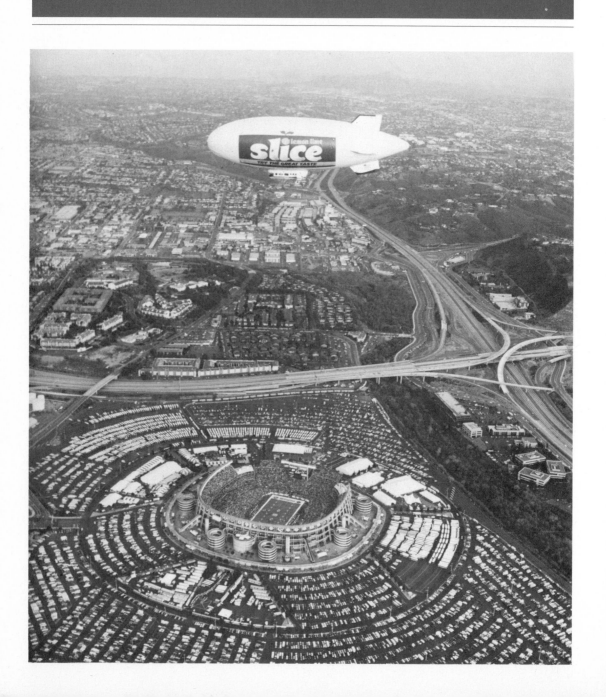

Chapter 1

Culture and Communication: Basic Concepts

Communication is mankind's most
important single act. When
improperly performed it turns
friends into enemies and plunges
nations into wars.

—Anonymous

Rock concerts, beauty pageants and the Super Bowl all have something in common. They are cultural events that the mass media have created and perpetuate.

The mass media play an important role in our society. To understand that role better, we need to know a little about how our Western culture developed and how the mass media have helped to change and shape it.

If you are wondering why you should be interested in such things as culture and its relationship to the mass media, stop for a minute and look around you. Did you ever wonder why you comb your hair the way you do, why you wear a certain style of clothing and why you spend your money on the things you do? Most people would answer by saying they do these things because they want to. But the answer goes much deeper than that.

Other questions you might ask yourself are "Why and how did the Super Bowl come to be one of the biggest mass-media events in American society?" and "How and why did alcohol and drug abuse become such a serious problem in middle-class culture?" The answers to these questions and many more may be found by studying our American popular culture and its interrelationship with the mass media.

CULTURE

To understand clearly our study of culture and media, it is essential to define precisely what we mean by *culture*. For anthropologists, culture includes everything that occurs in a society—all the customs and practices handed down from generation to generation. Culture covers the various forces that contribute to our behavior in society. These contributions usually come from our formal institutions, such as churches, the state, and now, the media; mores, or standards of behavior; laws; and conventional practices and customs.

Popular Culture.   *Popular culture* can be defined as the culture of everyone in a society. It can be so pervasive that we seldom notice it. In order for us to notice it, we must step back and consciously observe it. We can do this by really looking around us at the objects in our society and asking ourselves why we idolize the things we do, why we buy the things we do, and why we believe in the things we do.

Popular culture plays an important role in the lives of young and old alike. Here a trio of teenagers looks for bargains at a discount records and tapes store. *(Spencer Grant/The Picture Cube)*

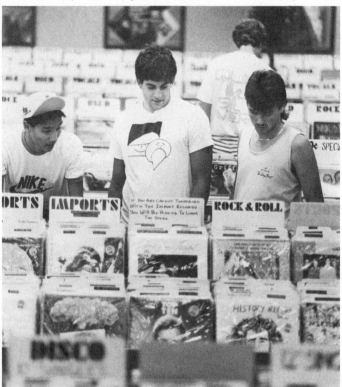

Throughout history, every society has had its own popular culture. Most of today's popular culture is mass-produced and is disseminated in large quantities through the mass media. Popular music, cheap paperback novels, soap operas, videocassette movies and a myriad of advertised products from designer jeans to disposable razors make up our everyday environment. Stephen King novels, Levi's jeans and the golden arches of McDonald's are instantly recognizable symbols in our modern-day pop culture.

Because of the mass mediation of our popular culture, another term, *mass culture*, has developed. This refers to the things in our culture that are mass-produced and/or shared through the mass media. In today's American society, that represents almost everything in our popular culture. It is so difficult to think of anything in our modern popular culture that isn't either mass-produced or promoted in the mass media that the terms mass culture and popular culture have come to be used almost interchangeably.

THE DEVELOPMENT OF MASS MEDIA THROUGH TIME: THE EPS CYCLE

While our mass culture today is a popular one, with distinctions between classes blurry at best, this was not always the case. Throughout this book we will be referring to a media progression cycle called the elitist-popular-specialized (EPS) cycle. This progression cycle concept was developed by mass-communication scholars John Merrill and Ralph Lowenstein, who in 1971 first pointed out that all media develop in three stages.[1]

A mass-communication medium usually starts out in the elite stage. Here the media appeal to, and are consumed by, the affluent leaders in the culture. After a nation breaks through the barriers of poverty and illiteracy, its media enter the popular stage and are enjoyed by the mass culture. Eventually, as the elements of higher education, affluence, leisure time and population growth coalesce, the mass media begin to enter a third stage of the EPS cycle—specialization. In this stage the media are consumed by highly fragmented segments of the population, each with its own interests and cultural activities.

While media in the United States are entering the age of specialization, in many underdeveloped nations the media are still in the early stages of this cycle. A closer look at these stages can help us see where we've been and where other countries may be headed.

Elite Stage. Down through the ages, *elite culture* has been the culture of the educated, aristocratic and wealthy. Elite culture is sometimes referred to as *high culture*. Until less than two hundred years ago, there was a distinct separation between high culture and that of the common, peasant class, which was known as *folk culture*. The elite were people whose lives revolved around fine art, literature and classical music. The peasants had their folk culture, which consisted of street carnivals, tavern drinking and singing and the telling of folktales. Although people who participated in the elite culture could also enjoy folk culture, the reverse was not true.

Popular Stage. In the nineteenth century, the distinction between elite and folk culture began to blur following the development of political democracy, public education of the masses and the Industrial Revolution. These forces ushered in the era of popular and mass culture. Although folk culture can be described as a forerunner of popular culture, the term popular culture was not coined until the nineteenth century. Pop culture scholar Ray B. Browne defined *popular culture* as

> *the cultural world around us—our attitudes, habits and actions: how we act and why we act; what we eat, wear; our buildings, roads and means of travel, our entertainment, sports; our politics, religion, medical practices; our beliefs and activities and what shapes and controls them. It is, in other words, to us what water is to fish: it is the world we live in.*[2]

Americans still gather for both elite and popular culture events. The top photo is a view from the stage of the Metropolitan Opera in New York City. Below, nearly 80,000 spectators attend a Farm Aid concert, organized by some of the top stars of rock, pop, and country music. The receipts went to American farmers faced with foreclosure. *(Top: Courtesy of the Metropolitan Opera; Photo by James Heffernan; Bottom: Jean-Louis Atlan/Sygma)*

Thus we use the term *popular* or *pop culture* in this book to describe what surrounds us in our everyday lives. Pop culture is our mainstream culture; it encompasses all the objects, customs, fads and activities we take for granted.*

Specialized Stage. The United States was the first nation in which all the factors necessary for specialization converged. During the latter half of the twentieth century, there has been a great deal of movement by the American mass media toward specialization. Futurist Alvin Toffler calls this trend the "demassification of the mass media," and he believes it will continue as we complete our move from the industrial age to the information age.[3]

Although magazines are the most specialized of the mass media (see Chapter 5), during the latter part of this century all American mass media have been accelerating toward specialization.

THE COMMUNICATION PROCESS

Communication can be defined simply as *the process by which individuals share information, ideas and attitudes*. A key word in this definition is "share." The word means to give or receive a part of something, or to enjoy or assume something in common. Some people use the term send rather than share when they discuss the communication process. However, "sending" merely implies transmitting a message with little concern for the person receiving the message, while "sharing" implies that the source and the receiver are actively working together for common understanding.

You will also note that we call communication a *process*. This means that communication is ongoing and dynamic. It also means that it encompasses various components that interact with one another, causing specific consequences. For example, what information, ideas and attitudes are shared, how much is shared, when is it shared and what tools are used to share it are all variables in the process.

Types of Communication. Various types of communication exist. *Intrapersonal communication* describes a person talking to himself or herself. In *interpersonal communication,* two or three people are talking with one another in close physical proximity. *Group communication* describes a process whereby groups of people communicate with one another in a face to face encounter. In *mass communication,* communicators use a mass medium to communicate over some distances to large audiences.

---

*Even today, however, a few things remain in the elite culture. Going to the movies is considered popular culture, but attending the opera is deemed elite. A Rembrandt painting is part of the elite culture, whereas a poster of Vanna White is a popular culture artifact. Bowling is a leisure activity of the popular culture, while polo is definitely a part of elite culture.

However, the differences between elite and popular culture are subject to change. Golf and tennis were once considered elite sports. Increased mass-media exposure has led to greater availability of public golf courses and tennis courts and has shifted these activities to the popular culture.

Figure 1.1. Communication model

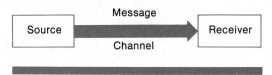

There are several basic components in the communication process. While these components can be presented in a variety of diagrams or models, our basic model includes the source, the message, the channel and the receiver (see Figure 1.1).

Source. The *source* (sometimes called the *sender, communicator* or *encoder*) is the person who shares information, ideas or attitudes with another person. The writer of this textbook is sharing his ideas on the definitions of the term *source* with you. The message is being disseminated to you through the process of mass communication— in this case, book publishing.

In mass communication, the source is usually a professional communicator who shapes the message to be shared. He or she might be a newspaper or television reporter or an entertainer who must gather information or ideas and then share them with the audience.

Message. The *message* is whatever the source attempts to share with someone else. It originates with an idea, which then must be encoded into *symbols* that are used to express that idea.

Symbols are words or objects that the source uses to elicit meaning in the mind of the receiver of the message. Words and pictures are the most common symbols used in communication. Words attempt to describe an object or concept, while pictures actually show a representation of the object or idea. If you were to give some friends directions on how to find your home, you might use words to identify the directions they should follow and the various cross streets that they need to look for. Or, if you preferred, you could draw them a map.

The process of selecting symbols for an idea or object is a very important step in communication because poorly selected symbols will result in a confusing or misunderstood message. Care must be taken to choose symbols that will elicit responses in the mind of the message receiver that are similar to those intended by the source.

In selecting symbols for their messages, communicators must keep in mind that each person has a different frame of reference and that, as a result, certain symbols may mean different things to different people. A *frame of reference* (sometimes called *field of experience*) is the set of individual experiences each person possesses; no two people have exactly the same experiences.

Each experience or event in our life leaves some sort of an impression on us, and we use the accumulation of these experiences to give meaning and interpretation to symbols. For example, a person who has been rescued by a police officer will respond

The source of a message in mass communication is a professional communicator, like this journalist working at a video display terminal (VDT). *(Brent M. Jones)*

differently from a criminal to the message "The police are coming." These different reactions are based on the meanings given to the word *police* that have been developed as a result of the individual's experiences.

Although we primarily use words and pictures to send our messages, we also communicate in other ways. Facial expressions, gestures and body language can effectively send messages. For example, a television newscaster might be reporting on the outcome of a presidential election by stating only the facts about the vote, while his facial expressions and/or tone of voice reveal his biases against the winner.

Channel. The *channel* is the way in which we send our message. In interpersonal communication we use the senses of sight, sound and touch to communicate messages. These are our channels. In mass communication such technological devices as books, newspapers, magazines, movies, radio and television are our communication channels.

Mass communication differs from interpersonal communication in that its messages must be moved over greater distances. This movement is achieved through the use of technological devices. Radio and television messages are transmitted electronically, while newspaper and magazine messages are reproduced on high-speed presses and distributed through the mails or via carriers. Today, however, even some print-media messages are transmitted electronically. Wire services send news via satellite, and *USA Today* transmits the entire contents of the newspaper by satellite to printing plants around the country.

Receiver. The *receiver* (sometimes called the *destination, audience* or *decoder*) in the communication process is the person with whom the message is intended to be shared. Without a receiver, there is no communication. In fact, if any one of the above four communication components is missing, there is no communication. To properly share your message, you also must be sure that the receiver is listening and understanding what it is you have to communicate.

Just because a story is carried in a newspaper or broadcast over radio or television does not mean that everyone has received the message. If some people do not read the story or pay attention to the broadcast, it has not been communicated to them.

In mass communication the receiver is usually a large audience that is often referred to as the *masses*. Because of the audience's size and diversity, mass communication requires careful choice of symbols that will elicit correct interpretations among receivers, who each has a different frame of reference.

Feedback. If the receiver or audience in the communication process transmits back to the source an observable response to the message, you have an added component called *feedback*. Feedback provides the source with an opportunity to determine if the message was correctly understood and, if it wasn't, with an opportunity to modify it (see Figure 1.2).

Feedback can take many forms. It can consist of words, gestures, facial expressions or any other observable act. A person making a pass at an attractive member of the opposite sex might get a clear message to "get lost" without a word being spoken.

Feedback is absent or at best very much delayed in mass communication. This makes mass communication much more difficult than face-to-face communication. Messages in mass communication must be clearly constructed because there is seldom a chance to restate their meaning. It is true that if a newspaper story is erroneously interpreted, people will write letters to the editor, and if a broadcaster's statement is incorrectly perceived, the station may get telephone calls. However, this feedback comes too late to do much good.

Certain additional factors—called communication noise—can complicate the communication process. Three examples of this are channel noise, semantic noise and psychological noise.

Channel Noise. *Channel noise* refers to external interference in the communication process. The message doesn't make it through as sent. You might be listening to

Figure 1.2. Communication process with feedback

your car radio when, all of a sudden, a large blast of static blocks out the music. This is a case of channel noise in mass communication. Other examples of channel noise might be print that is too small, a voice that is too soft or a picture that is blurred.

Semantic Noise. What if you heard on the radio that someone had just found a Polyphemus moth or that your mayor was suffering from hyperbilirubinemia? Chances are you would not clearly interpret the messages. This act of communication would be suffering from *semantic noise*.

When semantic noise occurs, the message gets through as sent but you don't understand what is means. Symbols causing semantic noise do not have to be long, technical terms. If a receiver of the message does not have a background in electricity, for example, he or she may find ohm and watt just as confusing as hyperbilirubinemia.

Semantic noise can occur even when we know the other person is familiar with the symbol we have selected. We must remember that words evoke mental pictures in the minds of both the source and the destination. For example, if a newspaper article mentions that a dog seriously injured a child, the reporter might have had a German shepherd in mind. However, the story can lead to misunderstanding if the receiver of the message, who has been aware of numerous stories describing attacks on humans by pit bull terriers, automatically pictures a pit bull when reading the story. Or perhaps the reader owns a Mexican hairless and pictures her pet when reading the word *dog*. In fact, we have no assurance that certain people will even think of a four-legged animal when the word *dog* is used; perhaps they are accustomed to using the term to describe members of the opposite sex whom they dislike.

Semantic noise can also occur when words take on connotations or emotional meanings that are based on experiences rather than on the word's dictionary meanings. Take the words *socialist, liberal* and *conservative*, for example. These mean different things to different people, based on individual political points of view. A great deal of confusion can thus arise in mass communication if these terms are thrown around too loosely.

The mass media also run into problems with semantic noise when reporters get caught up in the jargon of the beats they are covering. Government and education are two areas in which jargon is used extensively. When a reporter quotes the mayor as saying that the city has a "long-range strategic plan to interface the environmental negative declaration process with the private sector," the reader may decide to turn to the comic pages. Mass communicators must interpret ideas and information and select clearly understood symbols to transmit that information to the masses. In other words, they must constantly guard against semantic noise.

Psychological Noise. We refer to internal factors that lead to misunderstandings in the communication process as *psychological noise*. People try to protect themselves from information that they might find offensive in three ways: selective exposure, selective perception and selective retention. The concept of psychological noise comes from a series of consistency theories that were developed in the 1950s.

Selective exposure holds that, as a general rule, we expose ourselves to information that reinforces rather than contradicts our beliefs or opinions. For example, Republicans are far more likely than Democrats to watch a Republican candidate on television.

Selective exposure also helps to explain why people with extreme political views have difficulty getting their ideas across to the general public: the audience just "tunes them out."

One of the most colorful episodes in American journalism in the twentieth century—the flourishing of the underground press movement during the 1960s—best demonstrated this phenomenon. Various countercultural groups expressed a frustration that the "Establishment" press was not telling people about their ideas, such as opposition to the war in Vietnam, "blissful" experiences with psychedelic drugs and the joys of sexual freedom. So, in an effort to get their message out to the masses, many of these countercultural movements started up alternative, "underground" newspapers.

After a few years the messages were still not reaching the masses, and the underground press movement started to decline. The reason was selective exposure: the only people reading the newspapers were those who already subscribed to the philosophy of the counterculture. One survivor of this era is the *Village Voice*, a Manhattan weekly that has maintained its left-wing perspective.

The second kind of psychological noise is *selective perception:* we tend to see, hear and believe only what we want to see, hear and believe. As the late Canadian philosopher Marshall McLuhan pointed out, "Everyone has his own set of goggles," and we all think that what we see with our set of goggles is what everyone else sees. The Swiss biologist and psychologist Jean Piaget, who has been influential in twentieth-century educational philosophy, called this autistic thinking and defined autism as "thought in which truth is confused with desire."

Many studies have demonstrated selective perception at work. One involved showing people an editorial cartoon from a Northern newspaper ridiculing the Ku Klux Klan; the cartoon was repeatedly interpreted as pro-Klan when shown to Southern Klan sympathizers.

Paul Conrad, the popular and controversial *Los Angeles Times* political cartoonist, deals with this phenomenon all the time. Letters to the editor in response to his June 13, 1985, cartoon on the death of Karen Ann Quinlan—whose parents had much earlier obtained a court order to get her released from a hospital life-support system— included the following two:

> *Conrad's work of art on the death of Karen Ann Quinlan was so touching it brought tears. He outdid himself this time. I do hope he sent the original to the Quinlan family. It would be a precious gift I'm sure they would treasure.*
>
> L.C.M.

> *Conrad's cartoon with regard to Karen Ann Quinlan was repugnant.*
>
> L.W.S.

Another classic example of selective perception appeared in the early 1970s, when television producer Norman Lear first started experimenting with controversial situation comedies (sitcoms). After much effort, he persuaded CBS to air *All in the Family*, which featured Archie Bunker, a classic bigot. Bunker's prejudices were reflected

KAREN ANN QUINLAN IS FINALLY GRANTED THE RIGHT TO DIE.

Selective perception may cause an editorial cartoon, such as this one by Paul Conrad, to produce opposing reactions among readers; people see what they want to see. *(Paul Conrad)*

in a number of controversial topics, such as sex, religion and racism, that previously had been considered unsafe topics for discussion on prime-time television. The character of Archie Bunker was designed to satirize American bigotry. But what developed were Archie Bunker fan clubs and Archie Bunker T-shirts proclaiming America's No. 1 television bigot a folk hero. Many people thought what he said was true and thus failed to get the message or see the satire.

In the late 1980s selective perception was evident during the congressional Iran-Contra hearings. When Lt. Col. Oliver North testified before the committee, millions of Americans proclaimed him a national hero and wanted him to run for president—while others were convinced he should be sent to jail for breaking the law and figuratively "shredding" the Constitution.

Selective retention is the third basic psychological defense. It means that we tend to remember those things that reinforce our beliefs better than those that oppose them. For example, try to remember some good things about someone you dislike. Or try to come up with a list of faults for someone you really idolize. Chances are you will remember mostly bad things about your enemies and good things about your idols.

By now you should see that the communication process is more complicated than indicated by the simple definition first offered. Let's consider a more operational definition that attempts to recognize some of the complexities we've covered.

> **Communication** is a process involving the sorting, selecting and sharing of symbols in such a way as to help a receiver elicit from his or her own mind a meaning similar to that contained in the mind of the communicator.

Mass Communication. We also need to define the more complex process of mass communication. Before we do, however, we will describe one more aspect of mass communication that makes it controversial and important to study if we are to better understand our culture. Previously we noted that mass communication consists of (1) professional communicators shaping and sharing messages, (2) then transmitting them over some distance using technological devices called mass media, (3) to reach large audiences.

These three factors have an effect on the receivers of the message, and this effect should be included in a definition of mass communication. The effect, for example, can be as simple as expanding a person's knowledge about a certain topic by describing an injury someone received in an automobile accident. Or the effect might consist of making people feel good after they watch a movie or television show. However, media effects can also be far more significant, such as changing a person's cultural attitudes and behavior.

This latter, more complex effect causes many people to be disturbed by the mass media and their influences on our culture. Concern about excessive sex and violence in the media and explicit rock-music lyrics has generated a great deal of mass-media criticism in recent years. These issues will be discussed in more depth later in this book.

If we take these factors of mass communication and place them into an operational definition, we might say that:

> **Mass communication** is a process whereby professional communicators use technological devices to share messages over some distance to influence large audiences.

Channels of Mass Communication. The technological devices or mass media used to send messages over some distance include books, pamphlets, magazines, newspapers, direct-mail circulars, newsletters, radio, records, audiotapes, television, motion pictures, videotapes and computer networks.

You will note that we have not included telephones, stage plays or rock concerts. One could certainly argue that telephones transmit messages over some distance and that long-running plays or huge rock concerts are seen by large audiences. Then why aren't they considered mass media? Let's examine each of these in relation to our operational definition of mass communication.

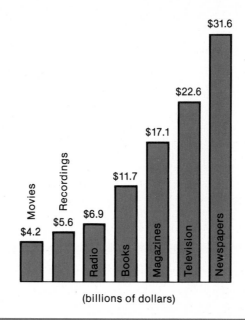

Figure 1.3. U.S. mass media annual income (in billions of dollars). SOURCE: *U.S. Industrial Outlook, 1988* (Washington, D.C.: U.S. Government Printing Office, 1988).

The telephone does use technological devices to transmit messages across some distance, but it does not reach large audiences. Instead, it usually transmits a one-on-one conversation and is an electronic extension of interpersonal communication. Although new technologies such as teleconferencing expand the size of the audience, it is still not sufficient to meet the concept of a *large* mass-media audience.

Although stage plays and rock concerts use some technological devices (lighting and sound systems) to reach large audiences, such shows are limited to a confined area and thus do not transmit those messages over some distance. If these events are broadcast or if audio or videotapes are made, then the broadcast medium or the tapes become the mass medium, not the stage play or concert itself. The Live Aid concert in 1985, for example, made an impact on our popular culture largely because it was shown on network and cable TV.

There is one more thing about the media that we must always keep in mind—the American mass media are businesses and their purpose is to make a profit. If they don't, they go out of business. Collectively, the mass media in the United States are one of the largest industries, with an annual income of nearly $100 billion, and they employ more than one million people (see Figure 1.3).

INFORMATION PROCESSING BY THE MEDIA

The importance of mass communication increases as we develop into adulthood. After early childhood, we learn very little firsthand. Once we learn to talk, we start gathering information from secondhand sources—other people, and eventually, the mass media.

In our early education, television and textbooks become important sources for our secondhand information. Other media, such as newspapers and magazines, join them as we grow older. For example, we might "know" that terrorists have taken hostages in the Middle East or that an earthquake has devastated a major city, but we probably didn't experience this information firsthand. We relied on secondhand sources—usually the mass media—to inform us. Because we depend on secondhand sources for information, the mass media play a major role in determining the content of our culture.

Agenda Setting. A process whereby the mass media determine what we think and worry about is called *agenda setting*. The word agenda means a list, plan, outline or the like of things to be considered. Mass-media agenda-setting theory contends that the mass media, not we, determine what will be news and what won't.

According to researchers Maxwell McCombs and Donald Shaw: "Here may lie the most important effect of mass communication, its ability to mentally order and organize our world for us. In short, the mass media may not be successful in telling us what to think, but they are stunningly successful in telling us what to think about."[4]

The professional communicators working for the mass media set the news and information agenda for us. If they determine that something isn't important, it most

A newspaper editorial board sets the news agenda during daily meetings. *(Dan Chidester/ The Image Works)*

likely won't be, because it will receive very little, if any, media attention. And, of course, the reverse is true. Often the media give far more extensive coverage to stories than they actually deserve. Sensational murder cases, for example, sometimes get week after week of front-page news coverage, even when very little new information has been uncovered. Such headlines as "No New Clues in Hillside Strangling" are not uncommon.

Most professional communicators, particularly those involved in processing the news, attempt to be objective and fair in their selection of news items. Very few purposely slant the news to fit their own particular biases. Yet there is far more news than space or time available to disseminate it. This means that selections must be made as to what is news on any given day and how much space or time will be devoted to it. Stories of limited interest, such as activities of the local water district, church ladies' aid society or Boy Scout troop, frequently go unreported.

Political candidates have a great deal of trouble with media agenda setting at election time. For example, in 1980 President Jimmy Carter felt that there were other important issues in the presidential election besides the American hostages being held in Iran. The media, however, seemed to disagree, and for over a year a count of the number of days Americans had been held hostage and a recap of the hostage story led the evening news each day. The American people were frustrated by the government's inability to free these Americans, and the media would not let them forget the incident. Jimmy Carter lost the election.

In 1984, while President Ronald Reagan was seeking a second term, seven Americans were being held hostage in the Middle East. This time the news media didn't feel the situation was that important, and the plight of the hostages went largely unreported. Ronald Reagan won reelection.

Media treatment of the hostage issue was obviously not the sole reason for Reagan's victories in 1980 and 1984, but the examples do illustrate inconsistencies in media agenda setting. These examples also do not suggest that the news media favored Reagan over Carter. In fact, in October 1986, this "tough-on-Iran" Reagan found his administration in turmoil after the news media revealed that members of his staff had been secretly selling arms to Iran and using the profits to fund rebel forces in Nicaragua. Much to President Reagan's displeasure, the content of the mass media during the summer of 1987 dealt primarily with the congressional hearings on the Iran-Contra scandal. It was their agenda, not his.

It is important to understand, however, that agenda setting can differ greatly from one news medium to another. The content of a suburban weekly newspaper will not be the same as that of a nearby metropolitan daily, for example. The suburban weekly may set as its primary agenda local activities in the community, while the metropolitan daily probably feels obligated to include more coverage of national and international news.

Gatekeeping. Another way that the media controls our access to news, information and entertainment is through *gatekeeping*. This sociological term was coined in 1947 by Kurt Lewin, who used it to describe the fact that news must travel through a series of checkpoints (or gates) before it reaches the public.

In the gatekeeping process, numerous people make decisions as to whether or not we are going to see or hear a story or be exposed to a new musical or entertainment performer or group. A story about the United States shifting its policy toward a Central American country may or may not reach the American people, depending on the decisions made by the gatekeepers. A group of rock musicians may or may not make it to the top of the charts, depending on decisions by gatekeepers.

Let's take a hypothetical example of the president of the United States changing his policy on a Central American country. Whether the American people learn about this shift in policy is not necessarily in the hands of the government. Government officials may issue a press release or hold a press conference announcing the change. However, a number of news media personnel must determine that the announcement is important before it becomes news.

Before appearing in a newspaper, the news item must pass to the reporter as a news release or in a news conference. He or she then decides whether the item is important enough to be covered and how much coverage should be given to it. If the reporter decides the item is important, he or she may rewrite the press release or write a story about the press conference or perhaps dictate the item over a telephone to a rewrite person at the newspaper. The rewrite person then functions as the next gate in evaluating the story's importance. Next a copy editor edits the item and judges its importance. The story may also appear before additional gates—the national or international editors and perhaps even the entire editorial board of the newspaper—before a determination is made as to if and where the story will be run in the next edition.

Before this same story appears on television, it must go through a similar set of gates: writers, editors and videotape editors all make judgments as to what portions of

Even the personnel in a television studio making decisions as a program airs serve as gatekeepers in the communication process. *(Stanley Rowin/The Picture Cube)*

the press conference will be aired. (If no videotape footage accompanies the news item, it might be stopped at this gate because television depends on visuals to keep the news interesting.)

Similarly, a rock group that may be the rage at a local college may never "make it" in the entertainment world because gatekeepers feel that they have enough performers with a similar sound. A pilot program for a new television series may never make it on the air because gatekeepers decide that it is not what the public wants. A potential best-selling book may never see print because a gatekeeper makes a decision to reject the manuscript.

INFORMATION PROCESSING BY THE CONSUMER

Although the mass media determine what news and entertainment the public will see and hear, people take in only a fraction of all the information that they receive. Instead, people process information by condensing it, selecting aspects of interest to them and integrating what they select into their own thinking.

People pay attention to only a small amount of the information available to them. To do otherwise would be to risk *information overload*. Can you imagine reading or remembering everything that has been printed or broadcast during your lifetime? As the years go by, most of us accumulate a substantial backlog of information. This allows us to filter new information into our memories to update and refresh previously developed perceptions and to reject information that we deem unimportant.

Communication researcher Doris Graber found that people "tame the information tide quite well." Her study in Evanston, Illinois, discovered that newspaper readers ignored two out of three stories, read no more than 18 percent of the stories in full, and looked at only the first and second paragraphs of the rest.[5] (Reading only the beginning of a story is actually an efficient process because it takes advantage of the inverted-pyramid writing style, the most common style of news writing: the most important aspects of the story are summarized in the first paragraph, the next most important information follows and the least important angles appear at the end.)

Graber also found that a similar screening process goes on for television news: of all the stories on a typical half-hour newscast, only one is retained sufficiently to be recalled shortly afterward. Despite this haphazard news-selection process, however, she found that people manage to stay on top of the most important stories.

In addition to ignoring large numbers of stories, people reduce the amount of information they need to store by extracting only the essential points from news stories they do pay attention to.

An example of how this works is the public's understanding of the reasons for the space shuttle *Challenger's* explosion in January 1986. A presidential commission was appointed to determine the cause of the tragedy, and volumes of testimony and study were printed and broadcast during the six months of the investigation. However, most people read, heard and remembered only enough to know that the failure of a booster rocket's O-ring had caused the tragedy.

As a result of her study, Graber concluded:

Average Americans are capable of extracting enough meaningful political information from the flood of news to which they are exposed to perform the moderate number of citizenship functions that American society expects of them. They keep informed to a limited extent about the majority of significant publicized events. They also learn enough about major political candidates to cast a thoughtful vote and make some judgments about post-election performances.[6]

These are the basic definitions and concepts needed to understand your study of popular culture and mass media. In the next chapter we will provide an overview of how popular culture and mass communication have been influencing one another since the fifteenth century.

SUMMARY

Culture is a term that refers to everything that occurs in a society. It represents all of the customs and practices handed down from generation to generation. Popular culture is the culture of everyone in a society. It is so pervasive that we seldom see it. Mass culture is a term often used synonymously with popular culture. It refers to everything in our culture that is either mass produced or disseminated through the mass media.

Most mass media evolve through a progression cycle called the elitist-popular-specialized (EPS) cycle. The media usually start out in the elitist stage, then progress to the popular stage and finally settle into a stage of specialization.

Several basic components are important to the proper functioning of the communication process. These include the source, message, channel and receiver. In addition, communication has such important elements as feedback, symbols, frames of reference and a variety of noises that include channel, semantic and psychological noise.

Mass communication is one of the more complex forms of communication. It is a process whereby professional communicators use technological devices to share messages over some distance to influence large audiences.

The mass media are the channels used in mass communication. In addition to providing information and entertainment, U.S. mass media are in the business of making money, nearly $100 billion a year.

Information processing by the media includes agenda setting and gatekeeping. Agenda setting is a process whereby the mass media determine what we think about by helping us decide what is important and what isn't. The media also serve as gatekeepers, determining what news, information and entertainment reaches us.

Consumers also exercise information-processing techniques that help them prevent information overload. They very selectively filter information of interest to increase their knowledge about that which they deem important while screening out a great deal of nonessential material.

NOTES

1. John C. Merrill and Ralph L. Lowenstein, *Media Messages and Men: New Perspectives in Communication* (New York: McKay, 1971), pp. 33–44.

2. Ray B. Browne, "Popular Culture—The World Around Us," in *The Popular Culture Reader,* ed. Jack Nachbar, Deborah Weiser and John L. Wright (Bowling Green, Ohio: Bowling Green University Press, 1978), p. 12.

3. Alvin Toffler, *The Third Wave* (Des Plaines, Ill.: Bantam Books, 1980), pp. 155–167.

4. Maxwell E. McCombs and Donald L. Shaw, "The Agenda-Setting Function of the Press," in *Enduring Issues in Mass Communication,* ed. Everette E. Dennis, Arnold H. Ismach and Donald M. Gillmore (St. Paul, Minn.: West, 1978), p. 97.

5. Doris A. Graber, *Processing the News* (New York: Longman, 1984), pp. 201–216.

6. Ibid., p. 204.

ADDITIONAL READING

Berlo, David K. *The Process of Communication.* New York: Holt, Rinehart & Winston, 1960.

Browne, Ray B., and Ambrosetti, Ronald J. *Popular Culture and Curricula.* Bowling Green, Ohio: Bowling Green University Popular Press, 1972.

Dance, Frank E. X., and Larson, Carl E. *The Functions of Human Communication: A Theoretical Approach.* New York: Holt, Rinehart & Winston, 1976.

Fisher, B. Aubrey. *Perspectives on Human Communication.* New York: Macmillan, 1978.

Fishwick, Marshall, and Browne, Ray B. *Icons of Popular Culture.* Bowling Green, Ohio: Bowling Green University Popular Press, 1970.

Glessing, Robert J. *The Underground Press in America.* Bloomington: Indiana University Press, 1970.

Hopper, Robert. *Human Message Systems.* New York: Harper & Row, 1976.

Schramm, Wilbur. *Men, Women, Messages and Media.* New York: Harper & Row, 1982.

Chapter 2

Culture and Mass Communication: How They Interact

The unexamined life is not
worth living.
—*Socrates*

On July 23, 1986, millions of Americans electronically joined the congregation in London's Westminster Abbey to witness the wedding of Prince Andrew and his bride, "Fergie." Why were so many Americans interested in this event, which took place 210 years to the month after the American colonies had declared their independence from Britain?

The answer had nothing to do with any reevaluation of the American Revolution. Americans tuned in because the mass media had turned the event into the "wedding of the year" in both countries.

The wedding was carried live on all three American television networks and was viewed in some 50 to 55 million American households. To build interest in the event, television crews from *CBS Morning News*, ABC's *Good Morning America* and NBC's *Today* spent part of the week broadcasting live from London. Even the evening news featured the impending wedding. And for days after the wedding, American newspapers and magazines were filled with pictures and stories about it.

The Duke and the Duchess of York, Prince Andrew and Sarah Ferguson, after their wedding at Westminster Abbey. *(AP/Wide World Photos)*

This is only one example of how the mass media influence American popular culture. Recognizing and understanding this pervasive influence is critical in understanding our basic cultural institutions, customs and behavior.

THE BEGINNING OF MASS COMMUNICATION

In Western culture, mass communication began in the fifteenth century when the German printer Johannes Gutenberg (1398–1468) invented the process of movable type. Movable type allowed molds of alphabet characters to be rearranged to form any message desired. After enough copies of a particular page were printed, the letter molds could be reused to form new words and pages.

Prior to that time, most books were handwritten and very time-consuming to produce. Because of this, reading material was scarce and limited to those in the elite culture—the clergy and nobility. Printing from carved wooden blocks was attempted in the fourteenth century, but they were not well received. Gutenberg's invention increased the number of books and made them available for a new emerging middle class.

Cultural Changes. The development of printing, which led to the spread of literacy to the middle classes, plus the development of trade and commerce caused major cultural changes. The medieval economy, particularly from the eighth to the twelfth centuries, was very regional and agrarian. Except for religious pilgrimages, wars and Crusades, people did not travel, and they produced consumer goods only to meet local needs.

During the Middle Ages, society was highly stratified; people belonged to one of three groups—clergy, nobility and peasants/artisans—and their social rank virtually never changed. Organizations such as guilds and monasteries, though established for different purposes, helped preserve the stratification of social ranks. Moreover, a strict equality was enforced among peers. Guild masters, for example, had to follow closely a set of rules governing their output and their conduct; no master was allowed to produce more work than any other.

Life in medieval society was very stable. People were born into a social class and remained there throughout their life. However, by the fourteenth century, Europeans had started to travel and explore the world beyond them. They began to discover different cultures and different types of consumer goods, and these discoveries led to the development of long-distance trade.

Pictorial Prints. Printing became the first mass-produced and mass-distributed commodity in this new Western culture. And pictorial prints had a special place in the early history of printing: they were the first form of mass-produced images for popular markets. Albrecht Dürer (1471–1528) was one of the most successful Renaissance artists to use the art forms of woodcuts and engravings to mass-produce pictorial prints. These prints became an early form of mass culture that helped foster consumerism in the lower classes of society.[1]

Modern scholars do not consider works of mass-produced graphic art made before the eighteenth century as examples of mass culture; their antiquity and their display in museums give them the status of fine art. But this view reflects a social redefinition that began in the late seventeenth century, when collectors in Holland and France started treating prints as works of art that could be enjoyed, like paintings, both for their esthetic merits and as investments. Before this time, printmaking primarily involved images for a popular audience.[2] (This same phenomenon can be found today as such popular cultural items as old comic books, posters and magazines are collected and exhibited as art. The current value of such items far exceeds their original selling price.)

In addition to books and pictorial prints, maps were also widely published and circulated. They not only facilitated trade and travel, but were used like pictorial prints as decorative wall hangings.

Early Books. Most books published during the first century of printing were repro-
ductions of traditional religious works, such as the Bible, the Book of Hours (which
contains the prescribed order of prayers, readings from the Scriptures, etc.) and the
like. Although produced with movable type, they were made to look like their handwritten predecessors by using traditional layouts and typefaces designed to resemble
handwriting. Woodcut illustrations were used in these books not so much to illustrate
a scene but rather to decorate the pages.[3] As the accuracy of illustrations became more
important in the latter half of the fifteenth century, woodcuts gave way to metal
engravings, which could be reproduced better.[4]

According to the Canadian media theorist Marshall McLuhan, the development of
printing had a profound impact on the thinking process in Western culture. In his
popular books written in the 1960s—*The Gutenberg Galaxy* and *Understanding
Media*—McLuhan contended that print restricted our thinking to linear patterns—
one thought follows the next in an orderly fashion. Not until the advent of the electronic media was our culture liberated from linear thinking. Electronic media—particularly television—he said, give us an "all-at-onceness" that breaks down the logic
of linear thought.[5]

THE PROTESTANT REFORMATION AND MASS COMMUNICATION

Although printing flourished during the fifteenth century, mass distribution of these
first mass-produced products was not yet possible. Then in the sixteenth century, as
the Protestant Reformation spread across Europe, rulers began to fear printing
because it permitted the wide distribution of pamphlets criticizing political and religious authorities. They attempted to control it by licensing printers and suppressing
books. King Henry II of France, for example, vowed to stamp out all heretical books,
and both books and printers were put to the torch during his reign.[6]

Mass Movement. The Reformation, led by a German monk, Martin Luther, was
the first mass movement made possible by mass communication. Print was used to
mobilize people of all social classes. Luther's main argument was that the pope and
his agents should no longer be the sole authority for the interpretation of the Bible
and that people should read and study the Bible on their own. He translated the Latin
Bible into German, and through mass communication it was made available to the
people.

Luther and his followers used mass-produced pamphlets to distribute the new religious thoughts to the masses. They communicated with the illiterate through pictorial
prints, much like present-day editorial cartoons, which carried propaganda messages
against the Catholic church and the pope.

Despite the efforts to censor these materials by rulers who remained faithful to the
Catholic Church, the Reformation spread. In fact, censorship led to the development
of international printing. Publishers in one country would print a book censored in
another for distribution in the prohibited country. Protestant Geneva, Switzerland,
for example, became a center for the publication of the works of French Protestants.

Also developing at this time were agents who worked as book distributors. Printing became firmly entrenched as the first successfully mass-produced and mass-distributed technology. Venice was the center of printing in this early period, and Italy had the most print shops, 50, followed by Germany, with 30.

DEVELOPMENT OF THE NOVEL

After mass communication developed, more and more people learned to read and write, especially among the middle classes. However, in those days, the elite did not think of literacy as being merely the ability to read and write. Only those who could read critically and understand the Greek and Roman classics were considered truly literate.

Chapbooks. The new readers were not interested in the ancient classics, however. In addition to the Bible, they read small, inexpensive books called chapbooks, which contained folk stories and romances. People read chapbooks simply for enjoyment, not to produce erudite literary analysis. Reading was a new way to enjoy the ancient art of storytelling, only now stories were told in printed versions rather than orally.

The Novel. Middle class readers also provided a market for a new form of book in the eighteenth century—the novel. Writers, no longer reliant on the patronage of the elite and obliged to satisfy their expectations of elevated, stilted language, began to use the everyday language of the masses.

A major characteristic of the novel was its realism. Each new novel was supposed to be different. Novels emphasized individual experience over collective experience. They were concerned with morality and attempted to present moral themes. To make the novels affordable and widely available, many—such as the works of Charles Dickens in the nineteenth century—were published in serial form. (That is, a few chapters would be published each week or month in pamphlet form.) With the evolution of the novel, the language of the written word became descriptive rather than conceptual or abstract.

INDUSTRIALIZATION

Printing technology remained virtually unchanged during the first several centuries of mass communication. Movable type and hand-cranked presses were state-of-the-art until the early nineteenth century, when a steam-powered cylinder press was perfected in England. This new development allowed for the rapid reproduction of printed materials. In 1846 a rotary press was developed that could produce about 20,000 copies of a newspaper per hour.

The rotary press was just one tiny part of the great technological explosion known as the Industrial Revolution. The Industrial Revolution irreversibly changed Western culture and lifestyles. It opened up new jobs in the cities and caused a migration of people from family farms to urban areas. Immigrants and migrants left their traditional popular culture behind and moved into the cities, where their work was regimented, standardized and homogenized.

Artisans and craftsmen were displaced by semiskilled workers who could operate machines. The use of these machines caused society to be restructured into one that focused on mass production and mass consumption. It also brought about the eventual lowering of the workweek from 12-hour days, six days a week, to the current 40-hour (or less) week.

Sociologist Louis Wirth described the new urban culture as one that saw "the weakening of bonds of kinship, and the declining social significance of the family, the disappearance of the neighborhood, and the undermining of the traditional basis of social solidarity."[7] Set adrift from their familiar surroundings and the age-old rhythms of rural life, the new urban working class had new needs—a way to learn about their new environment and ideas for spending their leisure time. These needs helped transform our culture.

The Metropolitan Newspaper. One of the first things to develop to meet these needs in the new industrial society was the metropolitan newspaper—often called the penny press—which was aimed at common people in the city. The first such paper in the United States was the *New York Sun,* which was established in 1833, shortly after the invention of the steam-driven press.

Although newspapers had existed since the late seventeenth and early eighteenth centuries, they had been read by the educated elite, not the general public. The costs of printing were too high to reach a mass audience, and the content was not everyday news items but rather dated information from abroad and political reports and essays.

Early issues of the *New York Sun* sold for a penny—rather than the usual six cents—and carried stories about ordinary people. Other penny-press newspapers followed, running news items about local events and common people's problems and interests. This new form of journalism helped to reduce anxiety and solitude by revealing to the lonely, displaced city dwellers their common humanity and their mutual pursuit of money as the common denominator of urban life.[8] According to sociologist Michael Schudson, the penny papers "expressed and built the culture of a democratic market society, a culture that had no place for social or intellectual difference."[9]

Entertainment. Although not directly related to mass communication at that time, two other institutions developed during the latter part of the nineteenth century to meet the needs of the new urban dwellers—the ballpark and vaudeville. Both kinds of entertainment helped to fill the growing amount of leisure time that workers enjoyed. Both later were transformed into mass-mediated activities.

The first professional baseball team, the Red Stockings, was founded in 1869, and soon there were teams in all the major Eastern and Midwestern cities. The *ballpark* brought together crowds of strangers who could experience a sense of community within the big city as they watched a baseball game. Immigrants were able to shake loose their ethnic ties and become absorbed in the new national game, which was becoming representative of the "American spirit." The green fields and fresh air of the ballpark were a welcome change from the sea of bricks, stone and eventually asphalt that dominated the city scene.

Workers could temporarily escape the routine and dullness of their daily lives by vicariously participating in the competition and accomplishment that baseball games symbolized. Baseball reflected the competitiveness of the workplace and the capitalist ethic, as players were bought and sold and were regarded as property. The ballpark also provided a means for viewers to release their frustrations against authority figures: the umpire became a symbol of scorn and frequent cries of "kill the umpire" were heard, accompanied by tossed debris.

As professional baseball emerged as a popular pastime, it became an increasingly commercial enterprise. Stadiums were built to seat the spectators, and the hawkers of beer, soda, hot dogs, peanuts and Cracker Jack soon appeared. Advertising on signboards, streetcar posters, handbills, balloons and in newspapers helped "sell" the ballpark to the public.[10] With the advent of the electronic media in the twentieth century, baseball and other sports would become a form of mass-mediated entertainment.

Vaudeville was the other popular form of entertainment in the nineteenth century. Vaudeville took the traditional forms of popular entertainment or folk art, such as ethnic humor, juggling, dancing and clown acts, and made them part of the new mass culture.

The vaudeville team of Drane and Alexander, photographed in 1912. (*The Bettmann Archive*)

Vaudeville set the mold for entertainment programs on the electronic media that eventually displaced it in the twentieth century. Radio incorporated the style and humor of vaudeville, and television in turn took over the entertainment format of radio when it developed in the late 1940s and 1950s. The quick cuts and action of modern-day television are ultimately based on the conventions of vaudeville entertainment.[11]

In the late nineteenth century the ballpark and vaudeville were followed by the first two electronic mass communication media—the phonograph and motion pictures. These media and their cultural impact will be discussed in separate chapters.

MASS MEDIA IN MASS SOCIETY

In the nineteenth century the role of mass communication was to supplement face-to-face communication and provide a means of disseminating—and creating—the new mass culture.

Cultural Niches. As new technologies developed in the industrial age, they had to find a way to serve the new society. Among the mass media, for example, the newspaper found its niche by becoming a medium where the common person could learn about what was happening in his or her city.

The *telephone* was invented to be used for broadcasting. However, its developers found a better use for it as an electronic extension of interpersonal communication.

Photography was invented in the nineteenth century as a quicker and less expensive alternative to family portraits produced by an artist. It later became an essential part of the way metropolitan newspapers covered events. Today photography is important in many fields of mass communication.

Radio was developed in the early twentieth century for ship-to-shore communication and for military use; messages could now be transmitted without having to string wire between two points. However, radio's more important function was as a mass medium for news and entertainment. For the first time people could hear news as it was happening and listen to a variety of free vaudeville entertainment in their own homes. Radio became a mass medium just before the Great Depression hit in 1929, and free entertainment was one of the few bright spots in the bleak 1930s.

Besides providing free entertainment, radio allowed members of the newly mobile society to take their favorite entertainment with them when they moved from the family farms and small towns to the large cities. Still to be able to hear such familiar voices as Amos 'n' Andy and Jack Benny when they left their homes in Iowa or Oklahoma for the impersonal cities or agricultural lands of California was an enormous comfort to the migrants of this era.

Television was invented as a potential replacement for radio by adding a picture to the sound. When radio programs—comedies, variety shows, and soap operas—moved to television, the format of radio changed to specialized music and news. Radio became a different medium, thus finding a new place for itself in mass society. This trend continues as new technologies come on the scene.

MASS MEDIATION OF LEISURE

As leisure became an important ingredient in the new mass culture—both as a means of stimulating consumerism and of providing activities for the increased hours away from the workplace—the mass media started to promote this leisure.

Sports. The metropolitan press began to cover the ballpark in the latter part of the nineteenth century. First came the sports page, pioneered by Joseph Pulitzer in his *New York World*, followed by the sports section, introduced by his rival, William Randolph Hearst, in the *New York Journal*. Sports magazines also developed during this period.

When radio came along in the 1920s, it started broadcasting from the ballpark. The first World Series game was broadcast in 1925; the first coast-to-coast broadcast was the 1927 Rose Bowl game.

As television developed, network executives decided that baseball—the national pastime—was not as "visual" a sport as football, so TV turned professional football into that medium's number-one electronic ballpark entertainment. It is also interesting to note that football was the first team sport to call time-outs for commercials.

Prior to this time, professional football had not become a major sport because of the popularity of collegiate football and the long tradition of baseball as America's favorite professional sport. The National Football League (NFL) was barely holding its own,

Instant replays on large TV screens mounted on scoreboards are now available for fans attending the games. *(Corky Trewin/NFL Photos)*

BOX 2.1.

THE SUPER BOWL: EXPORTING POPULAR CULTURE

On January 15, 1967, CBS and NBC gathered in the Los Angeles Coliseum for a television ratings battle and the enactment of one of the biggest popular cultural events in American history—Super Bowl I. Also in battle that day were the NFL's Green Bay Packers and the AFL's Kansas City Chiefs.

CBS won the ratings battle 16–12, but NBC had a large share of the audience, having promoted the event on its highly rated *Today* and *Johnny Carson* shows. CBS's victory was attributed to the fact that it had been broadcasting NFL football since the 1950s and its television signal reached more American households. NBC had been broadcasting AFL football only since 1965.

The unusual arrangement of two networks broadcasting the same football game had its complications. CBS provided the pictures for both networks from 11 cameras set up in the stadium. Each network provided its own commentators. Ray Scott and Jack Whitaker did the play-by-play for CBS, with Frank Gifford as commentator and Pat Summerall working the sidelines.

NBC had Curt Gowdy doing play-by-play, Paul Christman doing commentary, Charlie Jones working the sidelines and the losers' locker room and George Ratterman working the winners' locker room.

The Super Bowl has come a long way since those early days. It is now the highest-rated television show in the United States, with 30-second commercial spots selling for $600,000. Americans gather in front of their TV sets on Super Bowl Sunday; many hold parties. Some who normally don't watch professional football find themselves cheering for one team or the other. Some retail outlets that once closed only on Christmas and Easter are now closing on Super Bowl Sunday as well.

An entire cultural souvenir industry has developed around the Super Bowl, with everything from T-shirts to team photographs available for those lucky enough to actually attend the event itself. Even the coin that is flipped to determine who will kickoff at the beginning of the game sells for $4,000.

What really is the Super Bowl? It is a mass-media-created and promoted cultural event. Is it strictly an American phenomenon? In the beginning, but not any more.

Twenty years after Super Bowl I, Super Bowl XXI was broadcast on January 25, 1987, via satellite to 60 countries around the world. In some countries TV stations competed to obtain the rights to broadcast the event. In Britain, for example, Channel 4 began broadcasting Super Bowl XXI at 11 P.M. with Frank Gifford doing the British commentary. It was estimated that 3.6 million people watched the late-night event in the United Kingdom.

Rupert Murdoch's News Corporation broadcast the Super Bowl live in several countries, and the satellite Sky Channel beamed the game into 18 other countries. Super Bowl XXI aired at 10 A.M. Monday in Australia, just prior to the America's Cup sailing competition finals. In Japan, the Tokyo Broadcasting System had 20 sponsors for a delayed broadcast of the game on Monday night. China Central Television, which carried Super Bowl XX in 1986 as its first-ever televised football game, taped Super Bowl XXI for airing on May 24, 1987. It had an estimated audience of more than 300 million people.

Thus in 20 years the Super Bowl had profoundly affected not just the American popular culture but international popular culture as well.

and the American Football League (AFL) was about to disappear when the television networks came to the rescue. If NBC hadn't put down money for the television rights to its games, the AFL would have folded long before it merged with the NFL.

A third professional football league, the United States Football League (USFL), began play in 1983. However, in 1986 the USFL had to suspend operations when it secured only $1 in damages in a lawsuit it had filed against the NFL. The USFL claimed that the NFL had kept the television networks from giving the USFL a broadcasting franchise—and a guaranteed source of income. The need for mass mediation for a professional sport to survive was made brutally clear.

One of the biggest popular cultural events in American society today comes, after months of media hype, on the third or fourth Sunday of January. It is the media-created and media-promoted culmination of the professional football season—the Super Bowl (see Box 2.1).

Super Bowl Sunday, like Monday night football, fulfills many of the socialization functions that the early ballpark met. People come together for Super Bowl parties or Monday night football cocktail hours in order to share a common interest. Strangers with nothing else in common can talk about the electronic ballpark festival for days and weeks afterward. Those who attend a football game in person are happy to find the same features of the electronically broadcast version available to them—instant replays shown on a large TV screen on top of the scoreboard.

Consumer Goods. By covering a variety of other leisure-time activities, the mass media influence people to buy things so they can participate too. Recreational vehicles, boats, all-terrain scooters, ski outfits and designer jeans are just some of the consumer goods that have become a part of our popular leisure culture through the mass media's establishment of a need. Advertisements and reflections of active lifestyles on TV and in the movies create these needs.

CRITICISM OF MASS SOCIETY

The new mass culture ushered in by the Industrial Revolution was not accepted without criticism. Intellectuals found the new society debased and felt that it encroached on the elite or high culture. This critique by some European intellectuals, Germans in particular, led in the nineteenth century to the development of Romanticism and the first real study of popular culture. Leaders of the Romantic movement examined the traditional folk culture that was symbolic of the good old days. Such things as folk costumes, customs, foods and history took on a new importance. (Perhaps the most famous and enduring of these efforts was the collection of fairy tales by the Brothers Grimm.)

Other critics of mass culture believed that it had transformed our culture into just another commodity to be bought and sold and that it was intellectually destructive because it provided escapism and created a narcotic function in society. They saw the new mass culture consuming rather than preserving cultural objects that were being mass produced to meet society's entertainment needs. These critics also detested the fact that the mass media conformed to average tastes and did nothing to elevate the cultural level of the masses.

Current Complaints. This criticism of mass culture still exists today (and in fact seems to be increasing), with primary focus on the mass media and their influences on society in general. Some intellectuals still believe that television entertainment is "low culture" and is undermining the elite arts. Critics complain that most TV programming is nothing more than a mindless pacifier with no educational or artistic value. Sociologist Dwight MacDonald theorized that a significant part of the population is "chronically confronted with a choice of going to a concert or to the movies, of reading Tolstoy or a detective story, of looking at old masters or at a TV show."[12]

Defenders of high culture express concern that the proliferation of commercialized mass culture is blurring the distinction between elite and mass culture. They point out that this fusion of the two types of culture is not raising the level of mass culture but instead is corrupting high culture. MacDonald says, "There is nothing more vulgar than sophisticated kitsch" (a German term for mass culture).[13]

Critics contend that art in popular or mass culture is predigested so that spectators are spared the effort of understanding genuine art and given a shortcut to appreciating its pleasures. It is much easier to view a Norman Rockwell painting and instantly understand it than it is to quickly comprehend the meaning from an expressionistic Van Gogh.

This democratization of art, critics continue, leads to a homogenization of our culture that is analogous to the homogenization of milk—the globules of cream are evenly distributed throughout the milk, instead of floating separately on top.[14] In other words, the qualities of high and low culture have been blended together, and the demand for the "cream" has all but disappeared.

Another major criticism leveled at the mass media, particularly television, is that both news and entertainment are treated superficially. Critics charge that there seems to be a preoccupation with conflict and celebrity status and the major focus is to entertain rather than inform or educate.

In the 1980s a new criticism of the mass media developed. A group of Americans, led by the Reverend Jerry Falwell and his Liberty Foundation (the new name for his Moral Majority political lobby), began expressing fear that the mass media were corrupting our society sexually and morally. In 1985 a group called Fairness in Media attempted, without success, to take over the CBS network so that it could "take the bias out of its programming." Other groups attempted to get Congress to investigate allegedly obscene lyrics and satanic messages in recorded music, and a mid-1980s government commission on pornography was urging chain stores to stop selling erotica magazines like *Playboy* and *Penthouse*.

Criticism of the mass media has grown in recent decades as a result of the rapid expansion of paperback novels, popular music, television soap operas, violence-ridden movie thrillers and X-rated videocassettes, which are now available at video rental stores, in vending machines and even at some supermarkets. Although the artistic merits of media-produced culture and its impact on society have been debated for generations, at no time has the criticism been greater than in recent years (see Box 2.2).

BOX 2.2.

MASS CULTURE SHAPES THE MASS MEDIA

Although the mass media have long been criticized for the way they shape our popular culture, the culture itself plays a roll in shaping media content.

An example of this came in the late 1980s, when the movie and television industries started reversing their trend of showing promiscuous sex and began returning to the era of old-fashioned romance. This was prompted by the life-and-death AIDS (acquired immune deficiency syndrome) issue, which had become one of the most serious health threats facing the culture in the late 1980s.

Television was one of the first to address the problem in such specials as NBC's *An Early Frost*, about a young man trying to cope with the disease; CBS's *An Enemy Among Us*, about a teenager with AIDS; Showtime's *Brothers*, produced by Gary Nardino and Paramount Productions; and in individual episodes of such programs as *Hill Street Blues*, *St. Elsewhere*, and *L.A. Law*. By the 1987–88 season, the producers of such shows as *Cagney & Lacey*, *Cosby*, *The Golden Girls* and *Cheers* were attempting to address the issue.

The most dramatic change in media sexual attitudes came in daytime soap operas, which had frequently featured regular characters engaging in casual sex. By 1987 casual sex was on the decline, and soap-opera themes were returning to old-fashioned romance. NBC's *Days of Our Lives*, one of the pioneers in teenage sexuality, began inserting story lines about a young boy going to a pharmacy to "get protection" and eventually toned down its use of promiscuity. When Justin Kirakas first joined the show, he had a girl in every port and plenty in Salem. By 1987 Justin was involved in a serious relationship and was not going to touch the woman until after they married.

The motion-picture industry also felt the need to recognize the AIDS threat. Producers were concerned about showing unsafe sex yet were reluctant to go back to the days of stringent self-censorship. One of the ways they dealt with this issue was to include a box of condoms in the bedroom during love scenes. Among the first to do so in 1987 were *Dragnet* and *Masquerade* (which incidentally had changed its title from *Dying for Love* because of the AIDS sensitivity). Other producers required scripts to be altered to take out the unsafe sex scenes. Producer Steve Tisch told a *Los Angeles Times* reporter that his biggest hit, *Risky Business* (1983), "could not and should not be made in 1987."

Even the advertising industry was affected by the AIDS problem. Many media that had shied away from condom ads, such as local TV stations, now carried sensitive ads promoting condom use for safe sex.

The media and our culture are closely entwined, and what happens to one affects the other.

COMMERCIALIZATION OF CULTURE

The Industrial Revolution brought into our culture the concept of rapid production and consumption of goods and services. As our mass culture grows and expands and new forms of mass media develop, consumerism grows with it.

Individuals in our new mass society are still struggling to regain their identity, but many of them now seem to believe that the best way to establish that identity is through the purchase of the "right" types of consumer goods. The automobile they drive, the clothes they wear and the type of house they live in tell the world "who they are." The industrial-age American myth holds that the more material goods a person acquires, the better off he or she is. Since having more symbolizes being better, there is never enough, and the society of production and consumption continues to grow.

Product Images. The meanings symbolized by these material goods are disseminated to the masses through the media. The multibillion-dollar industry of advertising in the United States is not the only way in which consumer goods are "sold." The way products are portrayed on television, in motion pictures, in popular songs, on record-album covers and in special-interest magazines plays a very important role in transmitting meaning and generating desire for products.

The importance of the role the media can play in transmitting product images can best be illustrated by the roller-coaster successes and failures of the hat industry. Hats were an important element in men's wearing apparel in the new mass society. Until the 1940s well-dressed gentlemen always wore a hat when they went outdoors. Then Clark Gable and a few other Hollywood stars appeared outdoors in movies without hats. The bottom dropped out of the hat industry as thousands of men started copying the new hatless style. It took the character of J. R. Ewing in *Dallas* and the one played by John Travolta in the film *Urban Cowboy* to stimulate the desire for 10-gallon hats before the hat industry bounced back in the late 1970s.

An entire profession, called product brokerage, has developed around the need to portray consumer goods favorably in the entertainment business. Product brokers work with the people responsible for acquiring props for movies and TV shows to encourage them to use certain products in their shows. For example, Mercedes-Benz

Reese's Pieces helped cement the relationship between these two characters in the film *E.T.* The scene caused sales of this Hershey candy to skyrocket. *(AP/Wide World Photos)*

of North America Inc. will lend its automobiles to film producers free as long as they agree not to let the "bad guys" drive them. The best-known of these brokers is Associated Film Productions (AFP), which represents more than 150 brand names. Examples of product-broker efforts in the past ten years include the placement of Wheaties in *Rocky III,* Pampers in *Three Men and a Baby,* Milk Duds in *The Formula,* a Nikon camera in *Hopscotch,* Coca-Cola in *Missing,* Blue Diamond almonds in *Arthur,* and a Dynavite exercise machine in *Being There.*[15]

The effectiveness of product portrayal in movies can best be illustrated by the results of the use of Reese's Pieces, the candy used to cement a friendship between the extraterrestrial creature and the young boy, Elliott, in Steven Spielberg's film *E.T.* With promotional help from Hershey, sales of Reese's Pieces jumped 70 percent the month after the film was released, and within two months the candy was being sold at the refreshment counters of 800 theaters that previously had not carried it.[16]

CULTS IN POPULAR CULTURE

The words *cult* or *cultists* may evoke the image of religious worshipers in long white togas and shaved heads passing out literature at airports. Or we may remember the Jonestown suicides by followers of the Reverend Jim Jones or recall some of the TV specials on satanic cult worship.

Cults, however, do not necessarily have to be bizarre or evil. The *Random House College Dictionary* includes among its definitions of cult: "an instance of great veneration of a person, ideal, or thing, esp. as manifested by a body of admirers; the object of such devotion."

Rock Stars. In recent decades many kinds of cults have developed in Western culture. Many of them are interrelated with the mass media. Rock stars, for example, often become the objects of cultist devotion. In the eyes of their followers, they can do no wrong. Long after the Beatles split up and Elvis Presley died, cultlike followings still worship these performers.

Movie–TV Buffs. A large cultlike following developed around the movies *Star Wars, The Empire Strikes Back,* and *Return of the Jedi.* Some people say they have seen these movies hundreds of times, and box-office receipts seem to support these claims.

Probably the largest and most interesting television-produced cult has been the "Trekkies," who are devoted followers of the *Star Trek* series (see Box 2.3). The Trekkies have long outlasted the original TV series of the late 1960s. Each year thousands gather at conventions, many of them dressed in Star Trek costumes complete with pointed plastic ears. Exhibitors at these conventions sell a variety of Star Trek memorabilia.

Gang Members. Inner-city gangs provide still another form of subcultural identification for individuals attempting to establish their own identities in a mass society.

BOX 2.3.

THE TREKKIES "STAR TREK" THROUGH THE MEDIA

Star Trek was a 1960s television series that wouldn't die. Instead it became the catalyst for a complete subculture, called the Trekkies, and became a multimedia entertainment genre.

The science-fiction show had been modeled after a previously popular television genre—the Western. As Robert L. Shayon pointed out in *Saturday Review*, "*Star Trek* is a space version of *Wagon Train*."* The ratings for the series were not very high and it was taken off the air after three seasons. Although its viewers had not been many, they were loyally devoted fans. An effort to cancel the show after its first season produced one of the largest outpourings of protest mail in television's history.

The story of *Star Trek* continues to live, thanks to the high-tech world of multiple mass media. The science-fiction adventures of the spaceship U.S.S. *Enterprise* and its crew are now disseminated in a variety of mass-media forms. Although canceled by the network, *Star Trek* continued on TV in syndicated reruns. The story later spawned books, fotonovels, movies and audio books (see Chapter 4). Simon & Schuster's audio division brought out the audio book *Star Trek IV: The Voyage Home* as the first in a series in the fall of 1987. It was based on Vonda McIntyre's novelization of the 1986 *Star Trek* movie by the same name. Also released at the same time was *Strangers from the Sky* by Margaret W. Bonanno, an audio book based on the latest installment of Pocket Books' *Star Trek* series. Finally in 1987—some 20 years after its first television debut—a new version of *Star Trek*, called *Star Trek: The Next Generation*, was introduced to television audiences.

What makes *Star Trek* so popular? According to Wm. Blake Tyrrell, writing in a 1977 issue of the *Journal of Popular Culture*, *Star Trek* was a product of the dreams and nightmares of the 1960s. The show blends the imagination of a high-tech world of the twenty-third century with the human needs and emotions of the twentieth century. It gives *Star Trek* fans hope for the future by showing them that good old American values and ingenuity will still be important in the world of tomorrow.

*Robert L. Shayon, "Interplanetary Spock," *Saturday Review*, June 17, 1967, p. 46.

In 1988, according to the Los Angeles Police Department, there were 250 street gangs with an estimated 25,000 members in Los Angeles alone. These gangs usually reflect ethnic and territorial identities. However, rival gangs with similar ethnic origins often find themselves "at war" because of territorial disputes.

Subcult Characteristics. It is important to examine cults or subcultures to see how they fit into the larger cultural scene and to see how mass media affect them. Many of our subcultures, particularly those involving youth, are music oriented. Subcultures consist of the practices, fashions and styles of subgroups in society. Members of subcultures tend to self-stigmatize themselves and thus establish roles as social outcasts.

Members of a subculture use signs or badges of identification. Punk rockers, for example, use safety pins, patches, earrings and so forth to set themselves apart from and ridicule mass society. Styles become a signal to the mass culture that the subculture wants to be "different."

Punks give hidden meanings to style and objects. They use their badges and style to symbolize anarchy, and they want people in mass society to dislike them. Their goal is to be in opposition to the usual practices of society.

Thus the style of a subculture has two points: (1) to oppose everyday life and (2) to establish acceptance within the subculture. This need to establish an identity different from the masses through dress existed at the beginning of the Industrial Revolution, when workers in different occupations adopted certain wearing apparel to give them collective identities. Their clothes became their badges of identity and set the "blue-collar" workers apart from the merchants. Among punks, hair color, tattoos and markings on leather jackets all signify something within the subculture and at the same time attempt to provoke disgust from the mass culture. Contrary to popular myth, which portrays subcultures as lawless forms, "the internal structure of any particular subculture is characterized by an extreme orderliness: each part is organically related to other parts and it is through the fit between them that the subcultural member makes sense of the world."[17]

Although punk started in England as an effort by some young people to reject mass society, it wasn't long before the mass media had transmitted their styles and customs throughout the world. People with spiked and dyed hair, tattoos and safety pins in the cheek could soon be seen in such scattered locations as San Francisco, Vienna, and Tokyo.

Cultural Industries.   Although subcultures attempt to reject the larger mass culture and establish their own identities, they are an important part of the mass-culture industries. They are promoted and perpetuated by the mass media and mass industry—and not just the music industry, around which many of them develop.

Manufacturers of mass-produced consumer goods soon get on the bandwagon and merchandise the subculture. Even major chain drugstores carry washable colored hair spray for today's punk rockers. Sales of safety pins, earrings and leather jackets multiplied after the punk movement began. In the United States, the mass media toned down the punk subculture into "new wave" and the subcultural fashions entered the main culture. Women paid several hundred dollars for ripped dresses because they were part of the trendy "new wave" fashion.

Another subculture, the biker subculture, started out as youth-oriented in the 1940s, but today its members are gray-haired and middle-aged men and women. This subculture grew dramatically after the motion picture *The Wild One*, starring Marlon Brando, was released for a youth-oriented audience in the 1950s. The movie, based on a true incident that took place in Hollister, California, depicted a motorcycle gang taking over a town and wreaking havoc. Brando played a tough-talking gang leader who was seen as an anti-Establishment hero. As numerous biker cults developed, it became necessary for them to establish their own subcults within the larger subculture by adopting their own gang names and proudly displaying "their own colors," which give them individual identities.

The Harley-Davidson Motorcycle Company has made millions from this subculture. All kinds of paraphernalia have been marketed with the now-famous Harley-

Music is an international language that transmits popular culture world-wide. Here two young visitors try out the equipment at a consumer's electronic fair in West Germany. (*Reuters/Bettmann Newsphotos*)

Davidson wings on them. Several new products entered the marketplace in the late 1980s, including a wine cooler and a brand of cigarettes catering to the "macho" smoker. The cigarettes were produced by Lorillard, the nation's fourth-largest cigarette maker. The Harley insignia has become an icon as commonly recognized as McDonald's golden arches and the Coca-Cola logo.

Although subculture members try to be different from and antagonistic to the mass culture, they cannot escape from the commercialization of mass society. Each time a new subculture develops, the economy of the main mass culture benefits by providing products for the subculture, and the mass media also are right there to get a piece of the action—either through recorded music or special-interest magazines catering to the new subculture.

Wherever possible, marketing efforts of subcultural products are designed to expand the market into the mass culture as well. The blue jeans of the youth subculture of the 1950s and 1960s, for example, eventually found their way into the mass culture as an acceptable form of dress. The mass culture also attempts to water down the subculture until it becomes acceptable to the masses. For example, the health-food movement was once a fringe subculture but now is big business in the mass culture.

This interrelationship among our mass society, its subcultures and the mass media will be further explored when we examine the various media and how they function later in the book.

SUMMARY

Political democracy, public education and the Industrial Revolution of the nineteenth century ushered in a new mass society that depended on mass production and mass consumption of goods and services. The mass media developed as an integral part of this new mass society and became the disseminators and creators of the new mass culture.

With the new culture came more leisure time; to fill people's leisure hours new cultural industries were developed, which the mass-media marketed. Among the first cultural institutions to develop in the new mass society were the metropolitan newspaper, the ballpark and vaudeville. Each helped the new city dwellers to cope with their new lifestyle.

As new technologies developed, they had to find a niche in society. Some of the communication media finding a role in the new mass society were newspapers, telephones, photography, radio and television.

Our new mass culture has been commercialized to the extent that our economy revolves around selling us consumer goods as cultural items. The mass media play an important role in this commercialization of culture.

Even the subcultures in our society that consciously reject mass culture and are antagonistic to it are caught up in the cultural industry. Members of these subcultures buy items that identify their subcultures. These items are produced by the mass society and often become fads in the mainstream culture.

NOTES

1. Chandra Mukerji, *From Graven Images* (New York: Columbia University Press, 1983), p. 38.

2. Ibid.

3. Ibid., p. 53.

4. William Ivins, *Prints and Visual Communication* (Cambridge, Mass.: MIT Press, 1953), pp. 47–49.

5. Marshall McLuhan, *Understanding Media: The Extensions of Man* (New York: Signet Books, 1964), pp. 84–90.

6. Mukerji, p. 45.

7. Louis Wirth, "Urbanism as a Way of Life," *American Journal of Sociology* 44 (July 1938): 21.

8. Gunther Barth, *City People* (Oxford: Oxford University Press, 1980), pp. 58–109.

9. Michael Schudson, *Discovering the News: A Social History of American Newspapers* (New York: Basic Books, 1978), p. 60.

10. Barth, pp. 148–191.

11. Ibid., pp. 192–228.

12. Dwight MacDonald, "A Theory of Mass Culture," in *Mass Media and Mass Man*, ed. Alan Casty (New York: Holt, Rinehart & Winston, 1968), pp. 13–14.

13. Ibid., p. 17.

14. Ibid.

15. Michael Schudson, *Advertising, The Uneasy Persuasion: Its Dubious Impact on American Society* (New York: Basic Books, 1984), p. 102.

16. Joseph Winski, "Hershey Befriends Extra-Terrestrial," *Advertising Age,* July 19, 1982, pp. 1, 66.

17. Dick Hebdige, *Subculture: The Meaning of Style* (London: Methuen, 1979), p. 113.

ADDITIONAL READING

Burke, Peter. *Popular Culture in Early Modern Europe.* New York: Harper & Row, 1978.

Cantor, Norman F., and Werthman, Michael S., eds. *The History of Popular Culture.* New York: Macmillan, 1968.

Geist, Christopher D., ed. *Popular Culture and the Mass Media: A Reader.* Bowling Green, Ohio: Bowling Green University Popular Press, 1977.

Jacobs, Norman, ed. *Culture For The Millions?: Mass Media in Modern Society.* Princeton, N.J.: Van Nostrand, 1959.

McLuhan, Marshall. *The Gutenberg Galaxy: The Making of Typographic Man.* Toronto: University of Toronto Press, 1962.

———. *Culture Is Our Business.* New York: Ballantine, 1970.

Real, Michael R. *Mass-Mediated Culture.* Englewood Cliffs, N.J.: Prentice-Hall, 1977.

Williams, Raymond. *Television: Technology and Cultural Form.* New York: Schocken, 1975.

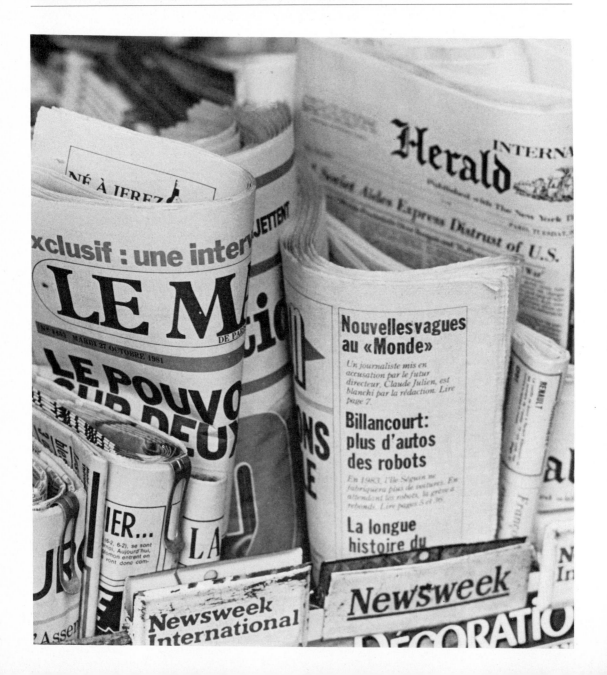

Chapter 3

Political Press Theories and Foreign Media

Congress shall make no law
respecting an establishment of
religion, or prohibiting the
free exercise thereof; or
abridging the freedom of
speech, or of the press or the
right of the people peaceably
to assemble, and to petition
the Government for a redress of
grievances.
—*First Amendment*

"There is a bitter bile in my throat these days," President Ronald Reagan told a *Time* magazine editor in 1987. (He was responding to a question about the press's coverage of his secret decision to sell arms to Iran in exchange for help in getting American hostages released.) "I've never seen the sharks circling like they now are with blood in the water. What is driving me up the wall is that this wasn't a failure until the press got a tip from that rag in Beirut and began to play it up. I told them that publicity could destroy this, that it could get people killed. They then went right on."[1]

Every American president since George Washington has had trouble with the press. In the Soviet Union, on the other hand, open confrontation between the press and government is almost nonexistent. Why hasn't the American government corrected this "problem" after two hundred years? The reason can be found in the basic philosophy under which the press functions in the United States, a philosophy made explicit in the First Amendment.

To get a better understanding of how and why the media operate differently in different countries, it is necessary to understand the various political philosophies about the purpose of the mass media. For the way in which the media function in a given society depends on the society's political system.

Two basic political approaches to the operation of mass communication exist, and each of these has an offshoot. The four theories are described by Siebert, Peterson and Schramm in their classic book *Four Theories of the Press.*[2]

The oldest is the *authoritarian theory*. It holds that people's lives must be regulated by a well-structured authoritarian government. This theory was based on the political philosophy of the Middle Ages: since the truth had been revealed once and for all in the Bible, dissent, which could only be error, could have no role.

Under this theory the press must be regulated by the government so that it will not threaten the government or the religious order and will instead help promote social harmony and unity.

The opposing viewpoint, called the *libertarian theory*, emerged in the seventeenth century. It holds that the press should serve the people rather than the government and that the best way to find the truth is to have as many opinions aired as possible. An adversarial relationship often results between the press and the government under this theory.

Siebert, Peterson and Schramm's offshoots include the *Soviet Communist theory* of a state-owned and controlled press, which evolved from the authoritarian theory, and the *social responsibility theory*, which they believe is needed to make a free press function effectively under the libertarian theory.

AUTHORITARIAN THEORY

When mass communication began expanding in the sixteenth century, the authoritarian theory held sway across Europe. Most nations had powerful, autocratic monarchies and strong, established Churches.

After the invention of the printing press, authoritarian states saw it as an important tool. Many attempts were made to use printing to unify the people. This was done by printing only *wisdom* and *truth*—which, of course, were identified by the heads of the church and state.

Thus the early press—starting with Gutenberg—published mostly authorized religious materials and, as people became more literate, chapbooks, the forerunner of the romance novel. Only after Martin Luther's challenge to the Catholic Church in 1517 led to the Protestant Reformation did books begin to appear that threatened the authoritarian state or religious order. Attempts were immediately made to censor "heretical" books, including by burning them. Less drastic, in order to limit printing to those who would operate for the "good of the state," governments established a system of state licensing for printers.

American Colonies. England was one of the countries to require the licensing of printers, and this policy, as well as other aspects of the authoritarian theory, was carried over to her American colonies. Although the English parliament allowed the

Licensing Act to expire in 1694, colonial governors retained controls on the press. When John Campbell received permission to establish the first regularly published newspaper in the colonies in 1704, he agreed to permit the authorities to screen all material before it was published.

The official attitude toward printing in the American colonies was best summed up in a 1671 statement attributed to Sir William Berkeley, governor of the Virginia colony: "But, I thank God, we have no free schools nor printing; and I hope we shall not have [them] these hundred years. For learning has brought disobedience and heresy and sects into the world, and printing has divulged them and libels against the government. God keep us from them both."[3]

After licensing laws were allowed to expire, authoritarian states attempted to exercise prior censorship by requiring that all material be approved by a government censor before it could be printed and distributed. As the number of presses and the volume of printed materials grew, however, this approach proved too cumbersome.

In the eighteenth century, control by *prior* restraint was largely replaced by the threat of punishment *after* publication. The laws of treason (the act of intending to

The front page of the *Weekly Mail* from Johannesburg, South Africa, shows crossed-out lines in an attempt to protest government censorship. Note the box about the paper's seizure to the right of the nameplate. *(AP/Wide World Photos)*

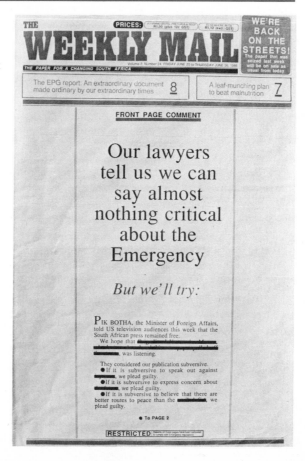

overthrow the government) and sedition (the act of showing disrespect for the government) were used to prosecute printers of materials that were considered dangerous to the state.

Modern Examples. Although the authoritarian theory of the press waned in many Western countries by the second half of the eighteenth century, versions of it still exist in authoritarian states today. In 1986, for example, the People's Republic of China, which had been undergoing a cultural liberalization, announced a new crackdown on literary freedom, outlawing all books, magazines and newspapers published without government approval. Publishers were required to register with the government, and authorities were empowered to confiscate all materials printed by those who did not. In addition, all publishers and printing firms were put on notice that if they were involved in putting out unauthorized material they would be fined and have their income confiscated. Again, in 1987, the Chinese Communist Party announced a new set of rules that banned large-circulation newspapers from writing about controversial subjects, such as China's political reform movement. These topics could only be discussed in specialized, limited-circulation magazines for scholars and researchers.

South Africa imposed stringent press and reporting controls during the struggles against apartheid in the 1980s. Journalists were prohibited from being "on the scene, or at a place within sight of any unrest, restricted gathering or security action" and were forbidden to report any "subversive" comments criticizing the government. Violators faced jail terms up to 10 years and fines up to $9,000. Similar censorship restrictions exist in other authoritarian African and South American countries.

LIBERTARIAN THEORY

In contrast to the authoritarian view that the press should be controlled so that it does not interfere with the mission of the government, the libertarian theory developed from a premise that the government should exist solely to serve the interests of the individual. As communication theorist Wilbur Schramm has noted, the libertarian theory was "foreshadowed in the sixteenth century, envisioned in the seventeenth, fought for in the eighteenth and finally brought into widespread use in the nineteenth."[4]

The Age of Enlightenment, during which the libertarian theory emerged, resulted from a number of developments in Europe during the early modern period (fifteenth to eighteenth centuries). These developments included scientific and geographical discoveries; the rise of trade and consumerism; the rise of the merchant class, which led to the growth of a middle class; the Protestant Reformation, which freed the individual from established church dogmas; and political and social revolutions that challenged the authoritarian concept and championed individual rights and freedoms.

Libertarians. Many philosophers and writers contributed to the formation of the libertarian concept. Among them were John Milton (1608–1674), John Locke (1632–1704), Isaac Newton (1642–1727), Adam Smith (1723–1790), Benjamin Franklin (1706–

1790), Thomas Jefferson (1743–1826), James Madison (1751–1836) and John Stuart Mill (1806–1873). The philosophy behind the libertarian theory of the press is described in the following letter, which Thomas Jefferson wrote to a friend in 1787:

> I am persuaded that the good sense of the people will always be found to be the best army. They may be led astray for a moment, but will soon correct themselves. The people are the only censors of their governors; and even their errors will tend to keep these to the true principles of their institution. To punish these errors too severely would be to suppress the only safeguard of the public liberty. The way to prevent these irregular interpositions of the people, is to give them full information of their affairs through the public channel of the public [news]papers, and to contrive that those papers should penetrate the whole mass of the people. The basis of our government being the opinion of the people, the very first object should be to keep that right; and were it left to me to decide whether we should have a government without newspapers, or newspapers without a government, I should not hesitate a moment to prefer the latter.[5]

Jefferson, who also felt strongly about the need for a literate society, qualified his statement favoring a society with free newspapers by saying "I should mean that every man should receive those papers, and be capable of reading them."

James Madison, another framer of our Constitution, expressed his views on the importance of a free press to our country's experiment in democracy as follows:

> Nothing could be more irrational than to give the people power and to withhold from them information without which power is abused. A people who mean to be their own governors must arm themselves with power which knowledge gives. A popular government without popular information or means of acquiring it is but a prologue to a farce or a tragedy, or perhaps both.[6]

American Democracy. Because of people like Jefferson, Madison and others, the libertarian theory of the press was an inherent part of the American experiment in democracy. The First Amendment in the Bill of Rights guarantees not only free speech but a free press as well.

Under the libertarian theory, it is the press that keeps the individual informed about the operations of government. It is important to remember that the American experiment in democracy was based on a system of checks and balances. Three separate and independent branches of government were established—the judicial, legislative and executive branches. In addition, the First Amendment provided that the press serve as a "watchdog" of government. This is why the press is often considered a fourth branch—the "fourth estate"—of the governmental power structure. Likewise, with the recent advent of the electronic press, those media have been referred to as the "fifth estate."

In the First Amendment the founders of our country installed a mechanism to protect the public's right to be informed. Thus the American press operates under the libertarian premise that the people's right to know is an essential ingredient of a free society. This right prevails over that of any government official to silence a critical press. (Limited efforts to restrict this press freedom, such as the Alien and Sedition Acts, will be discussed in Chapter 6.)

THE SOVIET COMMUNIST CONCEPT

The Soviet Communist theory, a modern offshoot of the authoritarian theory, holds that the media should be extensions of the state and should foster unity and social cohesiveness. The Soviets contend that theirs is a "people's press"; the Communist Party serves the people and the press helps the party carry out that function.

In the Soviet Union, all the mass media are owned and operated by the state. The mass communicators must be loyal party members so they know how to interpret all communications correctly, from the party's point of view. Westerners criticize this control of the press, saying that the media cannot serve two masters: the press is either a publicist for the government or a voice of the people.

Thus this state-owned and state-operated press is even more regulated than the authoritarian press. Lenin, the founder of the Soviet state, explained why an unregulated press would be such a threat to Soviet society:

> *Why should freedom of speech and freedom of the press be allowed? Why should a government which is doing what it believes to be right allow itself to be criticized? It would not allow opposition by lethal weapons. Ideas are much more fatal things than guns. Why should any man be allowed to buy a printing press and disseminate pernicious opinion calculated to embarrass the government?*[7]

How They Differ. Although the authoritarian and the Soviet Communist theories are similar in their belief that the state must be protected from a free and unregulated press, only the latter system makes use of the media to communicate party and state doctrines to the masses. Governments adhering to the authoritarian theory merely exercise control to ensure that the media do not publish anything that might harm the state. The mass media in an authoritarian system can be private as long as they are subject to licensing, prior censorship, postpublication prosecution, government subsidization or some other form of government control. Thus the Soviet Communist theory results in a *planned system*, whereas the authoritarian theory results in a *controlled system*.

Under the Soviet Communist system, there are two basic truths—the Marxist doctrine and the policies of the state. The Marxist doctrine is basically unchanging and unchallengeable. The state truth, however, changes from communist nation to nation and from leader to leader. In the Soviet Union, for example, Joseph Stalin, during his quarter-century rule, made the Soviet mass media virtually a parrot of his thoughts. Nikita Khrushchev, although more permissive of conflicting opinion than Stalin, also managed the news.[8] In the late 1980s, however, Mikhail Gorbachev introduced the concept of *glasnost* (openness) to the Soviet media. Under this new policy the press was allowed to openly criticize some government actions and policies.

THE SOCIAL RESPONSIBILITY CONCEPT

As early as the late nineteenth century, critics began to identify flaws in the libertarian theory. The free press was evolving in a manner that fell short of the idealistic libertarian goals.

As the metropolitan press developed, it became large and centralized. More and more media outlets became controlled by fewer and fewer owners, as chain ownership of newspapers grew. The press also became profit-oriented: selling newspapers and advertising space took precedence over the need to keep the public fully and accurately informed.

Major criticism of how the press was functioning in the American society began to be heard. The main areas of concern were the following:

1. *The press has wielded its enormous power for its own ends. Its owners have propagated their own opinions, especially in matters of politics and economics, at the expense of opposing views.*

2. *The press has been subservient to big business and at times has let advertisers control editorial policies and content.*

3. *The press has resisted social change.*

4. *The press has often paid more attention to the superficial and sensational in its coverage of current happenings, and its entertainment has often been lacking in substance.*

5. *The press has endangered public morals.*

6. *The press has invaded the privacy of individuals without just cause.*

7. *The press is controlled by one socioeconomic class, loosely the "business class," and access to the industry is difficult for the newcomer; therefore, the free and open market of ideas is endangered.*[9]

In 1947 an influential report issued by the Commission on Freedom of the Press, chaired by Robert Maynard Hutchins, then chancellor of the University of Chicago, called for a socially responsible press. The report made it clear that freedom and responsibility go hand in hand and that the press should be periodically reminded of its responsibility. Siebert, Peterson and Schramm later expanded on this theory:

> *Freedom carries concomitant obligations; and the press, which enjoys a privileged position under the Constitution, is obliged to be responsible to society for carrying out certain essential functions of mass communication in contemporary society. To the extent that the press recognizes its responsibilities and makes them the basis of its operational policies, the libertarian system will satisfy the needs of society. To the extent that the press*

(text continues on page 54)

BOX 3.1

THE SOCIETY OF PROFESSIONAL JOURNALISTS, SIGMA DELTA CHI CODE OF ETHICS

The SOCIETY of Professional Journalists, Sigma Delta Chi, believes the duty of journalists is to serve the truth.

We BELIEVE the agencies of mass communication are carriers of public discussion and information, acting on their Constitutional mandate and freedom to learn and report the facts.

We BELIEVE in public enlightenment as the forerunner of justice, and in our Constitutional role to seek the truth as part of the public's right to know the truth.

We BELIEVE those responsibilities carry obligations that require journalists to perform with intelligence, objectivity, accuracy, and fairness.

To these ends, we declare acceptance of the standards of practice here set forth:

I. RESPONSIBILITY: The public's right to know of events of public importance and interest is the overriding mission of the mass media. The purpose of distributing news and enlightened opinion is to serve the general welfare. Journalists who use their professional status as representatives of the public for selfish or other unworthy motives violate a high trust.

II. FREEDOM OF THE PRESS: Freedom of the press is to be guarded as an inalienable right of people in a free society. It carries with it the freedom and the responsibility to discuss, question, and challenge actions and utterances of our government and of our public and private institutions. Journalists uphold the right to speak unpopular opinions and the privilege to agree with the majority.

III. ETHICS: Journalists must be free of obligation to any interest other than the public's right to know the truth.

1. Gifts, favors, free travel, special treatment or privileges can compromise the integrity of journalists and their employers. Nothing of value should be accepted.

2. Secondary employment, political involvement, holding public office, and service in community organizations should be avoided if it compromises the integrity of journalists and their employers. Journalists and their employers should conduct their personal lives in a manner that protects them from conflict of interest, real or apparent. Their responsibilities to the public are paramount. That is the nature of their profession.

3. So-called news communications from private sources should not be published or broadcast without substantiation of their claims to news values.

4. Journalists will seek news that serves the public interest, despite the obstacles. They will make constant efforts to assure that the public's business is conducted in public and that public records are open to public inspection.

5. Journalists acknowledge the newsman's ethic of protecting confidential sources of information.

6. Plagiarism is dishonest and unacceptable.

IV. ACCURACY AND OBJECTIVITY: Good faith with the public is the foundation of all worthy journalism.

1. Truth is our ultimate goal.

2. Objectivity in reporting the news is another goal that serves as the mark of an experienced professional. It is a standard of performance toward which we strive. We honor those who achieve it.

3. There is no excuse for inaccuracies or lack of thoroughness.

4. Newspaper headlines should be fully warranted by the contents of the articles they accompany. Photographs and telecasts should give an accurate picture of an event and not highlight an incident out of context.

5. Sound practice makes clear distinction between news reports and expressions of opinion. News reports should be free of opinion or bias and represent all sides of an issue.

6. Partisanship in editorial comment that knowingly departs from the truth violates the spirit of American journalism.

7. Journalists recognize their responsibility for offering informed analysis, comment, and editorial opinion on public events and issues. They accept the obligation to present such material by individuals whose competence, experience, and judgment qualify them for it.

8. Special articles or presentations devoted to advocacy or the writer's own conclusions and interpretations should be labeled as such.

V. FAIR PLAY: Journalists at all times will show respect for the dignity, privacy, rights, and well-being of people encountered in the course of gathering and presenting the news.

1. The news media should not communicate unofficial charges affecting reputation or moral character without giving the accused a chance to reply.

2. The news media must guard against invading a person's right to privacy.

3. The media should not pander to morbid curiosity about details of vice and crime.

4. It is the duty of news media to make prompt and complete correction of their errors.

5. Journalists should be accountable to the public for their reports and the public should be encouraged to voice its grievances against the media. Open dialogue with our readers, viewers, and listeners should be fostered.

VI. PLEDGE: Adherence to this code is intended to preserve and strengthen the bond of mutual trust and respect between American journalists and the American people.

The Society shall—by programs of education and other means—encourage individual journalists to adhere to these tenets, and shall encourage journalistic publications and broadcasters to recognize their responsibility to frame codes of ethics in concert with their employees to serve as guidelines in furthering these goals.

(Adopted 1926; revised 1973, 1984, 1987)

does not assume its responsibilities, some other agency must see that the essential functions of mass communication are carried out.[10]

This concept of placing power in the hands of other agencies to ensure that the press acts responsibly has been applied to some extent to the broadcast media in the United States because they are licensed by the government. Although there have been recent efforts to deregulate the broadcast media, the Federal Communications Commission (FCC) has the authority to revoke a broadcaster's license if it is determined that he or she is not serving the public interest. This type of regulation does not apply to the print media in this country, although some other Western democracies do license their journalists. Thus social responsibility for the print media in the United States is a voluntary act adhered to by some print media officials, but not all.

Early Proponents. During the latter part of the nineteenth century, newspaper editors such as Horace Greeley of the *New York Tribune* and Henry J. Raymond of the *New York Times* recognized the need for some form of press responsibility and started to promote social good and community welfare. Then at the turn of the century, Joseph Pulitzer, whose *New York World* had been embroiled in a war of sensationalism with William Randolph Hearst's *New York Journal,* began reflecting on the dangers of circulation at any cost and started speaking out for more press responsibility. He wrote: "Without high ethical ideals a newspaper not only is stripped of its splendid possibilities for public service, but may become a positive danger to the community."[11]

Shortly thereafter, journalism education programs began to be established in colleges and universities. These programs not only offered career training in journalism but also stressed higher ideals and professional standards consistent with the social responsibility concept.

Self-regulation within the industry also reflected the press's acceptance of social responsibility. The American Society of Newspaper Editors adopted its Canons of Journalism in 1923. These guidelines call for the press to serve the public with truthfulness, impartiality, a sense of fair play, decency, respect for individual privacy and concern for the general welfare. Since then other professional journalism associations have stressed ethics and standards as a means of upgrading the profession (see Box 3.1).

Current Efforts. Today some American media organizations voluntarily adhere to the social responsibility theory. Others do not. Those that do attempt to present all sides of issues and strive to see that minority views and issues, as well as those of the Establishment, are covered. They may even open up editorial comments to dissenting opinions, usually on the "op-ed" (opposite editorial) page.

THE PRESS IN FOREIGN LANDS

In order to understand the mass media in American society better, it might be well to review briefly how the media operate in a few other countries today. It probably is already clear how the media in authoritarian or Communist states differ from those in the United States, but there are also differences in media operations among Western countries—particularly when it comes to the broadcast media.[12]

Soviet Union. Since we are already aware of the Soviet Communist theory of the press, let's begin our examination of the press in foreign lands by looking at the media in the Soviet Union.

Tass is the official Soviet news service, which provides the official news to media outlets. It operates similarly to the major wire services in this country (Associated Press [AP] and United Press International [UPI]) except that it is state owned and controlled. *Pravda (Truth)* is the Soviet party newspaper, which serves as the official record of party policies and government actions. It usually carries a front-page photograph glorifying the common person to stress that the party is dedicated to the "good of the common man." *Izvestia* is a government-published newspaper that is more popular and less theoretical than *Pravda.* In addition to these national publications, many ministries of government publish their own newspapers, and each of the 15 republics of the Soviet Union has its own regional and local media.

Unlike Western newspapers, which operate as businesses, the Soviet press does not carry advertisements. Because the Soviet press operates under the principles of the Soviet Communist concept, all of the newspapers in the country function as interpreters of the "truth" as seen by the Communist party. The press's function is to

A Soviet newspaper employee examines a front-page negative of *Pravda,* the official newspaper of the Soviet Communist Party. The page features a photograph of an ordinary citizen, a common practice of this newspaper. *(Sovoto)*

provide proper information for the people. Sometimes national and international news events are not covered in the Soviet press because they are considered not to be in the best interests of the state.

In 1986, for example, the Soviet Union initially attempted to keep secret the explosion and fire at the Chernobyl nuclear power plant. However, when high radiation levels were recorded in Scandinavia and other parts of Western Europe, the Soviet news media were forced to disclose some information. This terse radio broadcast seven days after the disaster released the first information of the event inside the Soviet Union: "There has been an accident at the Chernobyl nuclear power plant in the Ukraine. One of the nuclear reactors has been damaged. Measures for eliminating the consequences of the nuclear accident have been undertaken and victims are being rendered assistance. And now sports."[13]

Because of the lack of information from the Soviet Union, the Western press contained a great deal of misinformation about the disaster. At one point, reports that 2,000 people had died were printed and broadcast in the Western press, when in reality the figure was more like 31.

By the last 1980s Mikhail Gorbachev's new openness policy, *glasnost*, was changing this situation, however. The Soviet press was becoming much freer to print news and information critical of government officials. In fact, during the 1987 trial of six Chernobyl plant employees charged with causing the nuclear accident, the foreign press was even allowed to cover some of the court proceedings. While certain stories critical of Soviet life have appeared in print, there were still glaring omissions. The Soviet press made no mention, for example, of physicist Andrei Sakharov's public accusations against fellow members of the Soviet Academy of Sciences that they had spread "cock-and-bull stories" about his supposedly "tranquil life" in exile in the closed city of Gorky or his claims that he had suffered psychological torture and frequent harassment.

The four radio and four television networks in the Soviet Union are also state owned and operated. Programming consists of music (more than half of the music broadcast in the country is classical), drama and news. Unlike news media in this country, the Soviet news outlets do not attempt to scoop one another and prefer to wait on late-breaking stories until the leaders issue the official perspective. (Somber music is usually played for a number of hours before the death of a Soviet leader is officially announced, for example.)

United Kingdom. Great Britain has a large and successful national press, which is conveniently divided into two categories, the *popular* press and the *quality* press. The popular press has by far the higher circulation with the most widely read newspaper, the *Sun*, selling more than 4 million copies per day. The popular press is tabloid in format (half the size of a regular newspaper) and has content resembling parts of our *National Enquirer* and parts of the New York *Daily News*. These tabloids are designed to cater to the working class. The *Sun*, for example, features a "page 3 girl" (a different topless model appearing each day on page 3) and bingo to entice readers.

The *Sun* is owned by Rupert Murdoch, the Australian press baron who became a U.S. citizen in 1985. He also owns the *Times* of London and a major European satellite movie channel. His international media holdings as of 1987 included over 50 news-

Newspaper choices in Great Britain range from "popular" publications like the *Sun* to "quality" papers like the *Times*.

papers in Australia, the United States, Britain and Hong Kong; film companies and 18 magazines and trade publications in Australia and the United States; and television outlets in Europe and America.

An alternative to the popular press in the United Kingdom is the quality press, which consists of full-size newspapers written in a sophisticated manner for the more discriminating reader. Unlike most newspapers in this country, in the British quality press no effort is made to write down to the average reader. Only one quality newspaper, the *Daily Telegraph*, has a circulation more than a million. All others, including the famed *Times* of London, have national circulations of a few hundred thousand. Local and regional newspapers are also published in Great Britain, but none is as popular as the national popular and quality papers, which are distributed daily by train and plane to all parts of the United Kingdom.

The broadcasting media in the United Kingdom are also quite different from those in this country. For example, only four television channels are available to viewers in the United Kingdom, all of them closely regulated to protect consumer interests. Two of these channels are operated by the British Broadcasting Corporation (BBC), which was formed in the 1920s, when radio was becoming a mass-communication medium. The BBC is financed by government funds and by license fees levied on everyone who owns a television set.

The BBC also operates four radio channels. BBC 1 and BBC 2 carry popular music, one similar to American Top-40 and the other to American album-oriented stations. BBC 3 airs classical music, drama and other educational discussion programs. BBC 4 broadcasts news and talk-oriented programs, including popular newsmagazine shows.

BBC television, which started broadcasting in 1936, produces more than 85 percent of its own programming. The remainder includes independently produced shows and a few American imports, such as *Dallas* and *Dynasty*. BBC-produced programming is considered to be high quality and is distributed worldwide; more than a hundred stations carry its shows.

The BBC was the only broadcasting outlet in Great Britain until 1954, when Parliament, after years of debate, established the Independent Broadcasting Authority (IBA). The IBA operates the Independent Television (ITV) and Independent Local Radio (ILR) stations throughout the country.

Unlike the BBC stations, these independent radio and television stations carry commercials. However, the IBA regulates their number and types and even the points at which they interrupt the programs. Protection of consumer interests is the regulating criterion for the IBA.

ITV channels are regional in nature, and one is broadcast in each of the 15 regions (two stations broadcast in the London area at different times on the same frequency, for a total of 16 ITV stations). In addition to the two BBC channels and one ITV channel, Britishers receive a fourth channel—also independent and regulated by the IBA—called Channel 4. This channel was authorized by Parliament in 1982 to provide for "minority" programming needs.

Channel 4 programming originates in London and is fed throughout the kingdom. Local ITV stations, which subsidize this fourth network, are allowed to insert commercials where appropriate and can retain the revenue from those commercials.

For some time British television channels have carried teletext signals on their programs' blanking intervals (the blank space between picture frames). These teletext signals broadcast printed news and information that can be accessed by a remote-controlled converter. Several hundred pages (screens) of information, ranging from news to weather to travel information, are available on each channel's system. The basic difference between BBC and ITV teletext is that ITV carries commercials and the BBC channels do not. Nearly 2 million television sets in the United Kingdom are equipped with teletext converters. (For a more thorough description of teletext technology, see Chapter 14.)

Austria. The Federal Republic of Austria stretches from the Communist-bloc countries on the east to Switzerland. It has a population of only 7.5 million, mostly German-speaking, and nearly 100 percent literacy. The Austrian Republic was reestablished in 1945 after the end of World War II and regained full sovereignty in 1955, when the State Treaty was signed and foreign occupation ended. Permanent neutrality was declared in October of that year.

Because of its neutrality and its location at the eastern edge of Western Europe, Austria plays an important role in relaying information between the East and the West. News from American and Soviet satellites are monitored in Austria, and Austrian television personnel exchange information between the two blocs.

Newspapers in Austria are owned either by private individuals or by political parties. Two very large mass-circulation newspapers and 22 other dailies are published. The total circulation of these papers is 2.7 million, with the *Neue Kronen-Zeitung*, the *Kurier*, the *Graz* and the *Klagenfurt Kleine Zeitung* accounting for two-thirds of

In Austria newspapers are either privately held, like *Die Presse* and *Kurier*, or published by political parties, such as the government-run *Wiener Zeitung*.

this circulation. *Die Presse* is considered to be the most prestigious Austrian daily (equivalent to our *New York Times*). However, its circulation is only 59,000 Mondays through Thursdays and 77,000 on Fridays and weekends.

The two largest dailies, the *Neue Kronen* and *Kurier*, are privately owned. The Socialist party publishes the daily *Arbeiter Zeitung*, the Communist party publishes the *Volksstimme*, and the government publishes the semiofficial *Wiener Zeitung*. Another large political party—the People's party—publishes small provincial dailies. The Catholic church publishes a weekly called *Die Furche*. Editorial content of Austrian newspapers is determined by their ownership.

One state-regulated public monopoly, known as the Austrian Broadcasting Corporation, or ORF *(Österreichischer Rundfunk)*, is responsible for all Austrian broadcasting. ORF broadcasts two television channels, 13 locally originated radio stations and a teletext system similar to the one that operates in the United Kingdom.

By law, ORF television and radio signals must reach every valley and province in Austria, which includes the Austrian Alps in the western part of the country. This requires an expansive microwave operation. ORF has 2.5 million viewers in Austria and an estimated 6.5 million in the Communist-bloc countries of Hungary, Czechoslovakia and Yugoslavia.

Austria is Western in tradition, culture and political orientation, and ORF broadcasting reflects this. Since its television signal reaches Eastern Europe and its radio

signals travel into the Soviet Union, ORF is an influential medium for Western pen-
etration into Iron Curtain countries—more so than the Voice of America.

ORF is governed by a board composed of members of the various political parties
of Austria. The ruling party dominates the board membership, in accordance with the
Broadcasting Law of 1974. The general policy of ORF is one of neutrality and
objectivity.

ORF radio is more than 60 years old, and the television portion of the broadcast
system began in 1955, after the Soviets left the country. ORF television was politically
oriented until 1967, when a successful newspaper referendum forced a change.

ORF has 3,200 employees and receives its revenue from two sources: 60 percent
comes from user fees (about $10 per month from each radio and television set owner),
and 40 percent comes from commercials. Commercials are regulated by law and cannot exceed 20 minutes per day for television and 120 minutes a day for radio. Like
most European television, ORF does not broadcast 24 hours a day; it offers programming for three hours in the morning and from about 5:00 P.M. until midnight.

There are many similarities in operation, funding and structure between ORF and
the British Broadcasting Corporation. As a state-owned monopoly, ORF does not
have to make a profit and can spend a lot of money on experimental and cultural
programming.

Canada. Turning closer to home, we find British as well as American influences on
the mass media in Canada. Canada's vast size (the third largest country in the world)
and small population (26 million) has resulted in the domination of most media by two
or three giant companies in each medium. Since approximately one-fourth of the population is French-speaking, Canada has developed both French and English systems
of mass media.

Most of Canada's major newspapers are controlled by two companies—Southam
Communications, Ltd., which owns many papers, including Toronto's influential
Globe and Mail; and Thomson Newspapers, a syndicate founded by Roy Thomson,
the owner of the *Times* of London before Rupert Murdoch. There are very few independent newspapers.

Canadian Press (CP), co-owned by over 100 Canadian daily newspapers, is the only
Canadian wire service. Most papers supplement it by subscribing to America's AP
and UPI, Britian's Reuters or France's AFP.

Books and magazines in Canada consist of a mixture of Canadian-owned and foreign publications. The dominant Canadian book publisher is McClelland and Stewart,
although the most successful Canadian publisher internationally is Harlequin Enterprises, king of the romance novel market. Subsidiaries of American and British firms,
such as Random House of Canada and Penguin Books Canada, also play an important
part in Canadian book publishing.

Until the late 1960s, both *Time* and *Reader's Digest* marketed a Canadian version
in Canada. *Time*, for example, included an 8–10 page section on Canadian news
before the section of U.S. news. When the Canadian government passed legislation
limiting the deductibility of advertising costs in foreign media (including radio and
television), advertising support for the Canadian version of *Time* died. Today, there

is an occasional page of Canadian news in the issues of *Time* distributed in that country, but that's about it.

Filling the void has been *Maclean's*, formerly a Canadian news and opinion monthly along the lines of *Harper's* or *The Atlantic*. It is now Canada's weekly newsmagazine and the flagship of the country's dominant magazine publisher, Maclean-Hunter.

Lifestyle publications are as big in Canada as they are in America. In addition to Canadian magazines like Chatelaine, the magazine racks are filled with American, British and French publications.

Radio and television in Canada are provided by both national networks and independent stations. The first national networks were the Canadian Broadcasting Corporation (CBC) for English speakers and Radio Canada for French speakers (that name is somewhat confusingly used for both the radio and television networks. These networks are similar to the British BBC in that they are funded by the government. However, unlike the BBC, they do carry commercials. Despite the government funding, these networks are independent of political control. The government does, however, require all radio stations playing popular music to have at least 30 percent Canadian content.

The nation's second TV network, CTV, provides television programming that is a little less "highbrow" than the CBC's. The newest television network, Global, provides programming only to major metropolitan areas. In addition to the networks, there are numerous independent radio and television stations. All stations are regulated by the Canadian Radio-Television Commission (CRTC), a government agency similar to Britain's IBA or America's FCC.

Until recently, Canada's main contribution to the motion picture industry was to export its most talented citizens—from Mary Pickford to Michael J. Fox—to Hollywood. However, in recent years many Hollywood movie producers have been lured by generous tax breaks to make their pictures on location in Canada. Although the tax breaks have now been scaled back, the practice still continues because of lower production costs in Canada. The most famous Canadian movie production company is the National Film Board, which has been making award-winning documentaries for decades. It is funded by the government.

Mexico. The mass media in Mexico operate somewhat differently from those of the neighboring United States. The first newspaper in Mexico was started in 1722, 18 years after the first one was established in the British colonies in America. Because the Mexican literacy rate lagged behind that of the United States, the Mexican press lingered longer in the elite culture.

Although Mexican newspapers are privately owned, they do not operate with the same freedom as American newspapers. The Mexican government, for example, owns all of the nation's newsprint. The fact that a newspaper is able to get newsprint suggests that it has the blessing of the government.

One antigovernment newspaper, *Zeta*, which circulates in Baja California, survives only because it prints its copies across the border in nearby San Diego, where newsprint is available. Ominously, in 1988 the co-owner and editor of *Zeta* was murdered on his way to work in Tijuana. He joined more than two dozen Mexican journalists who have been murdered in the past 16 years. None of the murders has been solved.

Broadcasting in Mexico is much like that in Western Europe and Canada. Government entities regulate broadcasting, which consists of a combination of government-owned stations and strictly regulated private stations that must give up to 12.5 percent of their air time to the government.

Third World Nations.   The developing nations in Latin America, Africa, the Middle East and Asia are considered Third World nations. (The First World consists of the so-called Western powers and the Second World the Communist-bloc nations.) In some Third World countries media operations are strikingly different from those in more developed Western nations.

Economic, political and cultural factors strongly influence Third World countries. In the East African nation of Tanzania, for example, the average person's income is

---

The *Barricada*, published in Managua, Nicaragua, is the official newspaper of the Sandinista government. It is consistently critical of the United States and the Contra forces. Note the armed Sandinista soldier in the nameplate.

$136 a year. The media do not carry any advertising; the reason is not political, as it is in the Soviet Union, but economic—people cannot afford to buy what would be advertised.

In most Third World countries, advertising-supported media are possible only in large urban centers where there are large numbers of middle- and upper-middle-class citizens. Thus, for the most part, the Third World media exist for the elite class.

Many Third World nations operate state-owned television stations, which are used more to impress neighboring countries than to inform the people (the majority of whom don't own televisions sets). Yet, that doesn't mean that TV doesn't sometimes reach large audiences. In Egypt and Kenya, for example, many people will come together to share a single TV set.

Government-operated radio, on the other hand, is emerging in many Third World countries as the first mass-communication medium to reach the masses because radios are relatively inexpensive and can reach the illiterate. Mass media censorship is prevalent in Third World countries, and in many regions—Africa, for example—this censorship traces its heritage to earlier days of colonialism.

Foreign press domination in Third World countries, particularly from the Communist East and the capitalist West, has caused resentment because much of the news flowing in and out of these emerging nations must come from the communist-controlled *Tass* or Western press services such as AP and UPI. This resentment has led in recent years to numerous discussions at the United Nations Educational, Scientific, and Cultural Organization (UNESCO) on how to protect the sovereignty of nations from the flow of international information.

Several UNESCO-sponsored conferences have recommended a "new world information order," which would give each country the right to control who could send information out and what information could come in. A system of licensing all journalists (both foreign and domestic) working within the country would be used to control what news could leave a nation.

The UNESCO recommendations generated a great deal of controversy in the international journalistic community and strong resistance from many Western journalists. The United States cited these recommendations as one of the reasons why it dropped its membership in UNESCO in 1985.

SUMMARY

In this chapter we have examined the political philosophies under which the mass media operate and we have taken a look at how print and broadcast media function in certain countries.

The authoritarian theory of the press is the oldest and requires that the press be regulated so as to not hinder the state in any way.

The libertarian theory offers the opposing viewpoint that the press should function to serve the governed, not the governors.

Each of these theories has an offshoot. The Soviet Communist theory is an extension of the authoritarian theory and makes the press a planned, integral part of the state. Under this theory, the media are state-owned and controlled for the purpose of advancing the state's ideals and beliefs.

Social responsibility is an offshoot of the libertarian theory. After determining that the libertarian theory was not functioning as intended by the founding fathers, proponents of social responsibility contend that freedom of the press must go hand in hand with responsibility.

The mass media in the Soviet Union, United Kingdom, Austria, Canada, Mexico and Third World nations differ from those in the United States. The media in each country reflect economic conditions, the government's political philosophies and the popular culture.

NOTES

1. Hugh Sidey, "An Interview with the President," *Time*, Dec. 8, 1986, p. 18.

2. Fred S. Siebert, Theodore B. Peterson and Wilbur Schramm, *Four Theories of the Press* (Urbana: University of Illinois Press, 1956) p. 33.

3. Frank Luther Mott, *American Journalism,* 3rd ed. (New York: Macmillan, 1962), p. 6.

4. Wilbur, Schramm, *Responsibility in Mass Communication* (New York: Harper & Row, 1957), p. 72.

5. Quoted in Warren K. Agee, Phillip H. Ault and Edwin Emery, *Introduction to Mass Communications,* 6th ed. (New York: Harper & Row, 1979), p. 31.

6. Quoted in *Speaking of a Free Press* (New York: ANPA Foundation, 1970), p. 15.

7. Speech in Moscow, 1920, quoted in

H. L. Mencken, *A New Dictionary of Quotations on Historical Principles from Ancient and Modern Sources,* (New York: Knopf, 1966), p. 966.

8. Mark W. Hopkins, *Mass Media in the Soviet Union* (New York: Pegasus, 1970), p. 20.

9. Siebert, Peterson and Schramm, pp. 78–79.

10. Ibid., p. 74.

11. Joseph Pulitzer, "The College of Journalism," *North American Review* 178 (May 1904): 667.

12. Much of this information was gathered from personal interviews with media personnel in various countries.

13. This Radio Kiev broadcast was monitored in Annapolis, Maryland, and a report of it was carried by United Press International on May 4, 1986.

ADDITIONAL READING

Cullen, Maurice R, Jr. *Mass Media and the First Amendment.* Dubuque, Iowa: Brown, 1981.

Handlin, Oscar. *The History of the United States,* 2 vols. New York: Holt, Rinehart & Winston, 1968.

Lipscomb, A. A., ed. *The Writings of Thomas Jefferson.* Washington, D.C.: Thomas Jefferson Memorial Association, 1904.

Mill, John Stuart. "On Liberty [1858]," in *Great Books of the Western World.* Chicago: Encyclopaedia Britannica, 1952.

Schramm, Wilbur. *Mass Media and National Development.* Palo Alto, Calif.: Stanford University Press, 1964.

Part 2

The Development of Print Media

Chapter 4

Book Publishing: Past and Present

A book is the only place in
which you can examine a fragile
thought without breaking it, or
explore an explosive idea
without fear it will go off in
your face. . . . It is one of the few
havens remaining where a man's mind
can get both provocation and privacy.
—*Edward P. Morgan*

Exactly 47 hours and 29 minutes after the President's Special Review Board, better known as the Tower Commission, released its report on the Reagan administration's involvement in the Iran-Contra scandal, the first copy of a paperback book containing the entire report rolled off the press. This *instant book* had been produced in record-breaking time by a joint venture between Bantam Books and Time Books, a division of Random House.

Copies were rushed by air to bookstores across the country, and the book became an "instant" best-seller. Within a week 700,000 copies had been printed, and large bookstore chains like B. Dalton were selling out of the books as quickly as they were getting them in.

Although book publishing is the oldest form of mass communication, it is still a very successful and profitable enterprise. More than 1,700 regular publishing houses exist in the United States, and they gross $11.7 billion in sales a year. In addition, there are 14,000 small publishing firms, many one-person operations dedicated to preserving a particular literary point of view. In the late 1980s the combined effort of these publishers were producing more than 40,000 books each year.

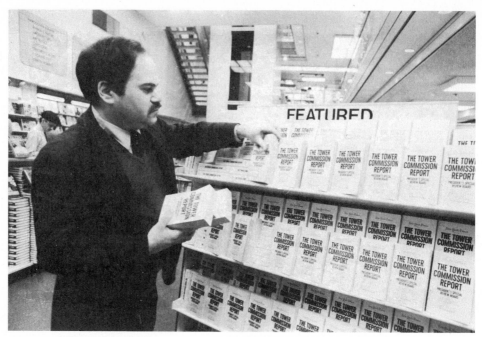

The Tower Commission Report, an "instant book" issued by Bantam Books, set a record by being on bookstands a mere 47 hours and 29 minutes after the report was released. *(AP/ Wide World Photos)*

Books are sold across the country in retail outlets ranging from large chain-owned bookstores, department stores, supermarkets and variety stores to gas stations, train depots, airports and convenience stores. Books are ever-present in our popular culture. For although books are one of the few mass media that do not rely on advertising to produce revenue, the book-publishing industry does use advertising—and talk shows—to stimulate sales.

Books also play an important role in preserving the ideas, thoughts and histories of civilizations. Since these records are handed down from generation to generation and are collected in libraries—a practice that has been going on for thousands of years—books have become the most permanent of all the mass media. For example, to learn about the Persian Wars of 500 years B.C., one need only to read *The History of the Persian Wars* by Herodotus, who lived at that time. To learn about early Greek literature and the Homeric age, which fell between the thirteenth and ninth centuries B.C., one can turn to Homer's *Iliad* and *Odyssey*, written around the eighth or ninth centuries B.C.

ORIGINS OF BOOKS

In order to understand how books influence our culture today, it is necessary to review how this mass-communication medium developed and how it has been influencing and changing cultures for centuries.

EPS STAGES — Elitist	Popular	Specialized	THE CULTURAL HISTORY OF BOOKS	
●			c. 2500 B.C.	Sumerian clay tablets.
●			c. 600 B.C.	Papyrus scrolls used in Egypt.
●			540 B.C.	First public library founded, in Athens.
●			1st century A.D.	Books regarded as household treasures by the elite.
●			5th century	Great Library of Alexandria, Egypt, destroyed.
●			5th–10th centuries	Books preserved in monasteries.
●			9th century	Chinese invent printing.
●			13th century	Rise of European universities.
●			1456	Gutenberg Bible printed from movable type.
●	●		16th century	Books become the first mass-produced and mass-distributed commodity.
●	●		16th century	Books help spread the ideas of the Protestant Reformation; authorities invoke censorship to control printers.
●	●		1640	*Bay Psalm Book* published at Harvard College.
	●		18th–19th centuries	Industrial Revolution.
●	●		19th century	Rise of American novelists and publishing houses.
	●		1852	*Uncle Tom's Cabin* is published; sells 7 million copies, helps spark Civil War (1861–65).
	●		1867	Horatio Alger, Jr., publishes his first "rags-to-riches" story, *Ragged Dick*.
	●		1873	Anthony Comstock founds the New York Society for the Suppression of Vice.
	●		1920s	Novelists used publicity from having their books "banned in Boston" to promote sales elsewhere.
		●	1945	Books begin serving a variety of specialized interests as post–World War II years change American culture.
		●	1957	Supreme Court begins to liberalize its interpretation of obscenity in *Roth* v. *United States*.
		●	1960s	Wide range of books published, reflecting new subcultures and protest movements.
		●	1973	Supreme Court adopts stricter "contemporary community standards" test to define obscenity (*Miller* v. *California*).
		●	1980s	Book publishers begin marketing electronic books.

Early Forms. We can trace book publishing back to Sumerian clay tablets, which were used 4,500 years ago to record various items of religious, legal and medical interest, as well as narrative tales. These are the oldest written documents known to mankind.

Next came papyrus scrolls, which were used throughout ancient Egypt, Greece and Rome. These large rolls of papyrus were attached to two rods that permitted the book to be held and rolled from either end. Although the lengths of the manuscripts varied, some rolls contained entire books. Archeologists have unearthed ancient handwritten scrolls in Egyptian, Greek, Latin, Arabic, Hebrew and Syrian. In addition to religious writings, these scrolls contained the philosophies, history, oratory, drama, poetry and anthologies of such ancient writers as Eustathius, Plato, Aristotle, Demosthenes, Homer, Sophocles, Euripides, Archilochus and Ascepiades.

Public Libraries. The first public library was established in Athens in 540 B.C. Later, around 300 B.C., Ptolemy I founded the Great Library in Alexandria, Egypt. The library became the intellectual center of the Hellenistic Empire, and the most famous scholars, scientists, poets, philosophers and artists of the day gathered there to study and work.

At its peak, the library contained between half a million and a million hand-copied papyrus volumes—almost all of Western civilization's recorded knowledge. Transcribers were often sent there to copy manuscripts for other libraries. This great repository of learning was burned and ravaged by Romans, civil war and even the Christian emperor Theodosius I; by A.D. 400 the world's greatest intellectual treasury up to that time had been lost forever.

The selling and collecting of papyrus scrolls in ancient Rome reached its peak around the time of Christ, with some households reportedly having libraries containing thousands of volumes. As the Roman Empire began its decline and libraries were ravaged and burned during barbarian invasions, books found sanctuary in Christian monasteries, especially in Ireland.[1]

Middle Ages. Although relatively little is known about the development and use of books during the Middle Ages (A.D. fifth through fourteenth centuries), there were some improvements in how knowledge was recorded. For example, in the fifth century the Saxons began using books made of animal skins; these more resembled paged books as we know them today. About this same time the Romans were replacing the awkward scroll with the codex, which was a stack of folded leaves that was bound along one side and protected by wooden covers. The more durable animal parchment was replacing papyrus as the medium on which books were written.

Also at about the same time, the Chinese were perfecting and using paper made from tree bark, old rags, hemp waste and fishnets. The art of making paper slowly spread through Europe around the twelfth century, although paper wasn't produced in England until the late fifteenth century or on the American continent until the late seventeenth century. The Chinese were also the first to develop printing, sometime during the ninth century. The oldest existing printed book is *The Diamond Sutra*, printed in China in A.D. 868 from carved wood blocks and containing Buddhist wisdom.

However, printing did not spread from China to the Western world. Bookmaking and manuscript copying by cloistered clergy in monasteries remained a handcrafted process in Europe through the Middle Ages. Thus most of the medieval codex production consisted of sacred works such as Bible texts and interpretations, liturgical manuscripts and the works of those philosophers and classical authors whose thoughts were believed to contribute to Christian principles.

However, by the thirteenth century, a secular stirring was felt throughout Europe, and there was a renewed interest in science, philosophy, contemporary languages and literature. This led to the emergence of the European universities and a new, secular interest in classical books.

The Renaissance. Six centuries after the Chinese began to print books, printing technology was introduced into the Western culture. Credit for bringing mass communication to the Western World belongs to the German inventor Johannes Gutenberg, who used movable type and a converted wine press to publish a 42-line-per-page Bible in 1456. This large-sized Bible, in Latin, was a replica of existing hand-copied manuscripts. Gutenberg's Bible was a work of great precision and beauty, and the reproduction of 200 identical copies was astonishing in a world that was used to handwritten books.

Although Gutenberg died a pauper shortly after his press was confiscated to pay his debts, by the end of the fifteenth century this new craft was established in every major capital in Europe. The first printer in England was William Caxton, who published his first book in 1476.

EARLY BOOKS AND THE ELITE

From the days of clay tablets to well beyond the invention of mass communication, books were limited to the elite. Thousands of years passed before the medium began to enter the popular culture.

Even after Gutenberg's new technology spread throughout Western Europe, books remained in the elite culture in accordance with the EPS curve (see Chapter 1). Poverty and illiteracy were the main causes. Books were read primarily by the clergy, educators, scientists, professionals and members of the aristocracy.

However, the Renaissance also saw a great expansion of trade and commerce and the creation of a new middle class. These prosperous merchants and bankers had a practical interest in secular learning and proved a ready market for books. Thus the first mass-communication medium began at last to reach people beyond a tiny elite.

The Reformation. By the time of the Protestant Reformation, in the sixteenth century, printing was able to reach the developing middle class. In the 1520s, for example, Martin Luther became the first person to use this new mass-communication technology for propaganda purposes. He wrote a series of pamphlets in German attacking the doctrines of the Roman Catholic Church. Luther's revolt caused the printing of books in Germany to rise from 150 in 1518 to 990 in 1524. Four-fifths of these books favored the Reformation. Soon his works were being printed in other languages and were spreading throughout Western Europe. As one historian has written, "Printing was the Reformation; Gutenberg made Luther possible."[2]

Part of Luther's new religious doctrine was the idea that the people—not the Catholic Church—should be the interpreters of the Bible. To facilitate this premise, he translated both the Old and New Testaments of the Latin Bible into conversational German. During his lifetime, 100,000 copies of the New Testament were printed, and it became and has remained the best-selling book in Germany.[3]

Censorship. The practice of censorship developed at the same time as the Protestant Reformation. It did not take long for those in authority—kings and popes—to realize that Gutenberg's new technology, which allowed ideas to be mass produced and distributed, posed a threat to those in power. As noted in Chapter 2, King Henry II in Catholic France made it a practice to burn books and printers who attempted to distribute Protestant thought. In England, King Henry VIII established a list of prohibited books and by 1529 had developed a system of licensing printers. Even Martin Luther advocated the censorship of books written by Huldreich Zwingli and John Calvin—Protestants with views different from his own. This era of religious censorship and suppression lasted over a hundred years, and many people were executed for expressing their beliefs. The voice of religious and political dissent was never completely stilled, however, as printers could always find a haven somewhere to publish "heretical" writings.

STAGES OF BOOK PUBLISHING IN THE UNITED STATES

England's policy of strict censorship of the press and the licensing of printers was transported to the new English colonies in America in the seventeenth century. Although this helped curtail the early development and spread of books in the colonies, book publishing did eventually grow and flourish. To better understand the development of book publishing in America, we will examine this industry as it evolved through each stage of the EPS cycle.

The Elitist Stage. Printing remained in the elite culture in the American colonies from the seventeenth to the nineteenth century. The conditions necessary for books to enter the popular culture (see Chapter 1) were slow to develop. Most colonists had few luxuries. Like all frontiersmen, they worked hard and had very little leisure time for the cultivation of aesthetic and intellectual values. With the exception of the elite and clergy, most colonists could not read nor write.

Religion, which played a major role in the expansion of book publishing in sixteenth century Europe, was also instrumental in getting this industry started in the colonies. Many settlers belonged to strict religious sects, such as the Puritans who settled in the Massachusetts Bay colony. The Puritans were responsible for establishing the first printing press in North America in 1638 at Harvard College near Boston; two years later it published the first book in the Thirteen Colonies, the *Whole Booke of*

Psalmes, better known as the *Bay Psalm Book*. Harvard controlled this press until 1662, when the Massachusetts legislature took it over. The early Harvard press was used to produce religious books, pamphlets and sermons, as well as some government and educational materials.

One of the first successful secular contributors to the development of book publishing in the American colonies was Benjamin Franklin. He began publishing one of America's most famous early books, *Poor Richard's Almanac*, in 1733. It became successful—selling about 10,000 copies a year—by giving people something besides the Bible to read in the home. The almanac contained a wide variety of useful and entertaining information, including poetry, short stories, mean temperatures in various parts of the country, lists of public officials and public affairs articles. In 1744 Franklin published the first novel in America, *Pamela*, by English novelist Samuel Richardson. Franklin was also the first person to establish a subscription library in the colonies.

Publishing developed slowly in the North American colonies. However, a number of important pamphlets produced by political dissenters around the time of the American Revolution stimulated an interest in reading. In 1774 three separate publications challenged the right of England's Parliament to govern the colonies: James Wilson's *Considerations on the Nature and Extent of the Legislative Authority of the British Parliament*, Thomas Jefferson's *A Summary View of the Rights of British America* and John Adams's *Novanglus Papers*. In 1776 Englishman Thomas Paine, who had come to the colonies two years earlier, published *Common Sense*. In 47 pages it spelled out the meaning of the American revolutionary movement and made it clear that the Americans were not quibbling over the details of taxation but were standing up for their liberties as a nation. The pamphlet sold 120,000 copies in three months, a tremendous number when one considers that the population at the time was only about 400,000.[4]

Following the Revolutionary War, book-publishing centers were established in New York, Boston and Philadelphia, and the new industry began to expand. According to historian Oscar Handlin, "the exciting current events of the Revolution fortified the desire for printed matter. Americans wished to learn what was going on in every part of the continent, and they were anxious to follow the political arguments provoked by the debate over their rights. The result was a steady rise in the volume of publications."[5]

A number of American novelists soon began publishing. Although some were writing in a style similar to their European counterparts, others were developing a uniquely American style of writing. Examples include Hugh Henry Brackenridge's *Modern Chivalry* (1792), a satire on the first few years of the politics of the new nation; Charles Brockden Brown's *Wieland* (1798), a romantic tragedy in a genre of horror and remorse that Edgar Allan Poe would later cultivate; and Washington Irving's *A History of New York, By Diedrich Knickerbocker* (1809), a humorous parody of an earlier work about New York City. Noah Webster helped establish an American language by publishing a national dictionary.

The Popular Stage. As the new nation struggled with its destiny as a republic dedicated to the common wealth of all its people, its economy and culture began changing. The nation underwent an expansion to the West. To accommodate this vast new country a transportation system of canals and eventually steam-engined railroads developed. The new methods of transportation furthered economic, political and social unity by bringing the vast regions of the nation closer together. This growth stimulated trade and commerce, and the nation's cities grew.

Conditions in Europe—landlords were ousting tenants from their land to put larger acreages together for more profitable farming and famine was sweeping across Ireland and Germany in the 1840s—caused hundreds of thousands of people to immigrate to the United States annually. This large unskilled labor pool stimulated the growth of industries, and by the mid-nineteenth century the agrarian American culture was being transformed into an industrial society as the Industrial Revolution swept the land.

The Industrial Revolution also brought new technology to printing. Cylinder and rotary presses and Ottmar Mergenthaler's Linotype machine greatly sped up book production. Large numbers of trees were also available, making wood-pulp paper abundant.

At the same time the concept of compulsory public education was taking hold; only an educated citizenry, it was argued, could uphold and protect the new democracy from the threat of new tyrannies. By the 1840s universal public education had been established in most Northern cities, and a large literate population began to emerge. By the 1850s all states had accepted the principle of tax-supported elementary schools. (In the South, however, blacks were barred from this education.) By 1861 the United States had the highest literacy rate in the world: 94 percent of the population in the North and 83 percent of the whites in the South (58 percent of the total population). Industrialization and universal public education together created the conditions that moved book publishing from the elite into the popular culture.

Books by American writers like Ralph Waldo Emerson, James Fenimore Cooper, Henry David Thoreau, Catherine Sedgwick, Lydia Sigourney and Edgar Allan Poe were finding their way into the popular culture. In addition, many Americans enjoyed the works of popular British authors such as Charles Dickens and William Wordsworth. By 1855, U.S. book sales far exceeded sales figures in England.

Recognizing the immense market for books, an entrepreneur named Erastus Beadle decided to mass produce a line of cheap books that appealed to common interests. He and his brother Irwin published huge printings of paperback books that followed a set formula of praising the spirit of individuality and the virtue of common people. A typical title was *Malaeska: Indian Wife of the White Hunter,* by Mrs. Ann S. Stephens. He sold these books—called Beadle's Dime Novels—for ten cents each and began advertising them as "Dollar Books for a Dime!" Between 1860 and 1865 he sold over 4 million copies.

During this period a number of other individuals established major publishing houses, many of which are still prominent today. Among these entrepreneurs were the brothers James and John Harper, John Wiley, George Palmer Putnam, Dan Appleton, Charles Scribner, E. P. Dutton, Henry Oscar Houghton and George Harrison Mifflin (Houghton Mifflin) and Charles Little and James Brown (Little, Brown).

These publishing houses opened up opportunities for a newly developed crop of American authors to publish their works, and many outstanding literary works resulted. Nathaniel Hawthorne's *The Scarlet Letter* (1850) is said to be one of the greatest books ever written in the Western hemisphere. Herman Melville's *Moby-*

Beadle's Dime Novels, like the one shown here, helped bring book publishing into the popular culture.

Dick (1851) is still considered one of the finest novels in American literature. Harriet Beecher Stowe's *Uncle Tom's Cabin* (1852), which helped forge antislavery thinking before the Civil War, established the American novel as a powerful literary and social force. The story of a literate, kindly slave known as Uncle Tom, who was abused and finally killed by the evil Simon Legree, was published first in serial form in a magazine and later as a two-volume novel. Although banned from sale in the South, the book was an early success, selling about 1,000 copies a week; a total of 7 million copies were eventually sold. *Uncle Tom's Cabin* had a profound influence on public opinion and evoked sympathetic responses from various national leaders, including the future president of the United States, Abraham Lincoln.

By the end of the nineteenth century a number of writers had large followings and fan clubs similar to those that idolize today's rock stars. They included Mark Twain, who wrote about growing up on the Mississippi with Tom Sawyer and Huckleberry Finn, and the English poets Robert Browning and Rudyard Kipling.

However, the most commercially successful author of this period was Horatio Alger, who wrote over 120 books about growing up in the new industrial society. His books, which offered hope for the young in the new mass culture, were all rags-to-riches tales of the American dream—a pious, intelligent young boy makes his way to the top by hard work and virtue. The theme of upward mobility seemed to strike a responsive chord in the hearts of many (see Box 4.1).

This era also saw the development of a free public library system, which made books available to all segments of the public regardless of whether they could afford

BOX 4.1

FACING THE WORLD OR THE HAPS AND MISHAPS OF HARRY VANE, BY HORATIO ALGER, JR.

One of the many Horatio Alger heros was Harry Vane, a poor orphan boy in *Facing the World*. After his father dies, Harry goes to live with a mean, stingy guardian who plots to steal his money after he is given a $300 reward for saving the lives of passengers on a train that was about to crash into a washed-out culvert. Harry, referred to throughout the book as "our hero," is reluctant to accept money for saving the train. "'Oh Sir!' said Harry, as soon as he understood what was going forward, 'don't reward me for what was only my duty. I should be ashamed to accept anything for the little I have done.'"

Harry finally takes the money, outsmarts his guardian's efforts to steal it, and runs away to join up with a traveling magician as an intermission singer and ticket collector. The two then decide to take their show to Australia, only to be shipwrecked. Harry, who saves the life of a young cabin boy on the ship who is about to be killed by the drunken captain, remains brave and heroic throughout the ordeal. After months on a desert island, the shipwrecked sailors and passengers take to lifeboats and are discovered by another ship headed for Australia. The book ends with Alger writing: "In due time they reach Melbourne, without further mischance ... What befell the two boys [Harry and the young cabin boy], in whom I hope my readers have become interested, will be told in a new story, entitled: 'In a New World; or, Harry Vane in Australia.'"

The plots of all Horatio Alger books were simple and melodramatic. His series of some 120 novels were all rags-to-riches stories for boys. His formula for success was simple but effective. The stories recounted the trials and tribulations of young, energetic, hard-working young boys who develop into "honorable, manly characters."

Alger's books had such evocative titles as *Ragged Dick, Only an Irish Boy, The Cash Boy, Making His Way, Strong and Steady, Try and Trust, Bound to Rise, Tony the Tramp, Joe's Luck* and *Julius the Street Boy*. Publishers promoted the books by pointing out that "their high moral character, clean, manly tone and the wholesome lessons they teach without being *goody-goody*, make Alger Books as acceptable to the parents as to the boys."*

Alger made an important contribution to American popular culture by transmitting the idea that upward mobility was possible as long as one was honest and worked hard. These virtues became an important part of American mythology.

*Quoted from inside cover of *Facing the World* (New York: New York Book Company, 1909.)

to purchase them. This library system helped to establish the concept of egalitarianism in the American culture.

As industrialization spread and the number of immigrants in the United States increased (there were 4 million foreign born in 1860 but 9 million by 1890), worker exploitation through poor working conditions and low wages became common. To expose these conditions, a new kind of book emerged in the popular culture. Novels like Upton Sinclair's *The Jungle* (1906), which described intolerable working and sanitation conditions in Chicago's meat-packing plants, helped raise the public's social consciousness during this era. This and other books like it were instrumental in changing public attitudes about the benefit and dangers of unfettered free enterprise. Eventually laws were passed to protect consumers and employees, such as statutes that required federal inspection of food products and child-labor laws, which prevented the exploitation of children in sweatshops.

Meanwhile, as book publishing became firmly entrenched in the popular culture, major efforts were still being made to censor books. The first such effort in the new nation came in 1821 when the book *Fanny Hill*, published before the Revolution by the famed printer Isaiah Thomas, was found to be obscene at a trial in Massachusetts.

A major push came in 1873 when Anthony Comstock, a New York City dry-goods store employee, founded the nonprofit New York Society for the Suppression of Vice. Its stated purpose was to "clean the filth out of the wickedest city in the world." Comstock devoted 40 years to this effort and was succesful in getting federal legislation passed that made it illegal to send anything obscene through the mail. One result was that providing information about contraception was illegal in many states for almost a hundred years (until a Supreme Court decision in 1965).

According to historian Paul Boyer, the vice-society movement grew "in response to the deep-seated fears about the drift of urban life in post–Civil War years." As Boyer notes, the migration of Americans away from the familiar sources of guidance and support—family, church and close-knit communities—and into the metropolitan areas made people like Comstock feel there was a need to protect the nation's young from the "filth" that could be found in popular literature.[6]

Efforts at censorship continued well into the twentieth century. It took court action before certain books, like Erskine Caldwell's *God's Little Acre* and James Joyce's *Ulysses*, could be sold in the United States. (Both books were attacked by censors because they contained sexually explicit language.)

One of the most famous censoring efforts of this century was conducted in Boston. This community, which still had strong religious influences, established a book-censoring commission; books found objectionable by the commission were "banned in Boston." Some of the writers whose works were banned were John Dos Passos, Theodore Dreiser, Ernest Hemingway, Sinclair Lewis, Upton Sinclair and H. G. Wells. Boston's strict censorship codes did not reflect national attitudes toward literature and conflicted with many people's desire for a wide range of reading material. As a result, the city's efforts seemed to do more to stimulate sales in other parts of the country than to suppress books in Boston. As Upton Sinclair once said, "We authors are using America as our sales territory and Boston as our advertising department."

Whatever impact censorship had on sales, there is no doubt that publishing houses flourished in the first half of the century, as reading became one of the most popular leisure activities in both the elite and popular cultures. An example can be found in the success story of Bennett Cerf and Donald S. Klopfer. In 1925 Cerf—a book salesman for Boni & Liveright—persuaded his wealthy friend Klopfer to invest $100,000 to purchase the Modern Library, Boni & Liveright's classical-book division. Two years later the partners formed an additional company so that they could print books other than classical reprints, "sort of at random," Cerf later noted. To suit their aim, they called this new publishing operation Random House. In 1966, they sold Random House to RCA for $40 million (RCA later sold Random House to Samuel I. Newhouse, Jr.). The value of book-publishing firms has continued to climb. In 1987, the Australian—turned American citizen—media baron Rupert Murdoch paid $300 million for Harper & Row.

The Specialized Stage. The period from 1945 to the present has seen a dramatic shift in the book-publishing industry, as the business responded to new and changing audiences. For example, after World War II ended, many military personnel enrolled in college under the GI Bill, which paid veterans' educational expenses. As a result, the textbook business boomed, and it wasn't long before textbook publishing led the list in revenue generators for the book-publishing industry (a position it for the most part still retains).

In addition, people began to take up or renew other interests, such as their family and children, suburban living, and leisure activities like hunting, fishing, bowling, tennis, golf and spectator sports. The book-publishing industry responded by bringing out more nonfiction "lifestyle" titles each year, rather than relying so heavily on a few blockbuster popular novels. Child care manuals, books on how to landscape the backyard or fix up the house and tell-all biographies became hot sellers in the marketplace. Book publishing had begun to enter the third stage of the EPS cycle—the age of specialization. (See Box 4.2 for perhaps the ultimate specialized book.) The ratio of literary works—fiction, biography, poetry and drama—to nonliterary works, such as textbooks, professional books, reference books, cookbooks and "self-help" and "do-it-yourself" guides, shifted dramatically. By the 1970s new *non*literary works outnumbered new literary works by more than two to one.[7]

Textbooks, used in nearly every classroom in America, generate the highest income of any U.S. book publishing category. (*Woodfin Camp & Associates*)

BOX 4.2.

BARBIE: HER LIFE AND TIMES BY BILLYBOY

Books have been reflecting our culture for thousands of years. These reflections can take many forms. Even a twentieth century popular-culture icon—the Barbie doll—has been chroniclized for future civilizations in a book called *Barbie: Her Life and Times*. Written by the French jewelry designer BillyBoy, the book includes over 300 full-color photos of the doll, taken from Billy-Boy's collection of over 11,000 Barbie dolls.

This study of the Barbie doll does more than reflect BillyBoy's affection for it, however. It also provides an insight into changing American attitudes toward the role of women in our culture by charting the evolution of the Barbie doll from its early days as a petticoated prom queen to a doctor, astronaut and fitness-conscious business-woman in the 1980s.

Perhaps someday sociologists will be able to study the role children's toys play in changing sexist stereotypes by reading BillyBoy's book on his doll collection.

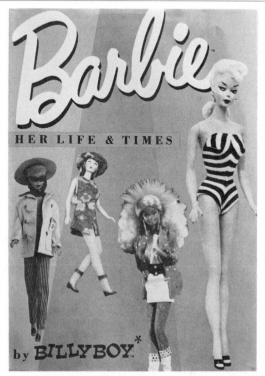

Courtesy of Crown Publishers, Inc., New York, 1987

How-to books represent one of the most successful categories of specialized book publishing. As people became absorbed with "who they were" and "self," the publishing industry started catering to their interests. Popular topics included such things as how to pan for gold, fix up your home, straighten out your psyche, exercise your body and lose weight through the "perfect" diet plan. Many of these how-to-books feed on the American myth that everyone in this country can succeed if he or she is determined and has the "inside scoop" on how to do it.

Representative titles of books in this genre in the late 1980s were *The Country Garden Book, Never Be Nervous Again, Nutrition Prescription, Glorious Needlepoint* and *Mary Emmerling's America Country Cooking.*

As the book-publishing industry adapted to providing reading material for special interests, the promotion of these books helped expand the special-interest area into larger segments of the culture. Specialized books on diets and exercise, for example, helped form a new cultural belief that "being thin" meant being healthy and "everybody should lose weight." It is interesting to note that with this new cultural attitude came an increase in cases of anorexia being reported in the late twentieth century.

The *U.S. Industrial Outlook* projected total book publishing revenues of $12.8 billion for 1988. As in previous years, the largest portion was expected to come from textbooks, 29 percent, and trade books, 23 percent, with technical, scientific and professional books contributing 18 percent, religious books 5 percent, and all other categories the remaining 25 percent.

Instant books, another extremely successful form of specialization, has put book publishing in competition with news-oriented mass media by providing more in-depth coverage of news events. The instant book is a paperback about a current topic that is published almost immediately after the event. When newspaper heiress Patty Hearst was kidnapped in 1974, several paperbacks about the kidnapping were on sale shortly thereafter. It was reported at the time that FBI investigators were buying the books in search of leads in the case. When rock idol John Lennon was murdered outside his New York apartment in December 1980, instant books about his life and its tragic end were on the market within days. Such rapid publication is unheard of for other kinds of books. Most books take at least six to nine months to manufacture.

Nonfiction novels also compete with the news media by presenting more in-depth coverage and interpretation of news events. Some of the pioneering examples of this approach are Truman Capote's *In Cold Blood,* a nonfiction novel based on the true story of two murderers who killed a Midwestern farm family, and investigative works like Bob Woodward and Carl Bernstein's *All the President's Men* and David A. Yallop's *In God's Name: An Investigation into the Murder of Pope John Paul I.* (The Woodward-Bernstein book details how the two *Washington Post* reporters uncovered the Watergate scandal; Yallop's book alleges that the death of Pope John Paul I was not due to natural causes, as reported.)

Personalized books have become possible as a result of new computer technology. These publications, composed and printed entirely by computer, are designed primarily for children. The computer stores a complete text of the book, with a few key items left blank. To purchase such a book, a person gives the publisher the name, address and other personal data about the child who will be given the book. This information is fed into the computer and out comes a book (obviously not a great literary work, but rather something simple or mundane) that incorporates the specified data in the story. Thus the recipient of the book becomes the hero of the story.

Fotonovels are part printed text, part picture book and part comic book. They usually develop as spinoffs of a popular movie or television program. *Star Trek* became one of the first successful topics for a fotonovel in this country. The books were a hit with the "Trekkies" (see Chapter 2). Although fotonovels have been popular in South America and Europe for more than 40 years, they are relatively new in the United States and seem to reflect the fact that specialized interests in our multimedia world tend to overlap from one medium to another.

Graphic novels are a spinoff of the comic book that have been gaining popularity in the late 1980s. This new book form, which began appearing in the late 1970s, consists of an original self-contained story told in the comic-book format. Two popular sellers in 1987 were *Maus,* a story about the author's relationship with his father, who was a Holocaust survivor, and *Dark Knight,* a takeoff from the old Batman comic-book character. *Star Trek* was also a popular topic for graphic novels. By the late 1980s numerous publishers were beginning to publish them, and many were optimistic that this new genre would appeal to people who didn't often read. Publishers were hopeful

BOX 4.3.

COMIC BOOKS: INTERNATIONAL CLASSICS

The comic book is a relatively new American publishing genre that has become an international phenomenon. These books became popular in the late 1930s with the introduction of *Detective Comics* and *Action Comics*, publications that featured original stories rather than comic strip reprints.

Soon youngsters in the American popular culture were reading about the fantastic achievements of such superheros as *Superman* and *Batman and Robin*. Following these flying crime fighters onto the comic-book pages were animal characters developed by *Terrytoons Comics* and *Walt Disney's Comics and Stories*. In 1939 60 different series of comic books were being published. This figure grew to 650 by 1954 (the year a strict self-censorship code was enforced), and included such comic characters as Airboy, Captain America, Captain Marvel, The Phantom, Dick Tracy, Popeye, Flash Gordon, Donald Duck, Mickey Mouse and Tarzan. There was even a series of classical literature tales told in the comic-book format, such as Huckleberry Finn, Robin Hood, Ivanhoe and King Arthur and the Knights of the Roundtable.

The development of the American comic book was influenced by other twentieth century mass media, particularly motion pictures, radio and eventually television. The Western genre of the motion picture became a popular subject for comic books. Even singing cowboy radio and movie stars like Gene Autry and Roy Rogers became comic book characters, as did fictitious action/adventure characters like *The Lone Ranger*, *The Shadow*, *Sergeant Preston of the Yukon* and *The Green Hornet*. In the 1950s, following television's entry into the popular culture, some comic books began featuring TV action/adventure themes such as *Have Gun Will Travel, Gunsmoke, Lawman* and *77 Sunset Strip*.

Although created in the United States, the modern comic book never really gained respectability here as an art or literary form. It was perceived as children's entertainment and as such became a target for concerned parents and others who feared that the comic book would corrupt the youth. Strong objections developed over the use of themes of sex and violence in comic books. The Comics Magazine Association of America (CMAA) attempted to establish a code of ethics in the 1940s.

The government got into the act when the Kefauver Crime Committee began holding hearings on the effect of comics on children. A stringent code of conduct was enforced by the CMAA in 1954, and approved comics began carrying a seal indicating that they contained only wholesome material. In 1955 the State of New York passed a law making it illegal to sell obscene, objectionable comics to minors or to carry such words as crime, sex, horror or terror in the title of any comic book. Other states followed with similar legislation. The number of comic books in this country declined significantly after that. It wasn't long before those who had been concerned about sex and violence in comic books shifted their efforts toward the newer medium of television.

In Europe, Japan, Central and South America, on the other hand, people of all ages read comic books. Some of the American superheros, such as Superman, became popular speaking in foreign tongues. The American genre of the Western became very popular abroad. Other comic characters were developed that were unique to the foreign cultures. In France and Japan, for example, comic books represent a very large publishing market. In Japan in the late 1980s, 20 percent of all publications sold were comic books. This translated into approximately 70 million copies a month. The themes or plots of these comic books range as widely as American popular novels and are mostly aimed at adults. Sex, violence and even nudity is not uncommon in many of these foreign comic books.

There is new hope for the comic-book genre in the United States, however. As this country prepares to enter the last decade of the twentieth century, numerous book publishers are bringing back a version of the American comic book with a new name and a new target audience—adults. These new comics are called graphic novels. Each graphic novel contains a complete story—like any other novel—and the quality of writing is very high. The graphics are also more spectacular than the old comic books and the production quality is far superior to ordinary paperbacks.

that the graphic novel would introduce these visually oriented individuals to reading and that this would lead them to try other types of books (see Box 4.3).

Novelization is a book genre that developed in recent years from the book industry's symbiotic relationship with motion pictures. Books and motion pictures have been linked together since the early days of film. Many books have been made into movies through the years, and the ability to sell the movie rights to a best-seller means a great deal to publishers and authors. Recently a reverse trend, called *novelization*, has occurred, whereby book publishers print novels based on successful movies.

Mass-market paperback books, often sexy romance, western or mystery novels, also account for large revenues in book publishing. These high-volume books often have press runs that exceed a million copies. These paperbacks, which once sold for around

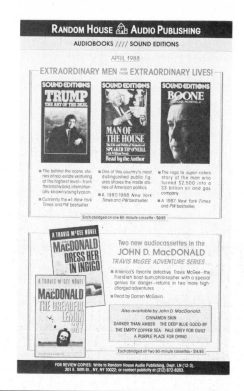

Electronic books expanded the bestseller categories from print to audio cassettes in the late 1980s. (*Random House Audio Publishing*)

75 cents, now bring $3 to $5 a copy and prove that despite the variety of other media for recreation and escape the novel still appeals to the masses.

Electronic books are a new publishing industry genre that by the mid-1980s had become very lucrative. As more and more people found themselves on freeways fighting the traffic to and from work, the concept of listening to books on audio cassette tapes became popular. Major publishing houses such as Random House, Simon & Schuster and Bantam Books joined other publishers in producing spoken versions of their books on audio cassette. After its first year in the audio book business Bantam Audio reported in 1987 that it had sold over a million cassettes. That same year Random House purchased Warner Audio Publishing and expanded its audio line from book-based fiction to self-help/health books.

Cassettes, which can be either rented or purchased, seem to be a godsend to commuters. Ironically, one of the most popular books in the mid-1980s was Thoreau's classic *Walden,* which describes a much more peaceful existence.

Censorship. Efforts at censorship not only continued but increased during the period of specialization. In the late 1940s and 1950s the book-publishing industry was attacked for printing materials that critics believed to be pro-Communist or anti-American. Alleged obscenity also remained a popular target for censors. For example, in 1950 the Chicago Police Bureau of Censorship banned a novel called *A Diary of Love* which had been written by Maude Hutchins, the estranged wife of the president of the University of Chicago.

Finally, in 1957, in a case against a New York publisher of erotic books, Samuel Roth, the U.S. Supreme Court issued a decision that liberalized the definition of obscenity throughout the United States. From now on the test of obscenity would be "whether to the average person, applying contemporary community standards, the dominant theme of the material taken as a whole appeals to prurient interest."[8] Although Roth went to jail, this decision was the first in a series that liberalized the interpretation of obscenity. (Prior to that time obscenity was defined as anything that had a tendency to deprave or corrupt anyone's mind. Thus if one page of a book contained a statement that could corrupt anyone—a child, for example—the book was judged to be obscene.) Then in 1973 the Supreme Court tightened up the standards again, setting these new guidelines for defining obscenity (*Miller v. California*, 1973):

- The work taken as a whole must appeal to the prurient interests of the average person applying contemporary community standards.

- The work must depict or describe, in a patently offensive way, sexual conduct specifically defined by the applicable law.

- The work taken as a whole must lack serious literary, scientific, political, or artistic value.

One of the problems resulting from this interpretation was the difficulty of measuring "contemporary community standards" and the inconsistencies that could exist in various regions of the country. What might be judged obscene in one part of the country might not be so judged in another.

In 1987 the Supreme Court (*Pope v. Illinois*) applied the "reasonable person standard" rather than the "contemporary community standard" in judging the third part of the Miller test. In this latest court interpretation of obscenity, the Court said:

> Only the first and second prongs of the Miller test—appeal to prurient interest and patent offensiveness—should be decided with reference to "contemporary community standards." The ideas that a work represents need not obtain majority approval to merit protection, and value of that work does not vary from community to community based on the degree of local acceptance it has won. The proper inquiry is not whether an ordinary member of any given community would find serious value in the allegedly obscene material, but whether a reasonable person would find such value in the material, taken as a whole.[9]

Along with the liberalization of the definition of obscenity has been a gradual change in the culture toward acceptance of sexual discussions and representations heretofore considered taboo. Sexually explicit themes in books, magazines and movies have become acceptable to many in the popular culture, though others still find them immoral and pornographic. As a result there have been numerous efforts to curb the proliferation of this so-called pornography. In 1967 a presidential commission was set up and funded with $2 million to study the effects of pornography on our culture. The two-year study found no causal relationships between the dissemination of pornography and crime and other antisocial behavior. Government panels in Great Britian in 1979 and in Canada in 1984 came to similar conclusions.

However, in 1986 an 11-member panel put together by U.S. Attorney General Edwin Meese released very different and controversial findings. The Meese commission, which had spent a year and $500,000 studying pornography, issued a 1,960-page report that said that it had found a casual relationship between exposure to sexually violent books, films and magazines and aggressive behavior toward women. It called for stringent enforcement of the nation's antismut laws and the extension of those laws into new areas. Soon after, a new harsh antiobscenity law was passed in North Carolina; supporters of the legislation hoped that it would set a nationwide precedent.

The American Civil Liberties Union and other opponents of censorship in any form immediately criticized the commission's findings. Even two of the commissioners, both women, wrote dissenting opinions, claiming that "no self-respecting investigator would accept conclusions based on such a study." However, the report was lauded by religious, conservative and feminist groups that had been complaining about pornography for years.

Opponents claimed that the report was not objective because the commission had been stacked with conservatives who supported the Reagan adminstration's point of

Cries for censorship of printed material come from a wide variety of people, as this antipornography rally in New York City demonstrates. (J. Ross Baughman/Visions)

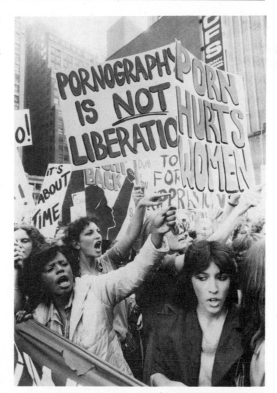

BOX 4.4.

THE DIARY OF ANNE FRANK

On July 6, 1944, four months before Anne Frank was arrested and sent to a German concentration camp where she died, she wrote in her now-famous diary the following thoughts about her first and only boyfriend, Peter van Daan:

> *Poor boy, he's never known what it feels like to make other people happy, and I can't teach him that either. He has no religion, scoffs at Jesus Christ, and swears using the name of God; although I'm not orthodox either, it hurts me every time I see how deserted, how scornful and how poor he really is.*
>
> *People who have a religion should be glad, for not everyone has the gift of believing in heavenly things. You don't necessarily even have to be afraid of punishment after death; purgatory, hell and heaven are things that a lot of people can't accept, but still a religion, it doesn't*

matter which, keeps a person on the right path. It isn't the fear of God but the upholding of one's honour and conscience. *

Do you think this statement is blasphemous and unworthy of the eyes of teenagers with religious backgrounds? In 1986, because of this passage, a group of parents in Greenville, Tennessee, went to court to prevent the local schools from making their children read the book. A judge ruled in their favor.

Although the book provides an earnest and humane statement about the value of religion by a young girl who died at the hands of men who believed in a doctrine of supremacy that had no room for religious freedom, it ended up on a list of books some people felt should be banned in the United States—200 years after the country was founded on a premise of religious freedom.

*The Diary of Anne Frank (London: Pan Books, 1954) p. 212.

view against pornography. Supporters said that the report was the first step in the "defense of decency and the sanctity of the family."*

Throughout the 1980s attacks on books have been increasing. From 1980 to 1984 censorship complaints brought to the attention of the American Library Association increased from 300 to almost 1,000 cases a year.[10] Efforts were being made to censor a variety of books for various reasons. Topics popular for attack included sex, race, politics, religion and drugs. Some of the more popular works targeted by mid-1980s censors because they contained references to one or more of these tabooed topics were *Adventures of Huckleberry Finn, 1984, Slaughterhouse Five, Go Ask Alice, The Diary of Anne Frank* and Doris Day's autobiography (see Box 4.4).

In 1987 a federal judge in Alabama upheld a fundamentalist Christian group's effort

*Even before the report was issued, lawsuits had been filed alleging that the commission had intimidated major retail chains into removing magazines like *Playboy* and *Penthouse* from their shelves. Letters signed by Alan Sears, executive director of the commission, had been sent to 23 major American companies, advising them that they had been identified in testimony before the commission as being "involved in the sale or distribution of pornography." Several of these companies, including the 7-Eleven chain, subsequently removed "adult"-type magazines from their inventory.

to ban 44 state-approved textbooks that allegedly contained "secular humanism," a philosophy that the judge equated with a religion. He ruled that secular humanism was a form of religion because it places man, not God, at the center of existence and advocates situational ethics and morals instead of absolute values. The banned books covered such fields as home economics, history and social studies. This decision was later overturned by a federal appeals court.

Although book banning is usually a tactic of conservative movements and tends to be criticized by liberals, there are no clear-cut political categories when it comes to reacting emotionally to the contents of books. Twain's *Huckleberry Finn*, which describes the evils of racism in the nineteenth century, has been branded as racist by many who find its use of the word nigger offensive. Other books have been condemned by feminist groups who claim that pornography degrades women. On the more conservative side of the political spectrum, in the 1980s the Reverend Jerry Falwell was condemning the censorship of conservative books (see Box 4.5).

According to historian John Tebbel, this "virtual epidemic of censorship" that has been sweeping the country in recent years is the result of a combination of cultural factors: (1) a militant advocacy of fundamentalist values by nearly 70 million evangelicals organized by radio and television evangelists; (2) a large number of traditionalists who found themselves unable to accept a changed world and longed for what they considered the peaceful days of repression and rigid traditional morals and manners; and (3) the Supreme Court's decision to leave the definition of obscenity to local community standards.[11] Others say that this trend is a reflection of cultural paranoia, and they cite Supreme Court Justice Potter Stewart's comment that "censorship reflects a society's lack of confidence in itself."

Another way the courts have been used in the latter part of the twentieth century as a tool of censorship is through the threat or institution of libel suits. One reason for this trend may be the fact that there are more attorneys per capita in the United States than in any other major civilized nation in the world. Although libel laws were designed to protect the innocent from defamation by the mass media and were clearly not intended as a form of censorship, some people have used the threat of a suit to pressure publishers into removing material from books before they go to press.

Book publishers started taking this new threat very seriously in 1979, when Doubleday and its author Gwen Davis Mitchell lost a $75,000 judgment to a California psychologist. (He argued that although his name wasn't used in the novel *Touching*, one of the fictitious characters who used nude therapy had been modeled after him.) Since then, many book publishers have involved lawyers in the review and editing of manuscripts. As a result, much of the content of these books has been altered.

Some of the books that were threatened with libel suits before publication were *Two of a Kind: The Hillside Stranglers* and biographies of John F. Kennedy, Ernest Hemingway, Frank Sinatra, Errol Flynn, Katherine Graham and Claus von Bülow. According to Rodney Smolla, author of *Suing the Press*, more and more books are being censored because of the threat of a libel suit.

In the 1980s, even the government was using the courts to censor the contents of books. A 1980 U.S. Supreme Court decision upheld an injunction against Frank Snepp, a former CIA officer, that required him for the rest of his life to get the CIA's approval before speaking or writing on the CIA's activities. The case resulted from a book written by Snepp that was critical of the way the CIA had treated Vietnamese

BOX 4.5.

KEEP BOOKBUSTERS OUT OF OUR LIBRARIES

The following is an editorial that appeared in the July 12, 1985, issue of USA Today.

If you're spooked by a story or a thought or a word, who're you going to call? Bookbusters!

In the past several years, attempts to get books pulled from library shelves have tripled, the American Library Association reported this week.

This year, the ALA expects to hear about 1,000 efforts to remove books from classrooms or libraries. Volumes that have come under fire recently include literary classics, like *Adventures of Huckleberry Finn* and *1984*.

Some communities have a review process that gives a book a chance to stay on the shelves once it has been challenged. Others simply yank the book.

In Racine, Wis., it was *Slaughterhouse Five*—Kurt Vonnegut's novel of the firebombing of Dresden. In Rankin County, Miss., it was *Go Ask Alice*, which describes a teenager's death from drug abuse. In Anniston, Ala., it was—yes—Doris Day's autobiography.

In New Jersey, Arizona, and many other states, the banned books were the novels of Judy Blume, who writes about the growing pains of adolescents.

Conservatives complain they are the victims of censorship, too. For example, Jerry Falwell says libraries tend to exclude books that have conservative or fundamentalist Christian points of view.

Lately, books thought to be racist have been targets. In Waukegan, Ill., an alderman tried to rid classrooms of *Uncle Tom's Cabin* and *Huckleberry Finn*—he didn't like the way they portrayed blacks. In Fairfax, Va., a teacher succeeded in getting *Huck Finn* temporarily banned from—ironically enough—Mark Twain Intermediate School.

The educator published his own version that substituted "slave" or "black man" for the word "nigger." Never mind that part of the book's purpose was to underscore the evils of the racism of that day. It's all been smoothed over now.

In the 19th century, it was bad grammar and blasphemy that helped get books banned. Today, it is racism, ageism, and sexism. Books are targeted because they promote creationism, or because they don't promote creationism.

The Bookbusters must think that words will hurt us. And not just words, but—eeeeek!—ideas.

Of course, ideas need a context. A kid who knows nothing of the racism that thrived when *Huckleberry Finn* was written won't understand the author was attacking racism.

Parents who object to depiction of premarital sex or drug abuse in novels intended for teens should use the opportunity to explain their family's values to their children.

But censorship is dangerous. There's no limit to beefs about books. If Mark Twain and Doris Day offend, why stop there? There's always the Constitution: Censorship is a hallmark of totalitarian regimes everywhere.

When the world has been made safe from ideas, the Bookbusters will have won. The library shelves will be empty—and ignorance will have triumphed.

intelligence aides, including leaving their names behind in files when the United States withdrew from Vietnam. Before writing the book he attempted to get the CIA to investigate the incident. When they refused, he wrote *Decent Interval*, describing what happened. The CIA charged that he had violated a secrecy agreement by publishing the material; the Supreme Court agreed and ordered him to turn over his profits from the book—some $180,000—to the government. In 1986 CIA director William J. Casey warned two journalists who were working on books about his agency that they would be violating the law if their books included any secret "communications intelligence."

If we use history as a basis for predicting the future, it is safe to assume that there will always be attempts to impose censorship as long as book publishing and other forms of mass communication play a major role in disseminating information and ideas in our culture.

Current Business Trends. As a major industry in the United States, book publishing has not been immune to the takeover fever that swept American business in the 1980s. Many privately owned houses—as well as small and even medium-sized companies—have been taken over by large conglomerates. Some worry that this trend will eventually limit the number and variety of books available, as profit-minded executives are less willing to take chances when deciding which books to publish.

Just as troubling to many people in the industry is the fact that many of the buyers have been foreign investors. Doubleday, Dell and Henry Holt were sold to West German publishers; New American Library, E. P. Dutton, South-Western, Gale Research and Grove Press were acquired by British companies; and Harper & Row was sold to Australian-born Rupert Murdoch. Although Murdoch is now a U.S. citizen, he invited the British book company William Collins & Son (on whose board he sits as a 42 percent shareholder) to become directly involved in the management of Harper & Row. A minor reversal of this trend occurred in 1987 when Random House, which is owned by the Newhouse publishing conglomerate, acquired Chatto, Virago, The Bodley Head and Jonathan Cape, a leading British book publishing group.

Publishers Weekly reported that 15 percent of the revenue generated by the U.S. publishing industry in 1986 was generated by foreign-owned companies.[12]

SUMMARY

Books are the most permanent form of mass communication because they are durable, designed to be passed from person to person and are housed in libraries. Civilizations have been recording permanent messages in portable form since the Sumerians used clay tablets 4,500 years ago. Other ancient forms of books included papyrus scrolls and the codex; these were the predecessors to the handwritten book on paper made from wood pulp.

In the mid-fifteenth century Johannes Gutenberg's invention of movable type turned the ancient art of bookmaking into a mass-communication medium. Soon after the invention of mass communication, those in authority saw the medium as a threat to their rule and took steps to regulate it. Despite these efforts at censorship, books became an important part of the Protestant Reformation in the sixteenth century.

In the United States, book publishing has gone through three stages of development—the elitist, popular and specialized stages. Specialized books outsell novels by two to one, and book publishing is a major cultural industry.

Throughout the history of book publishing, censorship and book banning have remained an integral part of society. In recent years many people have used the courts in an effort to censor books.

Book publishing is a major industry in the United States, generating over $9 billion in sales annually. In the 1980s many smaller firms were taken over by huge conglomerates, and some of the major American publishers were sold to foreign companies.

NOTES

1. Edward Edwards, *Libraries and Founders of Libraries: From Ancient Times to the Beginning of the Nineteeth Century* (Amsterdam: Gerard Th. Van Heusden, 1968; originally published 1865), p. 25.

2. Will Durant, *The Reformation: A History of European Civilization from Wyclif to Calvin: 1300–1564* (New York: Simon & Schuster, 1957), p. 368.

3. Ibid., p. 369.

4. Oscar Handlin, *The History of the United States*, vol. 1 (New York: Holt, Rinehart & Winston, 1967), p. 234.

5. Ibid., p. 258.

6. Paul S. Boyer, *Purity in Print: The Vice Society Movement and Book Censorship in America* (New York: Scribner's, 1968).

7. Curtis G. Benjamin, "Book Publishing's Hidden Bonanza," in *Readings in Mass Communication: Concepts and Issues in the Mass Media*, ed. Michael C. Emery and Ted C. Smythe (Dubuque, Iowa: Brown, 1972), p. 182.

8. *Roth v. United States*, 354 U.S. 476 (1957).

9. Quoted in *Publishers Weekly*, May 22, 1987, p. 20.

10. Barbara Palmer, "Censorship: The Battle Is Heating Up," *USA Today*, June 21, 1984, p. D1.

11. John Tebbel, *Between Covers: The Rise and Transformation of Book Publishing in America* (New York: Oxford University Press, 1987) p. 460.

12. Gayle Feldman, "Going Global," *Publishers Weekly*, Dec. 19, 1986, p. 20.

ADDITIONAL READING

Cerf, Bennett. *At Random: The Reminiscences of Bennett Cerf.* New York: Random House, 1977.

Compaine, Benjamin M. *The Book Industry in Transition.* White Plains, N.Y.: Knowledge Industry Publications, 1978.

Dessauer, John P. *Book Publishing: What It Is, What It Does*, 2nd ed. New York: Bowker, 1981.

Exman, Eugene. *The House of Harper.* New York: Harper & Row, 1967.

Handlin, Oscar. *The History of the United States*, 2 vols. New York: Holt, Rinehart & Winston, 1968.

Lehmann-Haupt, Hellmut. *The Book in America: A History of the Making and Selling of Books in the United States.* New York: Bowker, 1951.

Madison, Charles A. *Book Publishing in American Culture.* New York: McGraw-Hill, 1966.

Merryweather, F. Somner. *Bibliomania in the Middle Ages.* London: Woodstock Press, 1933.

Reitberger, Reinhold, and Fuchs, Wolfgang. *Comics: Anatomy of a Mass Medium.* London: Studio Vista, 1972.

Smolla, Rodney A. *Suing the Press.* New York: Oxford University Press, 1986.

Stern, Madeleine B. *Publishing for Mass Entertainment in Nineteenth Century America.* Boston: G. K. Hall, 1980.

Tebbel, John. *A History of Book Publishing in the United States*, 4 vols. New York: Bowker, 1972, 1975, 1978 and 1981.

Wroth, Lawrence C. *A History of the Printed Book.* New York: Limited Editions Club, 1938.

Chapter 5

Magazines:
The Specialized Medium

Of all the literary scenes
Saddest this sight to me:
The graves of little magazines
Who died to make verse free.

—*Keith Preston,* The Liberators

Jeffrey Dickey and Randy Achee, now both in their 30s, have been friends since their high-school days in Orange County, California. In the 1970s they started publishing a magazine aimed at college students. Today they operate a $6-million-a-year business that caters to the specialized college student market. Their publications—including *College Entertainment Guide, College Woman* and *Moving Up*—are published quarterly and emphasize entertainment and life-style topics for students. Their combined circulation is 2.3 million on 170 college campuses.

Dickey and Achee persuaded many manufacturers of products for the nation's 12.4 million college students that the best way to reach them was through publications distributed on campuses. Unlike the book-publishing industry, which uses advertising only to sell books, the magazine industry gets its greatest revenue from carrying ads in its publications. Typical products advertised in college magazines are records and tapes, perfumes and colognes, beer, motor scooters and condoms. The army, air force, navy and marine corps also make good use of these publications to advertise armed forces careers.

However, just as their business has grown, so has the competition. The field was wide open when Dickey and Achee began Alan Weston Communications in 1977. By the late 1980s at least 16 publications were distributed on campus, including entries from both major news magazines. Newsweek's *Newsweek on Campus* appears six times a year and has a circulation of 1.3 million. Time Inc. entered the lucrative college market in 1987 by acquiring Campus Publishing from its 23-year-old president, Douglas Ranalli. Campus had been publishing *Dorm* magazine since 1984. In addition to taking over *Dorm*, Time Inc. also started up a campus edition of *Time*.

The college market is just one of thousands of specialized audiences American magazines are catering to. Magazines are the most specialized of all the mass media, with new magazines appearing every year to reflect our ever-changing popular culture.

Although it took thousands of years for books to move from the elite stage to the popular stage and a hundred more years before they reached the specialized stage, magazines evolved much more rapidly. In fact, magazines have been specializing in one way or another since they began in the eighteenth century.

According to mass media scholars John Merrill and Ralph Lowenstein, all magazines have either *unit* specialization or *internal* specialization.[1] Unit specialization occurs in magazines that target audiences with special interests: *Hot Rod Magazine*, *Surfer* and *Personal Computing*, for example. Most magazines produced in the United States today fall into this category. Internal-specialization magazines are general-interest publications that appeal to a larger audience and offer a wider variety of articles. The readers then select the articles that are of interest to them. Although many of these magazines have gone out of business during the past 30 years, some are still very successful—consider *Reader's Digest*.

Magazines are generally targeted to a very specific audience, as these examples suggest.

THE CULTURAL HISTORY OF MAGAZINES

EPS STAGES: Elitist | Popular | Specialized

Elitist	Popular	Specialized	Date	Event
■			1704–14	First English-language magazines—*Review, Tatler,* and *Spectator*—published in London.
■			1741	First two American magazines published within days of each other.
		■	1743	*Christian History* founded, America's first unit-specialization magazine.
■			1821	*Saturday Evening Post* founded.
	■		1830	*Godey's Lady's Book* becomes first women's magazine.
	■		1865–1900	First magazine boom, following the end of the Civil War.
	■		1893	McClure and Munsey reduce prices of their magazines to make them truly affordable; *Saturday Evening Post* follows.
	■		1890s–1900s	Magazine muckrakers expose political corruption and unsafe working conditions.
	■		1920	Magazine advertising tops $129 million annually.
	■		1922	*Reader's Digest* is founded to serve the busy culture of the Roaring '20s.
	■		1923	Henry Luce starts *Time,* America's first newsmagazine.
	■		1936	Luce starts *Life* to fill the visual void created by radio.
	■		1947	*Reader's Digest,* with more than 9 million subscribers, becomes largest-selling publication in U.S.
	■		1948	*TV Guide* begins in New York City; later expands nationally.
	■		1950s	General-interest magazines begin to decline in circulation as specialized publications develop.
	■		1952	*Mad* is founded; pokes fun at consumer culture.
	■		1953	Hugh Hefner's *Playboy* gives popular culture a sex life.
		■	1960s	Specialized publications take over circulation lead from general-interest magazines.
	■		1972	*Life* ceases publication.
	■		1972	*Ms.* becomes first magazine with a feminist veiwpoint.
	■		1974	Time Inc. introduces *People* magazine as a smaller version of old movie fan magazines.
	■		1978	*Life* resumes publication as a monthly.
		■	1980s	More than 12,000 specialized magazines are available; new ones start daily. Computer, family and life-style magazines are the latest to find a niche in the specialized culture.

HISTORY OF MAGAZINES

British Publications. The first English-language magazines were started in London in the early eighteenth century. The first such publication, the *Review*, was actually a cross between a newspaper and a magazine. It was published by Daniel Defoe (the author of *Robinson Crusoe*) in 1704. In 1709 Richard Steele began publishing the *Tatler*. He was soon joined by Joseph Addison, and together they published both the *Tatler* and its short-lived successor, the *Spectator*. In 1731 the first British publication to carry the word magazine in its title began: Edward Cave's *Gentlemen's Magazine*. Cave later hired the famed man of letters Dr. Samuel Johnson as one of his writers. Johnson started his own magazine, the *Rambler*, in 1750. These magazines sought an audience among the elite—both men and women—by providing witty and stimulating reading in periodical form.

The SPECTATOR.

Non fumum ex fulgore, sed ex fumo dare lucem Cogitat, ut speciosa dehinc miracula promat. Hor.

To be Continued every Day.

Thursday, March 1. 1711.

I Have observed, that a Reader seldom peruses a Book with Pleasure 'till he knows whether the Writer of it be a black or a fair Man, of a mild or cholerick Disposition, Married or a Batchelor, with other Particulars of the like nature, that conduce very much to the right Understanding of an Author. To gratify this Curiosity, which is so natural to a Reader, I design this Paper, and my next, as Prefatory Discourses to my following Writings, and shall give some Account in them of the several Persons that are engaged in this Work. As the chief Trouble of Compiling, Digesting and Correcting will fall to my Share, I must do my self the Justice to open the Work with my own History.

I was born to a small Hereditary Estate, which I find, by the Writings of the Family, was bounded by the same Hedges and Ditches in *William* the Conqueror's Time that it is at present, and has been delivered down from Father to Son whole and entire, without the Loss or Acquisition of a single Field or Meadow, during the Space of six hundred Years. There goes a Story in the Family, that when my Mother was gone with Child of me about three Months, she dreamt that she was brought to Bed of a Judge: Whether this might proceed from a Law-Suit which was then depending in the Family, or my Father's being a Justice of the Peace, I cannot determine; for I am not so vain as to think it presaged any Dignity that I should arrive at in my future Life, though that was the Interpretation which the Neighbourhood put upon it. The Gravity of my Behaviour at my very first Appearance in the World, and all the Time that I sucked, seemed to favour my Mother's Dream: For, as she has often told me, I threw away my Rattle before I was two Months old, and would not make use of my Coral 'till they had taken away the Bells from it.

As for the rest of my Infancy, there being nothing in it remarkable, I shall pass it over in Silence. I find, that, during my Nonage, I had the Reputation of a very sullen Youth, but was always a Favourite of my School-Master, who used to say, *that my Parts were solid and would wear well.* I had not been long at the University, before I distinguished my self by a most profound Silence: For during the Space of eight Years, excepting in the publick Exercises of the College, I scarce uttered the Quantity of an hundred Words; and indeed do not remember that I ever spoke three Sentences together in my whole Life. Whilst I was in this Learned Body I applied my self with so much Diligence to my Studies, that there are very few celebrated Books, either in the Learned or the Modern Tongues, which I am not acquainted with.

Upon the Death of my Father I was resolved to travel into Foreign Countries, and therefore left the University, with the Character of an odd unaccountable Fellow, that had a great deal of Learning, if I would but show it. An insatiable Thirst after Knowledge carried me into all the Countries of *Europe*, where there was any thing new or strange to be seen; nay, to such a Degree was my Curiosity raised, that having read the Controversies of some great Men concerning the Antiquities of *Egypt*, I made a Voyage to *Grand Cairo*, on purpose to take the Measure of a Pyramid; and as soon as I had set my self right in that Particular, returned to my Native Country with great Satisfaction.

I have passed my latter Years in this City, where I am frequently seen in most publick Places, tho' there are not above half a dozen of my select Friends that know me; of whom my next Paper shall give a more particular Account. There is no Place of Publick Resort, wherein I do not often make my Appearance; sometimes I am seen thrusting my Head into a Round of Politicians at *Will's*, and listning with great Attention to the Narratives that are made in those little Circular Audiences. Sometimes I smoak a Pipe at *Child's*; and whilst I seem attentive to nothing but the *Post-Man*, over-hear the Conversation of every Table in the Room. I appear on *Sunday* Nights at St. *James's* Coffee-House, and sometimes join the little Committee of Politicks in the Inner-Room, as one who comes there to hear and improve. My Face is likewise very well known at the *Grecian*, the *Cocoa-Tree*, and in the Theaters both of *Drury-Lane*, and the *Hay-Market*. I have been taken for a Merchant upon

Joseph Addison and Richard Steele published *The Spectator* in London in the early eighteenth century. (*Culver Pictures*)

Early American Efforts. In 1741 two prominent printers in Philadelphia—Andrew Bradford and Benjamin Franklin—vied to publish the first magazine in the American colonies. Bradford was the victor, publishing his *American Magazine, or a Monthly View of the Political State of the British Colonies* three days before Franklin's *General Magazine, and Historical Chronicle, for All the British Plantations in America.* Franklin was more successful, however, as his magazine lasted for six issues compared to Bradford's three. The content of these American magazines consisted mostly of material reprinted from British magazines; only about 10 percent of the material in the six issues of the *General Magazine* was original.[2]

These early American magazines were designed for the elite, the relatively few literate members of society. Thus they carried essays and articles on religion, philosophy, natural science, political affairs and literature.

In 1743 a publication that might be described as the first specialized magazine in America was printed. It was *The Christian History*, a religious magazine. Due to the low literacy rate in the eighteenth century and the slowness of the mails, the development of magazines during this period was less than spectacular. Indeed, prior to the nineteenth century, no American magazine lasted for more than 14 months.

Successful Expansion. By the 1820s, however, American magazine publishing began to develop into a lucrative and long-lasting enterprise. One of the more famous magazines of this era was the *Saturday Evening Post*, which was founded in 1821. It lasted as a weekly publication until 1969. In 1825 there were fewer than 100 magazines in the United States. Twenty-five years later, there were 600.

This tremendous growth in magazine publishing resulted from advances in printing technology (steam power and cylinder and rotary presses), the eventual development of a literate society as a result of compulsory education, and major reform movements that generated topics for printed discussion. In 1820, for example, the first abolitionist magazine, *The Genius of Universal Emancipation*, was published in Ohio. As slavery became hotly debated and as the nation moved toward the Civil War, magazines played an important role in informing and influencing the people. As mentioned in Chapter 4, Harriet Beecher Stowe's *Uncle Tom's Cabin* first appeared as a series of magazine articles before it was published in book form.

Nevertheless, before the Civil War, magazine readership was still drawn primarily from the elite. The *Saturday Evening Post* and other successful publications founded in this period—the *North American Review* (1815), *Harper's* (1850), and *Atlantic Monthly* (1857)—carried mostly short stories, novels, poems, scholarly essays and political and social commentaries.

Expansion into Popular Culture. By the end of the Civil War (1865), compulsory education had helped give the United States the highest literacy level in the world and the railroads had provided a means of transporting people and goods (including publications) across the continent. American magazines could now start to enter the popular culture. Numerous publications featuring both unit and internal specialization appeared. Two of the most popular genres of unit specialization were farming and women's magazines. Some of the more popular publications of the late nineteenth century were *Ladies' Home Journal, McCall's* and *Woman's Home Companion.* (*Godey's Lady's Book,* the forerunner of these specialized women's publications, was first published in 1830.)

The 1880s and 1890s saw the debut of a number of mass-circulation, general-interest magazines featuring fiction and nonfiction articles. The most important were *Collier's, Cosmopolitan* and *McClure's. McClure's,* founded by the newspaper magnate Samuel S. McClure, was the first inexpensive mass-circulation magazine, selling for 15 cents a copy. This prompted Frank Munsey to cut the price of his *Munsey's Magazine* to 10 cents. Soon the *Saturday Evening Post* was selling for a nickel. Now that they were very affordable, magazines became entrenched in the popular culture. The variety of their articles enabled these magazines to appeal to a wide range of Americans. Farmers in the Midwest could enjoy certain stories in *Saturday Evening Post,* for example, while other articles appealed to merchants and bankers in New York. The magazine industry thrived. In 1865 there were about 700 magazines, by 1900 more than 5,000.

The Muckrakers. The millions of Europeans who immigrated to the United States during the latter part of the nineteenth century provided a large labor force for the new industrial economy. Many workers were forced to live in deplorable slums and work long hours in sweatshops for abysmally low wages. Reformers turned to such magazines as *The Nation* and *Harper's Weekly* for support in their efforts to improve living and working conditions. In the 1890s, the Populist movement attacked the great disparity between rich and poor and accused industrial capitalists of a greedy disregard for the common welfare. The medium for their crusading articles was magazines.

By the beginning of the twentieth century, this new form of journalism, called *muckraking,* had become an important part of magazine content. Muckraking journalists sought out and exposed corruption and scandal. President Theodore Roosevelt coined the term *muckraker* to express his dislike for this negative form of journalism. For him, these journalists were like the "Man with the Muckrake" in *Pilgrim's Progress,* who would not look up from the filth on the floor even when he was offered a glittering crown. But the muckrakers themselves considered the term a compliment to their crusading efforts.

Although *Harper's Weekly* had exposed political corruption in New York as early as the 1870s and the nineteenth-century magazine *The Arena* had attacked slums, sweatshops and prostitution, it was not until the turn of the century that campaigns against corruption became commonplace in such mass-circulation magazines as *McClure's, Everybody's* and *Collier's.* Soon both general-interest and opinion magazines were carrying muckraking articles exposing deplorable living conditions, corrupt business practices, exploitation of workers and political corruption.

Among the more prominent muckrakers were Lincoln Steffens, Ida Tarbell, Ray Stannard Baker, David Graham Phillips and Upton Sinclair. Steffens tackled the slums in his widely praised "Shame of the Cities" series; Tarbell exposed the corrupt business practices of John D. Rockefeller in the "History of the Standard Oil Company"; Baker wrote a series on the problems of corrupt labor unions entitled "The Right to Work"; Phillips attacked politicians who favored special interest groups in "Treason in the Senate"; and Sinclair wrote about worker exploitation and unsanitary conditions in Chicago's meat-packing houses in "The Condemned Meat Industry."

Muckrakers created popular sentiment for reform legislation, most notably the Pure Food and Drug Act and the Meat Inspection Act, both sponsored by President Theodore Roosevelt.

World War I. As World War I approached, muckraking journalism declined—attention was increasingly focused on the war in Europe. Magazines played a role in eventually getting the United States involved in the war. The British conducted an overt campaign to get pro-Allies propaganda before the American people, some of which made its way into American magazines. Numerous stories (many of them false) about German atrocities in Belgium circulated throughout the United States. Even President Woodrow Wilson was influenced by the British magazines that he regularly read.[3]

Postwar Trends. Although Wilson overcame considerable domestic opposition to secure the entry of the United States into World War I in 1917, he was unsuccessful in persuading the nation to guarantee the peace. The U.S. Senate refused to ratify the treaty that would have made the United States a member of the new League of

BOX 5.1.

MAGAZINES REFLECT CULTURAL CHANGES

American popular culture changed dramatically during the first part of the twentieth century. As the culture changed, so did the content of the nation's magazines. One of the best ways to study the changing popular culture is to look at magazines over a period of time. Each new trend, fad, hobby or subculture is reflected in our magazines. These changes are seen in general-interest as well as special-interest publications.

One of the first studies of our changing culture as seen through the pages of magazines was published in *Radio Research* (edited by Paul F. Lazarsfeld) in 1942–43. In this study, Leo Lowenthal compared the biographical articles in *Collier's* and the *Saturday Evening Post* for 1901 and 1940–41; he found that in the 40-year interval the proportion of articles about business and professional men and political leaders had declined, while those about entertainers had gone up 50 percent.

The study showed how our culture had changed from the days of the Industrial Revolution—when men of production played a paramount role in society—to a new age preoccupied with leisure pursuits and the popular, rather than the elite, arts. It confirmed too that our popular culture had moved from an interest in elite or high culture to mass-cultural interests: in 1901 the entertainers featured were mostly serious artists, such as opera singers, sculptors, or pianists, while the 1941 entertainers were all movie stars or baseball players.*

Probably more so than any other mass medium, magazines serve as a barometer for measuring our changing American culture.

* Alan Casty, *Mass Media and Mass Man* (New York: Holt, Rinehart & Winston, 1968), p. 20.

Nations. Many Americans believed that peace and economic prosperity could best be achieved by isolating our nation from alliances and commitments with other countries. This isolationist attitude grew after the war. As the country turned inward, it began to focus on the cultural changes that were occurring in the 1920s. They included changes in the family structure, women's suffrage, prohibition, growth of urban life, a rising crime rate and more permissive moral attitudes—which many people blamed on the invention of the automobile (which allowed young people to court one another away from the home), jazz music and dance halls.

As the culture changed, so did magazine content (see Box 5.1). A variety of new magazines emerged. For example, as our popular culture became fast-paced with prohibition, popular music and fast living during "The Roaring 20s," the stage was set for a magazine that would save the reader time by condensing its articles. In 1922 *Reader's Digest* was founded by DeWitt and Lila Wallace; their idea was to take the best articles from other publications and reprint them in a condensed form, and their magazine became the largest-selling one in the nation.

Because the United States did not have a strong system of nationally circulating newspapers, as in England, magazines filled the void. The first "newsmagazine," a term coined by its founders Henry B. Luce and Britton Hadden, was introduced in 1923 as *Time. Newsweek* followed in 1933 and in 1948 *U.S. News & World Report* entered the field.

As the trend toward urbanization continued, metropolitan magazines, featuring articles about life styles in our large urban centers, became popular. The first and most successful was the *New Yorker,* introduced in 1925.

Life. Henry Luce had another idea for making magazine history in 1936, when he brought out a large-size pictorial weekly called *Life.* By this time radio had become an important mass-communication medium and was taking listeners to the scenes of important news events. (It also competed with magazines for consumers' leisure time.) *Life* was able to fill the visual void radio created by providing pictures of major news events each week.

Life was an almost instant success and soon was found in most households. Its excellent photojournalism is still admired today. Teams of *Life* photographers were sent out on news and feature stories, and only the very best of the photos were used.

Although *Life* became a very popular magazine, its development was not without controversy. A 1938 photo essay on the birth of a baby shocked many people, and the magazine was banned in 33 cities—to cite just one instance in which the content was too graphic or controversial for the conservative elements in the popular culture.

A year after *Life* began publishing, Gardner Cowles introduced *Look* magazine as an imitator. It too became a popular general-interest magazine. In 1945, *Ebony* was founded as another version of *Life,* this time aimed at a burgeoning black audience.

TV Guide. When television started entering the popular culture in 1948, *TV Guide* was established as a magazine catering to New York television-set owners. Sold soon after to Walter Annenberg's Triangle Publications, it became *the* national television guide, offering local area listings. In 1974 it replaced *Reader's Digest* as the

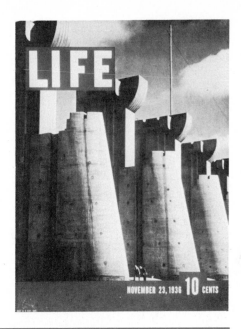

LIFE magazine provided Americans with a weekly pictorial report on world news for 36 years. This spectacular photo of a dam at Fort Peck, Montana, on the cover of the first issue was taken by the famous *LIFE* photographer Margaret Bourke-White. *(Margaret Bourke-White/Life Magazine)*

largest-selling magazine in the country, and today its weekly circulation figures approach 17 million. These two publications have been competing for first place ever since, with both publications exceeding 18 million circulation at one time or another (see Table 5.1). In 1988 media baron Rupert Murdoch agreed to pay $3 billion for Triangle Publications, publishers of *TV Guide, Seventeen,* and *Racing Forum.*

MAD magazine started out in a comic-book format and evolved into a humor magazine that satirizes the consumer-oriented popular culture of the United States. True to its own code, it remains the largest circulation magazine without paid advertising. *(Barbara Rios/ Photo Researchers)*

Table 5.1.
The 30 Top U.S. Magazines

TV Guide, followed closely by Reader's Digest, is the nation's leader in magazine circulation. These two publications have tied with each other for first place for years. The rest of the top 30 is dominated by women's interest magazines, though news, senior citizen, health, lifestyle, sports and erotica publications also do well.

Magazine	Circulation (millions)
TV Guide (Triangle)*	16.8
Reader's Digest	16.2
Modern Maturity (American Assn. of Retired Persons)	15.8
National Geographic	10.7
Better Home and Gardens (Meredith)	8.0
Family Circle (New York Time)	6.2
Woman's Day (CBS)	5.5
McCall's	5.2
Good Housekeeping (Hearst)	5.2
Ladies' Home Journal (Meredith)	5.0
Time	4.7
Redbook (Hearst)	4.0
Cable Time (Telegyde)	3.7
Playboy	3.4
Newsweek	3.1
People (Time)	3.0
Cosmopolitan (Hearst)	2.9
Sports Illustrated (Time)	2.9
Prevention (Rodale)	2.8
Smithsonian	2.3
U.S. News & World Report	2.3
Glamour (Conde Nast)	2.3
Penthouse	2.3
Southern Living	2.2
Field and Stream (CBS)	2.0
Seventeen (Triangle)	1.8
Popular Science (Times Mirror)	1.8
Parents (Gruner & Jahr)	1.7
Motorland (California Automobile Assn.)	1.7
Popular Mechanics (Hearst)	1.6

SOURCE: Gale Directory of Publications, vol. 2 (Detroit: Gale Research, 1988).
*The corporate owner is included only when it differs from the name of the magazine.

Mad. As the American popular culture became ever more obsessed with techology and conspicuous consumption, it was not surprising that a magazine developed to criticize these trends. In 1952 William Gaines established *Mad*, a satirical humor magazine that used a sophisticated comic book format.

Much of *Mad's* success seems to come from its ability to poke fun at the materialistic and commercialized American culture and mass media's role in it. *Mad's* willingness to satirize the very commercial products that other magazines rely on for advertising revenue endears it to many Americans. Today *Mad* holds the distinction of being the only large-circulation magazine to survive without accepting paid advertisements.

Playboy. A year after *Mad* began publishing, *Playboy* appeared on the scene. It has since been credited by some and criticized by others for launching the sexual revolution in America. The first issue in 1953 was put together on a card table in the kitchen of the founder, Hugh Hefner, a former *Esquire* magazine employee.

Hefner enlisted the assistance of a freelance artist on the promise of some stock in his new company, and the first issue of *Playboy* was polished and released featuring a nude centerfold of movie actress Marilyn Monroe. By 1954 *Playboy* was selling more than 100,000 copies a month, and this figure climbed to nearly 800,000 two years later. It now sells 4.5 million copies a month, down from its best years, when it sold more than 7 million.

Intent on building a sophisticated image for his nudie magazine, Hefner also ran articles by well-known and respected writers. At first he refused to accept advertising, but later he carefully added this form of revenue by accepting only "quality-image" advertising; he rejected more than 80 percent of the ads submitted for publication. His plan paid off, as in a few short years his magazine became accepted by many in the popular culture. John Brady, former editor of *Writer's Digest*, said that Hefner "gave popular culture a sex life."[4]

DECLINE OF GENERAL-INTEREST MAGAZINES

As many new special-interest magazines were launched in the 1950s, it soon became apparent that general-interest magazines were in trouble. In 1956 *Collier's* was the first modern mass-circulation general-interest magazine to go bankrupt and cease publication.

Demographic and Regional Breakouts. By 1967, *Look* turned to alternative ways to survive. It began publishing *demographic breakout* editions, which allowed advertisers to pay less by placing their ads in editions of the magazine that went only to certain demographic categories. An advertiser could run an ad, for example, in a portion of the copies printed, such as those going to people with incomes above $24,000. Despite these efforts, *Look* went out of business in 1971.

Many surviving general-interest magazines and the successful national newsmagazines sell ads on a *demographic* or *regional breakout* basis. Regional breakouts allow advertisers to purchase ads in the copies circulated in particular geographic regions.

The biggest shock for the millions of people who depended on general-interest magazines came in 1972, when *Life* announced that its December issue would be its last. Although American popular culture had changed greatly in the 36 years since *Life* was born, the magazine had reared a generation of Americans—and life without *Life* seemed too much for many of them to take.

A number of factors contributed to the demise of these general-interest magazines. One was higher production costs and postal rates. Another was the competition for leisure time posed by the new medium of television. Television filled the same visual void for pictures of news events that *Life* did. It provided both pictures and sound— and did it daily. Another factor in the demise of many general-interest magazines was the fact that many readers were turning to more specialized magazines.

Since advertising revenue is the "life's blood" of the magazine industry, the nail in the coffin for many general-interest magazines came when advertisers realized that they could better target the specialized audiences they were seeking by using specialized publications. With the increase in numbers and variety of special-interest magazines available, many advertisers no longer wanted to pay the higher cost of reaching the general-interest masses. The homogeneous interests of specialized magazine readers were superior to regional and demographic breakouts.

Despite *Life*'s demise, 1972 was not all gloom for the magazine business. This was the year that a new special-interest magazine, *Ms.*, was founded. Devoted to women's rights and the feminist movement, it found a niche in American popular culture by recognizing that women should be something more than sex objects and housewives. The magazine was an overnight success and remains popular today.

In 1974 Time Inc. launched *People* magazine, a smaller, livelier version of the old movie fan magazine. (Movie magazines had been popular during the heyday of the movies in the 1930s and '40s, but their readership had declined after the motion-picture industry was forced to move into the era of specialization in the 1950s.) Some felt that *People* was an attempt to satisfy some of the diehard former *Life* readers with a more focused publication that was less expensive to produce. It has become successful, with 85 percent of its sales coming from newsstands, particularly in supermarkets.

Life's Rebirth. Despite these new magazines, many who had grown up with *Life* still missed it. In response, Time Inc. began issuing a number of special editions of *Life*. Their success prompted Time to reintroduce the magazine as a monthly in 1978. The new *Life* still features quality photojournalism but does not have the weekly "news" orientation it once had.

High Risk. In 1983 Time Inc. created yet another new magazine, this time with disastrous results. As cable television spread across the nation, Time Inc. decided to try to reach this affluent and growing market by publishing a cable TV program guide. In April it produced the first issue of *TV-Cable Week*, spending $100 million to move into the specialized market dominated by *TV Guide*. The goal was to supply cable TV subscribers with better information than was available from Annenberg's publication.

TV Guide, however, did not stand still, and it easily fought off the competition by simply adding cable programs to its listings. In September 1983, after five months, Time Inc. published its last issue of *TV-Cable Week*. A staff of 250 was laid off, and losses totaled $50 million.

Many other new magazines have had similar experiences. The costs of establishing and sustaining a new publication are great and many magazines go under before they can establish themselves in the market place.

TYPES OF MAGAZINES

According to the 1988 *Gale Directory of Publications* (formerly the *Ayer Directory of Publications*), by the late 1980s over 12,000 magazines were being published in the United States. This figure had increased from 6,950 in 1950. Of these 12,000-plus publications, about 800 were general-interest magazines; the rest were devoted to special interests. This large assortment of magazines can be divided into the following ten main categories.

Family Magazines. One of the newest categories of magazines to become popular in the late 1980s was the family magazine. These publications reflected a revived interest in the family by a segment of the population that had previously been regarded as interested in the self only—the Yuppie generation. New magazines in this category include *Parenting, Fathers, Child, Children* and *Grandparents*.

Computer Magazines. Another successful new magazine category in the 1980s was computer magazines. As more and more people used computers at home and at work, they created a market for publications like *Byte, PC World, MacWorld, PC Magazine* and *Publish* (see Box 5.2).

Erotica Magazines. Erotica or sex magazines began reflecting more permissive attitudes toward sex and nudity in the 1950s. Always controversial, this category came under renewed criticism in the 1986 report by the Meese Commission on Pornography (see Chapter 4). Letters from the executive director of the Commission were sent to a number of chain stores that carried these magazines telling them that testimony before the Commission indicated that they were involved in the sale of pornography. Several companies, including 7-Eleven, removed the publications from their shelves. The popularity of these magazines seems to have peaked in the 1970s, however, as circulation figures had started to decline even before the Meese Commission report. Publications in this category include *Playboy, Penthouse, Playgirl, Hustler, Oui* and *Screw*.

BOX 5.2

MAGAZINES OF THE 1980s

In 1981, an investor approached David Bunnell with the idea of starting a magazine about computers. Bunnell jumped at the chance, and he put together the first issue of *PC Magazine* in his home. This was not Bunnell's first experience in the computer field, however. In 1974 he stumbled onto a job writing instruction manuals for a small electronics firm in New Mexico. In 1975 the firm brought out the first personal computer—the MITS Altair.

In 1982, after Ziff Davis Publishing purchased a majority interest in *PC Magazine*, Bunnell and 48 of his 52 staff members started a competing publication, *PC World*. The 324-page publication made history as the fattest first issue ever published. By 1986 the 38-year-old Bunnell, serving as editor-in-chief of *PC World* and *MacWorld*, was making over $1.6 million a year.

Bunnell is one of a number of people who became successful during the 1980s by publishing specialized magazines. Other new publications that found success in the 1980s were family-oriented magazines, which were popular with the Yuppie generation in the late 1980s, and health and sports magazines, which reflected growing interests in health-oriented leisure activities. In 1986, for example, 33 new sports magazines began publishing in the United States. Six of them were wrestling magazines, including one called *Beauties of Wrestling* about female grapplers.

One of the best ways for a person to stay abreast of the changing popular culture in the twentieth century is to browse in the magazine section of newsstands or read the latest directory of publications.

Sports Magazines. A genre that caters exclusively to our culture's interest in leisure activities is the sports magazine. These publications range from the specialized general-interest magazines like *Sports Illustrated* and *Sport*, to more specialized publications covering just one sport—such as *Runner's World*, *Boating*, *Backpacker*, *Flying* and *Skiing*. Sports magazines, like erotica magazines, once seemed to be intended for men only. However, women now make up a large segment of the audience for general sports magazines, and some sports magazines are designed just for women.

Men's Magazines. Although men are the prime audience for most erotica and sports magazines, there are many other men's magazines, especially ones that focus on adventure and fashion. *Field & Stream*, *Gun & Ammo*, *Esquire*, and *Gentlemen's Quarterly* are well known publications in this category. *Gentlemen's Quarterly* reflects a new trend in our popular culture, as many men become as caught up in consumer fashions as women have long been.

Women's Interest. As discussed earlier, women's magazines have been around since the nineteenth century and today include some of the magazines with the highest circulations in the country. *Vogue*, *Glamour*, *Better Homes and Garden*, *Good*

Housekeeping, Woman's Day, Modern Bride and *McCall's* are just a few of the many traditional women's magazines. As we have seen, *Ms.* was the first women's magazine to depart from the traditional mold and reflect a feminist viewpoint. By the late 1980s, magazines designed for a more sophisticated American woman were making an impact, including *Woman, New Woman, New York Woman,* and *Complete Woman.* Women's interest in health and fitness was reflected in new publications like *Self* and *Shape.*

Youth Magazines. Magazines for young people—ranging from *Boy's Life* to *Seventeen*—have been around for a long time. As American teenagers mature earlier, their magazines have been tackling more adult topics. In 1988 an Australian publishing firm began challenging *Seventeen* in the U.S. market by bringing out a sexier publication for teenage girls. Called *Sassy,* the magazine's first issue included articles on "How to Flirt" and "Losing Your Virginity." An important subcategory of youth magazines is the wide range of rock-'n'-roll fan magazines commonly referred to as *teenzines* (see Box 5.3).

Ethnic Magazines. Virtually all ethnic minorities have found magazines to be an effective way to communicate with one another. Some of the more successful ethnic publications are *Ebony, Black World, Tan, Essence* and *Identity.*

A teen-age girl reads a copy of *Seventeen.* In 1988, an Australian publishing company challenged *Seventeen's* domination of the market with a racier publication called *Sassy.* *(Barbara Rios/ Photo Researchers)*

Box 5.3

THE TEENZINES

One of the most popular categories of youth-oriented magazines is the *teenzines*. These magazines play an important role in shaping and reflecting the popular culture of teenagers. Most teenzines are fan magazines for 11- to 13-year-old girls. They are offshoots of such traditional movie magazines as *Photoplay* and *Motion Picture* that focus primarily on rock stars rather than movie stars. Teenzines got their start in the 1950s, when popular music and the motion-picture industry first started targeting young people as a potential audience.

The early teen fan magazines had a preachy, parental tone that attempted to set and preserve moral standards. The popularity of these magazines grew in the 1960s, as Beatlemania and Monkeemania caused monthly circulation figures to skyrocket. Since then, rock music has dominated the content of the magazines. As a result, the magazines have reflected the changing attitudes in popular music and given their young readers what they want: the inside scoop on the public and private lives of their rock stars. Today these magazines feature intimate interviews with sexy superstars such as Billy Idol and Prince and discuss rock stars' attitudes on romance, drugs and sex.

Although the content of the female-oriented teenzines is more worldly than it was in earlier days, these publications still attempt to avoid four-letter words and lewd poses. Their goal is to feature "wholesome" pinup shots of rock stars that girls can post on their bedroom walls and school lockers.

Some of the more popular teenzines are *Tiger Beat, Teen Beat, Bop, Topless Hunks* and *16*, all for girls. Male-oriented teenage fan magazines include *Circus, Hit Parade, Metal,* and *Creem*. These publications have macho overtones and are not immune to four-letter words or photos that border on lewdness.

The teenzines, like all magazines, must reflect the desires of their audience if they are to remain successful. In so doing, they reflect the popular culture that influences teens today, even to the exasperation of adults. As one teenzine editor noted in an interview with a *Los Angeles Times* reporter, "It's not our role to play the part of parents. Kids are picking up the magazines to get away from that. To read about these people [rock stars]—it's sort of rebellious."

Subcultural Magazines. Other subcultures, from motorcycle gangs to marijuana smokers, have magazines specializing in their interests. Such publications include *Easyriders* for bikers, *Advocate* for gay-rights supporters and *High Times* for marijuana smokers.

Other magazine categories are newsmagazines; opinion, intellectual, quality and humor magazines; city and regional magazines; and special-interest publications devoted to business, travel and exploration, hobbies, religions, romance, cars and motorcycles, gourmet foods and life styles.

Additional Periodicals. In addition to the 12,000 publications that are widely available, there are thousands of periodicals with limited circulation. The *Standard*

Periodical Directory lists over 62,000 journals and magazines in this category, including academic publications, alumni magazines, trade journals, monthly reports from professional associations, industry magazines, free-circulation magazines (like those produced by airlines) and business publications.

SPECIALIZATION AND POPULAR CULTURE

Many people have tried to explain the trend away from general-interest publications to highly specialized periodicals. The trend was slow at first, starting in 1945 at the end of World War II, and has rapidly accelerated in recent years.

In 1973 sociologist Richard Maisel suggested that the United States had moved from an industrial society to a postindustrial society, which is characterized by increased specialization and the growth of service industries. In such a society, he says, the populace tends to fragment into segments with various interests and concerns.[5]

Jean-Louis Servan-Schreiber, a Frenchman, made the same point in his book *The Power to Inform:* "Americans today find that, as a result of an era of progress from which their country benefited before any of the other industrialized nations, their immense, reputedly homogeneous society of 200 million individuals is fragmenting."[6] In other words, the human resistance to the mass culture that developed during the Industrial Revolution has finally caused that culture to fragment into subcultures with individualistic interests.

Meeting Consumer Needs. This fragmentation has caused magazines to specialize. From their beginnings in the eighteenth century, magazines have had to give readers what they wanted in order to survive. As Americans had more money to spend and more leisure time to spend it in, people developed special interests to consume their time and money. Coupled with this has been the desire of individuals to find their own identities in our mass culture.

The need to break away from the mass identity created by the Industrial Revolution and find individuality through cults and other subcultural forms (see Chapter 2) has created an interesting paradox. It seems that in addition to our desire to be valued as individualists, we also need to "belong" to some identifiable group—smaller, of course, than the masses as a whole. Thus we seem to be seeking a compromise in the American popular culture between being faceless entities in mass society and individuals who belong to something. As one mass-media scholar puts it:

> We are young, middle-aged, or old. Many of us find an attachment to a racial
> or ethnic minority more important than a status as an American. We are
> Easterners or Southerners or Westerners or Texans or Californians—and
> proud of it. We are environmentalists, runners, women's liberationists, part of
> the counter culture, Jesus freaks, skiers, sports car enthusiasts, concerned
> parents, swinging singles; we collect stamps and coins and beer cans and
> model trains and antique cars and nostalgia items; we ski, surf, hike, climb
> mountains, scuba dive, sail, camp, fish, hunt, bowl, golf, ice skate, and swim.[7]

Almost every month a new magazine is launched to reach a previously untapped group of consumers.

All consumer industries have tried to cater to at least some of these widely varying interests. Our mass media—particularly the magazines—have simply done so more visibly.

One policy of the Hearst Corporation, one of the more successful publishing firms, helped it move quickly into the age of specialization: "Find out what your readers want and give it to them."[8] By 1955 Hearst was already publishing mostly special-interest magazines, including *Motor*, *Motor Boating*, *American Druggist*, *Harper's Bazaar*, *House Beautiful*, *Town and Country*, *Good Housekeeping*, *Sports Afield* and *Cosmopolitan*. And when *Cosmopolitan*, for example, started to show signs of decline, the old, rather conservative format was abandoned and a new format developed to appeal to a sophisticated, sexually liberated woman. Its circulation climbed as a result.

Advertising's Role. A magazine's success depends on its ability to attract advertising, and advertisers want magazines that can deliver readers. But not all readers are equally valuable to advertisers. As reader interests began to fragment, advertisers found that they could reach their target audience more effectively and at a lower cost by advertising in special-interest publications with smaller circulations. Magazine advertisers have changed their focus from a "shotgun blast" at the masses to a rifle shot at particular groups. From the first, the success or failure of any magazine has depended on its ability to predict reader interests and meet those interests with appropriate reading material. Specialization has made it easier to do so.

SUMMARY

Since their beginning in the eighteenth century, magazines have provided a wide variety of material for their readers. All magazines, by their very nature, specialize in some way. They either have unit specialization or internal specialization.

Magazines did not really begin to flourish until the 1820s, when new technologies, coupled with a new literate society brought on by compulsory education, paved the way for their expansion. By the end of the nineteenth century, magazines had entered the popular culture with general-interest, special-interest, and low-cost publications.

The beginning of the twentieth century was the heyday of muckraking articles in magazines, but by 1917 the public's attention had shifted to concern about World War I in Europe. In the 1920s a new variety of magazines developed to meet the needs of the new, fast-paced American culture. After World War II, general-interest magazines started to decline, and the age of specialization was firmly established.

Magazines can be classified in a variety of ways, but what is abundantly clear is that there seems to be a magazine for just about every interest and taste in both our popular and elite cultures.

Individuals in our culture have gone from faceless cogs of a mass society to members of one sort or another in a variety of interest groups. Magazines, which must deliver readers to their advertisers, have changed to cater to these various special interests and as a result have become the first mass medium to effectively reflect these changes.

NOTES

1. John C. Merrill and Ralph L. Lowenstein, *Media, Message and Men: New Perspectives in Communication*, 2nd ed. (New York: Longman, 1979), p. 39.

2. Frank Luther Mott, *History of American Magazines 1741–1850* (New York: Macmillan, 1930), p. 232.

3. Oscar Handlin, *The History of the United States*, vol. 2 (New York: Holt, Rinehart & Winston, 1968), p. 322.

4. John Brady, "The Nude Journalism," in Edward Jay Whetmore, *Media America: Form, Content and Consequences of Mass Communication*, 3rd ed. (Belmont, Calif.: Wadsworth, 1985), p. 76.

5. Richard Maisel, "The Decline of Mass Media," *Public Opinion Quarterly* (Summer 1973), p. 161.

6. Jean-Louis Servan-Schreiber, *The Power to Inform* (New York: McGraw-Hill, 1974).

7. Don R. Pember, *Mass Media in America*, 4th ed. (Chicago: Science Research Associates, 1983), p. 89.

8. John Tebbel, *The American Magazine: A Compact History* (New York: Hawthorn, 1969), p. 211.

ADDITIONAL READING

Anderson, Elliott, and Kinzie, Mary. *The Little Magazine in America: A Modern History.* Yonkers, N.Y.: Pushcart Press, 1978.

Ford, James L. *Magazines for the Millions.* Carbondale, Ill: Southern Illinois University Press, 1970.

Mogel, Leonard. *The Magazine: Everything You Need to Know to Make it in the Magazine Business.* Englewood Cliffs, N.J.: Prentice-Hall, 1979.

Mott, Frank Luther. *History of American Magazines 1850–1905,* 3 vols. Cambridge, Mass.: Harvard University Press, 1938–1957.

Peterson, Theodore. *Magazines in the Twentieth Century.* Urbana: University of Illinois Press, 1964.

Riley, Sam G. *Magazines of the American South.* Westport, Conn.: Greenwood Press, 1986.

Taft, William H. *American Magazines for the 1980s.* New York: Hastings House, 1982.

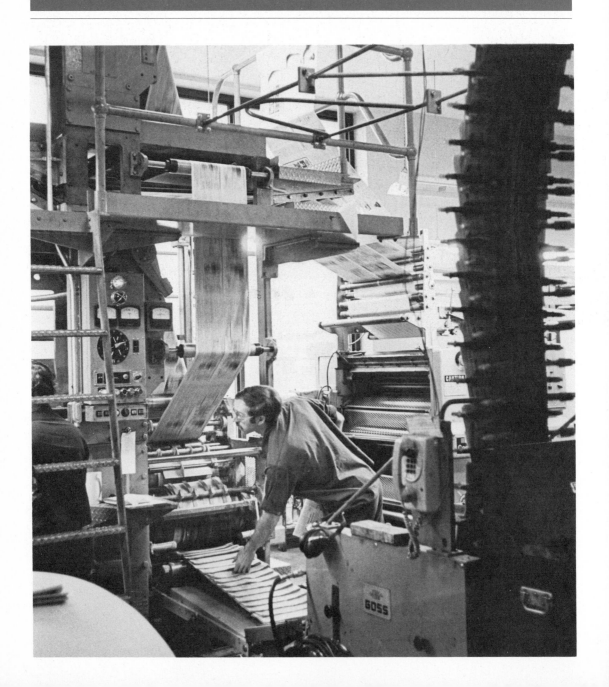

Chapter 6

Newspapers:
Past, Present and Problems

It is well to remember that
freedom through the press is
the thing that comes first.
Most of us probably feel we
couldn't be free without
newspapers, and that is the
real reason we want the
newspapers to be free.
—*Edward R. Murrow*

After 30 years of losing readers to television, the newspaper industry finally started fighting back in 1982 by using some of the same techniques and space-age technology that had made television so successful.

In the fall of that year, Gannett, the largest newspaper chain in the United States, launched a new national newspaper that was filled with short "TV style" news stories and ample color and graphics. Distributed to printing plants around the country by satellite, the newspaper was called *USA Today*.

Many traditional newspaper readers were critical of the new newspaper because its stories were so brief and necessarily lacked in-depth coverage. These critics felt Gannett's efforts were foolish and doomed to failure. This criticism began to subside in a few years, however, as many people who had previously been getting all of their news from television began purchasing the newspaper regularly. In May of 1987 *USA Today* reported its first profits—revenue had climbed 40 percent during the first five months of the year—and its daily circulation was over 1.6 million, second only to that of the *Wall Street Journal*.

USA Today is put together in Arlington, Virginia (just outside of Washington, D.C.) and then transmitted by satellite to various Gannett newspaper plants through-

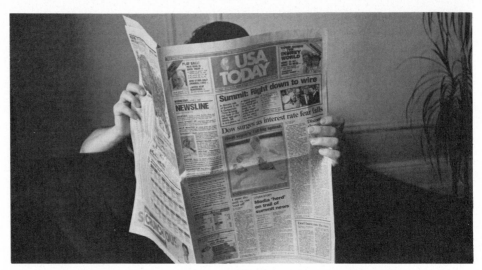

USA Today was launched in 1982 using satellite technology to create a daily national newspaper. Its use of bold color and graphics and its relatively scant hard-news coverage has become a model for many local papers. By the late 1980s, *USA Today* had a circulation of more than 1.6 million.

out the United States, where the signal is converted to printing plates. The paper is printed and distributed locally. For the reader, though, what made *USA Today* stand out were its color graphics, short capsule news stories and extensive use of human-interest features.

Soon other newspapers were utilizing computerized color graphics and condensing much of their news into brief summaries to allow more space for human-interest articles. The look and content of newspapers, which had remained relatively unchanged during the past century, was undergoing a transformation in an effort to adapt to an electronically visual popular culture.

This was not the first time the new medium of television had had an impact on newspapers, however. TV's more immediate coverage of news events brought an end to the use of sensationalism to sell newspapers. Home delivery subscriptions replaced street hawkers screaming out lurid headlines.

Since their nineteenth century introduction into the popular culture, newspapers have been the recorders of the first rough draft of cultural history. Newspapers quickly chronicle and disseminate to the masses the daily actions within any given culture. Although newspapers are not as quick to disseminate information as the newer electronic mass media, they are the fastest of the print media.

EARLY ORIGINS OF NEWSPAPERS

Early attempts to disseminate printed information to the public can be traced back some two thousand years to the official news sheets, called *acta diurna* (daily acts), posted by the Roman government in public places. However, it wasn't until the mid-sixteenth century that efforts to sell printed news began. Leaders in Venice made

CULTURAL HISTORY OF NEWSPAPERS

Elitist	Popular	Specialized		
■			1st century	Romans post news sheets in town squares.
■			16th century	Italians sell printed news sheets for a coin called a *gazetta*.
■			17th century	Corantos (newspaper forerunners) begin in Germany.
■			1665	*Oxford Gazette* founded, first English-language newspaper.
■			1690	First newspaper published in 13 Colonies, *Publick Occurrences*; lasts one issue.
■			1704	*Boston News-Letter* becomes first regularly published American newspaper.
■			1735	John Peter Zenger tried in New York for libeling the governor.
■			1765–83	American newspapers promote revolution.
■			1791	Bill of Rights ratified: press is given protection from government censorship by First Amendment.
■			1798	Alien and Sedition Acts passed, leading to prosecution of newspaper editors for criticizing government.
		■	1827	*Freedom's Journal* founded, first black newspaper in the United States.
	■		1833	*New York Sun* founded, first penny press.
	■		1841	Horace Greeley begins *New York Tribune*; introduces the editorial page and attacks slavery.
	■		1848	Associated Press (AP) founded, first news wire service.
	■		1883	Joseph Pulitzer begins publishing *New York World*.
	■		1895	William Randolph Hearst buys *New York Journal*; circulation war with Pulitzer is branded "yellow journalism."
	■		1896	Adolph Ochs buys *New York Times* and ushers in objective journalism.
	■		1907	United Press (UP) becomes second news wire service.
	■		1909	Hearst starts third news wire service, *International News Service* (INS).
	■		1920s	Tabloids begin reflecting Roaring '20s life styles.
	■		1923	Society of Newspaper Editors adopts Canons of Journalism, stressing social responsibility.
	■		1958	United Press and International News Service merge to become United Press International (UPI).
	■	■	1965–70	Underground newspapers reflect new American subcultural life styles.
	■		1972	Two *Washington Post* reporters expose the Watergate scandal that eventually leads to President Nixon's resignation.
	■		1982	*USA Today* founded as a national daily, using satellite technology and innovative color graphics.
		■	1985	Desktop publishing, using computers, makes possible inexpensive publication of specialized newspapers.

news regularly available to the public on printed sheets that sold for a coin called a gazetta. Later many newspapers would adopt the name *Gazette* for their publications.

Corantos. Another forerunner of today's newspaper began appearing in Germany around 1609 and in London in 1621. Called corantos, they consisted of printed single sheets containing current news that was published at regular and frequent intervals—often once or twice a week.[1] Amsterdam, where corantos were published in Dutch, German, French and English, became the first major newspaper center.

First English Papers. In 1665 the first real English-language newspaper—the *Oxford Gazette*—started publishing twice weekly under the authority of the English Crown. Later renamed the *London Gazette*, it continued publishing into the twentieth century.

The first daily newspaper in English was the *Daily Courant*, which began publication in London on March 11, 1702. This high-quality, highly literate paper was aimed at the educated elite. Like newspapers of today, it relied on advertising for its revenue.

Like all other publications, these early English newspapers were subject to censorship by the Crown, although censorship was rarely enforced after the late seventeenth century. In the American colonies, however, colonial governors continued to censor newspapers well into the eighteenth century.

THE COLONIAL AMERICAN PRESS (1690–1820s)

The Cradle of American Journalism. Credit for the first effort to found a newspaper in the American colonies belongs to Benjamin Harris, a former London publisher. He brought out the first edition of *Publick Occurrences Both Foreign and Domestick* in Boston on September 25, 1690. Harris had fled to the colonies after being arrested in England for printing seditious material against the Crown.

The first issue of *Publick Occurrences* apparently didn't please those in authority any better than his previous efforts in England. Among other things, the paper carried unfavorable comments about some Indians who were allies of the English and about the French king, who, it was alleged, had seduced his daughter-in-law. The newspaper's first issue was therefore its last. The governor of Massachusetts colony banned Harris's paper on the grounds that it had been published without authority and contained material disapproved by the government.

In putting Harris out of business, the authorities reaffirmed their right to *prior* censorship: publishers had to first secure permission from the government before publishing anything. A firmly established authoritarian principle dictated that the press be controlled to protect the interests of the Crown, and in the colonies the governors represented the Crown.

It was not until April 1704 that the *Boston News-Letter* became the first newspaper to be published regularly in the colonies. Its publisher was the postmaster of Boston, John Campbell, and under its nameplate were the words "published by authority."

The post-office connection was important for several reasons. First, the postmaster was the governor's appointee and in effect was "approved" by him. Second, the post office was an effective place for gathering news because people assembled there to read aloud to each other letters from England.

Because most colonists were English, it was not surprising that the *Boston News-Letter* was similar in appearance and content to the *London Gazette*. Two-thirds of the *News-Letter* consisted of news taken from London journals. Thus most stories concerned English politics and European wars. The rest of the space was filled with very brief articles about ship arrivals, sermons, deaths, political appointments, court actions, the weather, and the activities of Indians and pirates.

When Campbell retired from his job as postmaster in 1718, his successor, William Brooker, seemed to consider newspaper publishing a part of the job. But when Campbell refused to relinquish the *News-Letter*, Brooker started a second paper, the *Boston Gazette*, in 1719. Unlike Campbell, when Brooker lost his job as postmaster a year later, he turned the paper over to his successor. Five postmasters, including Brooker, served as publisher of the *Gazette*.

The Spread of Newspapers. Philadelphia's first newspaper, *The American Weekly Mercury*, was founded by the William Bradford family in 1719. Although it too was an authorized publication, Bradford's son Tom, the publisher, soon got into trouble for writing that he hoped the General Assembly "will find some effectual remedy to revive the dying credit of the Province and restore to us our former happy circumstances."[2] Tom went to jail for the statement; he was later released and was allowed to continue publishing the paper until his death in 1742.

In 1721 James Franklin, the older half-brother of Benjamin Franklin, started the *New England Courant* in Boston. Unlike the two older Boston papers, the *Courant* was not "published by authority" and had no connection with the post office.

The *Courant* did not resemble the *London Gazette*, as its predecessors had, but modeled itself after English literary essay papers such as the *Spectator* and *Guardian*. Its content was thus more entertaining than informative. The *Courant* ran humorous literary essays, most of them satirically critical of the Puritans and the colonial government. Eventually James Franklin was thrown in jail for a month and forbidden to publish the *Courant* or any paper "of like nature." Franklin circumvented that government order by naming his brother, Benjamin, an apprentice in his print shop, publisher.

Ben Franklin, who had perfected his writing style by reading and rewriting Joseph Addison's essays in the *Spectator*, which his brother kept in the print shop, started contributing satirical essays to the *Courant*. Appearing under the pseudonym of Silence Dogood, the articles soon became a popular feature.

In 1723 Benjamin Franklin left his apprenticeship to strike out on his own. He moved to Philadelphia, where he worked for Tom Bradford for several years. Then, in 1729 he bought an interest in an unsuccessful newspaper, *The Universal Instructor in all Arts and Sciences and the Pennsylvania Gazette*. He shortened the name to the *Pennsylvania Gazette* and turned it into a highly regarded newspaper—thus launching a successful publishing career that was to include a chain of newspapers as well as *Poor Richard's Almanac* and his *General Magazine*.

The *Pennsylvania Gazette* thrived after its acquisition by Benjamin Franklin on September 25, 1729. (*The Bettmann Archive*)

New York became the third colonial city with a newspaper when William Bradford started the *New York Gazette* in 1725. Bradford had left Philadelphia to become the official printer for the New York colony. Although not a postmaster, he benefited from the status of being an agent of the government.

Struggle Against Authority. In 1733 a young German immigrant by the name of John Peter Zenger began publishing the *New York Weekly Journal.* Zenger had the backing of a number of anti-Establishment merchants who disliked the colonial governor, William Cosby. Zenger printed one attack after another on the governor and his council until he was arrested for seditious libel. During the nine months he was held in jail awaiting trial, Zenger continued to edit his newspaper, which was printed and distributed by his wife and friends.

The trial began ominously, as Zenger's two attorneys were disbarred for attempting to get the judge to disqualify himself (on the grounds that he had been appointed by Governor Cosby). Zenger's supporters then hired Andrew Hamilton, a Philadelphia attorney, to represent him. At that time truth was not a defense in a libel suit (it is today), and the jury needed only to decide whether or not Zenger had printed the papers in question. The judge would decide if the material was criminally libelous.

During the trial in 1735, Hamilton argued for truth as a defense of libel. He challenged the jury to ignore the technicalities of the law and recognize the greater issues at stake: "The question before the court . . . is not the cause of the poor printer. . . . No! It may in its consequences affect every freeman . . . on the main[land] of America.

It is the best cause; it is the cause of Liberty ... the liberty both of exposing and opposing arbitrary power ... by speaking and writing Truth."[3]

The jury responded to Hamilton's oratory, ignored the letter of the law and returned a verdict of not guilty. Although the Zenger decision set no legal precedent, it sent a clear signal that the people were no longer compliant toward government suppression of the press. The press was beginning to play an important role in shaping cultural attitudes in the colonies.

Following the Zenger case, other newspapers started up in the colonies. By 1765 all but two—Delaware and New Jersey—had newspapers. There were four papers in Boston, three each in New York and Philadelphia, and two each in Connecticut, Rhode Island and North and South Carolina. The other four colonies had one paper each, published weekly at the seat of government.

With the exception of Benjamin Harris, John Campbell and the various postmasters who published the *Boston Gazette,* most newspaper editors and publishers in colonial days were printers by trade. Besides publishing a newspaper, these printers usually had a job-printing business and also printed books and pamphlets. Sometimes the printer-publisher was the postmaster, a magistrate and in many cases, the official printer for the colony. Frequently they ran bookstores where they sold their own publications as well as books from London—and occasionally general merchandise. Ben Franklin, for example, advertised coffee, soap, wines, patent medicines, eyeglasses, Rhode Island cheese and lottery tickets for sale along with his books and stationery.[4]

The Press and the Revolution. Slowly the colonial culture, with its strong loyalty to England, was changing. This loyalty was severely strained in 1765, when the British Parliament passed the Stamp Act imposing a tax on all legal documents, official papers, books and newspapers. To ensure that the tax was collected, all printing had to be done on taxed paper. This law was followed by the Townshend Acts, which placed taxes on tea, wine, oil, glass, lead and paint.

Hostility toward this "taxation without representation" was building in the colonies, and colonial printer-publishers started speaking out boldly against second-class colonial citizenship. Soon many newspapers were at the center of the controversy. Samuel Adams's *Boston Gazette* and Isaiah Thomas's *Massachusetts Spy* were leaders in the patriotic movement that was sweeping the colonies. A number of those prominent in the American Revolution were writers for the colonial press: John Adams, John Dickinson, Benjamin Franklin, Thomas Jefferson, Richard Henry Lee and Thomas Paine.

When the Revolution broke out in 1775, the press attempted to cover the war. However, there were no effective ways of gathering the news, and papers often had to rely on hearsay and secondhand reports from the battlefield. Facts were not always a major element in some of the war reports, as the partisan press helped to sustain the spirit of the American people. Typical was the May 3, 1775, *Massachusetts Spy* report on the first battle of the war:

Amercians! forever bear in mind the BATTLE OF LEXINGTON!—where British troops, unmolested and unprovoked, wantonly and in a most inhuman manner, fired upon and killed a number of our countrymen, then robbed,

*ransacked, and burnt their houses! Not could the tears of defenseless women,
some of them were in the pains of childbirth, the cries of the helpless babes,
not the prayers of old age confined to beds of sickness, appease their thirst for
blood!—or divert them from their design of MURDER AND ROBBERY!*

The Press in the New Republic.

The Press in the New Republic. Neither the Articles of Confederation of 1781
nor the Constitution drawn up in 1787 included protection for the press. Nevertheless,
the practice of prior censorship had died with the end of British rule, and newspapers
participated vigorously in public debate. In particular, the New York newspapers
played an important role in securing the ratification of the Constitution by publishing
the *Federalist Papers,* a series of essays in defense of the new document. Finally, in
1791 the First Amendment, the constitutional foundation for freedom of the press in
the United States, was ratified.

In the early days of the new republic, the press played a major role in American
politics. The new nation split into two parties—the Federalists, led by Alexander
Hamilton, and the Republicans, or anti-Federalists, led by Thomas Jefferson. Newspapers became partisan, lining up with one party or the other. Some even became
party organs, directly subsidized by the party. The development of a highly partisan
press has caused some historians to see the 1790s as the beginning of the "dark ages"
of American journalism.

Pro-Federalist papers included John Fenno's *Gazette of the United States,* William
Coleman's *New York Evening Post,* Noah Webster's *American Minerva* and William
Cobbett's *Porcupine's Gazette.* Pro-Republican newspapers included Philip Freneau's *National Gazette,* Samuel Harrison Smith's *National Intelligencer* and Benjamin Franklin Bache's *Aurora* (Bache was a grandson of Ben Franklin).

The content of these postrevolution newspapers was not all political, however. The
American culture still placed a great deal of importance on foreign news, particularly
from England. Even though the new nation had won its independence through a
bloody war, the culture was still dependent on the "mother country" for many things,
including cultural leadership, the models for newspapers and magazines and news
about English customs and thought.

However, the partisan postrevolutionary press differed in many ways from the tame
colonial newspapers with their noncontroversial accounts of foreign and domestic
news. Now the papers were run by strong-minded editors, who routinely expressed
their political convictions and attacked those who held opposing points of view.

Alien and Sedition Acts.

Alien and Sedition Acts. In 1798—just seven years after the First Amendment
gave the press explicit constitutional protection from government interference—the
Federalist-controlled Congress passed the Alien and Sedition Acts. The Sedition Act
placed serious restrictions on a person's right to criticize the government, the president or any members of his cabinet. Some Republican newspaper editors, at least one
Republican congressman and other critics of the government were tried under the
new law. Those convicted were fined and sent to jail. Citizens became so angry at
this government high-handedness that they voted Federalist President John Adams
out of office in 1800 and elected Thomas Jefferson, who had campaigned against the

acts. Jefferson pardoned those who had been imprisoned under the acts, and all fines were repaid with interest. The laws expired with the end of the Federalist reign.

Early Nineteenth Century. The dark ages of American journalism continued into the nineteenth century, as Thomas Jefferson, a long-time defender of a free press in a democratic society, suffered outrageous personal attacks from Federalist newspapers. Even President James Madison, the "Father of the Constitution" and the author of the First Amendment, was harshly criticized by certain elements of the press when he succeeded Jefferson to the presidency.

In the meantime, a new kind of paper, the mercantile newspaper, had emerged in the new nation. The *Courier*, the *Enquirer*, and the *Journal of Commerce* carried business news, shipping information and advertisements. In the early nineteenth century the mercantile press and the political press began to merge, forming the prototype of today's American newspaper.

As the American experiment in democracy unfolded in the years after independence, the press played an important role in shaping and reflecting political culture and values. Political leaders and thinkers differed on how the new democracy should function, and their lively war of ideas was amplified and disseminated through the mass medium of newspapers.

It is important to note, however, that in this period newspaper readers consisted primarily of a rather select, educated elite of politically aware citizens and merchants. Newspapers did not reach out to the general public until 1833.

THE PENNY-PRESS ERA (1833–1865)

By the 1830s New York had emerged as the metropolitan center of America's emerging industrial culture. Its population quadrupled to over 800,000 people between 1830 and 1860, as immigrants from Europe and migrants from rural New England arrived daily.

Popular Culture Newspapers. On September 3, 1833, Benjamin Day, a printer, launched a daily newspaper called the *New York Sun*. This paper represented a major departure from previous newspapers in terms of its content, cost and target audience. Instead of aiming the paper at the elite, who could afford to pay the customary six cents per copy, Day priced his paper at one cent, within reach of the new urban masses—the industrial-age immigrants and migrants.

Day hired newsboys to sell the four-page newspaper on the streets. He borrowed this "London plan" of circulation from English newspapers. To capture the interest of the newly arrived city dwellers Day concentrated on stories of crime, violence, murder, fires, trials, executions and other sensational topics. Another popular feature in the *Sun* was a humorous column that summarized the daily police-court activities in New York (see Box 6.1). Day's approach proved successful, and by the end of his first year the *Sun* had a circulation of 10,000.

BOX 6.1.

POLICE OFFICE

One of the most popular items in the New York Sun *was George W. Wisner's report of the police-court news. The following example of his work appeared in the July 4, 1834, edition.*

Margaret Thomas was drunk in the street—said she never would get drunk again "upon her honor." Committed, "upon honor."

William Luvoy got drunk because yesterday was so devilish warm. Drank 9 glasses of brandy and water and said he would be cursed if he wouldn't drink 9 more as quick as he could raise the money to buy it with. He would like to know what right the magistrate had to interfere with his private affairs. Fined $1—forgot his pocketbooks, and was sent over to bridewell.

Bridget McMunn got drunk and threw a pitcher at Mr. Ellis, of 53 Ludlow st. Bridget said she was the mother of 3 orphans—God bless their dear souls—and if she went to prison they would choke to death for the want of something to eat. Committed.

Catharine McBride was brought in for stealing a frock. Catharine said she had just served out 6 months on Blackwell's Island, and she wouldn't be sent back again for the best glass of punch that ever was made. Her husband, when she last left the penitentiary, took her to a boarding house in Essex st., but the rascal got mad at her, pulled her hair, pinched her arm, and kicked her out of bed. She was determined not to bear such treat-

ment as this, and so got drunk and stole the frock out of pure spite. Committed.

Bill Doty got drunk because he had the horrors so bad he couldn't keep sober. Committed.

Patrick Ludwick was sent up by his wife, who testified that she had supported him for several years in idleness and drunkenness. Abandoning all hopes of a reformation in her husband, she bought him a suit of clothes a fortnight since and told him to go about his business, for she would not live with him any longer. Last night he came home in state of intoxication, broke into his wife's bedroom, pulled her out of bed, pulled her hair, and stamped on her. She called a watchman and sent him up. Pat exerted all his powers of eloquence in endeavoring to excite his wife's sympathy, but to no purpose. As every sensible woman ought to do who is cursed with a drunken husband, she refused to have anything to do with him hereafter—and he was sent to the penitentiary.

Dennis Hart was fighting in the street. Committed.

John Movich, of 220 Mott st., got drunk and disturbed his neighbors. Committed.

With such a large audience, the *Sun* was very attractive to advertisers, and increasing advertising revenues meant new independence for the newspaper. Up to now, most papers had either served the business interests (the mercantile press) or been tied to political parties, which restricted editorial freedom. But with advertisers footing the bills instead, Day could take the editorial stands he believed in.

There were 11 competing newspapers in New York when Day started the *Sun*. After five years, the *Sun*'s circulation was over 30,000—more than the combined circulation of all the other papers. Day had successfully launched the metropolitan newspaper as a mass medium of popular culture.

Others soon copied Day's innovations. In 1835 James Gordon Bennett founded the *New York Herald,* which refined and expanded the popular content of the penny press. He designed his paper to "cover the city" by sending reporters to Wall Street, churches, social events and the courts.

Bennett's newspaper took a middle-of-the-road approach. Although it too featured crime news as an essential ingredient, it was more serious and responsible than the *Sun.* Just as important, it was more lively and entertaining than the mercantile, or Wall Street, papers, which quickly struck back. In an effort to discourage sophisticated New Yorkers from reading the *Herald,* the Wall Street press implied that Bennett's newspaper was "not suitable for ladies and gentlemen."[5] This was the first major struggle between the elite and popular press in the United States.

Many other penny-press newspapers followed Day's and Bennett's lead. One of the more significant was Horace Greeley's *New York Tribune,* which was founded in 1841. Greeley—whose exhortation "Go West Young Man, Go West" is legendary—hired others to handle the business side of the newspaper and concentrated his efforts on editorial work. He introduced the idea of separating news and opinion and developed the editorial page as we know it today. Greeley became one of the most influential editorial writers in the nineteenth century. He even ran unsuccessfully for president of the United States in 1872 on the Republican ticket.

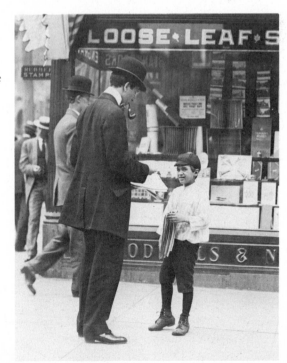

Benjamin Day introduced news carriers to the streets of New York to sell his successful *Sun,* the newspaper that launched the penny press and made newspapers available to the masses. *(Lewis Hine/Culver Pictures)*

Ten years after Greeley established the *Tribune*, Henry J. Raymond founded the *New York Times*. Modeling his newspaper after the *Times* of London, Raymond concentrated on news interpretation and background reporting and developed a strong editorial policy. He personally accompanied presidential candidates so he could write campaign stories firsthand. He also hired European correspondents to cover foreign stories exclusively for the *Times*.

New Technology. The Industrial Revolution had a major impact on printing technology, which had been virtually unchanged since the mid-fifteenth century. Newspapers began using the new rotary and cylinder presses, first driven by steam and later by electricity. It was now possible to print nearly 100,000 copies of a 12-page newspaper in an hour—a far cry from the early days of hand-fed presses.

The Associated Press. Soon after Samuel F. Morse invented the telegraph in 1844—the first glimmer of the electronic age—American newspapers started to take advantage of this new technology. By 1848 six New York newspapers had joined together to use the telegraph to pool their news-gathering resources. This first wire service was called the Associated Press of New York, later simply the Associated Press.

The debut of electronic technology affected the content of newspapers, just as television would in the second half of the twentieth century. Because telegraph lines were sometimes cut and news transmissions were often interrupted for military use during the Civil War, journalists started to put a complete summary of the story in the first paragraph. All of the traditional elements—who, what, when, where, why and how—were crowded into the lead paragraph so that the important information could be received before the transmission was interrupted. This style of newswriting, called the *inverted pyramid*, is still used in a modified version today. Use of the telegraph also spelt the demise of editorial comment in news stories. Because editorial opinions varied from newspaper to newspaper, a reporter writing for a number of newspapers could not come up with a slant that would fit them all. It was better to stick to the facts and let the individual newspapers editorialize as they wished.

Newspaper Syndicates. The first independent newspaper syndicate was founded in 1865 to supply feature materials to rural newspapers. Then, in 1884, Samuel S. McClure (who later published *McClure's Magazine*) established the first large-scale newspaper syndicate to furnish nonnews features and entertainment material to participating newspapers. McClure concentrated on women's features and the serialization of popular novels. Today's syndicated materials include comic strips, editorial cartoons, columnists, humor material and crossword puzzles.

THE YELLOW JOURNALISM ERA (1865–1900)

Between 1865 and 1900 the United States was transformed into a major industrial state. According to Agee, Ault and Emery,

*Industrialization, mechanization and urbanization brought extensive social,
cultural and political changes: the rise of the city, improved transportation and
communication, educational advances, political unrest and the rise of an
extensive labor movement. The mass media could not fail to go through great
changes along with the society they served.*[6]

The 35-year period between the end of the Civil War and the turn of the century is
known as the "yellow journalism" era to some and the period of "new journalism" to
others. It was a time when the metropolitan press took on a flamboyance characteristic
of the new industrial age. Newspapers became a major force in disseminating the new
mass culture.

During this period the population of the country doubled, the national wealth quadrupled and manufacturing output increased sevenfold. The United States was completing its transformation from an agrarian culture to an industrial society. One-third
of the population was urban, and by 1900, 62 percent of the labor force was engaged
in nonagricultural work.

As the nation changed, so did its newspapers. Urban workers looked to the press
for crusading reporting on corruption and editorial support for laws to ban the worst
abuses in mines and factories. Among the many crusading journalists who led the
effort to provide newspapers for the new mass audience, three stand out. Of these,
two fought head-to-head in New York in one of the century's fiercest circulation battles: Joseph Pulitzer, later named by his colleagues as the leading American editor of
this period, and William Randolph Hearst. The third was Edward W. Scripps (see
page 130).

Joseph Pulitzer. The new nation of immigrants was ready for one of its own to
take a leading role in American journalism. Born in Hungary in 1847, Joseph Pulitzer
came to the United States at the age of 17 to fight in the Civil War.

After his discharge in 1865, Pulitzer moved to St. Louis, where he studied law and
worked as a newspaper reporter for a German-language newspaper. In 1878 he bought
the *St. Louis Post-Dispatch* and soon turned it into the city's leading newspaper. In
1883 he left the *Post-Dispatch* in the hands of an editor to move to New York. There
he bought the run-down *World*, with similar results. Within four years the *World*
was New York's leading newspaper, with a record-breaking circulation of 250,000.

Although Pulitzer was not above using entertainment and sensationalism to capture
readers' attention, he did not neglect the basic purpose of a newspaper. He believed
in accuracy, an aggressive and crusading editorial policy and good news judgment.
One of his famous commands to his staff was "Accuracy! Accuracy!! Accuracy!!!"
Another was: "Terseness! Intelligent, not stupid, condensation." Still another showed
his concern for the lighter side of the news: he reminded reporters to look for both
the significant news and the "original, distinctive, dramatic, romantic, thrilling,
unique, curious, quaint, humorous, odd, apt to be talked about" news.[7]

Pulitzer was constantly crusading for just causes. He was particularly concerned
about the plight of his fellow immigrants, who were the victims of discrimination,
poverty, ignorance and crowded slum conditions. Pulitzer believed that his paper
should

. . . always fight for progress and reform, never tolerate injustice or corruption, always fight demagogues of all parties, always oppose privileged classes and public plunderers, never lack sympathy with the poor, always remain devoted to the public welfare, never to be satisfied with merely printing news, always be drastically independent, never be afraid to attack wrong, whether by predatory plutocracy or predatory poverty.[8]

Despite his high ideals, Pulitzer allowed himself to be pulled into one of American journalism's most degrading circulation wars. His opponent was William Randolph Hearst, who had become a successful publisher by using some of Pulitzer's techniques of entertainment and sensationalism.

William Randolph Hearst. In marked contrast to Pulitzer, William Randolph Hearst was born into a wealthy San Francisco family. As part of his privileged upbringing, Hearst was sent to Harvard for an education. While there he served as business manager of Harvard's *Lampoon* and became familiar with Pulitzer's style of journalism by exposure to the *World*, which circulated along the East Coast. About this time Hearst's father, George, purchased the *San Francisco Examiner* to use to manipulate the California legislature into appointing him to the U.S. Senate. (U.S. senators were appointed by state legislators until the adoption of the Seventeenth Amendment in 1913.)

When Hearst returned to San Francisco in 1887 he persuaded his father (now a senator) to turn the *Examiner* over to him rather than sell it. Then, employing some of the techniques he had learned from Pulitzer's *World*, he turned the *Examiner* into a mass-circulation newspaper that found a niche in San Francisco's popular culture.

Hearst, like Pulitzer, attempted to protect the public from abuses by the rich and powerful and from political corruption. He even crusaded against his father's friend Senator Leland Stanford, the millionaire owner of the Southern Pacific Railroad. Hearst opposed Stanford's efforts to get government subsidies for the railroads and made that crusade a major topic of his paper. He also fought corruption in San Francisco politics.

In 1895 Hearst, seeking new worlds to conquer, moved to New York. There he bought the *New York Journal* to compete head-to-head with Pulitzer's *World*, which at the time had the largest circulation of any paper in the country. Although Hearst had Pulitzer's crusading zeal and his flair for sensationalism, he did not share his rival's concern for accuracy and fairness. As one book has pointed out, "Hearst did not blink at coloring, stealing, or even faking the news; he did not hesitate to appeal to jingoism and a variety of other cheap emotions; and the tone of discourse in his papers often fell to mere abuse."[9]

In the circulation war, which reached a peak in 1898, both publishers resorted to journalistic excesses, including bold, misleading headlines, intensive coverage of crime, sex and violence, sensationalistic photojournalism and bizarre promotional stunts. Hearst was even accused of provoking the Spanish-American War through his sensational coverage of Spain's activities in Cuba.

Eventually people started calling these tactics "yellow journalism." The term came from "The Yellow Kid" comic strip, which was drawn for the *World* by Richard

BOX 6.2.

WOMEN IN JOURNALISM

The term *sob sister* was coined around the turn of the century to describe the women who wrote sentimental human-interest stories for William Randolph Hearst's newspapers. Although the hiring of women by Hearst helped to open up the field of journalism to women, it was by no means a first for women in the field.

Ann Smith Franklin, widow of Benjamin Franklin's older brother, is considered to be one of the first female journalists. She took over her husband's printing business after his death in 1735. About this same time the wife of John Peter Zenger was helping her husband publish the *New York Weekly Journal* while he was in prison awaiting trial on a charge of libeling the governor. The first female printer, however, was Dinah Nuthead, who took over her husband's printing business after he died in 1695.

Today there are many women in the editorial offices of American newspapers. However, even in the late 1980s not too many women held top editorial positions. According to a 1986 survey by the American Society of Newspaper Editors, 12.4 percent of the country's senior newspaper editors were women, though only a fraction of them were top newsroom executives. In fact, by 1988 only seven women held the top editorial position in newspapers with circulations over 100,000. They were Katharine Fanning, *Christian Science Monitor*; Barbara Henry, *Rochester* [N.Y.] *Democrat & Chronicle*; Sandra Mims Rowe, *Virginian-Pilot/Ledger-Star* (Norfolk, Va.); Janet Chusmir, *Miami Herald*; Beverly Kees, *Fresno Bee*; Deborah Howell, *St. Paul Pioneer Press Dispatch*; and Jane Amsterdam, *New York Post*.

In addition to these top editors, several other women in the 1980s had distinguished careers as publishers after inheriting newspapers from their husbands. They include Katharine Graham, chairman of the Washington Post Co. and Helen K. Copley, chairman of the San Diego-based Copley Newspaper chain.

Outcault, one of the most popular comic-strip cartoonists of the time. (Pulitzer had introduced color comic strips to American newspapers in 1894.)

The strip featured a bald, toothless, grinning boy dressed in a yellow sacklike garment. Because of the strip's popularity, Hearst offered Outcault a tremendous salary to quit the *World* and draw for the *Journal*, an offer he couldn't refuse. But Pulitzer, claiming he had sole rights to the comic strip, simply hired another cartoonist to draw it. For a while New York had two "Yellow Kids."

Although the two newspapers together sometimes sold more than a million copies a day during the circulation war, Pulitzer eventually lost his appetite for the competition and withdrew from the contest, leaving the field of yellow journalism to Hearst and a few of his imitators.

Hearst went on to build a major publishing empire consisting of a chain of newspapers throughout the country, four feature syndicates (which merged in 1931 to form the King Feature Syndicate), a wire service (International News Service, which he founded in 1909 when his papers were denied membership in the Associated Press) and numerous magazines, including *Cosmopolitan, Good Housekeeping,* and *Harper's Bazaar.*

One of Hearst's more significant contributions to the field of journalism was the introduction of women reporters into the newsrooms, mostly human-interest feature writers who became known as "sob sisters" (see Box 6.2). He also hired promotion managers to increase readership and led the way in proving the importance of strong circulation departments.

Edward Wyllis Scripps. The third crusader during this flamboyant period of American journalism was Edward Wyllis Scripps (1854–1926). Scripps concentrated his efforts in the nation's smaller cities, building a chain of newspapers with headquarters at the *Cleveland Press* in Ohio.

Like Pulitzer and Hearst, Scripps used his papers to champion the people's rights, but he never stooped to sensationalistic abuses. Scripps's goal was to improve the position of the new industrialized masses through better education, labor-union organization, collective bargaining and a reasonable redistribution of wealth. In this way, he reasoned, the ideal of a peaceful and productive society could be realized.

Scripps started many newspapers by sending an editor and business manager into a community with $25,000 and instructions to establish a newspaper. If they succeeded, they received 49 percent of the stock; if they ran out of money, they were replaced. If the paper did not show a profit within 10 years, it was shut down. In addition to his chain of 30 newspapers, Scripps also founded the Newspaper Enterprise Association (NEA) syndicate in 1902 and the United Press wire service in 1907.

THE TWENTIETH CENTURY PRESS

By the late 1890s many readers were looking for something better than what Hearst, Pulitzer and others like them had to offer, and yellow journalism began to wane.

Objectivity. What was lacking in New York and many other cities was a newspaper that was objective in its coverage of the news. Seeing an opportunity to improve the state of journalism in New York, Adolph Ochs purchased the near-bankrupt *New York Times* in 1896 and set out to make it the "newspaper of record." He introduced the slogan that still appears on the paper's front page today: "All the news that's fit to print."

Ochs guided the *Times* for 40 years and turned it into a paper that was respected worldwide for its comprehensive, accurate and balanced news coverage. As Ochs hoped, the *Times* has become the newspaper of record, and today it can be found indexed in most scholarly libraries. The standards set by the *New York Times* became respected by readers and journalists alike and soon other papers followed its lead.

Social Responsibility. The second trend at work at the beginning of the twentieth century was an emphasis on the *social responsibility* of newspapers and journalists (see Chapter 3). Schools and departments of journalism were established in colleges and universities, and attempts were made to teach high standards. The Graduate School of Journalism established at Columbia University in 1912 by a legacy from Joseph Pulitzer took the lead in this field. (The school still administers the most prestigious awards in newspaper journalism, the Pulitzer Prizes.) Various professional newspaper organizations drew up codes of ethics during this period.

Many observers of the American press were convinced that the libertarian theory of the press, which forbade government interference with the press, would not work if the mass media were not socially responsible. Some of the major newspapers in the country accepted this view and tried to make their publications more socially responsive by striving for fairness in news coverage and downplaying sensationalism.

Jazz Journalism. Although newspaper content was more responsible and objective during this period, sensationalism was not dead. Hearst publications continued to use bold headlines, sensationalized photography and stunts to sell papers. Indeed, there was another wave of sensationalism during the "Roaring '20s." This was called jazz journalism, and it reflected the Jazz Age of the time.

Helping to usher in this period of jazz journalism was Joseph Medill Patterson, copublisher of the *Chicago Tribune*. Patterson introduced a tabloid newspaper (half the size of a regular newspaper and similar in size to today's *National Enquirer*) to New York City.

Patterson's *New York Illustrated Daily News* featured large photographs (sometimes one covered the entire front page), crime, violence, and sex stories and sensational headlines to sell papers at newsstands. There was still a huge market for this type of journalism, and the New York *Daily News* ("Illustrated" was later dropped) soon became the nation's largest-selling daily newspaper, with a circulation that exceeded 2 million copies for many years. It finally surrendered first place in 1980 to the *Wall Street Journal*.

Soon Hearst and others started bringing out tabloid newspapers in New York City too. It is interesting to note that the largest-selling *weekly* newspaper in the United States is also a sensational tabloid—the *National Enquirer*, which sells nearly 5 million copies per week (see Box 6.3).

The Electronic Press. The most significant change in the way people got the news was the introduction of electronic journalism—first radio and then television news. (These are discussed at length in Chapters 8 and 9.) In the following discussion, we use the term *press* to include both print and electronic news gathering.

Interpretative Reporting. Although *interpretative reporting* was first introduced in the 1930s, there has been a marked increase in this type of reporting during the past decade or so. These articles, often labeled "news analysis," appear alongside straight news stories and try to explain the implications and possible consequences of certain events. They have become an important part of modern journalism.

For example, after George Bush and Michael Dukakis had sewed up the nomina-

BOX 6.3.

SUPERMARKET JOURNALISM: GIVING US WHAT ENQUIRING MINDS WANT TO KNOW

Not all successful newspapers are delivered to the home or sold on newsstands. Some are strategically marketed at supermarket checkout counters. Here grocery shoppers are enticed with sensational headlines and teasers for unbelievable stories that supposedly will be found on the inside pages.

The leader of these supermarket journals also happens to be the largest-circulating newspaper in the United States—the *National Enquirer*. The *Enquirer's* success can be traced back to 1952, when Generoso (Gene) Pope purchased the *New York Enquirer*. He immediately began filling the newspaper with stories about sex and violence (topics that the *Enquirer* now downplays). In the 1960s Pope expanded it into a national publication and began selling it in supermarkets. He toned down the sex and violence to appeal to a broader audience and began focusing on stories about celebrity gossip, government waste, haunted houses, ghosts, psychic predictions, honest people who find and return money, life-threatening accidents, successful people who never went to college, heroic activities, fat people who learned how to lose weight, ideas on saving money and medical advice. In short, Pope had learned how to market our popular cultural interests through news columns.

Through the years the *National Enquirer* has become one of the most successful and controversial newspapers in American society. It has been sued by numerous celebrities and has reached out-of-court settlements with many of them. Lawsuits against the *Enquirer* have been filed by Carol Burnett, Johnny Carson, Frank Sinatra, Tom Selleck, Richard Pryor and Shirley Jones, to name a few. Despite large settlements to the plaintiffs, the *National Enquirer's* flamboyant style does not change.

In 1987 the *Enquirer* angered many by publishing a front-page photo of former Democratic presidential frontrunner Gary Hart with actress Donna Rice sitting in his lap. The headline read: "GARY HART ASKED ME TO MARRY HIM." Other newspapers, mag-

tions of their parties for president in May 1988, the *New York Times* carried an article on its front page about possible running mates. Written by the *Times'* leading political reporter, R. W. Apple, Jr., the article explained how the process of picking vice presidential nominees had worked in the past and speculated on who might be the best choices this time.

Investigative Reporting. Investigative reporting has a longer history; it dates back to the turn of the century, when muckraking reporters began exposing the corruption and abuses of the new industrial society (see Chapter 5).

Classic examples of investigative reporting are Seymour Hersh's revelations about the My Lai massacre during the Vietnam war and Bob Woodward and Carl Bernstein's uncovering of the Watergate scandal in 1972–74.

In 1969 Hersh discovered that American soldiers had killed over 300 Vietnamese civilians at the village of My Lai the previous year. His reports led to congressional hearings and the indictment of military personnel involved in the episode. The incident shattered the myth that American soldiers were always the good guys who protected the innocent in times of war.

azines and television networks had carried the Donna Rice–Gary Hart story in previous weeks, but none of the stories came near the revelations of the *Enquirer*. The *Enquirer* had reportedly paid $25,000 for the photograph, and the cover helped the publication climb above the 5 million circulation mark that week.

When Marine Lt. Col. Oliver North became a folk hero during his 1987 testimony before a congressional committee investigating the Iran-Contra scandal, the *Enquirer* began featuring him on its cover. Months after his testimony the *Enquirer* was still catering to his popularity by running cover photos proposing him as a candidate for president.

The *National Enquirer* does not represent anything new in American journalism, however. What it does represent is a continuation of the style of journalism that has been in existence here since newspapers first began catering to the popular culture in the early nineteenth century. The publications of Benjamin Day and James Gordon Bennett in the early days of the penny press, Wil-liam Randolph Hearst and Joseph Pulitzer in the yellow journalism period, and the tabloids of New York in the jazz journalism age of the 1920s were not too much different in content from the *National Enquirer*. And they too were popular with the masses. This style of journalism is also the most popular form of journalism in the United Kingdom.

National Enquirer reporters are among the highest paid in the nation, and the paper covers major news events with teams of journalists and photographers, as *Life* magazine did in its heyday. The *Enquirer* often rushes journalists to the scene of news events to sign up eyewitnesses to "exclusive stories." While the popular entertainer Liberace was dying of AIDS in 1987, for example, eight *National Enquirer* reporters and photographers camped outside his Palm Springs home attempting to arrange exclusive stories.

Although highly criticized for its approach and style, the *National Enquirer* seems to be giving many people what they want—sensational stories concerning events that "enquiring minds want to know."

The Watergate story started with a police report about a burglary at the Democratic National Headquarters in a Washington, D.C., apartment complex called Watergate. Woodward and Bernstein, investigative reporters for the *Washington Post*, tried to find out what was behind the break-in. With the help of an anonymous source within the government, called "Deep Throat," they began discovering a series of illegal activities that they traced to the White House. When President Richard Nixon himself was implicated in a cover-up, he resigned from office. This event shook the foundation of our American culture because it ran counter to the myth that we could trust our presidents to respect the laws of the land.

In both of these investigative news events, many Americans blamed the press for revealing the information. Nevertheless, in a free society the role of the press is to keep the people informed and reflect all of the culture, including its unpleasant secrets.

Advocacy, Subjective or New Journalism. Not all journalists subscribe to the standard of strict objectivity. In the 1960s some reporters began to practice what they called *advocacy journalism, subjective journalism* or even *new journalism.* Believing that they should report the truth "as they see it," these reporters became personally and emotionally involved in the events they covered. This type of reporting has not been welcomed by the Establishment press, but it has found a home in certain specialized publications. One of the more successful subjective journalists is Hunter S. Thompson, who wrote "Fear and Loathing: On the Campaign Trail 1972" for the magazine *Rolling Stone*.

Although new journalism has had many meanings over the years, today the term refers to a twentieth century writing style that applies literary techniques to journalism. The result is a semiobjective, journalistic view of reality written from a subjective, first-person viewpoint. Some writers who have used this style are Tom Wolfe, Jimmy Breslin, Truman Capote, Norman Mailer and Gay Talese.

Limited Specialization. As our popular culture continues to fragment, American journalism is changing only slowly. Although newspapers do specialize in the sense that they serve a specific community or region, they generally attempt to appeal to almost everyone in that area. Thus they trail the other media in moving into the final stage of the EPS cycle.

However, there are some newspapers that do cater to specialized audiences, particularly ethnic groups. The first black newspaper, *Freedom's Journal,* was founded in 1827 by John B. Russwurm and the Reverend Samuel Cornish. The most important black pre–Civil War newspaper was Frederick Douglass's weekly, *North Star.* By the mid-1970s there were more than 325 black newspapers in the United States, with a

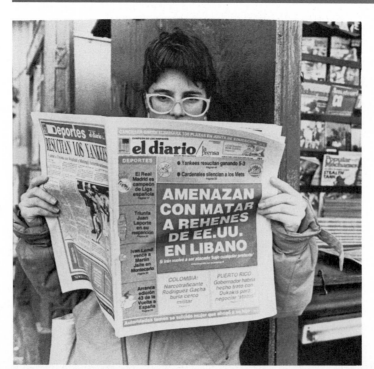

Ethnic newspapers have provided news for specialized interests in our culture since the early nineteenth century. *(Dion Ogust/The Image Works)*

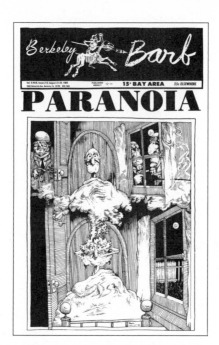

The *Berkeley Barb* was one of the best-known of the many underground newspapers that flourished during the late '60s and early '70s.

total circulation of more than 7 million. Most black papers represent the middle-of-the road black Establishment position. However, two—*Muhammad Speaks* and *Black Panther*—took a more militant position. Other ethnic newspapers in this country include the more than 50 Hispanic newspapers started since 1960 and the foreign-language newspapers originally founded to serve the wave of European immigrants at the turn of the century. Despite the number of minority publications, figures released in 1988 by the American Newspaper Publishers Association indicated that only about 7 percent of American newsroom employees are minorities.

Another type of newspaper specialization flourished in the 1960s to serve the alienated youth and political radicals of the period. Many people wanted an alternative source of news and information, and the *underground press* was born. Although thousands of underground newspapers were established, few were successful. Some of the better-known ones included the *Village Voice* and the *East Village Other* in New York, the *Los Angeles Free Press*, Chicago's *Seed*, Boston's *Avatar* and *Phoenix*, the *Berkeley Barb* and San Francisco's *Rolling Stone*. This latter publication is now an Establishment rock magazine.

NEWSPAPERS AS BUSINESSES

Although newspapers perform a crucial public service by keeping our society informed, we cannot forget that newspapers—like all mass media—are businesses that have to make a profit. It they don't, they die. Newspapers, in fact, generate the largest revenues of all mass media: $31.6 billion in 1987.

The price of a newspaper does not begin to pay for the cost of producing it; the major source of newspaper revenues is advertising. The more circulation a newspaper has, the more it can charge for its advertising. Fatter newspapers do not necessarily have more news. They do, however, carry more advertising and are usually more financially successful.

The need to turn a profit means that newspapers have to compete, and competition keeps them from stagnating. And, as we noted at the beginning of this chapter, the major competitor for newspapers today is television.

Soft News. One way many newspapers have responded to the challenge of television is to expand the amount of space devoted to *soft news,* or *fluff journalism.* Designed to entertain the reader, it includes such varied material as background stories that accompany news events, features on health, money management and diet, as well as comics, crossword puzzles and columns, from Erma Bombeck to Dear Abby. Soft news is contrasted with *hard news,* straight factual reports on current events.

Decline of Competition. The competitive nature of newspapers as businesses is causing other changes in American newspapers—some of them less desirable than others. For example, when Americans started moving out of the cities to the suburbia in the mid-twentieth century, the number of newspapers serving many metropolitan areas started a steady decline. Cities that once boasted many newspapers now had only one. Lack of competition within a city is always a cause for concern, since it can result in complacency and newspapers' shirking their responsibility to keep their community well informed.

Chain Ownership. Another trend in the newspaper business is the concentration of more and more newspapers in the hands of a few media conglomerates, called *chains.* The four largest newspaper chains in the United States are Gannett, Knight-Ridder, Newhouse and Times Mirror. The advantage of chain ownership is that their local newspapers enjoy strong financial backing. The disadvantage is that, as control of the nation's newspapers falls into fewer and fewer hands, local community interests may be subordinated to corporate interests. Where newspapers once acted as the voice of their communities, they now often serve as the mouthpiece of the corporation that owns them. Some chains have been known to require that their corporate philosophy be reflected on news and editorial pages.

And who controls the chain? Although most chains are media companies, there is nothing to stop a large oil company, for example, from buying newspapers. If this were to happen, would the newspapers remain impartial in reporting news about the oil business?

Some people worry that foreign investors may buy up American newspapers. What is there to prevent political leaders of a wealthy country with a controlled press from buying a major interest in Gannett, for example? Would these newspapers—many of them the only paper in their community—be unbiased in their coverage of the controlling country? This concern became a reality in the summer of 1986, when a Mexican newspaper magnate with reported close ties to the Mexican government purchased America's second-largest news service, United Press International (see below).

Libel Suits. Meanwhile, the recent rash of libel suits has already had a chilling effect on many newspapers. Since juries have awarded huge damages in a few well-publicized cases, some newspapers have cut back on their investigative reporting to minimize their risk of being sued.[10] This trend could have serious implications for a democracy based on the premise that only an informed citizenry can determine its political destiny.

But the bottom line cannot become the only consideration in deciding what to publish. After all, as Tom Goldstein reminds us in his book *The News at Any Cost,* the press is not merely a business; newspapers were given constitutional protection "because the founding fathers felt that a vigorous and independent press was essential to let people know what government was doing."[11] This conflict in roles will be discussed further in Chapter 15.

NEWS WIRE SERVICES

The American press's coverage of our popular culture has been greatly assisted since the nineteenth century by press wire services. Wire services were established as news-gathering and disseminating services for newspapers after the invention of telegraph in the 1840s. Today wire services work for radio and television as well.

American Wire Services. As mentioned earlier, the first wire service was the Associated Press, which was established in New York in 1848. AP, which remains the largest American wire service, has always been a nonprofit organization; newspapers

News wire services send photographs as well as stories to members and subscribers. Shown here is an Associated Press darkroom and laserphoto distribution center set up at the Democratic National Convention. *(Art Stein/Photo Researchers)*

that use and pay for the service "belong" to the Associated Press. Thus members share as well as receive news stories.

United Press International, the second major American wire service, was founded as United Press by E. W. Scripps in 1907. It operates like other businesses, with users subscribing to its service. Thus AP has members, while UPI has clients or customers.

The third wire service to be formed in the United States was International News Service, which William Randolph Hearst established in 1909. In 1958 United Press merged with International News Service to become United Press International.

Foreign Wire Services. AP and UPI are not only the two major news services in the United States; they are dominant worldwide services as well. However, three others are equally influential in global news coverage: Agence France-Presse (AFP), headquartered in Paris; Reuters, in London; and the Telegrafnoie Agentsvo Sovetskovo Soyuza (Tass), in Moscow.

AFP, which was organized in 1945 at the end of World War II, has 100 foreign bureaus. Like AP, it is a nonprofit service. Reuters was founded in the 1850s and has more than a thousand correspondents in 180 countries, including a half-dozen bureaus in the United States. In recent years its revenues have come to exceed AP's, thanks mostly to the addition of financial news and information-retrieval services.

Tass, like all Soviet news media, is the official voice of the Soviet Union. Its foreign correspondents in more than a hundred countries gather and report local and international news in accordance with official Soviet policy.

Although UPI was established as a profit-making wire service, it has been losing money since 1963. In 1982 it was sold by its co-owners, the E. W. Scripps Company and the Hearst Corporation, to the Media News Corporation. But the new owners were not able to turn the service around either, and in the summer of 1986, they sold UPI to Mexican newspaper magnate Mario Vazquez Rana, who owned Mexico's largest chain of newspapers. As just mentioned, this alarmed American journalists, who were concerned about Vazquez Rana's ties to the Mexican government.

Foreign ownership of such an essential news source was unprecedented. At the time of the sale, UPI's subscribers included about 850 American newspapers and some 3,300 radio and television stations. In addition, it was a major news source for numerous Third World nations, many in Latin America.

Thus many people were relieved when Vazquez Rana entered into a $55 million agreement with a California conservative Republican in 1988 to return control of UPI to an American. Dr. Earl W. Brian, a Health and Welfare Agency director under Governor Ronald Reagan, became the new executive officer of UPI. However, Vazquez Rana technically remained the owner of the wire service until the complicated ownership transfer could be completed.

BIASES AND OTHER PROBLEMS

There are five basic functions of the American press (both print and electronic): (1) to inform, (2) to entertain, (3) to influence through editorials, (4) to present advertisements, and (5) to transmit the culture. Most of the criticism of the press focuses on how it carries out the first of these—to inform. Reader, listener or viewer biases account for much of this criticism.

Blaming the Messenger. For one thing, it is simply human nature to blame the messenger for bad tidings. (In an ancient Greek play by Sophocles, for example, a king beheads a messenger who has brought him some bad news.)

For example, when there were riots on American streets and university campuses in the 1960s, many people blamed the press for causing the disturbances. They claimed that by publicizing riots in one place, the media were giving others the idea to riot elsewhere. Similarly, during the unraveling of the Watergate scandal in 1972–1974, many people criticized the press for "harping on Watergate" because they didn't want to hear about crimes being committed by the highest government officials. More recently, the press's coverage of terrorist activities in the 1980s has been criticized for encouraging more terrorist attacks. After particularly intense criticism of its coverage of the TWA hijacking in 1985, ABC television announced that it would no longer publicize the demands of terrorists.

This is one reason the press ranks near the top of most lists of the nation's most controversial institutions. Researchers have found that criticism of the press rises in direct proportion to the amount of unpleasant news being reported.

Watchdog Function. Of course, under the libertarian theory, it is an essential function of the American press to serve as a watchdog of government. Keeping the citizenry informed about its government necessarily puts the press and government in an adversarial relationship, at least some of the time. When the press reports on activities that do not reflect favorably on the government and its leaders, it often receives a great deal of criticism from the government.

Bad News Only Myth. Many people also suffer from a misconception that the press prints "only bad news because that's what sells newspapers." In fact, newspapers carry both good and bad news, but readers often ignore the good. Stories about the Boy Scouts, PTA and church socials tend to interest only Boy Scouts, PTA members and people who attend church socials.

There is some disagreement on just what constitutes bad news. Although an obituary should be considered bad news, just ask your newspaper editor what happens if he or she leaves one out of the paper. Editors are bombarded with angry telephone calls from family and friends. And for that matter, a story about a blizzard might be bad news for residents of a community but great news for people elsewhere planning a ski trip.

Myth of Media Truth. Another problem the media have is the popular misconception that if something appears in print or is heard over the airwaves, it has to be true. How many times have you heard someone attempt to win an argument by saying "I saw it in the newspaper" or "I saw it on television"? So when the media do make mistakes—as they inevitably will—people are bitterly critical.

Biases. Finally, many people blame the press for being biased. Certainly everyone has his or her own biases, and newspeople are no exception. Good journalists do try to keep their biases out of their stories and present all sides of the story fairly, objectively and accurately. However, most readers and viewers forget that they too have biases. And often when they read or hear a story that is trying to present several sides, they react negatively to those parts that conflict with their own biases.

More specific complaints about television news will be discussed in Chapter 9.

SUMMARY

The history of American newspapers has paralleled the history of our culture. As our society has changed, so have its newspapers.

Early colonial newspapers were designed for the elite—those who were interested in political and business information. With the advent of new technology, compulsory education and the major cultural changes brought on by industrialization and urbanization, newspapers moved into the popular culture with the advent of the penny press.

The significant changes in our society as the United States was transformed into a truly industrial nation between the end of the Civil War and the turn of the century brought about many changes in American journalism, including the era of sensationalism, or yellow journalism.

Twentieth-century newspapers, for the most part, have attempted to blend objectivity and social responsibility. This era also has seen the development of electronic news media, interpretative reporting, investigative reporting, advocacy journalism, "new journalism" and specialized newspapers.

Despite the role news media play in our democratic society, it must be kept in mind that they are businesses and that business decisions play an important role in their operation.

Unlike other mass media, most newspapers have resisted the trend toward specialization (other than local or regional specialization). However, there are some specialized newspapers, mostly religious and ethnic publications.

Wire services play an important role in gathering news and information for the mass media. The two largest American wire services are the Associated Press and United Press International. The other dominant worldwide news sources are AFP, Reuters and Tass, headquartered in Paris, London and Moscow, respectively.

Individual biases and other problems play a role in making mass communication a complex activity. Although the various functions of the media—to inform, entertain, influence, advertise and transmit culture—are criticized, the most severely criticized is the function to inform. Reasons for this are that people (1) tend to blame the messenger for unpleasant information, (2) fail to understand the *watchdog* function of the media, (3) believe the myth that the mass media dwell only on bad news and (4) bring their own biases into the information-sharing process.

NOTES

1. Peter Burke, *Popular Culture in Early Modern Europe* (New York: Harper Torchbooks, 1978), p. 264.

2. George Henry Payne, *History of Journalism in the United States.* (Westport, Conn.: Greenwood Press, 1970), p. 40.

3. Quoted in Warren K. Agee, Phillip H. Ault and Edwin Emery, *Introduction to Mass Communications*, 9th ed. (New York: Harper & Row, 1988), p. 67.

4. Frank Luther Mott, *American Journalism: A History 1690–1960,* 3rd ed. (New York: Macmillan, 1962), p. 49.

5. Michael Schudson, *Discovering the News: A Social History of American Newspapers* (New York: Basic Books, 1978), pp. 50–56.

6. Agee, Ault and Emery, p. 83.

7. Ibid., p. 85.

8. Quoted in Edwin Emery, *The Press and America: An Interpretive History of the Mass Media*, 3rd ed. (Englewood Cliffs, N.J.: Prentice-Hall, 1972), p. 311.

9. W. Phillips Davison, James Boylan and Frederick T. C. Yu, *Mass Media: Systems and Effects* (New York: Praeger, 1976), p. 15.

10. Michael Massing, "The Libel Chill: How Cold Is It Out There?" *Columbia Journalism Review* (May–June 1985), pp. 31–43.

11. Tom Goldstein, *The News at Any Cost: How Journalists Compromise Their Ethics to Shape the News* (New York: Simon & Schuster, 1985), p. 83.

ADDITIONAL READING

Boyd-Barrett, Oliver. *The International News Agencies.* Beverly Hills, Calif.: Sage, 1980.

Carlson, Oliver. *The Man Who Made News: James Gordon Bennett.* New York: Duell, Sloan & Pearce, 1942.

Chancellor, John, and Mears, Walter R. *The News Business.* New York: Harper & Row, 1983.

Glessing, Robert. *The Underground Press in America.* Bloomington: Indiana University Press, 1970.

Janowitz, Morris. *The Community Press in an Urban Setting.* New York: Free Press, 1967.

Liebling, A. J. *The Press.* New York: Pantheon, 1981.

Manoff, Robert, and Schudson, Michael, eds. *Reading the News: A Pantheon Guide to Popular Culture.* New York: Pantheon, 1986.

Mott, Frank Luther. *The News in America.* Cambridge, Mass.: Harvard University Press, 1952.

Peck, Abe. *Uncovering the Sixties: The Life and Times of the Underground Press.* New York: Pantheon, 1985.

Pickett, Calder M. *Voices of the Past.* Columbus, Ohio: Grid, 1977.

Rivers, William L. *News in Print.* New York: Harper & Row, 1984.

Sim, John Cameron. *The Grass Roots Press: America's Community Newspapers.* Ames: Iowa State University Press, 1969.

Swanberg, W. A. *Citizen Hearst.* New York: Scribner's, 1961.

———. *Pulitzer.* New York: Scribner's, 1967.

Van Deusen, Glyndon G. *Horace Greeley: Nineteenth Century Crusader.* Philadelphia: University of Pennsylvania Press, 1953.

Wolseley, Ronald E. *The Black Press, U.S.A.* Ames: Iowa State University Press, 1971.

Part 3

Development of Electronic Media

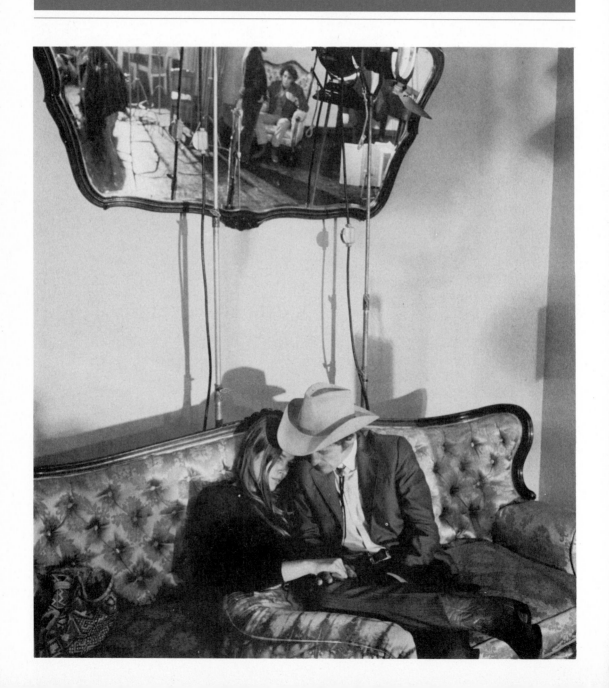

Chapter 7

Motion Pictures: Cultural Reflections

People tell me that the movies
should be more like real life.
I disagree. It is real life that
should be more like the movies.
—*Walter Winchell*

"The last time I checked, I owned the films that we're in the process of colorizing," media entrepreneur Ted Turner told an audience at a fundraiser in Beverly Hills in 1986. "I can do whatever I want with them, and if they're going to be shown on television, they're going to be in color."

Turner, who owns Atlanta satellite-cable television superstation WTBS (among others), had recently spent $1.2 billion to purchase the 3,650-title film library of MGM, RKO and early Warner Brothers. He then hired Color Systems Technology to apply the computerized system it had developed to add color to the black-and-white movies in the collection. He reasoned that this would make these old movies more acceptable to television viewers. This action plunged him into the center of a major controversy, as Turner found himself accused of destroying classics and committing "cultural butchery."

In a 1986 letter to Gilbert Cates, president of the Directors Guild of America, an angry committee of film directors urged that the organization put "all resources at its disposal to stop this process in its path." Cates agreed with the committee: "It [colorizing] is a process of dissembling the historical and artistic fabric of our landmarks. Once you can add color, why can't you add a different score, add shots, re-edit it, or do anything you want?"[1]

Some of Cates's colleagues condemned Turner's activities in even stronger terms. During a hearing before a subcommittee of the Senate Judiciary Committee, comedian/director Woody Allen said, "Determining the color that people wear, or what

Woody Allen testifying before a Senate panel considering the issue of colorization of motion pictures. *(UPI/Bettmann Newsphotos)*

colors the walls are and so on are major creative decisions. . . . To have a group of people from the outside making those decisions is criminal and ludicrous."

Director Billy Wilder said, "Those fools! Do they really think that colorization will make *The Informer* any better? Or *Citizen Kane* or *Casablanca?* Or do they hope to palm off some of the old stinkers by dipping them in 31 flavors? Is there no end to their greed?"

Another director, Joe Dante, said, "Black and white was an art form in the '40s. . . . By changing them [the films], they are tampering with history. It's the death knell of an entire art form."[2]

RKO Pictures filed a lawsuit to prevent Turner from colorizing its films. The suit alleged copyright infringement for the "unauthorized reproduction and adaptation through colorization" of 10 of the company's black-and-white films from the 1930s, '40s and '50s.

Turner responded by saying "All these guys are like Chicken Little, saying the sky is falling on their head. All I'm trying to do is protect my investment in MGM."[3] He claimed that colorization was necessary because television advertising rates for black-and-white movies were lower than those for color movies, and he noted that the original black-and-white versions of the films would still be available for those who wanted them. (He might also have pointed out that most of the outcry was coming from members of the elite culture who didn't want any tampering with the classics to make them more appealing to a mass audience.) In any case, RKO lost its suit.

CULTURAL HISTORY OF MOTION PICTURES

Elitist	Popular	Specialized	Year	Event
■			1888	First motion-picture camera developed in Thomas A. Edison's laboratory.
	■		1895	Lumière brothers start projecting motion pictures in a Paris café.
	■		1896	Films shown in vaudeville theaters.
	■		1903	Edwin S. Porter's *Great Train Robbery*, first American film to tell a complete story.
	■		1905–10	Era of the nickelodeon, movie theaters that charged a nickel for admission.
	■		1912	Mack Sennett begins Keystone Company, which specialized in slapstick comedy.
	■		1915	D. W. Griffith releases *Birth of a Nation*, first full-length film to have an impact on the culture.
	■		1917	Charlie Chaplin becomes first entertainer to earn $1 million a year.
	■		1923	Lee De Forest begins experimenting with sound motion pictures.
	■		1927	*The Jazz Singer* ushers in talking motion-picture era.
	■		1930	Motion-picture industry tightens its code of standards to avoid censorship.
	■		1930s–40s	Golden Age of movies; movies provide an escape from Depression and war.
	■		1939	*Gone With the Wind* breaks box-office records.
	■		1941	Orson Welles's *Citizen Kane* is released; voted greatest classic of all times in 1987.
	■		1941–45	Hollywood promotes patriotism during World War II with propaganda films and rousing war movies.
	■		1946	Hollywood's biggest box-office year—$1.7 billion gross income, 86 million Americans attending movies each week.
	■		1947	Red Scare leads to congressional investigation of Hollywood.
	■		1948	Supreme Court requires movie studios to sell their theaters.
	■		1948	Motion-picture audiences decline after television's breakthrough year.
		■	1950s	Hollywood experiments with 3-D, Cinerama, Cinemascope, and movies for youth subculture.
		■	1960s	Movie industry abandons self-censorship and adopts a movie-rating system.
		■	1960s	Youth, sex and violence help sell movies to new audiences.
	■		1970s	Disaster films become popular with movie audiences.
	■		1977	George Lucas's *Star Wars* is released; its computerized special effects give movies a new image and excitement.
	■		1980s	Video movies expand industry revenues; multiplexes replace large-screen theaters.

The controversy over colorization illustrates how many people in our culture resist the application of new technology to an older art form. The motion-picture industry had this problem earlier when it started adapting books as story lines for movies. Many people claimed that classic novels were being ruined by being subjected to the "Hollywood treatment." Changing mass-media technologies affect not only our culture but previously existing media technologies as well. The motion-picture industry was one of the first electronic media to affect our popular culture, and it was among the first to be forced into the age of specialization by the rapid expansion and changes in mass-media technology of the twentieth century.

EARLY HISTORY

In the late nineteenth century, as city dwellers were experiencing more leisure time, they began looking for new pastimes beyond reading, the ballpark and vaudeville (see Chapter 2). This was the industrial age, and mechanical inventions of all kinds were dramatically changing the American way of life. It was only natural that some inventors turned their attention to developing mechanical devices for leisure use.

Edison. The leading American inventor of leisure technology was Thomas A. Edison, probably best known for inventing the light bulb. But he was also responsible for devising the phonograph in the 1870s, and by the 1880s he was trying to come up with something similar for the eye. The concept behind motion pictures, however, actually dates back to the second century A.D., when the Greek astronomer Ptolemy discovered that the human eye retains an image on the retina for a moment after the image disappears. This is called persistence of vision. Over the years many people theorized that a series of still pictures of similar yet slightly different images could give the illusion of movement if flashed before the eye quickly, because persistence of vision would fill in the gaps. Experimentation with this theory took place in Edison's laboratory until his assistant, William Kennedy Dickson, constructed the first crude motion-picture camera.

The first commercial use of motion pictures was a kinetoscope—a four-foot-tall box that one person at a time could peer into to see a series of still photos "move" across a light source. Edison unveiled the kinetoscope to the world in 1894, and the "peep show" became a popular attraction in penny arcades. One of the first films made by the Edison Co. for the arcades was a 30-second strip called *Anabelle*. Sex and violence soon became the predominant theme for these arcade films.

Projection. In 1895 two brothers in France, Auguste and Louis Lumière, perfected Edison's invention by developing a projection device. They produced a film and began showing it for an admission price in the basement of a Paris café. The motion-picture industry was born.

In the United States the novelty of Edison's kinetoscope soon began to wear off. In the meantime, two inventors of a movie-projection system known as the vitascope, Thomas Armat and Francis Jenkins, joined forces with Edison, and in April 1896 motion pictures began showing in vaudeville houses, supplementing the live entertainment.

Vaudeville theaters remained the primary showplace for motion pictures until about 1905, when nickelodeons took over. These were motion-picture parlors where admission cost a nickel. The average length of a motion picture was about 12½ minutes, and most programs featured two to three films. By 1908 there were between eight and ten thousand nickelodeons in the United States.

Early Classics. Another major innovator was the Frenchman Georges Méliès, who began producing films in 1897 and soon became an international distributor. He introduced the concept of special effects. Méliès's most famous film, *A Trip to the Moon* (1902), showed a group of scientists and chorus girls launching a rocket to the moon. The rocket hit the "eye" of the man in the moon, and the space travelers encountered moon men. The special effects in the film, although not up to today's standards, were fascinating for the time and included the earth rising on the moon's horizon and moon people disappearing in smoke.

But the father of the story film was not Méliès but the American film producer Edwin S. Porter, an Edison Company camera man. In his most famous film, *The Great Train Robbery* (1903), he developed new editing techniques to piece together different scenes to create a story line. The film—filled with gunfights, chases and action as a band of desperadoes hold up a westbound train—was only 12 minutes long, but it set standards for drama and excitement that would become basic to American films for years to come. Incidentally, it also introduced the enduring Western theme into American filmmaking. The significance of *The Great Train Robbery* has been summed up this way:

> *For years* The Great Train Robbery *was the nickelodeon's most widely exhibited picture and it is said to have insured the permanence of the movies. It became the bible for all film makers until Griffith's films further developed Porter's editing principle. The efforts of all movie makers to imitate its form and content stimulated the industry as nothing—not even Méliès' films—had ever done before.*[4]

The next milestone in the development of American motion pictures was *Birth of a Nation,* directed by D. W. Griffith and released in 1915. Originally titled *The Clansmen, Birth of a Nation* was a three-hour masterpiece. Although all early films were silent, Griffith's film was accompanied by a complete musical score to be performed by a symphony orchestra. The movie impressed the nation and led President Woodrow Wilson to say it was "like writing history in lightning."[5]

Griffith began his career in motion pictures in 1907 as an actor for the Mutoscope and Biograph Company in New York. Because his acting skills were limited, he became a director there a year later. He was the first to use close-ups and a variety of camera angles to add emotional impact to his films. Through new editing techniques he showed how emotion and tension could be generated by the length of the scene, with shorter scenes creating greater excitement. An innovator who defied the conventions of moviemaking, Griffith insisted on hiring established stage actors and holding rehearsals. He was also the first to shoot on location—at the San Gabriel Mission outside Los Angeles in 1910.

Birth of a Nation, filmed in Los Angeles, used all of Griffith's innovations in shooting, lighting, and editing to capture the emotion of the Civil War. It was the first motion picture to attempt to portray a part of U.S. history in dramatic terms, covering the period from pre–Civil War days through Reconstruction. Griffith, the son of a Confederate officer, had a flawed, sentimental attachment to the old South. His sympathetic portrayal of the Ku Klux Klan and stereotyping of blacks offended many. The National Association for the Advancement of Colored People, the president of Harvard University and liberal politicians all damned the work for its bigoted portrayal of blacks. Despite this, the movie was a box-office success, and it clearly demonstrated what a dramatic impact this new art form could have on popular culture. As a result of its showing in major cities there were race riots and a rebirth of the Ku Klux Klan in the South.

Griffith was stung by the uproar created by his film. He decided to invest some $2 million of the profits from the film to create a new movie, *Intolerance*, which preached against the evils of bigotry. He reportedly chose the name because he felt that *he* had been a victim of intolerance. Despite high production costs and lavish sets, the film was a box-office flop and led to a steady decline of Griffith's directing career. He died a forgotten man in 1948.

THE RISE OF COMEDY

Unlike the print media, motion pictures did not spend a long period in the elite culture before moving into the popular stage of the EPS cycle (see Chapter 1). In fact, there are more culturally elite films today than there were in the early days of motion pictures. Both economic and social factors explain why this new medium moved immediately into the popular culture. Relatively inexpensive to produce, movies debuted as an affordable kind of entertainment at a time when people needed new outlets for their leisure time.

In addition, silent movies appeared at a time when American cities sheltered large numbers of foreign workers. Even though many of these immigrants spoke no English, they could still enjoy the comedy and drama of silent films: pantomime is a universal language.

Comedy had a special appeal for workers in the new industrial society because it gave them an opportunity to laugh at the disappointments, frustrations and confrontations of daily living.

Sennett. One of the first to make a major contribution to motion-picture comedy was Mack Sennett. Sennett, who worked for Griffith in his early days in the film industry, was the son of Irish immigrants. In 1912 he struck out on his own, founding the Keystone Film Company. Sennett fascinated his audiences by showing them the new twentieth century America. Typical scenes were of automobiles beginning to replace the horse and buggy, dusty roads, policemen in slapstick chase scenes, men with large moustaches and women wearing full-length dresses and huge hats. Sennett's comedy effectively brought to the screen the visual and physical elements of burlesque, and his Keystone Kops became a Hollywood trademark.

Chaplin. An English stage comedian, Charlie Chaplin came to this country in 1913 to tour vaudeville stages with a music-hall act. Although leery of the new medium of film, he was enticed to start working for Sennett at Keystone for an attractive salary of $150 a week. One year later he signed a contract with the Essanay Company of Chicago for $1,250 a week, plus a $10,000 bonus for signing and a guarantee of $75,000 for 1915 (a huge amount of money in those days). The contract allowed him to act, direct and produce his comedies. By 1917 Chaplin was making more than $1 million a year, a figure that was almost incomprehensible at a time when many people earned less than a thousand dollars a year and new automobiles sold for $500.

In 1915 Chaplin produced *The Tramp*, in which he played a vagabond in baggy pants who comes to the rescue of a pretty girl. The tramp and the girl were the heroes of many of the Chaplin movies that followed. While giving people an opportunity to laugh at the plight of the downtrodden in society, Chaplin also used comedy to make social commentary on good and evil in our society. Only relatively few had prospered from the years of unfettered industrial expansion, while a vast and growing army of workers struggled to cope with low salaries and harsh working conditions. Chaplin's films depicted the stark and often cruel distances between the haves and have-nots (see Box 7.1).

Chaplin became the first twentieth century superstar. Millions of fans rushed to novelty shops to purchase mechanical dolls and plaster Tramp statuettes in his image, much as later generations have bought Mouseketeer, Beatle, *Star Wars* and *E.T.* paraphernalia.[6]

Laurel and Hardy. Other popular comedy stars in the silent-film era were Stan Laurel and Oliver Hardy, who, in the Sennett and Chaplin style, portrayed the down-trodden against the world. Although they started out separately, they got together in 1926 and remained a popular movie comedy team well into the sound era. Indeed, of all the comedians from the silent-film era, they were the most successful in making the switch to sound motion pictures.

Keaton and Lloyd. Although not a team, two other master comedians of the silent era were Buster Keaton and Harold Lloyd. Keaton came close to rivaling Chaplin in his ability to provide funny and serious insights into human relationships and to dra-matize the conflict between individuals and the immense industrial society that surrounded them. Like Chaplin, Lloyd was small in physical stature, which was a disad-vantage as the characters he portrayed struggled against various misfortunes in a hostile world.

However, unlike Chaplin, Lloyd usually overcame the obstacles he encountered on the screen.

BOX 7.1.

THE KID, A CHARLIE CHAPLIN CLASSIC

One of Charlie Chaplin's greatest films was *The Kid* (1921) starring Chaplin and a four-year-old named Jackie Coogan. Coogan's performance established him as a child star and set a trend for many other child stars to follow.

Coogan's parents were vaudeville performers. One night when Chaplin was in the audience at the Orpheum Theater in Los Angeles, Coogan's father brought young Jackie on the stage to take a bow with him at the conclusion of his dance act. Chaplin, who had been a child vaudeville performer, was facinated by the four-year-old's personality and vowed to use him in one of his movies.

Chaplin came up with the idea of a film about the life of an orphan child who lives with a tramp. He taught the basic tricks of the art of pantomime to young Coogan, and *The Kid* was ready for production.

The 30-minute film tells a story of an impoverished mother who leaves her child in the seat of a car parked in front of a mansion, obviously so that the child will be found by the rich owners and brought up in wealth. After she leaves, two thieves steal the automobile. When they find the baby in the backseat, they abandon him in an alley.

Chaplin, playing the role of his now-famed baggy-pants tramp, discovers the baby and attempts to find its mother—to no avail. He finally takes the boy home to his one-room flat and raises him in poverty, but with love. To earn money, the tramp works as a window mender and uses the "kid" to go around the town breaking windows for him to fix. In one scene the "kid" is shown about to throw a stone at a window when a policeman walks up behind him. As he brings his hand back to throw, it touches the policeman's coat. He looks up at the policeman, playfully tosses the stone up and catches it, then innocently throws it away and ambles off, suddenly breaking into a sprint.

One day the "kid" gets sick and Charlie calls a doctor. When the doctor discovers that the tramp has no money, he calls the welfare workers. Learning that the child

SOUND JOINS MOTION

The genres of comedy and drama helped the American film industry flourish. Following Griffith's lead, the American film industry moved permanently to Hollywood, California, where good weather and wide open spaces allowed for year-round outdoor moviemaking. Since World War I inhibited European filmmakers from developing this new industry, American moviemakers took the lead. By the early 1920s, Hollywood was producing three-quarters of the world's films.

By 1925, 46 million Americans were attending movies weekly. The American film industry had become big business. Movies made in Hollywood set standards of excellence throughout the world. This was the decade that sound was synchronized with film and a new medium emerged.

Early Efforts. For 30 years inventors had attempted to connect sound to motion pictures. Dickson, Edison's assistant, claimed to have produced a rough synchronization of word and picture as early as 1889. Others experimented with synchronizing does not belong to the tramp, the welfare workers take the boy away to an orphanage hospital. After an emotional yet comic struggle with the tramp, the officals put the "kid" in the back of a flat-bed Model A and take him away. Charlie chases after the orphanage wagon on the rooftops of the tenement houses and eventually catches up with it and rescues the "kid." (The rescue scene is filled with emotion, with both the kid and the tramp crying real tears.)

After a series of comical hide-and-seek scenes, the child is reunited with his mother, who by this time has found fame and fortune. Both Charlie and Jackie Coogan turn in tear-jerking yet hilarious performances. The delicate mixture of slapstick comedy and sentimentality make this silent movie an all-time great.

The silent-movie era produced a number of memorable films. What made them so remarkable was the fact that the story is told without dialogue. With very little help from the few subtitles flashed on the screen to suggest a scene change, the stories develop clearly through the use of pantomime. Pan-

tomime as a cinematic art form vanished with the arrival of the talking motion pictures.

(The Bettmann Archive)

recording discs with motion pictures in France between 1896 and 1900. However, live sound was preferred during the nickelodeon days in the United States. Pianos, organs or trios of musicians provided musical accompaniment to many films. Actors sometimes recited the lines behind the screen. Sometimes narrators explained or commented on the scenes in the movies (Oliver Hardy's first job in cinema, incidentally, was singing in a quartet behind the screen at an Atlanta nickelodeon.)

Serious problems continued to exist with efforts to put sound and motion together. Separate disc machines, such as the Vitaphone, could easily get out of sync with the film. After World War I, three German inventors discovered a way of putting sound directly on film using light beams. In the United States, Dr. Lee De Forest developed a similar sound-on-film process. De Forest, whom many consider to be the father of American radio (see Chapter 8), started experimenting with sound motion pictures in 1923.

The Jazz Singer. However, it wasn't until audiences heard Al Jolson sing "Mammy" on screen in *The Jazz Singer* (1927) that people realized that sound motion

A scene from *The Jazz Singer*, the film that launched Hollywood into the new era of "talkies." *(Museum of Modern Art/Film Stills Archive)*

pictures were really possible. Produced by Warner Brothers, a small movie company that had very little capital to lose, the film was an instant success and changed the movie business forever.

In 1930 the trade paper *Variety* summed up the impact of sound this way: " . . . it didn't do any more to the industry than turn it upside down, shake the entire bag of tricks from its pocket and advance Warner Brothers from last place to first in the league."

The public's rapid acceptance of sound initially caught the film industry off guard, but soon all the studios were scrambling to produce "talkies." By 1930 the silent-film era was history, and so was its universal language of pantomime. Also at an end were the careers of actors and actresses with unsuitable voices or accents.

During this period some studios also experimented with Technicolor sequences in a few of their movies, though complete Technicolor films did not become common until the mid-1930s.

Cultural Changes. The 1920s were a period of immense technological and social change in American culture. The automobile, radio, advertising and the motion picture combined to change American lifestyles and help usher in an age of "New Morality." Many films glamorized the fast and loose life of the Roaring '20s. They showed men and women dancing, smoking and drinking in public, activities previously considered unacceptable, particularly for women. The movies helped break down these taboos and changed cultural attitudes. Today critics note that since the 1920s there has been an increase in the number of cases of lung cancer and alcoholism among women.

A number of scandals in Hollywood during the 1920s led some to refer to the movie capital as a "twentieth century Babylon."[6] A director named William Desmond Taylor was murdered and the case was never solved; actor Wallace Reid, on the screen a

symbol of virtuous young American manhood, died of a narcotics overdose; and comedian Fatty Arbuckle was charged with manslaughter in the death of a girl at a party
in his hotel suite.

Self-Censorship. In this era of Prohibition, when many people felt that government
should police public morals, it was not surprising that many people cried out for some
form of government censorship of the motion-picture industry. To forestall such an
effort, the industry established its own organization to draw up a code of ethics. The
Motion Picture Producers and Distributors of America (MPPDA) was founded in
1922. Its first president was Will H. Hays, who was a former postmaster general, the
chairman of the Republican National Committee and an elder in the Presbyterian
church. His credentials gave the office the political and moral stature needed to avert
government censorship.

The MPPDA established a list of forbidden subjects that corresponded to the most
frequent targets of critics. In 1927 this list was adopted as the Code of the Motion
Picture Industry. Criticism continued, however, primarily from the Catholic church.
In 1930 the MPPDA, now commonly called the "Hays Office," tightened the code to
spell out more clearly what could not be shown in motion pictures. Depiction of
immoral behavior and nudity was still permissible, so long as it was made clear that
such behavior was wrong and that those who indulged in it were punished. According
to film historian Arthur Knight, "The studios could present six reels of ticket-selling
sinfulness if, in the seventh reel, all the sinners came to a bad end."[8]

The fast and "loose" life portrayed in movies eventually led to the Catholic church's
formation of a Legion of Decency, which advocated boycotts of motion pictures that
the church felt were indecent.[9] Protestant and Jewish groups backed the legion's
efforts, and Hollywood felt the impact of the boycotts on a national scale.

The Hays Office responded to this pressure in 1934 by issuing a stringent set of
rules, the "Code to Govern the Making of Motion and Talking Pictures," to be
enforced by a new Production Code Administration (PCA). Movies released without
PCA approval were fined $25,000. These self-imposed guidelines prohibited profan-
ity, replaced skimpy-dress scenes with full clothing and restricted bedroom scenes to
married men and women only (and even they had to be shown in separate beds). Not
only were such words as God, hell and sex banned, but so were everyday slang terms
like guts, nuts and louse. The Hays Office even got involved in timing the length of
screen kisses. The movies became so pure during this period that there was a major
national furor in 1939 when Clark Gable used the word damn in his now-immortal
line, "Frankly, my dear, I don't give a damn," at the end of *Gone With the Wind*.

A WAY OF LIFE

In the 1930s and 1940s, moviegoing was not merely a form of entertainment but a way
of life. People no longer went to see a particular picture, they "went to the movies"
much as many people today sit down for an evening of watching TV.

Big Studios and Stars. To serve the rapidly growing audience, large motion-
picture studios developed. MGM, Paramount, Warner Brothers, 20th Century-Fox

and RKO all put actors and actresses under contract and made them into "movie stars." Some of the all-time greats were Mary Pickford, Douglas Fairbanks, W. C. Fields, the Marx Brothers, Gary Cooper, Jimmy Stewart, Clark Gable, Clara Bow, Jean Harlow, Spencer Tracy, Katharine Hepburn, John Wayne, James Cagney, Fred Astaire, Ginger Rogers, Humphrey Bogart, Rita Hayworth, Joan Crawford, Edward G. Robinson and Judy Garland.

Studios started mass-producing motion pictures. Since each major studio owned its own chain of theaters across the country, it had to produce one feature film and one "grade B" movie (an inexpensive film for second billing) for each of the 52 weeks in a year. Cartoons and newsreels were also needed to round out the evening's entertainment.

Great Depression. Offering a complete evening of entertainment for the price of one show became very important during the Great Depression of the 1930s. Although there was a decline in attendance in 1934, more than 60 percent of the American public found a way to afford to go to the movies during the Depression. The lavish spectaculars of this period helped people forget the dreary reality of daily living and escape into a make-believe world created by Hollywood.

Trends and Celebrities. Even in these lean years, movies played their role in keeping our consumer culture alive. For example, one of the top box-office stars of the decade was a curly-haired little girl named Shirley Temple. The star of 21 relentlessly upbeat films, she spurred the sale of Shirley Temple dolls, books and clothing.

What the stars did influenced everything in our popular culture from what people wore to how they did their hair. Peroxide hair-rinse sales skyrocketed in the 1930s, thanks to Jean Harlow, Carole Lombard and Mae West and movies like *Platinum Blonde* (1931). In 1934 Clark Gable nearly destroyed the undershirt industry when he took off his shirt and exposed a bare chest in *It Happened One Night*. Soon men all over the nation were following suit and abandoning their longstanding habit of wearing undershirts.

Motion-picture stars, beginning with Charlie Chaplin, became the first "celebrities" of our popular culture. Celebrities have replaced political and military heroes as the objects of public adulation. Although heroes do things, celebrities tend to be passive objects, whose popularity is created and maintained by the media. According to sociologist Daniel Boorstin, a celebrity is "a person who is well known for his well-knownness."[10]

Film Genres. In addition to the traditional film genres—like the Western, which began with *The Great Train Robbery*—a variety of new ones developed during the 1930s. One of the most popular was the gangster movie, which depicted the typical criminal activity of the Prohibition era (1920–1933). Since many normally law-abiding citizens violated the law and continued to drink, a large underground developed to supply their need. Gangsters got involved in the manufacture, distribution and sale of alcohol.

This world was graphically recreated in such films as *Little Caesar* (1930), *The Public Enemy* (1931), *City Streets* (1931) and *Scarface* (1932), which was based on the exploits of Chicago gangster Al Capone. These were followed by tough-talking cop movies and prison films. Although most of these movies depicted the gangster in an unfavorable light, some glamorized his get-rich-quick image.

One of the problems with the Western and gangster film genres was the fact that as Hollywood exported its films, they created a distorted view of American culture. For example, until very recently many foreigners believed that the United States was a land where gangsters ruled the cities and cowboys and Indians fought on the prairies. (These stereotypes have now been replaced by perceptions of wealth and ruthlessness, following the export of such TV shows as *Dallas* and *Dynasty*.)

Following the election of Franklin D. Roosevelt to the presidency in 1932 and the repeal of Prohibition the following year, the mood of the country seemed to be improving. This upswing was reflected in a series of musical extravaganzas that were produced in Hollywood as alternatives to the gangster films. Three Busby Berkeley musicals, for example, were 1933 box-office successes: *42nd Street*, *Gold Diggers of 1933* and *Footlight Parade*. These surrealistically choreographed fantasies allowed the audience to become absorbed in the singing, dancing and comedy depictions of back-stage show-business life.

Also popular during this period were a variety of comedies ranging from the slap-stick of the Marx Brothers in *Duck Soup* (1933); to more sophisticated, fast-paced romantic comedies such as *It Happened One Night* (1934), starring Clark Gable and Claudette Colbert; *Twentieth Century* (1934), starring John Barrymore and Carole Lombard; and *Bringing Up Baby* (1938), with Katharine Hepburn and Cary Grant. *It Happened One Night*, about a journalist in professional and amorous pursuit of a runaway heiress, established the romantic comedy as a popular genre for the rest of the 1930s.

Hollywood also developed the film series, featuring continuing episodes much like modern television. These included the Andy Hardy pictures, Charlie Chan films, Flash Gordon, Henry Aldrich, the Thin Man and *Young Doctor Kildare*.

The fantasies depicted in the films of this period gave Americans hope and a way to cope with the harsh realities of the Depression. Many films had strong moral themes and showed that decent, honest people could overcome obstacles. The films all had a warm, happy ending. One of the best at turning out these films was Frank Capra, who directed *It Happened One Night* (1934), *Mr. Deeds Goes to Town* (1936), *You Can't Take It With You* (1938) and *Mr. Smith Goes to Washington* (1939). One of his all-time classics, *It's a Wonderful Life* (1946) starring Jimmy Stewart, is still shown on television each year during the Christmas season. Its heart-warming message is that everyone's life has value because of the other lives it touches.

When the United States entered World War II in December 1941, Hollywood was there to rouse patriotic enthusiasm. Numerous propaganda films were produced during the war, while entertainment movies showed the Americans triumphing over their Japanese and Nazi enemies. Such movies as *30 Seconds over Tokyo* helped reassure Americans that they were winning the war and that the cultural myth of an indestructible American spirit was a reality.

Although Hollywood mass-produced many motion pictures during the Depression and war years, it managed to turn out a number of classics. Among the all-time greats were *Gone With the Wind*, which broke box-office records in 1939, and Orson Welles's *Citizen Kane* (1941), which did not do well at the box office at first but was later—in 1987—voted the best film of all time.

THE GIANT IS CRIPPLED

In 1946 the motion-picture business was on top of the world, with 87 million Americans going to the movies each week (about half as many go every *month* now). The industry was putting out between five and six hundred movies a year. This was the industry's peak box-office year; the American film business grossed $1.7 billion domestically. However, during the next two years, 1947 and 1948, three events rocked the industry and toppled it from its peak of success.

Red Scare. In 1947 a subcommittee of the House Committee on Un-American Activities (HUAC) alleged that members of the Communist party had infiltrated the movie industry and were using films to disseminate Communist propaganda.

After World War II ended in 1945, a Cold War broke out between the United States and the Soviet Union. As Americans saw country after country in Eastern Europe being occupied by the Soviet army, rumors ran rampant that the Soviet Union was attempting to take over our country as well, with the help of American Communists. The government responded by conducting congressional investigations to see whether national security had been breached, and the motion-picture industry became one of the targets for their inquiries.

The HUAC hearings, which began on October 20, 1947, led to the fining and imprisonment of 10 Hollywood writers who refused to answer the committee's questions about their alleged Communist party affiliation. The writers—who came to be

Humphrey Bogart and Lauren Bacall were among many Hollywood stars who appeared before the House Committee on Un-American Activities (HUAC) during its investigation of alleged Communist infiltration of the motion picture industry. *(Historical Pictures Services)*

known as the "Hollywood 10"—were also blacklisted by motion-picture executives, who feared that if they took no action the government, supported by public opinion, would take control and censor their industry. The blacklisting, which spread far beyond the original Hollywood 10, lasted for more than a decade. Many blacklisted entertainers and writers went without work for a dozen or more years.

The Hearst newspapers gave the hearings major coverage and called for restrictive laws: "The need is for FEDERAL CENSORSHIP OF THE MOTION PICTURES. The Constitution PERMITS it. The law SANCTIONS it. The safety and welfare of America DEMAND it"[11] Many Americans supported this point of view.

In fact, many Hollywood studios were more than willing to accommodate the new public mood. In the late 1940s the industry turned out such anti-Communist movies as *I Was a Communist for the FBI*, *I Led Three Lives*, *I Married a Communist* and *The Red Menace*, films which only helped to fuel the anti-Communist terror that gripped the nation.

A few films, however, subtly criticized the witchhunting of this period. The most successful was *High Noon* (1952), a Western that offered an allegory on McCarthyism.[12] The film, starring Gary Cooper, told the story of a courageous marshal who when facing the threat of attack from four gunmen found his friends and fellow town folks turning their back on him. Like many people during the witchhunting days, "they didn't want to place their own lives at risk by getting involved." Another, to be produced long after that period, was Woody Allen's *The Front* (1976), which told the story of Hollywood writers who had to get their work accepted under another name because they had been blacklisted.

Antitrust. The next setback for the motion-picture industry came in 1948, when the U.S. Supreme Court ruled that the major studios were operating an illegal monopoly on the production, distribution and exhibition of films (*U.S. v. Paramount Pictures, Inc., et al.*). At this time, for example, Paramount owned 1,239 theaters, 20th Century-Fox 517, and Warner Brothers 507. The five major studios owned 77 percent of the first-run movie houses in the 25 largest American metropolitan areas.

The Supreme Court decision forced the major studios to sell all their theaters. Warner Brothers sold its Stanley Warner Theaters, MGM got rid of its Loews Theaters, RKO divested itself of RKO Theaters, 20th Century-Fox sold its National Theaters and Paramount Pictures severed its connection with Paramount Theaters. No longer did the studios have guaranteed outlets for their movies; from now on they would have to compete in the marketplace to get theaters to show their films. This opened up movie production to many independent film producers and reduced the dominance of the large studios.

Television. But the greatest blow of all was yet to come. In 1948 two major radio networks began the process of transforming television from a rich man's toy to a new mass medium for the popular culture. At first major studio executives ignored TV and told themselves that it was a passing fad. After all, they thought, no tiny television screen could compete with the larger-than-life "silver screens" in motion-picture theaters. But they were quickly proved wrong, as more and more people chose the convenience of staying home to watch the free entertainment. One factor encouraging home viewing was a shift in demographics. After the war many Americans started moving from the cities to the suburbs, and most movie theaters were concentrated in the big urban centers.

Television also hurt movie viewing indirectly by creating new interests in the popular culture. Telecasts of team sports like baseball and football stimulated an interest in professional and collegiate sporting events. And TV programs featuring such previously elite individualistic sports as golf, tennis and skiing helped create an interest in these activities. Soon many more people were spending some of their leisure time enjoying these sports.

Fight for Survival. Movie attendance continued to decline in the 1950s. Weaker studios, such as Republic, Allied Artists and Monogram, soon collapsed. Others followed. While the number of television sets in homes was increasing 400 percent between 1948 and 1960, weekly theater attendance declined 50 percent. The demand for the second features eventually vanished altogether.

The motion-picture industry fought back by introducing a variety of technical gimmicks to attract audiences. For example, studios began experimenting with three-dimensional (3-D) films (which required special glasses, given to people at the theater, to view them). In 1952 alone Hollywood released such 3-D movies as *Bwana Devil, House of Wax, Creature from the Black Lagoon, The French Line, Kiss Me Kate* and *Murders in the Rue Morgue.* Audiences left their TV sets to experience the visual illusion of knives, arrows, avalanches and chemicals being hurled at them, but they quickly tired of the novelty. The industry even experimented with "smell-o-vision," where smells were piped into theaters. But movie audiences continued to dwindle.

Finally, the industry introduced Cinerama, a process of using three projectors and three screens to wrap around the audience. Whereas 3-D had attempted to bring the picture into the audience, Cinerama put the audience into the picture. Cinerama previously had been used for special-effect travelogues but not by Hollywood to tell a story. An MGM film editor, Harold Kress, disputed the claim of Cinerama executives that this special-effects film could not be edited. After he proved that a powerful story could be told in this new film technology, Hollywood talent banded together and produced the first Cinerama story—*How the West Was Won*—as a benefit for a Santa Monica, California, hospital. Many major Hollywood stars appeared *gratis* in the film. It was a box-office success in an era of low movie-theater attendance—and it won Kress his first Academy Award for film editing.

A second Cinerama production—*Brothers Grimm*—lost money, and Hollywood soon abandoned the new technology. Cinerama required larger screens as well as extra theater personnel to operate the three projectors and sophisticated sound equipment that gave the film its unique qualities. It was just too expensive to be practical.

The third gimmick the industry tried was CinemaScope. It too used a larger screen, but it was more successful than the other two techniques because it required no special glasses and only one projection system. The first CinemaScope film was *The Robe* (1953), a Biblical epic starring Richard Burton. It was followed by other large-scale, expensive films, such as *The Ten Commandments* (1956) and *Ben Hur* (1959). Some CinemaScope features were successful; others were not.

The film industry's struggle to regain its audiences from television was also partially responsible for the almost total conversion to color motion pictures in the 1950s. Although a few successful color films had been produced in the 1930s, including *Gone With the Wind* and *The Wizard of Oz* in 1939, color shooting was slow and expensive. Black-and-white films thus remained the rule rather than the exception until the more competitive years of the 1950s.

Despite all of these efforts to attract back its mass audiences, the motion-picture industry was finding that the popular cultural interests had changed and that the new medium of television was more than a gimmick—it had become a new way of life. By the mid-1950s the film industry decided to end its boycott and permit old films to be shown on television. Some companies even rented out their movie studios for TV productions.

YOUTH, SEX, VIOLENCE AND SPECIAL EFFECTS

The motion-picture industry now realized that, in order to survive as a mass-communication medium in the age of television, it had to move from the popular stage of the EPS cycle to specialization. This change in focus began in the mid-1950s, when the industry discovered that, though many adults were staying home to watch television, there was a potential audience among young people, who wanted to get out of the house and socialize.

Youth. Social-commentary films about young people, such as *Blackboard Jungle* (1955) and *Rebel Without a Cause* (1955), appealed to the young and made box-office idols out of young actors. For example, James Dean, an unknown actor from a small town in Indiana, became a teenage idol overnight after appearing in *Rebel Without a Cause*. Although he starred in only three hit movies before his death in a traffic accident in 1955, Dean remains a legend today. His memory has been kept alive in our popular culture in a number of ways: television stations have continued to show his movies, video stores feature his films, and poster companies still sell blow-ups of publicity stills from his movies.

The youth-oriented movies of the 1950s catered to a new American subculture— the youth subculture. These films portrayed the restlessness and rebellion of young people in a sympathetic way that they could easily relate to. Also developing at this time was a youth-oriented genre of popular music—rock-'n'-roll (see Chapter 10). In fact, the theme song for *Blackboard Jungle* was the first rock-'n'-roll hit of the 1950s, *Rock Around the Clock*.

The 1950s were also the years for such low-budget films as *I Was a Teenage Werewolf*, *I Was a Teenage Frankenstein*, *Joy Ride* and *Riot in Juvenile Prison*. Then as now, horror and violence were popular genres in the youth subculture. Braving a horror movie became a rite of passage for young men, while their dates screamed in terror. (Surveys show that among young dating couples the male usually chooses the movie; among older married moviegoers, the choice generally falls to the wife.)

A string of beach movies followed, featuring teenagers enjoying life at the beach, with all of its sun, bikinis, surfing, volleyball and romance. These films reflected the party flavor of the new youth subculture and featured similar plots with such titles as *Beach Blanket Bingo* and *How to Stuff a Wild Bikini*. Movies featuring the new rock-'n'-roll stars of the period, like Elvis Presley and the Beatles, were also box-office successes of the 1960s.

By the latter part of the 1960s, the influence of the youth "counterculture" began to be felt. Some films were now featuring antiheroes—social misfits, deviates or outlaws who usually lost out in the end, but for whom the audience felt sympathy. The youth subculture had become anti-Establishment, opposing the war in Vietnam and defying the laws against drugs. Thus when other lawbreakers, like the notorious bank-robbing team of *Bonnie and Clyde* (1967), were portrayed as heroes, the film was a hit with youths. Other films that glorified lawlessness were *The Dirty Dozen* (1967), *Cool Hand Luke* (1967), *Easy Rider* (1969) and *Butch Cassidy and the Sundance Kid* (1969). More sophisticated anti-Establishment films that satirized the "hypocrisy" of middle class values included *The Graduate* (1967), *Bob and Carol and Ted and Alice* (1969) and *Goodbye, Columbus* (1969).

Sex. A major departure for the film industry in the 1960s was the explicit presentation of sexual themes, reflecting the new sexual permissiveness of the time. Since sexual themes were not allowed on television at the time, movie producers saw a golden opportunity. As the sexual genre developed during this period of specialization, a more explicit variety with actual nudity became commonplace as an effective tool to pull people away from their relatively sexless TV sets.

The sexual themes of such films as *Barbarella*, *Midnight Cowboy* and *Carnal Knowledge* helped lure people to the box office. Three hard-core pornography films also became popular during this period: *Deep Throat*, *Behind the Green Door* and *The Devil in Miss Jones*.

Obviously, the industry could only make such films by completely ignoring the standards of the Production Code Administration. By the late 1960s the motion-picture industry officially abandoned the former self-censorship system by devising a rating system that placed the burden of censorship on the moviegoer. The ratings ranged from "G," which designated wholesome movies for the entire family, to "X," which prohibited anyone under 18 from attending and warned that anything might be found in the movie, from brutal violence to hard-core pornography. Although profanity and explicit sexual themes and scenes were originally restricted to R- and X-rated movies, they now can can be found in today's PG (parental-guidance recommended) films.

At first, most movies received a rating of either G or M (later changed to PG), with 25 percent of the films rated G and 43 percent M or PG. However, within a decade the movie industry found that moviegoers preferred more violent and sexually explicit films. By 1979 movies rated PG and a new category called PG-13 had content similar to that of the early-day R-rated movies. The R category grew from 25 percent in 1969 to 45 percent in 1979; the G category fell from 25 to 6 percent.

Disasters and Violence. When television began toning down its depiction of violence in the 1970s to comply with consumer group complaints, the motion-picture industry turned to disaster films and explicit violence as film genres. Disaster films became the big box-office draws of the 1970s. These films were filled with suspense as passengers scrambled for their lives in a sinking luxury liner *(The Poseidon Adventure)*, summer vacationers were gobbled up by a giant shark *(Jaws)*, Los Angeles was shaken to destruction *(Earthquake)* and a giant skyscraper was consumed by flames *(The Towering Inferno)*.

As people became accustomed to disasters, the films got more violent in an effort to keep the audience interested. Some of the more popular superviolent films were *The Wild Bunch* and *Dirty Harry*, a movie starring Clint Eastwood as a tough San Francisco cop who doesn't let the law get in his way of capturing, torturing and eventually killing a rooftop sniper. Although these films depicted people being gunned down in cold blood, it was still the "bad guys" who lost out in the end. However, as the 1970s drew to a close, many innocent people were being axed and mutilated in films such as *Halloween*, the *Texas Chain Saw Massacre* and *Friday the 13th*. All of these films had sequels.

Of course not everyone wanted to spend their Saturday nights watching people being hacked to pieces. Some viewers, especially women, wanted good, clean, wholesome family-type entertainment, and movies were also made for this segment of the market. Some of the more successful included the musical about the life of the legendary singing Von Trapp family of Austria, *The Sound of Music* (1965), *Oliver!* (1968) and a long string of Walt Disney movies.

Special Effects. As space-age technology and space exploration became part of our cultures, the movies began to use this technology and depict these themes. With the help of such directors as Steven Spielberg and George Lucas, films started featuring amazing computer-generated special effects. These special effects created graphic depictions of everything from interplanetary war to extraterrestrial beings. The first to dazzle audiences was Lucas's *Star Wars* (1977), which broke box-office records. It was followed by *Close Encounters of the Third Kind*, *The Empire Strikes Back*, *Return of the Jedi*, *Poltergeist*, *Raiders of the Lost Ark*, *E.T*, *Poltergeist II*, *Aliens*, *Indiana Jones and the Temple of Doom* and *The Fly*.

CURRENT TRENDS

Today movies deal with every social and antisocial theme; graphic scenes of violence, bondage and explicit sex are not uncommon. As a result, the motion-picture industry still finds itself under attack from a variety of groups, ranging from concerned parents and religious leaders to women's rights activists. All are calling for some form of censorship.

Censorship. Parent and religious groups are concerned that the movies' depiction of brutal violence, permissive sex, alcohol and drug abuse, reckless driving and wanton destruction of property encourages such behavior among young people. Women's groups believe that movies that show women in stereotyped roles, portray them as sex objects and show explicit scenes of bondage and violence are hurting women's

(text continues on page 168)

BOX 7.2.

THE BUSINESS OF MOVIES TODAY

In 1987 movie-theater ticket sales reached $4.2 billion, making it the biggest box-office year in motion-picture history. In addition, by late 1987 there were more movie theaters in the United States than ever before: 22,721 movie screens, with more opening every month. To fill these screens 511 movies were made in 1987, more than in any year since 1970.

The continued success of movies, which TV toppled from its number-one position in entertainment in the late 1940s, results from the fact that the industry has changed greatly from its former golden years in the 1930s and '40s. There are more independent producers, and the old movie giants that controlled our popular culture 50 years ago are no longer the same. Many of the names are the same—Metro-Goldwyn-Mayer, United Artists, 20th Century-Fox, Paramount, Warner Brothers, Columbia and Universal—but their methods of operation and financial bases are different. No longer do they have 250 stars under contract, as MGM did in 1935, and they are either large conglomerates with many other business enterprises or are owned by conglomerates. Paramount, for example, is part of Gulf + Western's Entertainment Group, which also includes the New York Knicks basketball team, Madison Square Garden and 894 movie theaters. Columbia is owned by the Coca-Cola Co.

In addition to the big motion-picture pro-

To offset the boom in home video, Toronto-based Cineplex Odeon has lured back viewers by offering such extras as plush seats, marble floors and gourmet food. (Cineplex Odeon, Universal City Cinemas)

The Major Studios: Veteran Movie, Television and Video-Cassette Producers

Columbia	Disney	MGM	Paramount
Founded 1924	Founded 1923; set up Touchstone in 1984 to produce films for adult audiences	Founded 1924	Founded 1912
14 film releases in 1987, including "Ishtar," "La Bamba" and "Roxanne"		8 film releases in 1987, including "Moonstruck" and "Spaceballs"	12 film releases in 1987, including "Beverly Hills Cop II," "The Untouchables" and "Fatal Attraction"
	13 film releases in 1987, including "Tin Men," "Three Men and a Baby" and rereleases of "Snow White" and "Cinderella"		
Parent company: **COCA-COLA CO.**			Parent company: **GULF AND WESTERN INC.**
Other Coca-Cola entertainment-related businesses:	Parent company: **WALT DISNEY CO.**		Other Gulf and Western entertainment-related businesses:
Radio stations			470 U.S. movie theaters (Festival, Trans-Lux, Mann; currently selling 50% to Warner Communications)
Merchandising	Other Disney entertainment-related businesses:		
(has merged Columbia Pictures and Tri-Star Pictures to create new company called Columbia Pictures Entertainment Inc.)	Theme parks and resorts		
	Merchandising		Canadian movie theaters
			Madison Square Garden the New York Knicks
			50% of USA Network

20th Century-Fox	Universal	Warner Bros.	United Artists
Founded 1935	Founded in 1912	Founded 1923	Founded 1919
13 film releases in 1987, including "Broadcast News," "Wall Street" and "The Princess Bride"	16 film releases in 1987, including "Jaws, the Revenge," "Cry Freedom" and "Batteries Not Included"	17 film releases in 1987, including "Lethal Weapon," "Full Metal Jacket" and "Empire of the Sun"	6 film releases in 1987, including "The Living Daylights" and "Baby Boom"
Parent company: **NEWS CORPORATION LTD.** (Rupert Murdoch and family own 49%)	Parent company: **MCA INC.**	Parent company: **WARNER COMMUNICATIONS INC.**	Parent company: **MGM/UA COMMUNICATIONS INC.** (Kirk Kerkorian and investor group own 79%)
Other News Corporation entertainment-related businesses:	Other MCA entertainment-related businesses:	Other Warner Communications entertainment-related businesses:	(MGM bought UA in 1981; sold rights to 3,000-title MGM film library, which includes "Gone With the Wind" and "The Wizard of Oz," to Turner Broadcasting System in 1986)
7 U.S. television stations	50% of Cineplex Odeon (1,567 screens)	Records and music publishing	
Fox Broadcasting (distributes programs to independent TV stations)	50% of USA Network	Part-owner of MTV and Nickelodeon	
	New York station WOR-TV		
Publishing and broadcasting properties in the U.S. and abroad	Records and music publishing	Currently buying 50% of Gulf and Western's U.S. movie theaters	
	Universal Studios Tour		
	Merchandising		

The Mini-Majors: Newcomers in the Movie Business

Cannon	De Laurentiis	Lorimar
Founded 1979	Founded 1985	Founded 1987
27 film releases in 1987, including "Barfly," "Tough Guys Don't Dance" and "Death Wish IV"	9 film releases in 1987, including "Tai-Pan," "King Kong Lives" and "Weeds"	6 film releases in 1987, including "Made in Heaven," "In the Mood" and "Orphans"
Owns Commonwealth Theaters (437 screens)		

New World Pictures	Orion	Tri-Star
Founded in 1983	Founded 1978	Founded 1982
20 film releases in 1987, including "House II," "Flowers in the Attic" and "Pinocchio and the Emperor of the Night"	13 film releases in 1987, including "Radio Days," "Robocop" and "House of Games"	18 film releases in 1987, including "Gardens of Stone," "Running Man" and "Ironweed"
		Owns Loew's Theater Corp. (300 screens)
		Recently merged with Columbia Pictures

Research by Stuart Rohrer, *New York Times*, Jan. 10, 1988. Copyright © 1988 by The New York Times Company. Reprinted by permission.

ducers are a number of smaller studios referred to as *mini-majors*. These companies, which sometimes own large groups of theaters and produce hit television shows, include Lorimar, Cannon, De Laurentiis, New World Pictures, Tri-Star and Orion. There are also a number of small independent producers.

The continued success of this industry can be summed up in three words: new delivery systems. The old single-screen movie theaters are being replaced with newer, smaller versions. Almost all of the new theaters are multiplexes, single buildings that usually house eight to 10 smaller screens, although some have as many as 18. Almost as important as an outlet for movies are videocassette sales. By the late 1980s, many low-budget movies were being produced with the idea that even though they would have a short box-office life, they would become profitable from videocassette sales.

The future for the motion-picture industry looks bright. Even more changes in delivery systems are on the horizon, the most promising being high-definition television that will allow transmission of motion pictures to multiplex theaters via satellites (see Chapter 14).

Table 7.1.
All-Time Film Rental Leaders

Although the motion-picture industry was slow to recognize the new technologies of TV and VCRs, it finally realized that they could be important additional sources of revenue. By the late 1980s, the industry was earning billions of dollars from the sale of video movies. These are the top 30 all-time film rental leaders, as reported by *Variety*.

Films	Rental Revenue ($ millions)
E.T.	228.4
Star Wars	193.5
Return of the Jedi	168.0
The Empire Strikes Back	141.6
Jaws	129.6
Ghostbusters	128.3
Raiders of the Lost Ark	115.6
Indiana Jones and the Temple of Doom	109.0
Beverly Hills Cop	108.0
Back to the Future	104.2
Grease	96.3
Tootsie	95.2
The Exorcist	89.0
The Godfather	86.2
Superman	82.8
Close Encounters of the Third Kind	82.7
Beverly Hills Cop II	80.8
The Sound of Music	79.7
Gremlins	79.5
Top Gun	79.4
Rambo: First Blood, Part II	78.9
Gone With the Wind	77.6
Rocky IV	75.9
Saturday Night Fever	74.1
The Sting	71.3
Crocodile Dundee	70.2
Platoon	69.7
Rocky III	66.2
Superman II	65.1
Snow White and the Seven Dwarfs	62.7

Reprinted by permission from *Variety*, 82nd show business annual edition, Jan. 20, 1988, p. 43.

movement toward equality and are contributing to an increase in violence against women.

The central issue in this ongoing controversy is whether motion pictures shape our popular culture or merely reflect it. The groups that advocate censoring motion-picture content believe that the "silver screen" is a powerful force in our culture that sets trends and life styles; directors and producers maintain that they merely reflect the life styles and interests that exist in our society and are giving people the type of entertainment they want.

Video Movies. The latest development to affect the motion-picture industry was the introduction of home video equipment in the late 1970s. This time the motion-picture industry was quick to welcome and find a use for the new technology. Movies found a whole new audience as many people who had not been to a theater in years began watching films on videocassettes.

As videocassette recorders (VCRs) and video-rental businesses spread throughout the country in the 1980s, Hollywood began rerecording old films onto videotape. New movies are also released after their run at the box-office for a considerable amount of extra income. Motion picture producers receive a percentage of the box-office receipts from theaters, but no such share from video rentals. However, the many rental outlets are a prime market for videocassette sales. When Steven Spielberg's *The Color Purple* was released on videocassette, for example, it had already made nearly $100 million at the box office. It was expected to sell over 275,000 videocassettes at $89 each to video-rental outlets, providing nearly $25 million in additional income (see Table 7.1).

The old motion-picture industry has successfully adapted to new niches and seems to be riding smoothly into the twenty-first century (see Box 7.2).

SUMMARY

The motion-picture industry has had a major impact on our popular culture, and our popular culture has in turn affected the industry, as new media, cultural attitudes and changing life styles have forced it to change.

Soon after the invention of the motion-picture camera in Thomas Edison's laboratory, film found its way to mass audiences. It was first used as a moving peep show in penny arcades, then in vaudeville shows and, beginning in 1905, in movie parlors called nickelodeons.

Films such as Edwin Porter's *The Great Train Robbery* and D. W. Griffith's *Birth of a Nation* proved that the motion picture could be a powerful storytelling medium. Film moved quickly into the popular culture because it was invented at a time when immigrants in our industrialized urban society needed an entertainment medium with no language barrier. The international languages of the silent film's pantomime and comedy provided that medium. Soon actors like Mack Sennett, Charlie Chaplin, Stan Laurel, Oliver Hardy, Buster Keaton and Harold Lloyd were silently communicating to the masses.

Although experimental sound pictures were made in the early days of the industry, it wasn't until Warner Brothers brought out *The Jazz Singer* in 1927, with Al Jolson singing on screen, that the full potential of "talking" pictures was realized. The success of the early "talkies" changed the industry and helped make Warner Brothers into a major studio.

In the 1930s and 1940s going to the movies became a way of life in the United States. The major movie studios turned out hundreds of films a year and created movie stars who became as familiar to American audiences as members of their own families. These films also provided an effective escape from reality during a time of depression and war.

In 1947 and 1948 three events rocked the industry and toppled it from its peak of economic success. First came the congressional hearings into alleged Communist infiltration of the motion-picture industry. The second was a Supreme Court ruling that forced major studios to sell their theaters. The final blow was the entrance of television into our popular culture.

The motion-picture industry changed from a big-studio-dominated industry that owned most of the stars and the distribution outlets to one of independent producers and theaters. The industry experimented with a variety of films and technology—such as three-dimensional pictures and large screens—but it could not win back its mass audience.

Soon Hollywood discovered that films aimed at specialized audiences helped revive box-office receipts. Finding popularity at the box office were films aimed at youth and films that contained sex, violence and special effects.

Today, despite continual efforts to censor the content of films, the motion-picture industry is prosperous. The industry's adaptation to the new videocassette technology has provided it with a significant additional source of revenue.

NOTES

1. Jack Mathews, "Film Directors See Red Over Ted Turner's Movie Tinting," *Los Angeles Times*, calendar section, Sept. 12, 1986, p. 1.

2. Ibid.

3. John Voland, "Turner Defends Move to Color Films," *Los Angeles Times*, calendar section, Oct. 23, 1986, p. 1.

4. Lewis Jacobs, *The Emergence of Film Art*, 2nd ed. (New York: Norton, 1979), p. 27.

5. Gerald Mast, *A Short History of the Movies*, 4th ed. (New York: Macmillan, 1986), p. 63.

6. Ibid. p. 93.

7. David Robinson, *The History of World Cinema* (New York: Stein and Day, 1973), p. 104.

8. Arthur Knight, *The Liveliest Art: A Panoramic History of the Movies* (New York: New American Library, 1957), pp. 112–113.

9. Robinson, p. 190.

10. Pamela S. Ecker, "My Affair With Farrah," in Jack Nachbar, Deborah Weiser and John Wright, eds., *The Popular Culture Reader* (Bowling Green, Ohio: Bowling Green University Popular Press, 1978), pp. 211–212.

11. Walter Goodman, *The Committee: The Extraordinary Career of the House Committee on Un-American Activities* (New York: Farrar, Straus & Giroux, 1964), p. 218.

12. Robinson, p. 253.

ADDITIONAL READING

Boorstin, Daniel J. *The Image: A Guide to Pseudo-Events in America.* New York: Harper & Row, 1964.

Bordwell, David, and Thompson, Kristin. *Film Art: An Introduction,* 2nd ed. New York: Knopf, 1986.

Charters, Werrett Wallace. *Motion Pictures and Youth.* New York: Arno Press & The New York Times, 1970.

Ellis, Jack C. *A History of Film.* Englewood Cliffs, N.J.: Prentice-Hall, 1979.

Fulton, Albert R. *Motion Pictures: The Development of an Art from Silent Films to the Age of Television.* Norman, Okla.: University of Oklahoma Press, 1960.

Griffith, Richard, and Mayer, Arthur. *The Movies,* rev. ed. New York: Simon & Schuster, 1970.

Higman, Charles. *Hollywood at Sunset.* New York: Saturday Review Press, 1972.

Jacobs, Lewis. *The Rise of the American Film: A Critical History.* New York: Harcourt, Brace, 1939.

Kauffman, Stanley. *A World on Film.* New York: Harper & Row, 1966.

Lee, David, and Berkowitz, Stan. *The Movie Business.* New York: Vantage, 1981.

Schickel, Richard. *Movies: The History of an Art.* New York: Simon & Schuster, 1963.

Chapter 8

Radio: A Wireless Wonder

> Radio was really do it yourself
> television. Instead of a big
> ugly glass picture tube, you
> saw the performers in your own
> mind. You were not restricted
> by the boundaries of a 21-inch
> tube, but instead painted your
> own big as life version of each
> moment with that loving creative
> brush we call imagination.
> —Jack Benny

On June 13, 1987, Ralph's Pretty Good Grocery, Bertha's Kitty Boutique, the Powdermilk Biscuit Company and the Chatterbox Cafe were discussed live on radio for the last time. These were the "hot spots" in the mythical town of Lake Wobegon, Minnesota, which had been featured for some 13 years on the Saturday radio show *A Prairie Home Companion*.

The town, where "all the women are strong and all the men are good-looking and all the children are above average," was created by one of the most popular radio personalities of the 1980s—Garrison Keillor. His radio show was produced by Minnesota Public Radio and aired over 275 public radio stations. In 1985 the publishing industry cashed in on Keillor's popularity by selling over a million copies of his book *Lake Wobegon Days*.

A Prairie Home Companion was a throwback to the earlier days of radio broadcasting, when live comedy monologues and variety acts were commonplace. Keillor's success with this format, which was rather unique at the time, demonstrated the continued strength of radio in the 1980s, some 60 years after the medium entered the popular culture.

Thus the announcement that the 44-year-old radio personality was going to quit so that he could return to being a "shy person" again shocked his cultlike following. Minnesota Public Radio received some 42,000 calls following the announcement from people wanting tickets for the remaining 17 shows. (The program was broadcast live each week from a 925-seat theater.) The last broadcast was televised and relayed by satellite to Los Angeles, where 2,500 Keillor fans paid up to $75 to watch the show on large-screen TV. Keillor's departure from the airwaves was featured in various magazines and newspapers and on radio and television news shows (see Box 8.1). Keillor's last show was so popular that in 1988 the second "annual farewell performance" was held in New York's cavernous Radio City Music Hall and carried live on cable TV's Disney Channel.

Ever since it first entered the popular culture in the 1920s, radio has had a profound impact on listeners. It was the first mass-communication medium to change American home life dramatically by bringing the sounds of live entertainment from vaudeville, theaters and ballrooms right into the nation's living rooms.

Today there is more than one radio for every person in the United States, and 95 percent of all automobiles in this country are equipped with them. Radio has a larger listening audience than television for a sizable part of the day, usually around the "drive times" of 6 to 10 A.M. and 3 to 7 P.M. According to statistics compiled by the Radio Advertising Bureau, on average high school and college students spend more hours a day listening to radio than they do watching television.

HARNESSING SOUND WAVES

The invention of radio was the culmination of 70 years of technological advances in communicating messages.

The need for instant communication first arose in the 1830s, as the great era of railroad building got under way. The efficiency and safety of the railroads required a system that could send messages to distant stations faster than the trains traveled. Experimentation soon began on harnessing sound waves to meet this need.

The Telegraph. In 1844 a portrait painter and experimental photographer named Samuel F. Morse invented a system of sending sound waves over long-distance telegraph wires. To demonstrate his discovery, he strung 40 miles of telegraph lines between Washington, D.C., and Baltimore, Maryland, and transmitted the now-famous message: "What hath God wrought?"

Soon telegraph lines were crisscrossing the country; by 1861 a transcontinental line was in place. This electronic communication system was adequate for the railroads' needs, but it was unsuitable for public use, since the telegraph messages were limited to coded signals of dots and dashes, the well-known Morse code.

The Telephone. Many scientists went to work to find a way to send the human voice over telegraph lines. The Scottish inventor Alexander Graham Bell came up with the first workable system in 1876. His telephone consisted of a microphone,

Elitist	Popular	Specialized	CULTURAL HISTORY OF RADIO	
■			1888	Henrich Hertz transmits wireless sound waves.
■			1901	Guglielmo Marconi sends wireless sound across the Atlantic.
■			1906	Lee De Forest adds grid to vacuum tube, making voice transmission possible.
■			1917	U.S. enters World War I; U.S. Navy takes over broadcasting from American Marconi Co.
■			1919	Radio Corporation of America (RCA) founded; Frank Conrad transmits music over the airwaves in Pittsburgh.
■			1920	KDKA (Pittsburgh) goes on the air for Westinghouse—first fully licensed station with continuous broadcasting.
■			1922	WEAF (New York) begins commercial broadcasting.
■	■		1926	AT&T gives up effort to build a radio network; NBC (an RCA subsidiary) starts two networks.
■			1927	UIB/Columbia network begins (later becomes CBS).
■			1927	Federal Radio Act sets up commission to regulate the airwaves.
	■		1928	*Sam and Henry* (later *Amos 'n' Andy*) becomes popular network sitcom.
	■		1930s	Radio soap operas offer escape from the Depression.
	■		1933–45	President Franklin Roosevelt uses radio for fireside chats with the nation.
	■		1934	Federal Communication Commission (FCC) established.
	■		1934	Mutual Broadcasting System goes on the air as fourth radio network.
	■		1938	Orson Welles's *War of the Worlds* panics nation.
	■		1939	First FM radio station goes on the air in New Jersey.
■	■		1940–45	Edward R. Murrow broadcasts vivid descriptions of the war in Europe on CBS for American audiences.
	■		1943	Federal government forces NBC to sell one of its two networks; it eventually becomes ABC.
	■		1948	Network radio revenues reach a peak.
	■		1950s	Radio loses its programs and stars to television.
		■	1950s	Radio begins to specialize with individual musical formats and disc jockeys; promotes rock-'n'-roll.
		■	1959	Payola scandal rocks radio industry.
		■	1970s	Country-and-western music and all-talk shows grow in popularity on radio.
		■	1981	FCC begins deregulated radio.
		■	1980s	AM radio adds stereo broadcasting to fight growing popularity of FM stations.

BOX 8.1.

COMPANION TO "PRAIRIE" LOVERS ENDS HIS REIGN

The following article was written for the Los Angeles Times by staff writer Dennis McDougal, who covered the last broadcast of Garrison Keillor's A Prairie Home Companion.

ST. PAUL, Minn.—Garrison Keillor shut down Ralph's Pretty Good Grocery, Bertha's Kitty Boutique and the Chatterbox Cafe with style and grace Saturday, declining to accept "cheap bronze plaques" commemorating his 13-year run as host of radio's *A Prairie Home Companion* and returning to the stage for no fewer than a half-dozen encores following his final public appearance.

Outside the World Theatre where the gangly, iguana-eyed radio personality has performed for nearly a decade, the mayor of St. Paul, George Latimer, released 10,000 yellow, orange and blue balloons and a local theater troupe serenaded Keillor. A crowd of 500 strong women, good-looking men and above-average children jockeyed for a glimpse of their departing hero while a brass band played.

It was wholesome Americana: a scene straight out of *The Music Man, Our Town* . . . or *Blue Velvet.*

The 44-year-old storyteller—hailed as the new Mark Twain—told a sold-out audience several times during the 2½-hour show that he would miss them more than they would miss him. He packs for Denmark next week, where he claims he will resume his life as a shy, retiring writer of fiction.

With his backup orchestra and the show's soloists playing a spate of melancholy melodies ranging from *Remember Me* to *Till We Meet Again,* his farewell radio program very nearly crossed over the line from the climax of a broadcast phenomenon to a sentimental sob fest.

Handkerchiefs and Kleenex came out all over the tiny World Theatre when Keillor

sang farewell to Lake Wobegon in his low flannel voice:

"I looked back and shed a tear, to see it in my rear-view mirror, I said I'd just be gone a couple of weeks, and now it's been 30 years," he sang.

Lake Wobegon, "The little town that time forgot," sprang from Keillor's own tragic-comic memories of his Midwestern fundamentalist upbringing just 50 miles north of St. Paul in suburban Anoka County.

But that all changed after his national radio audience grew in recent years to more than 3.5 million listeners. After more than a million sales of his novel, *Lake Wobegon Days,* in 1985, Keillor and his sad little Minnesota town became more American than Mayberry, Muncie or apple pie.

The Disney Channel has been televising the show since March, and fan mail protesting the demise of *A Prairie Home Companion* has poured in by the bag load at Minnesota Public Radio, the show's producer. Director Sydney Pollack bought the film rights to the novel and explored upper Minnesota with Keillor some months ago in search of the non-existent town and its archetypal residents for the purposes of making a movie.

In the most recent tour books, even the American Automobile Club has felt compelled to print a descriptive paragraph, warning summer travelers not to go searching for Lake Wobegon because it exists "only on a popular Saturday night radio program."

But true Keillor fans are undaunted by such facts. What they are after, says Van

Nuys resident Don Browne who personally paid more than $1,000 for tickets, air fare and hotel charges to see the last show, is Truth with a nostalgic capital *T*.

"I first heard the show in June of 1980 and I immediately went to the library looking for Lake Wobegon," said the UCLA research scientist. "They can say it doesn't exist, but there's a lot of it right here (in St. Paul). Everything's a lot simpler, a lot more honest. You try to cash a check in Westwood, they ask you for three pieces of ID and a blood sample. But it's not like that here at all."

In Lake Wobegon, Bob's Bank operates out of a green mobile home on Main Street, "where your money is safe and the door is always open," according to a "commercial" that aired from time to time on *A Prairie Home Companion*.

Every check issued by the bank carried both Bob's picture and the inscription: "Cash this. They're friends of mine," according to Keillor's vision.

Garrison's friends flocked in from all over the United States this last show: Philadelphia; Shreveport, La.; Honolulu; Los Angeles . . . In fact, there were very few from St. Paul or Minneapolis in the audience. When he asked for a hand from his fellow Minnesotans in the audience, the applause was scattered.

Carroll and Joyce Lehman drove all the way from Keene, N.H., to see the last of Keillor and counted themselves lucky to get $100 tickets. What more wholesome way could they spend their 22nd wedding anniversary.

"It was wonderful! It was just wonderful!" Joyce squealed.

"She grew up in Iowa and she says that Garrison knows just how it was," Carroll Lehman said of his effervescing mate.

Keillor spun his final weekly report of the news from Lake Wobegon by freezing Mayor Clint Bunsen, Pastor Ingqvist, a half-dozen Norwegian bachelor farmers and all the rest of his Minnesota characters in the timeless fantasy of a quirky wholesome town that disappeared amid freeways and fast-food franchises long before Keillor decided to abandon his show and go to Denmark.

In his finest storytelling hush, Keillor told his audience that the last day he spent in his imaginary hometown was Wednesday, June 10, 1987.

It was raining, ending a long spring drought. A great long rain, he called it.

Everyone crowded into the Chatterbox Cafe because it was that kind of a day—a cream of mushroom soup and toasted cheese sandwich kind of a day in Lake Wobegon. With Keillor's voice growing quieter and more confidential with each sentence, he described in loving detail how the rain turned into a surrealistic mist as his characters faded from view.

"And here it is. This mist. You could get to anywhere you wanted to get in it," he told his rapt and weepy audience. The talk in the cafe had turned to the planting of the last sweet corn, now that the drought was done. The great, long rain would mean that the crop would not fail, the river would rise and it would be possible to sail on down the river and see at last what was around the bend.

Outside the World Theatre on Saturday it was a hot, muggy June afternoon. Inside it was cold and misty and the 925 people who watched the last show shared a final grilled cheese sandwich with Keillor before he said goodby.

"That's where I leave them," he said. "If you see them, give them my best and tell them I think of them. That's the news from Lake Wobegon."

which converted sound into electrical energy, and a receiver, which changed it back into sound.

Three years earlier, the Scottish physicist James Clerk Maxwell predicted that someday it would be possible to generate electronic signals that could be sent through space at the speed of light without the use of wires. The German physicist Heinrich Hertz proved Maxwell's theory correct in 1888, when he sent a wireless signal from one point to another in his laboratory. (The unit of frequency called *hertz* is named in his honor.)

Development of the Wireless. A wealthy young Italian, Guglielmo Marconi, experimented with Hertz's theories in Bologna, Italy, where he successfully sent signals across the hillside near his family home. Unable to interest the Italian government in his invention, Marconi and his mother traveled to England, where his mother's family had important social contacts. There he demonstrated his invention and obtained support from the British Post Office Department. Marconi received his first patent on radiotelegraphy equipment in England in 1896, when he was 22 years old. The following year he formed the British Marconi Company, which continued to experiment with radio signal transmission over greater distances.

Marconi made history in 1901 when he set up a radio receiver in Newfoundland and picked up three dots (the Morse code for the letter S) that had been sent across

Guglielmo Marconi, a key figure in the development of wireless technology.
(Historical Pictures Services)

the Atlantic by a colleague in England. He then developed a number of companies that expanded the ability of Morse code communication to mobile points. Radio thus found its first niche in the culture transmitting messages ship-to-ship and ship-to-shore.

Meanwhile, scientists were still struggling to find a way to send voices through the air. They were looking for a wireless telephone. The essential step came in 1906, when an American, Dr. Lee De Forest, perfected the vacuum tube by inventing a grid that became an amplifier when inserted into the tube. This improved vacuum tube, called an Audion, enabled radio receivers to pick up voice and music sounds. The vacuum tube remained a fundamental component of radio receivers until the transistor was invented in 1947. Although De Forest is generally given credit for being the "father of radio," his patent rights to the Audion were disputed by J. Ambrose Fleming, who had patented a vacuum tube called the Fleming valve in 1904; De Forest's invention had been an improvement on Fleming's vacuum tube rather than a completely new invention.

On Christmas Eve 1906, University of Pittsburgh professor Reginald A. Fessenden, working with General Electric engineers, used wireless technology to broadcast music to ships at sea. Although a new era of wireless transmission had arrived, few people at the time had any idea that they were experimenting with a mass-communication technology that would transform the culture.

BEGINNING OF RADIO AS A MASS MEDIUM

One person who did foresee radio's future as a mass-communication medium—and who later became a force in making it so—first learned of radio's potential at the age of 21, while working as a wireless operator for the American Marconi Company on April 14, 1912. Through the static on his radio receiver came a series of dots and dashes that told that the S.S. *Titanic* had hit an iceberg in the North Atlantic and was sinking fast.

The young radio operator was David Sarnoff. The *Titanic,* which was considered unsinkable, had been on its maiden voyage from Europe to the United States and was carrying many socially prominent passengers. The news of the tragedy spread fast, and soon many amateur radio operators were trying to make contact with the sinking ship. President Taft ordered all of the stations shut down except one—David Sarnoff's.

Sarnoff received and transmitted messages about the disaster and fed the information, including reports about survivors, to the waiting nation. Although he gained fame during the event, Sarnoff later went to work for the Radio Corporation of America (RCA) and earned his place in radio history as the head of its subsidiary the National Broadcasting Company (NBC).

Voice transmission continued in the experimental stages for a number of years. In 1916 De Forest sent out an experimental transmission of the Wilson-Hughes presidential election returns, which is now considered to be the first radio news broadcast.

That same year, David Sarnoff sent the following message to his boss at the American Marconi Company:

> I have in mind a plan of development that would make radio a "household utility" in the same sense as the piano or phonograph. The idea is to bring music into the house by wireless.... The receiver can be designed in the form of a simple "Radio Music Box" ... supplied with amplifying tubes and a loud speaking telephone, all of which can be neatly mounted in one box.... Aside from the profit derived from this proposition, the possibilities for advertising for the company are tremendous for its name would ultimately be brought into the household, and wireless would receive national and universal attention.[1]

Like most memos, this "Music Box Memo" was largely ignored. However, in 1919 a Westinghouse engineer, Dr. Frank Conrad, started broadcasting music at an experimental station in Pittsburgh. A department store started running newspaper ads suggesting that people could hear "Dr. Conrad's magical music" come out of thin air by purchasing a crystal set (a small tubeless radio receiver that used a crystal detector) at their store.

Also in 1919 General Electric purchased the equipment and patents held by the American Marconi Company and joined forces with Westinghouse, American Telephone & Telegraph (AT&T), Western Electric Company and United Fruit Company to pool electronic patents and form RCA. Each company owned a percentage of RCA and Sarnoff became RCA's general manager in 1921. The decision to form an American radio distribution firm was prompted by the nation's involvement in World War I in 1917–18 and the realization that Marconi, the major company in the field of radio at that time, was foreign-owned. During the war, the U.S. navy took over all U.S. commercial and amateur wireless stations, dismantling some and operating others as part of its own facilities. (Marconi, incidentally, served in both the Italian army and navy during the war.)

The rapid sale of crystal sets to hear Dr. Conrad's music proved that Sarnoff had made a good suggestion in his 1916 music box memo. The next year, on November 2, 1920, Westinghouse went on the air in Pittsburgh with station KDKA, the first fully licensed commercial broadcasting station to have continuous programming. Its opening broadcast featured returns from the Harding-Cox presidential election, along with a request for people to write the station if they heard the broadcast.

Early Commercial Broadcasting.   The success of Westinghouse's KDKA led the other electrical companies to open their own stations. RCA went on the air with WDY in New York, AT&T began WEAF in New York and General Electric started WGY in Schenectady, New York. Westinghouse later added stations in Massachusetts, New Jersey and Illinois. The motivation for these electrical companies to start commercial radio stations was financial. While the sale of radio transmitters and receivers for ship-to-shore broadcasting was limited, by expanding radio to the masses, the entire population became a potential market.

WEAF went on the air in 1922 as a toll station; that is, it sold air time to advertisers.

The print media resented the competition and criticized the idea of radio advertising, calling it offensive. Even broadcasters disagreed as to whether commercials belonged on radio.

The Beginning of the Networks. As more and more stations were founded around the country, AT&T started linking them together in 1923 using its telephone lines. This "chain broadcasting," which allowed stations to share programming, was the forerunner to network broadcasting.

In 1926 AT&T bailed out of the broadcast distribution business and began leasing its wires to RCA's subsidiary NBC. This launched the era of network broadcasting, with NBC establishing and operating two radio networks—NBC Red and NBC Blue. The company operated both networks until the Federal Communications Commission intervened and forced the sale of the Blue network in 1943. The Blue network thus became the American Broadcasting Company (ABC).

In 1927 another broadcasting system was organized by the United Independent Broadcasters (a group of rival stations not affiliated with NBC), with the help of the Columbia Phonograph Record Company. First called UIB/Columbia, it was renamed the Columbia Broadcasting System (CBS) after it was reorganized and purchased in 1928 by a 27-year-old cigar-company heir named William S. Paley. Paley, who still chaired the board of CBS in the 1980s, had been impressed with the success of radio advertisements in boosting the sales of his cigars.

A fourth radio network, the Mutual Broadcasting System, was started in 1934 by four non–network-affiliated stations. By 1935 Mutual had 60 affiliates. It was the only major network to remain exclusively in radio after the other three expanded into television.

The Need for Government Regulations. By the latter part of the 1920s, the expanding radio industry found itself in need of stricter regulations to allocate radio frequencies and keep stations from jamming each other's signals. It turned to the federal government for help and the Radio Act of 1927 was passed, which set up the Federal Radio Commission (FRC). Soon the number of radio stations in the country was reduced to avoid interference in reception. The FRC was expanded and renamed the Federal Communications Commission (FCC) by the Communication Act of 1934.

DEVELOPMENT OF RADIO NEWS

Although KDKA's debut broadcast was a report on election returns, early radio newscasts were limited. For the most part, announcers simply read headlines from the local newspaper—with an advertising tag line that if listeners wanted the complete details, they should buy a copy of the paper. Some newspapers actually started radio stations to advertise themselves.

Early radio news was also unscheduled. Not until the 1930s were regularly scheduled newscasts offered—usually only one or two in the morning, one at midday and a couple in the evening.

Newspaper Opposition. Network radio grew rapidly after 1927, and by 1930 radio had become firmly entrenched in the popular culture. The new medium's popularity, coupled with the decline in newspaper advertising revenue following the Great Depression in 1929, alarmed many newspaper publishers.

Not only was the advertising revenue of radio increasing while that of newspapers was declining, but this new mass-medium was becoming a credible news source as well. For the first time in history, listeners could hear news events as they were happening without being on the scene. To many, this was far superior to reading about the event the next day. When the stock market crashed in October 1929, people became even more interested in "instant" news.

After radio broadcast both the Democratic and Republican conventions coast to coast in 1932 and the Associated Press provided radio with election returns for instant airing, the newspapers had had enough. The American Newspaper Publishers Association issued an ultimatum to the press associations: stop providing news to radio. Most AP members voted to comply with this request in 1933, and all three press associations stopped selling news to radio stations. Forced to gather news on its own, radio was soon giving newspapers more competition than they had bargained for.

CBS took the lead in creating a first-rate news-gathering service. Under the direction of former newspaperman Paul White, CBS opened bureaus in major U.S. cities and in London. A string of news commentators such as H. V. Kaltenborn, Boake Carter, Lowell Thomas, Edwin C. Hill and Gabriel Heatter became household voices.

Within several years after the wire-service ban, United Press and International News Service were selling news to radio again. UP even set up a service specifically for radio broadcasting. AP resumed its news feed to radio in 1940, and it too developed a special radio news service.

Radio Meets Cultural Needs. President Franklin D. Roosevelt assisted radio in becoming a major information source. After his election in 1932, Roosevelt started using the new medium to communicate directly with the people through broadcasts that he called fireside chats. Many Americans were in states of panic over their financial troubles. Their only hope, they believed, was the leadership of the new president. For the first time in history, average people had the opportunity to listen directly to the reassuring voice of their president. (In the 1980s, a new president, Ronald Reagan, used radio to talk directly to the people. His weekly Saturday broadcasts often included the first formal announcement of major policy decisions.)

Reports about the activities of a madman in Germany—Adolf Hitler—were also causing concern among Americans. Radio kept a concerned nation informed about Hitler's activities, as network radio newscasters took the ears of the American people to the scenes of the action.

Radio and World War II. In 1937 CBS sent a then-unknown Edward R. Murrow to Europe as its director of educational broadcasting. He and an assistant, newspaperman William L. Shirer, soon found themselves covering history in the making. On March 12, 1938, as Hitler sent his troops into Austria, Murrow described the scene

Franklin D. Roosevelt was the first U.S. president to use radio to communicate regularly with the public. His "fireside chats" reassured anxious Americans during the Depression. (*UPI/Bettmann Newsphotos*)

live from Vienna, while Shirer reported on reactions from London and other CBS reporters gave their impressions from Berlin, Paris and Rome. This was radio's first multiple pickup news broadcast; it demonstrated the scope and diversity of radio as a news medium and left no doubt about its importance in the American popular culture.

In 1940 Americans vicariously lived through the bombings of London, as Murrow broadcast eyewitness accounts of the air raids in his famous *This Is London* series. Murrow could describe any event in such a way that listeners could picture it in their minds (see Box 8.2). Americans could almost feel the impact of the war through Murrow's reports.

Radio's coverage of the war in Europe set the stage for the fateful Sunday on December 7, 1941, when radio bulletins announced to the nation that Japanese planes had bombed the American fleet in Pearl Harbor. The next day a record-sized audience listened to President Roosevelt deliver his war message to Congress. As FDR declared that December 7 was a "day that will live in infamy," he inspired a spirit of patriotism and dedication that has never been equalled in American history.

Throughout World War II radio reporters kept the people at home informed about the war with firsthand broadcasts from the battle scenes in the Pacific and Europe. For the first time, Americans experienced a war being fought on distant soil almost as it was happening. There was, however, a great deal of censorship of news from the front, self-imposed as well as governmental, and the horrors of war were downplayed.

BOX 8.2.

EDWARD R. MURROW: A TONGUE AS DESCRIPTIVE AS A PAINT BRUSH

Edward R. Murrow worked for the CBS network from 1935 to 1961, when he resigned to become director of the United States Information Agency. His ability to calmly describe news events on radio in a manner that left no confusion in the minds of the audience helped bring the realities and the horrors of World War II home to Americans. The following is an excerpt of Murrow's April 15, 1945, broadcast describing what he found when he visited the German concentration camp Buchenwald.

Permit me to tell you what you would have seen, and heard, had you been with me on Thursday. It will not be pleasant listening. If you are at lunch, or if you have no appetite to hear what Germans have done, now is a good time to switch off the radio, for I propose to tell you of Buchenwald. It is on a small hill about four miles outside Weimar, and it was one of the largest concentration camps in Germany, and it was built to last. As we approached it, we saw about a hundred men in civilian clothes with rifles advancing in open order across fields. There were a few shots; we stopped to inquire. We were told that some of the prisoners had a couple of SS men cornered in there. We drove on, reached the main gate. The pris-

oners crowded up behind the wire. We entered.

And now, let me tell this in the first person, for I was the least important person there, as you shall hear. There surged around me an evil-smelling horde. Men and boys reached out to touch me; they were in rags and the remnants of uniform. Death had already marked many of them, but they were smiling with their eyes. I looked out over that mass of men to the green fields beyond where well-fed Germans were ploughing.

A German, Fritz Kersheimer, came up and said, "May I show you round the camp? I've been here ten years." An Englishman stood to attention, saying, "May I introduce

DEVELOPMENT OF RADIO ENTERTAINMENT

Radio's impact on American culture was not limited to its "ear-witness" news coverage. It also became a powerful entertainment medium.

Shortly after radio entered the popular culture, the nation experienced the most serious economic depression in its history. Many wealthy families lost their fortunes in the stock market crash, large numbers of poor and middle-class families lost their sources of income as their breadwinners were laid off, and many people lost their life savings as banks collapsed across the country.

Radio had come along at just the right time. It provided free entertainment in the comforts of the home. Families that could no longer afford to go out for entertainment gathered together in their living rooms to escape reality by laughing, fantasizing and dreaming of happier times.

myself, delighted to see you, and can you tell me when some of our blokes will be along?" I told him soon and asked to see one of the barracks. It happened to be occupied by Czechoslovakians. When I entered, men crowded around, tried to lift me to their shoulders. They were too weak. Many of them could not get out of bed. I was told that this building had once stabled eighty horses. There were twelve hundred men in it, five to a bunk. The stink was beyond all description.

When I reached the center of the barracks, a man came up and said, "You remember me. I'm Peter Zenkl, one-time mayor of Prague." I remembered him, but did not recognize him. He asked about Benes and Jan Masaryk. I asked how many men had died in that building during the last month. They called the doctor; we inspected his records. There were only names in the little black book, nothing more—nothing of who these men were, what they had done, or hoped. Behind the names of those who had died there was a cross. I counted them. They totaled 242. Two hundred and forty-two out of twelve hundred in one month.

As I walked down to the end of the barracks, there was applause from the men too weak to get out of bed. It sounded like the hand clapping of babies; they were so weak. The doctor's name was Paul Heller. He had been there since 1938.

As we walked out into the courtyard, a man fell dead. Two others—they must have been over sixty—were crawling toward the latrine. I saw it but will not describe it.

In another part of the camp they showed me the children, hundreds of them. Some were only six. One rolled up his sleeve, showed me his number. It was tattooed on his arm. D-6030, it was. The others showed me their numbers; they will carry them till they die.

An elderly man standing beside me said, "The children, enemies of the state." I could see their ribs through their thin shirts. The old man said, "I am Professor Charles Richer of the Sorbonne." The children clung to my hands and stared. We crossed to the courtyard. Men kept coming up to speak to me and to touch me, professors from Poland, doctors from Vienna, men from all Europe. Men from the countries that made America.

Source: From Edward R. Murrow, *In Search of Light: The Broadcasts of Edward R. Murrow, 1938–1961* (New York: Knopf, 1967), pp. 91–92. Copyright © 1967 by the Estate of Edward R. Murrow. Reprinted by permission of Alfred A. Knopf, Inc.

Electronic Vaudeville. Radio had become a first-class entertainment medium after the networks were established in 1927. Variety shows, dramatic productions and comedy series soon dominated the airwaves. Most comedy programs consisted of a series of jokes, gags and short skits that were a form of burlesque comedy borrowed from vaudeville. Many vaudeville stars found jobs in this new entertainment medium, and eventually radio, coupled with motion pictures, led to the death of vaudeville.

Situation Comedy. After a few years, radio comedy shows had evolved into a new form of comedy—situation comedy (sitcom). Early radio sitcoms were originally 15 minutes long and ran five nights a week. Episodes were in serial form, with the aver-

A couple of microphones, some sound effects, and a handful of actors and actresses set the stage for a wide variety of entertainment on radio during its "Golden Age." *(The Bettmann Archive)*

age plot or story line lasting for most of the week. This format was later changed to the 30-minute, once-a-week, self-contained situation comedy, as we now have on television.

The first successful situation comedy, which started in the 15-minute format and then converted to 30 minutes, debuted in 1928 as *Sam and Henry*; it later changed its name to *The Amos 'n' Andy Show*. It soon became the nation's most popular radio program—so popular, in fact, that movie theaters stopped their shows and turned on the radio when it was "Amos 'n' Andy time."

The stars of this series, Freeman Gosden and Charles Correll (both white men), played four to five characters each, all black men (it was common for one radio actor or actress to play more than one part on the same show). Although not as racist as D. W. Griffith's *Birth of a Nation*, the show did perpetuate the negative stereotypes of black people that were common at the time.

Other popular situation comedy shows were Fred Allen and his *Allen's Alley*, which featured conversations between Allen and a cross-section of ethnic Americans, and *The Jack Benny Show*, which focused on Benny being a very stingy man. A number of other shows featured husband-and-wife teams where one spouse would handle the straight lines and the other would provide the comedy by being a dimwit. Popular among these shows were the *Burns and Allen Show* and *Fibber McGee and Molly*.

Many of these early radio entertainers had started their show-business careers in vaudeville. Edgar Bergen and his wooden dummy Charlie McCarthy, Eddie Cantor, Don Ameche, Nelson Eddy, Bing Crosby and Bob Hope were just a few of the entertainers who became well known as members of the family. Fictional heroes such as the Lone Ranger, the Green Hornet and the Shadow added suspense to the lives of

millions. Good radio drama, which required the audience to use its powers of imagination to visualize what was happening, was provided by such weekly shows as *Lux
Radio Theater* and the *Mercury Theater on the Air.*

The Soap Opera. Radio introduced another entertainment genre that is still with
us today—the soap opera. Radio soap operas (named after the early sponsors of the
shows, which were mostly soap companies) were similar to the daytime soaps on television today—with a couple of exceptions. First, radio soaps were only 15 minutes
long and their characters had "romances" (such as *The Romance of Helen Trent*)
rather than affairs. Today's TV soap opera characters also tend to be younger and
sexier than their radio counterparts.

Early radio soap operas, particularly during the Depression, provided listeners with
an escape from their troubles; they were often comforted to find that the radio characters had worse problems than their own. Up to 80 soap operas a day were broadcast
during radio's golden years (1930s–40s). Although many made the transition to television, only one—*The Guiding Light*—was still on the air in the late 1980s. Television, of course, has introduced new, faster-paced soap operas tailored for prime-time,
such as *Dallas, Dynasty, Knots Landing* and *Falcon Crest.*

A Mobile and Credible Medium. Radio has always been a mobile form of entertainment. The Great Depression forced many Americans to leave their homes in
search of jobs, but their favorite programs were always waiting for them when they
reached their destinations. And now that the transistor has made radios portable by
eliminating the need for bulky vacuum tubes, people can take radios with them anywhere. Sony "Walkmans" and other portable radios can be seen today as constant
companions for sunbathers, joggers, bicyclists and other people on the go.

Radio's credibility as a news medium also affected the culture. As radio news bureaus developed in the 1930s, regular programs were frequently interrupted for special
news bulletins. An ear-witness account in 1937 of the fiery crash of the German diri-
gible *Hindenburg*, which killed 36 people in New Jersey, helped establish radio's credibility. As more and more people came to depend on radio to take their ears to the
scenes of major news events, the stage was set for one of the most famous hoaxes ever
played on the American public.

On the eve of Halloween in 1938, a 23-year-old radio producer and actor, Orson
Welles, broadcast his rendition of H. G. Wells's novel *War of the Worlds* on the
Mercury Theater on the Air.

All week the cast had been struggling to adapt the story to radio and was finding it
difficult to make the drama believable. So Welles decided to present the story as an
interruption of a regular music broadcast, with news reporters breathlessly cutting in
to describe the landing of creatures from Mars.

Although the broadcast included four announcements that the attack was just a
dramatization, many people were listening to the Edgar Bergen and Charlie
McCarthy show on another network when *War of the Worlds* started. During the
first commercial on the McCarthy program, many people turned the dial to see what
else was on. They tuned in to an announcer describing a strange creature climbing
out of a vessel in Grovers Mill, New Jersey. Then they heard the announcer being

On Halloween eve in 1938, 23-year-old Orson Welles panicked the
nation with his radio adaptation of H. G. Wells's *War of the Worlds.*
(Culver Pictures)

annihilated by the creature's ray gun. National panic set in, as people telephoned
friends and relatives to warn them of the impending disaster.

By the end of the hour-long broadcast, people had attempted suicide, jammed long-
distance telephone lines and caused national pandemonium. Military personnel were
called back to their bases. In Concrete, Washington, a power failure during the broadcast caused a traffic jam, as most of the town's residents fled to their automobiles to
escape the invading Martians.

To understand how so many people could be fooled by a radio drama, one must
remember that times were tense. The nation was in its eighth year of economic
depression, Hitler had taken over Czechoslovakia and world war was imminent. And
radio was a new and believable news medium. Psychologists and sociologists spent
years afterward studying Welles's national panic. In the meantime, the FCC quickly
stepped in and banned fictional news bulletins from the airwaves.

RADIO LOSES ITS NICHE

Radio prospered during World War II and the years right after the war, but soon the
cloud of television began to cast its shadow over the medium.

The radio networks were turning their attention to TV, and numerous station owners were applying for TV licenses. Many people saw television as an improvement on
radio, since it provided pictures as well as sound.

The CBS Raid. Television's breakthrough year was 1948, when radio network advertising revenue reached an all-time high of $210 million. This was also the year that CBS made its famous raid on NBC radio personalities, signing such stars as Jack Benny, Amos 'n' Andy, Burns and Allen, Edgar Bergen and Bing Crosby to CBS television contracts.

According to broadcast historian Erik Barnouw, CBS's coup was made possible by the American income-tax laws. CBS convinced these radio stars that they could reduce their taxes by "selling" their shows to CBS, since money from the sales would be taxed at the lower capital gains rate. CBS succeeded in buying all of NBC's highly rated Sunday night entertainers and gained control of important talent for the new television age.[2]

NBC's Recovery Efforts. NBC responded by signing for its TV network the popular vaudeville and nightclub comedian Milton Berle. To ensure that he wouldn't be stolen away, they offered him a 33-year contract. It seemed like a wise investment as Berle became "Mr. Television" and gave NBC several years of high ratings. He used many of his vaudeville and burlesque routines on television, such as dressing in outlandish costumes (many times in drag or in gorilla suits), and he featured lots of slapstick. However, TV shows proved not to have the staying power of their radio predecessors. After eight years people began to tire of Berle, ratings declined and the show was taken off the air. Milton Berle was forced to retire—on full salary for another 25 years.

SPECIALIZATION GIVES RADIO A NEW NICHE

As the networks focused their attention on television, there was a steady decline in radio ratings and earnings. However, radio did not die, as some had predicted. Television had stolen radio's programming format and left it with a choice—change or die. It chose the former. After a period of transition it found its new niche in the specialization stage of the EPS cycle.

Music and News. Gradually radio eliminated its programming of ballroom music, quiz shows, soap operas, sitcoms, dramas and action/adventure shows and replaced them with a basic format of music and news. Network affiliate stations, which had formerly all sounded alike, now took on their own identities. One station in an area might play Top 40 music, while others would feature rhythm-and-blues, country-and-western, jazz, or classical music. Born with this new era of radio was the disc jockey—an announcer who developed a following for his or her on-the-air personality and choices of music.

The development of the disc jockey era was not without controversy, however. In 1959 the radio industry was rocked by the "payola scandal." A number of disc jockeys, including Alan Freed, the man who coined the term *rock-'n'-roll,* were charged with taking money and gifts from the recording industry to plug certain records. Many disc jockeys lost their jobs, and stations now hired program directors to select the music that would be played on the air. Radio-station employees must still sign a form acknowledging awareness of the FCC payola rules and promising to report to management any record company gift worth more than $25.

The new era of specialization of radio and its popular music formats coincided with the development of rock-'n'-roll as the most successful form of popular music. Ever since the 1950s, the success of radio and popular recordings have been dependent on one another.

Types of Music. Some of the most common music formats on radio today are Contemporary Hit Radio (formerly called Top 40), Album-Oriented Rock, Middle of the Road (MOR), Adult Contemporary, Country-and-Western, Beautiful Music, Classical, Big Band, Ethnic Music, Jazz and New Music (featuring the sounds of new wave and punk).

All-News and All-Talk. Not all radio stations feature music, however. All-news stations broadcast a complete news show every 20 minutes or so—20 minutes is the average driving time for an all-news listener.

All-talk shows feature a host with guests and/or telephone call-ins. Topics for the call-in shows range from personal and sexual problems to politics; popular hosts are psychologist Dr. Toni Grant, sex therapist Dr. Ruth Westheimer and political jour-

Mutual Broadcasting's Larry King, perhaps the most successful radio talk-show host. *(Mutual Broadcasting Systems)*

Radio has found an important niche in American popular culture, offering constant companionship for all ages. *(Alan Carey/The Image Works)*

nalist Larry King. The call-in format has become very popular in our culture, as it gives listeners a chance to get advice for personal problems or to "sound off."

Sports. Radio still plays a major role in broadcasting sports events, despite television's inroads in this field. Credit for this must be given to radio's mobility. Radio can be taken to work, on picnics and so forth. Some people even take their radios to the

Table 8.1.
Radio Station Formats

1. Adult Contemporary	15. Other Foreign Languages
2. Agricultural and Farm	16. Jazz
3. American Indian	17. Middle-of-the-Road
4. Beautiful Music	18. All News
5. Big Band	19. Other
6. Black	20. Polish
7. Bluegrass	21. Progressive
8. Christian	22. Religious
9. Classical	23. Spanish
10. Country-and-Western	24. Talk
11. Educational	25. Top 40
12. French	26. Urban Contemporary
13. Golden Oldies	27. Variety
14. Greek	

SOURCE: *Broadcasting Cablecasting Yearbook 1987* (Washington, D.C.: Broadcasting Publications, 1987).

sporting event, to give themselves an opportunity to "hear" as well as "see" the activities. In addition, the advent of pay-TV and cable sports networks with exclusive contracts has limited many people's access to televised sporting events.

Programming Potpourri. According to *Broadcasting Cablecasting Yearbook 1987*, radio stations are now categorized under no less than 27 programming formats (see Table 8.1). The advantages of this new formula radio are many. Not only do radio stations now focus on specialized listening needs, but they can deliver well-defined audiences to advertisers.

Recently TV has mounted a new challenge to radio, as TV enters the specialization stage. Cable channels such as MTV and VH-1 are competing with contemporary hit radio stations by showing music videos, while other channels have begun to feature talk shows and radio personalities such as Dr. Ruth.

TECHNOLOGY AND SPECIALIZATION

A number of technological improvements have also helped radio to find its new niche in our popular culture.

FM Radio. Radio reception quality was enhanced by the development of FM (frequency modulation) broadcasting. FM operates on a higher frequency and sends its signals in a straight line. Thus it avoids the atmospheric distortion that is common in AM (amplitude modulation) broadcasting, which bounces its signals off the ionosphere. FM has less static and higher quality and was the first to broadcast in stereo.

Although FM was introduced before World War II, it did not become a successful alternative to AM broadcasting at first. However, in the 1960s the FCC made several

Radio and rock-'n'-roll have been a profitable combination since the 1950s. (*Courtesy of K-Rock, NYC*)

decisions that assisted the development of FM radio. One was a freeze on the allocation of new AM licenses, leaving FM as the only avenue for new radio stations. The second was an FCC ruling that allowed FM to broadcast in stereo. The third was the 1967 "nonduplication rule," which required AM–FM combination stations to limit the duplication of their programming on both frequencies. (This regulation was abandoned in the mid-1980s.) In 1945 only 50 FM stations were on the air. In 1960 there were 688. By the late 1980s there were more than 5,000 FM stations reaching 95 percent of American households.[3]

In the late 1980s some AM stations were attempting to fight back against the growing popularity of FM radio by experimenting with AM stereo broadcasting.

The future of radio continues to look bright. Nearly 10,000 AM and FM stations are on the air serving the American popular culture[4] and advertising revenue generates nearly $7 billion annually.[5]

PUBLIC RADIO

Another avenue for specialization—primarily for elite rather than mass cultural tastes—is provided by noncommercial educational radio stations.

Since 1970 National Public Radio (NPR) has been the major network servicing this market. NPR receives its funding through the Corporation for Public Broadcasting, which was established by the Public Broadcasting Act of 1967. The sources of CPB's funding are the federal government, private donations and station membership fees. In the 1980s, however, the Reagan Administration adopted a policy that called for a 50 percent reduction in federal funds by 1990.

NPR provides about 50 hours of programming each week for some 250 affiliates. Two of its news programs, "All Things Considered" and "Morning Edition," are highly regarded. In 1979 NPR became the first radio network to use satellites to transmit its programming.

There are also smaller regional networks that distribute educational programming. The best known of these is Minnesota Public Radio.

SUMMARY

Although radio is a twentieth-century mass-communication medium, its beginnings date to the nineteenth century, when scientists were attempting to discover ways to convert sound waves into electrical energy. Samuel Morse's invention of the telegraph, Alexander Graham Bell's discovery of the telephone, Guglielmo Marconi's wireless telegraphy and Lee De Forest's amplifier vacuum tube all contributed to the development of radio.

Radio became a mass-communication medium in the 1920s, when stations started broadcasting music and news bulletins. Companies such as Westinghouse, General Electric, RCA and AT&T played major roles in converting radio from a maritime communication system to a mass medium. They did so to sell more radio receivers.

The development of the networks in the late 1920s launched radio into its golden age as a news and entertainment medium. American life styles were drastically changed as people were able to hear major news events live from the scene and enjoy the very finest entertainment free in their homes.

During the Great Depression, many people escaped their troubles by listening to radio. They were also able to take their entertainment with them when they migrated to find new jobs in distant places.

After television adopted radio's programming in the 1950s, radio entered the specialization stage. Stations learned to cater to distinct segments of the listening audience and adopted music and news as the basis of their programming. The development of FM radio also enhanced the medium. Since 1970 National Public Radio has been providing programming for elite cultural tastes.

Radio continues to have a strong impact on our culture, with nearly everyone owning radios and young people spending more time with radio than any other mass medium. The future of radio remains bright.

NOTES

1. Quoted in Archer Gleason, *History of Radio to 1926* (New York: American Historical Society, 1938), p. 85.

2. Erik Barnouw, *The Golden Web: A History of Broadcasting in the United States* (New York: Oxford University Press, 1968), p. 245.

3. *Broadcasting Cablecasting Yearbook 1986* (Washington, D.C.: Broadcasting Publications, 1986), p. H-55.

4. Ibid.

5. *U.S. Industrial Outlook 1988* (Washington, D.C.: U.S. Government Printing Office, 1988), p. 63-3.

ADDITIONAL READING

Aitken, H. G. *Syntony and Spark—The Origins of Radio.* New York: Wiley, 1976.

Allen, Robert C. *Speaking of Soap Operas.* Chapel Hill: University of North Carolina Press, 1985.

Archer, Gleason L. *History of Radio to 1926.* New York: American Historical Society, 1938.

Baker, W. J. *A History of the Marconi Company.* New York: St. Martin's, 1971.

Barnouw, Erik. *A Tower of Babel.* New York: Oxford University Press, 1966.

———. *The Image Empire.* New York: Oxford University Press, 1970.

Brooks, John. *Telephone: The First Hundred Years.* New York: Harper & Row, 1976.

Campbell, Robert. *The Golden Years of Broadcasting: A Celebration of the First 50 Years of Radio and Television on NBC.* New York: Scribner's, 1976.

Davis, Stephen. *The Law of Radio.* New York: McGraw-Hill, 1927.

Dunning, John. *Tune in Yesterday: The Ultimate Encyclopedia of Old-Time Radio, 1925–1976.* Englewood Cliffs, N.J.: Prentice-Hall, 1976.

Fang, Irving E. *Those Radio Commentators!* Ames: Iowa State University Press, 1977.

Friendly, Fred. *Due to Circumstances Beyond Our Control.* New York: Random House, 1978.

Head, Sydney W. *Broadcasting in America: A Survey of Television and Radio;* 3rd ed. Boston: Houghton Mifflin, 1976.

Hettinger, Herman S. *A Decade of Radio Advertising.* Chicago: University of Chicago Press, 1933.

Post, Steve. *Playing in the FM Band.* New York: Viking, 1974.

Sarnoff, David. *Looking Ahead: The Papers of David Sarnoff.* New York: McGraw-Hill, 1968.

Schubert, Paul. *The Electric Word: The Rise of Radio.* New York: Macmillan, 1928.

Settel, Irving. *A Pictorial History of Radio,* 2nd ed. New York: Grosset & Dunlap, 1967.

Sterling, Christopher H., and Kittross, John M. *Stay Tuned: A Concise History of American Broadcasting.* Belmont, Calif.: Wadsworth, 1978.

Chapter 9

Television:
From Soaps to Satellites

Children will watch anything,
and when a broadcaster uses
crime and violence and other
shoddy devices to monopolize a
child's attention it's worse
than taking candy from a baby.
It is taking precious time from
the process of growing up.
—*Newton Minow, former chairman,*
Federal Communications Commission

The ABC television network paid $225 million for the rights to televise the 1984 Summer Olympics and $309 million for the rights to the Calgary Winter Olympics in 1988. In addition to these staggering amounts, the network spent $100 million to produce the coverage for each event. Why would a sports event be worth so much money?

The answer lies in *audiences* and *advertisers*. The name of the game in American TV broadcasting since its inception has been "to package audiences for advertisers." Over 90 percent of America's households watched some part of the 1984 Olympics, and ABC had hoped for a repeat performance in 1988 (the ratings were lower in 1988, however). The promise of delivering large audiences to advertisers enables the networks to charge substantial sums for commercial time. In 1984 the Olympics also delivered large audiences for the network's preview of its fall line-up of prime-time programming.* This helped ABC to a "top rated" beginning for the fall 1984 season. During the 1988 Olympics, ABC used the same tactic to draw attention to its innovative programs for the yuppie audience, *The Wonder Years* and *thirtysomething*.

American television has been a commercially successful mass-communication medium during the latter half of the twentieth century. It started out in the 1940s as a novelty—radio with pictures—and by the 1960s had become this nation's most important entertainment medium. It also had become a powerful and controversial influence on our popular culture, one that not only held up a mirror to society but also magnified the forces of change within that society. Some have credited TV with raising the educational level of our young, while others blame it for destroying family life and individuality. Whatever its impact has been, one thing is certain—television is big business (nearly $23 billion a year) and it has played a major role in changing our popular culture.

HOW IT BEGAN

Early Experimentation. The story of electronic television begins in 1923, when Vladimir Zworykin, a Russian immigrant working for Westinghouse Corporation, developed the iconoscope, which was the first practical electronic tube for a television camera. Zworykin later developed the kinescope, or picture tube.

In 1927 Philo Farnsworth applied for a patent on an electronic television system, and by 1928 General Electric was experimenting with telecasting. NBC followed with experimental telecasting in 1930, and by 1939 its station in New York was offering regularly scheduled programs. In Great Britain the BBC began regular television broadcasting in 1936. However, it wasn't until the 1939 New York World's Fair that a large number of Americans saw television demonstrated for the first time.

Early TV Stations. The FCC authorized commercial television broadcasting in 1941. However, the nation's entry into World War II in December of that year put TV's development on hold, since all electronic research and development was diverted to the war effort. However, six stations remained on the air during the war: two in New York City and one each in Schenectady, N.Y., Philadelphia, Chicago and San Francisco.

Early Programming. Before 1948 only a small elite of Americans could afford this expensive novelty. In 1946 there were approximately 7,000 television sets in American households. Programming was limited, but it included sporting events, such as football, baseball, tennis, boxing, wrestling and hockey; news; studio productions of plays; dance recitals; musical shows; and old movies.

In the fall of 1947 TV began to generate interest in the popular culture. An estimated 3.5 million people watched the World Series on television that year, most of them in neighborhood taverns. Now they wanted TV sets in their own homes.

*Prime time is 8–11 P.M. on both coasts, 7–10 P.M. in the Midwest and mountain states.

Elitist	Popular	Specialized		CULTURAL HISTORY OF TELEVISION
■			1923	Vladimir Zworykin, working for Westinghouse, develops a television camera tube.
■			1927	Philo Farnsworth applies for electronic television patents.
■			1936	Great Britain is the first country to begin regular television broadcasting.
■			1939	Large numbers of Americans see television for the first time at New York's World Fair.
■			1941	FCC authorizes commercial television broadcasting in the United States.
■			1946	Color television demonstrated by CBS and NBC.
■	■		1948	Television's breakthrough year; CBS and NBC begin offering regular news and entertainment on TV.
	■		1951	Microwave provides coast-to-coast television broadcasts.
	■		1952	Edward R. Murrow changes radio's popular *Hear It Now* to *See It Now*.
	■		1952	FCC lifts the freeze on new stations that it had imposed in 1948.
	■		1954	Army–McCarthy hearings are televised; Murrow risks career to challenge McCarthy on *See it Now*.
	■		1956	*Playhouse 90* brings high-quality live drama to television.
	■		1956	Television begins extensive coverage of presidential elections.
	■		1959	Westerns dominate TV entertainment.
	■		1963	Television's coverage of Kennedy assassination demonstrates its power to unite nation in one emotion.
	■		1967	Congress establishes Corporation for Public Broadcasting to fund educational and cultural programs.
	■		1968	Riots outside Democratic convention televised; TV blamed for nation's unrest.
	■		1969	World watches man's landing on the moon live on television.
	■		1971	*All in the Family* brings Archie Bunker and controversial issues to TV comedy.
	■		1973–74	Watergate hearings and impeachment proceedings televised; Nixon resigns.
	■		1977	*Roots* becomes most popular mini-series; this program format becomes an effective way to increase ratings.
	■		1978	*Dallas* revives popularity of evening soap operas.
		■	1980s	Cable television and VCRs change American viewing habits; network popularity begins to decline.
		■	1982	Home Shopping Network debuts—advertising becomes programming.
	■		1987	Iran-Contra hearings televised; Oliver North temporarily becomes a folk hero.
		■	1988	ABC preempts two weeks of prime-time programming to televise the Calgary Winter Olympics.

Breakthrough Year. Television's breakthrough year was 1948, the year the CBS and NBC radio networks turned their attention toward it. Since television was offering radio programming with the added novelty of pictures, interest in network radio began declining and so did radio network advertising revenues. In this year CBS made its famous raid on NBC's radio stars, signing them for the new CBS television network; Milton Berle went on television for NBC, becoming "Mr. Television"; and New York newspaperman Ed Sullivan began his long-running variety show, *Toast of the Town*, on CBS (see p. 189).

In the fall of 1948 the FCC, recognizing that this new medium was going to grow rapidly, placed a freeze on TV-station authorizations, restricting the number to 124 (although only 108 stations actually got on the air). During the freeze, which lasted until 1952, the FCC developed a comprehensive plan to allocate television frequencies to all parts of the United States. The plan authorized 2,000 channels in 1,300 communities. The FCC also worked on a proposal to standardize color television systems and allocate educational television frequencies.

Despite the freeze, television expanded as a mass medium in 1948 to 1952. A microwave relay system was developed that allowed for the first coast-to-coast network broadcasts in 1951. The number of TV sets in American homes rose from 172,000 to 15 million during this period.

Lifting the Freeze. After the freeze was lifted, television expanded even more rapidly. NBC and CBS were far along in their efforts to shift their interests from radio to television. A third network—DuMont—was struggling to compete. ABC merged with Paramount Theaters and followed the other three networks into television. Mutual remained a radio-only network. DuMont was unable to compete with the three former radio networks and went out of business in 1955. However, DuMont earned its place in television history by producing *The Honeymooners*, with Jackie Gleason, and using kinescopes to preserve early television on motion-picture film. Thirty-some years later, Americans were enjoying *The Honeymooners* in syndicated reruns.

EVOLUTION OF TELEVISION ENTERTAINMENT

TV entertainment started out as nothing more than a novelty. The shows consisted of pointing a camera at some action and letting it be transmitted. The early programs included variety shows, puppet-comedy shows, stand-up comedians, domestic comedies and game shows. Many of these latter programs were carbon copies of radio shows, but with pictures. People watching early television were dazzled to be able to see action and watch their longtime radio stars present familiar sitcoms in their living rooms.

Early Entertainers. Some of the leading entertainers during the beginning years of television were Milton Berle, Ed Sullivan, the puppets Cecil the Seasick Sea Serpent and Howdy Doody, Sid Caesar, Imogene Coca, Lucille Ball, Art Carney, Jackie Gleason, Art Linkletter, Arthur Godfrey, Jack Benny, Amos 'n' Andy, ventriloquist Edgar Bergen and his dummy Charlie McCarthy, Bing Crosby, Red Skelton and the witty comedy team of George Burns and Gracie Allen.

Most of these entertainers had started their careers in vaudeville and made the transition to radio. Now they were transmitting re-creations of the early days of vaudeville into the living rooms of the United States. The content of popular cultural entertainment had not changed much since the nineteenth century. Only the delivery system had changed.

Live Drama. Some of the best dramas ever shown on television were the plays broadcast live from New York studios in the 1950s. The major Hollywood studios, fearing competition from the new medium, refused to allow their facilities to be used to produce television programs. Two of the best-known live dramas of this "golden age" of television were Rod Serling's *Requiem for a Heavyweight* (see Box 9.1) and *Days of Wine and Roses* starring Cliff Robertson and Piper Laurie. These high-quality dramas focused on character development and analysis, rather than on car chases and elaborate scenery.

Quiz Show Scandal. Quiz shows, which had been popular on radio, offered greater rewards when transferred to television. Radio's *$64 Question* became TV's *$64,000 Question*, for example. The popularity of these shows grew as people could vicariously share in the delight of winning big money by knowing the right answers to questions.

In 1959 television was rocked by its first major scandal when it was revealed that certain quiz-show contestants had been given the questions prior to the programs. This was done to ensure that the most popular contestants would win and return the next week. Until this time, TV programs had been produced by advertising agencies and the shows' sponsors. As a result of the scandal, the FCC required quiz shows to issue disclosures whenever assistance was given to contestants and the networks were forced to take over production of the programs to ensure compliance with ethical standards.

The Westerns. By the late 1950s TV entertainment had moved from live quiz and variety shows, domestic comedies and drama to prerecorded dramatic series. The first genre to develop was the Western, which had long been popular in movies and on radio. Such shows as *Gunsmoke* and *Have Gun, Will Travel*, which had been popular on radio, *Wyatt Earp*, *Colt 45*, *The Rifleman* and *The Virginian* occupied the TV screen during prime time. By 1959 there were 30 Westerns on prime time each week.

Also in 1959 *Bonanza* began airing on NBC at 7:30 on Saturday evenings to sell color television sets for its parent company, RCA. It was the only color show on TV, and its time slot was important because department stores were open at that time and color sets could be demonstrated by showing *Bonanza*.

Bonanza transmitted the American myth that the rugged rural life of the "good old days" was a glamorous and comfortable time. The program revolved around three

BOX 9.1

REQUIEM FOR A HEAVYWEIGHT

"I was almost heavyweight champion of the world," a battered and broken Mountain McClintock emotionally told the young woman at the employment agency. The powerful scene was a part of a 90-minute drama that launched the first episode of *Playhouse 90*, which would become one of the most popular drama series to ever be aired on television.

This historic live presentation of Rod Serling's *Requiem for a Heavyweight*, winner of the 1957 Emmy for best television writing, went on the air for CBS on October 12, 1956.

It was television's first 90-minute drama. It was live—being acted, produced and transmitted coast-to-coast at the very moment people were seeing it in their homes. Included among the many firsts attributed to this production was the debut of well-known stage comedian Ed Wynn in a serious dramatic role. In addition to Wynn as Army, the boxer's handler, was his son Keenan Wynn, who played Maish, the boxer's manager, and Jack Palance as Harlan "Mountain" McClintock. Kim Hunter played the part of Grace Carney, the young woman from the employment agency who saw beyond Mountain's ugly battered face to the tender man underneath.

The production, which was both tender and forceful, showed how live television drama focusing on character development could make a powerful statement. It told the story of a prizefighter, once ranked in fifth place as a heavyweight contender, who was realizing that his fighting career was over. The ring doctor had declared him finished, pointing out that a few more punches to the eye would blind, if not kill, him. What does a man who has done nothing but box for 14 years do with himself? Adding to the intrigue was the fact that Maish owed several thousand dollars to gangsters because he had bet that Mountain would not survive three rounds in his last fight. Mountain, who was proud of the fact that he had never taken a dive in 111 fights, stood in the ring and took the worst beating of his life for seven rounds.

Maish's efforts to get Mountain to dress up in a Mountaineer's costume and fake a fight as a wrestler failed as the proud ex-boxer emotionally told his manager/best friend, "I'm not a clown."

Playhouse 90 was one of the most successful live drama programs of the 1950s. Others that gave audiences oustanding live drama included *Goodyear Playhouse*, *Kraft Theater* and *Studio One*. The period is now referred to as the "golden age" of television.

grown sons, at least two of them in their 30s, still at home and subject to the authority of their father. Some sociologists felt that the show appealed to people who missed the parental authority and support they had given up to leave home and marry.[1] Whatever the reason, *Bonanza* was one of the most popular shows on the air for 15 years.

Urban Westerns. Other genres that became popular during this period were doctor, police, detective and courtroom shows, in which—as in the Westerns—good always prevailed over evil. These adventure stories were sometimes referred to as "urban Westerns" because the moral themes were the same as in the Westerns; only the location and time period were changed. Some of the urban Westerns were *Dragnet, Highway Patrol, Racket Squad, The Lineup, Perry Mason* and *The Defenders*. A few years later came *The Man from U.N.C.L.E.* and *Mission Impossible*, series dealing with international intrigue and spy chasing, as the "good guys" pursued the forces of evil around the world.

Variety Shows. Variety shows, hosted by such performers as Carol Burnett, Bob Hope and Sonny and Cher, provided cheerful escape during the 1960s. However, by the late 1960s one variety show—*The Smothers Brothers*—was introducing realism and social commentary into evening entertainment. In keeping with the cultural unrest and growing displeasure with the Vietnam war that was sweeping the country, the show ridiculed the war and other social ills and soon was canceled by CBS in a dispute over censorship. Audiences, the network executives felt, did not want controversy and realism mixed with their entertainment. (The show returned to television 20 years later, in 1988.)

Another variety show that debuted in 1968, *Rowan and Martin's Laugh-In*, became popular with younger audiences by dealing with sexual and political themes, topics that reflected the new openness that had swept the nation during the 1960s. Its hosts, Dan Rowan and Dick Martin, were able to touch on these topics without irritating network executives the way the Smothers Brothers did. This type of programming survived in the late 1980s on such shows as *Saturday Night Live* and *Late Night with David Letterman*. In the meantime, the more traditional variety shows had all but disappeared by the mid-1970s, except for an occasional special.

Sitcoms. From the beginning the most popular of all the TV entertainment genres has been the situation comedy. Other forms of television entertainment—such as the Westerns and variety shows—have come and gone, but the sitcoms have endured.

In an effort to appeal to middle-class America, early TV continued to produce the family sitcoms that had been popular on radio. The settings were always the same— a happy, white, middle-class home with humorous but bland family problems to cope with and solve by the end of each 30-minute show. *Father Knows Best, Make Room for Daddy, Leave It to Beaver, I Love Lucy, The Adventures of Ozzie and Harriet* and *My Three Sons* were a few of the more popular shows in this category. There were also sitcoms like *Bewitched, I Dream of Jeannie* and *The Munsters*, which featured supernatural characters trying to act like ordinary middle-class folks.

As the American culture passed through the troubled 1960s and entered the 1970s, TV sitcoms reflected changing cultural attitudes. One of the most innovative departures was *All in the Family*, a new kind of sitcom produced by Norman Lear, which debuted on January 12, 1971. For the first time, a TV sitcom was dealing with—and joking about—the culture's social issues: sex, politics and racial prejudice, issues that theretofore had been taboo on television. The show starred Carroll O'Connor as Archie Bunker, who was characterized as a classic bigot. Archie unexpectedly became a folk hero in American popular culture. Many people apparently did not recognize the satire in the program and felt Archie's bigotry reflected their own latent or not-so-latent feelings.

The show was so successful that it generated a number of spinoffs. Archie's wife, Edith, had a cousin named Maude, who eventually got a show of her own, as did Maude's maid, Florida, and the Bunker's black next-door neighbors, the Jeffersons. *All in the Family* and its spinoffs opened up the sitcom format to allow for biting social commentary in a humorous framework.

The Mini-series. In the mid-1970s the networks tried to break down traditional viewing habits by introducing a new format, the mini-series. The idea was to get people hooked on the series in the first episode—usually broadcast on Sunday night—so they would tune in again the next several evenings. Mini-series have proven very popular and they are often scheduled during "sweep periods," when TV stations are monitored to determine audience sizes. (Sweeps are usually conducted three times a year—November, February and May—and are used to set advertising rates. High ratings means higher ad rates for the local stations and networks.)

The mini-series concept actually came from public broadcasting, which began showing BBC-produced serials such as *The Forsyte Saga* in 1969 and *Upstairs Downstairs*. In 1975 CBS attempted to emulate PBS's successful *Upstairs Downstairs* with a short-lived American version called *Beacon Hill.* This led ABC to introduce a 12-hour version of Irwin Shaw's novel *Rich Man, Poor Man* in 1976.

The following season ABC introduced *Roots,* a mini-series based on Alex Haley's book of the same name, which kept millions of viewers glued to the TV set for eight nights. The series, which traced Haley's ancestors from Africa through American slavery and into the twentieth century, set ratings records and helped keep Haley's book at the top of the best-seller lists for months (see Box 9.2). Part of the popularity of *Roots* was its powerful portrayal of one of the darker aspects of American history.

TV Sports. Sports, which has played an important role in providing leisure enjoyment for the masses since the nineteenth century, has become an important part of television programming. The popularity of electronically mediated athletics grew rapidly after the development in the 1960s of such new technology as instant-replay television recorders. Television permanently took over as the "electronic ballpark" (see Chapter 2).

Last-place network ABC led the way with its innovative *Wide World of Sports,* which cut between live, taped and filmed sports events, some of which had taken place days before in various places around the world. In 1970 ABC paid $9 million for the rights to *Monday Night Football.* Eventually ABC found itself number one in the ratings thanks to its expanded sports coverage and a new lineup of popular sitcoms like *Happy Days* and *Three's Company.*

Daytime TV. Despite the fact that prime-time television has the largest audience and highest advertising rates, over the years daytime TV has been the biggest money-maker. Soap operas and game shows have always been extremely popular and are much cheaper to produce, even though the game shows give away money and prizes.

BOX 9.2

FRED SILVERMAN: TV'S TARNISHED "GOLDEN BOY"

Credit for breaking television ratings records with the successful mini-series *Roots* goes to television's "Golden Boy" Fred Silverman, whose influence on all three major networks has been unparalleled.

Silverman became the chief of programming for CBS in 1970. He was instrumental in leading the network through some major programming overhauls that gave it a wider audience age range and made it number one in the ratings. Some of his daring accomplishments included putting the controversial sitcom *All in the Family* on the air in 1971.

Last-place network ABC was so impressed with Silverman's accomplishments that it lured him away in 1975 with a higher salary and the title of vice president in charge of programming. Under Silverman's leadership, ABC quickly moved to first place in the ratings, thanks in part to the popularity of *Roots*. The successful mini-series broke audience viewing habits by getting viewers hooked on the series during the first episode and keeping them tuned to ABC each succeeding night while the network promoted its own line of regular prime-time programming during commercial breaks.

Silverman's successes at ABC enticed the now-last-place NBC to offer him the presidency of the network in 1978. Although his duties were broader—head of the entire network—NBC's intentions were clear. It wanted Silverman to lead the network into the number-one ratings spot. Things were different this time around, however. Silverman found himself competing with some very effective programming strategies that he had left behind at both CBS and ABC. After three years of unsuccessful efforts to boost NBC's ratings, in 1981 the network fired Silverman. Several years later under his successor, Grant Tinker, and with the help of some programs that Silverman had been instrumental in developing while president, like *Hill Street Blues*, NBC did take over the number-one spot in network ratings.

What is he doing today? Silverman is working as an independent producer of TV programs. After several failures with *Thicke of the Night* and *We Got It Made,* he was producing successful shows like *Perry Mason Returns* and *Matlock.* His talent was still contributing to the television industry, but the pressures to produce or else had been significantly reduced.

As we have seen, soap operas have been an important part of the American culture since the early days of radio. Today they appeal to a wide range of viewers, from homemakers to business executives (see Box 9.3).

In the 1980s, as our culture became more tolerant of open media discussions of such controversial topics as AIDS, child molestation, gay rights, spouse abuse, alcoholism and drug abuse, the popularity of daytime talk shows increased. Following the success of Phil Donahue, others like Oprah Winfrey and Geraldo Rivera were using this format to launch talk shows of their own.

Prime-time Soaps. In 1964, ABC premiered the first prime-time soap opera, *Peyton Place,* based loosely on a steamy best-seller by Grace Metalious. Shown two or

BOX 9.3

THE SOAP OPERAS OF TELEVISION
James R. Wilson

One of my students recently told me that she never schedules any of her classes between 2 and 3 P.M. because she has been hooked on *General Hospital,* a daily television soap opera, ever since she came to this country in 1982.

And she's not alone. By the mid-1980s it was estimated that nearly 35 million people watch at least one soap opera every day, and 56 percent of *all* college students watch at least one per week. Is it any wonder that in college union lounges across the nation students are gathered around the TV sets each day to watch the latest activities of Erica Kane, Jill Abbott or Rachel Cory?

The TV soaps have become extremely popular with college students in recent years, but others have "come out of the closet" and admitted that they watch soaps, including business executives who are joining their workers in the employee lounge during the lunch hour to watch the daytime shows. But most important, these programs remain quite popular with the homemakers of the United States—just as their radio counterparts were from the 1930s to the 1950s. During the depression years the radio soaps provided a form of escape for listeners—they had found a way to listen to stories of people who were having tougher times than they were.

Several radio soaps made the switch from radio to TV in the early days, but only one of these transplants remains on the air today: *The Guiding Light.* The original TV soaps followed the same basic format as their radio predecessors, including the daily length of 15 minutes. The first half-hour soap, *As the World Turns,* made its debut in 1956. One year later *The Edge of Night*—another 30-minute soap—debuted, and TV soap operas were changed forever as sponsors and producers found that it was a lot cheaper to put together one 30-minute program than to hire actors, writers and technical crews for two 15-minute programs.

In 1975 expansion hit the soap operas again as NBC's *Another World* went to 60 minutes daily. In 1979 it expanded to 90 minutes each day. However, this format was unsuccessful because it took so many story lines to fill the time that viewers were becoming confused. The program returned to its 60-minute format in 1980.

Several other soaps expanded to an hour in the 1970s, with two of them making a stop along the way. In 1976 ABC converted two of its half-hour soaps—*General Hospital* and *One Life to Live*—to 45-minute shows running back to back. Two years later they both expanded to their present one-hour format.

It was also in the 1970s that a new soap

three nights a week, it launched the careers of Mia Farrow and Ryan O'Neal and demonstrated yet again the durability and versatility of the genre. Other networks were slow to follow ABC's lead, but in 1978, CBS launched *Dallas* as a weekly serial. For 10 years it and its imitators, *Dynasty, Knots Landing* and *Falcon Crest,* topped the evening ratings by bringing the continuing stories and daytime troubles of TV families to nighttime viewers.

These shows appeal to the average person's interest in the rich and elite, and all seem to revolve around one central theme—that rich families are plagued with turopera was introduced in an attempt to lure younger viewers. The story lines of *The Young and the Restless* were about younger people, and the actors and actresses represented the gods and goddesses who had only been available in movies and high-fashion magazines. The program also established the technique of *extreme* character closeups to get the viewers more deeply involved.

Soap operas, begun as a radio escape in the depression of the 1930s, survived war and radicalism to become not only the most popular form of daytime programming, they have expanded into prime time as well. And

their popularity is overflowing into other media. There are now magazine and newspaper columns designed to keep readers up-to-date on the daily activities of their favorite soap characters. To top it off, a series of books has been published that deal with the original story lines of some of the more popular soaps for fans who weren't born when their favorite shows went on the air. Now those younger members of the audience of 35 million avid soap opera viewers can see how their favorite soaps began. And the way things are going, they may never end.

Soap operas, such as NBC's *Santa Barbara*, provide escapist fare for millions. Increasing tolerance among viewers has allowed the soaps to deal explicitly with highly controversial issues. *(Courtesy of NBC)*

James R. Wilson is an associate professor of radio and television broadcasting at California State University, Fresno.

moil and strife and the American cultural myth that money can't always buy happiness is true. It doesn't matter if your name is Ewing (on *Dallas* and *Knots Landing*), Carrington or Colby (on *Dynasty*), Channing (on *Falcon Crest*), Tyler (on *All My Children*), Quartermaine (on *General Hospital*), Abbott or Chancellor (on *The Young and the Restless*)—if you've got money you've got troubles. It is worth noting that *Dallas* and *Dynasty* were the most popular American TV shows in Canada, Australia, Chile and many western European countries.

BOX 9.4

HILL STREET BLUES: A 1980s TRENDSETTER

On May 12, 1987, the last regular episode of *Hill Street Blues* aired on NBC, ending six years of television trendsetting. When the program debuted on NBC in January 1981, it ranked at the bottom of the ratings. Since the program had been the brainchild of NBC president Fred Silverman, the network decided to keep it on the air for the 1981–82 season—a decision that helped the last-place network start its move to number one in the ratings. Created by the innovative TV producer Steven Bochco, the show won eight Emmys during its next season, the beginning of what became a record-setting 26 Emmys for one series.

Hill Street Blues was different. It developed a new style of programming that would later be copied by such shows as *St. Elsewhere* and *L.A. Law*. The program featured the day-to-day activities of the personnel in a rundown inner-city police station. Its characters were not macho cops but ordinary flawed men and women with problems on and off the job. The show used complex plots that interwove a variety of characters and multiple ongoing story lines. Its production techniques included the use of hand-held cameras that created an effect of actually being in the crowded downtown police precinct rather than being in an audience looking in on the scene.

Hill Street Blues represented a new genre of television programming—one that took bits and pieces from a variety of others. It had action/adventure, traditional drama, a police-detective story line, comedy and the continuing themes of the traditional soap opera. Unlike other action/adventure and police-detective story lines, *Hill Street Blues* minimized the violence and car chase scenes and instead focused on character development, borrowing from still another television genre—the live dramas of the 1950s. It ignored the typical formula patterns of development for entertainment programs and presented its material in a manner reflective of the complexities of the everyday world. It led the way for a new hybrid genre of television entertainment and eventually was replaced by other similar shows.

After it ceased production in 1987, *Hill Street Blues* continued on local stations in syndication.

Hybrid TV. As our culture evolved so did the entertainment genres on television. In the 1980s a new TV format developed that was a combination of a number of others. It borrowed the ongoing story line from soap operas, character development from early-day TV dramas, action/adventure from police and lawyer shows, comedy from sitcoms and fast-paced action from vaudeville and TV variety shows. This genre was pioneered by *Hill Street Blues* and was effective because it reflected the fast pace and ambiguities of twentieth century American culture. Other shows, like *St. Elsewhere, Miami Vice* and *L.A. Law,* were soon utilizing these same techniques as the trend continued its popularity into the late 1980s (see Box 9.4).

Docudramas. Another invention of the 1980s was the docudrama, which portrays a real-life situation in fictional form. While the shows take liberties with the facts to heighten the dramatic effect, the impression left in the viewer's mind is that the televised version is the way it actually happened. Although docudramas bring historical topics into the popular culture through the medium of entertainment, they cause some concern because they often blend truth with fiction.

In the summer of 1986, for example, NBC produced a docudrama about the people behind the planning and building of the Statue of Liberty in 1887. The show, called *Liberty*, ran the following disclaimer: "This story is based on actual events. However, some of the characters and incidents portrayed and the names used herein are fictitious." The producers never specified what was real and what wasn't, and viewers were left with a confusing view of a historical event.

But a docudrama can strive for accuracy and still be entertaining. The 1988 ABC mini-series *Baby M* carefully followed the sequence of events and court records of a famous surrogate motherhood case. Winning high ratings, this docudrama brought a complex social issue into focus for the masses.

As Americans became more concerned about social issues during the 1980s, some made-for-TV movies began providing information on such topics as alcoholism, AIDS, incest, child kidnapping and spouse abuse.

These educationally oriented movies were very helpful in disseminating important social information in the context of leisure entertainment.

Tabloid TV. By 1988 a TV version of the titillating sensationalism of tabloid newspapers had emerged as a new genre of television programming.

Leading the way was Rupert Murdoch, the king of tabloid newspapers in Britain and the United States. Murdoch's Fox Broadcasting Company was using sex, murder and mayhem in its attempt to establish a fourth TV network made up of independent stations (see Box 9.5).

Fox introduced a news magazine show, *A Current Affair*, which featured bloody murder scenes, titillating sex crimes and gore. Another popular Fox show, *America's Most Wanted*, gained invaluable publicity when a number of suspects wanted for crimes (which are re-enacted on the show) were apprehended as a result of the weekly broadcasts.

Fox was not the only one getting into the tabloid TV business. The networks were keen to add real-life crime shows to their line-ups, since they are so cheap and easy to produce. NBC began broadcasting *Unsolved Mysteries* as a weekly series in the fall of 1988, while ABC aired a special by Geraldo Rivera, *Murder: Live from Death Row*, which included actual film footage of the murder of a convenience store customer as well as interviews with several convicted murderers talking about their crimes. (The most celebrated of these was Charles Manson.)

On the *Morton Downey Jr. Show* the controversial talk-show host had a guest re-enact the strangling of a woman in New York's Central Park by her boy friend who claimed that he had accidentally killed her during "rough sex."

Planned to follow these shows were a series featuring actual murder trials, a series on missing children, and more re-enactments of real crimes, some using real-life victims playing themselves.

BOX 9.5

A FOURTH TELEVISION NETWORK IN THE 1990s?

Ever since the DuMont television network went out of business in 1955, American network TV has consisted of the big three—NBC, CBS and ABC. However, in the late 1980s there was a new network challenger: the Fox network.

In the spring and summer of 1987, Fox began introducing prime-time sitcoms in an effort to capture a share of the ratings that had previously been the domain of the big three. The move was timed to take advantage of the fact that at this time of year most network programs were reruns. It was a gamble—but one the controversial media-baron owner of Fox Broadcasting, Rupert Murdoch, considered worthwhile.

After acquiring numerous newspapers in Australia, London and the United States, Murdoch became an American citizen in 1985 so that he could acquire Metromedia, a chain of independent TV stations. (U.S. law prohibited foreign ownership of American TV stations.) He also acquired the 20th Century-Fox movie studio that year. His intent was to put together a fourth television network, linking his Metromedia stations and some independent affiliates into a 105-station network. The Fox movie studios would produce the network's programming.

Coincidentally, the Metromedia stations had been a part of the DuMont television network before it went out of business. DuMont had trouble surviving because the latest entry into TV broadcasting in the 1950s—ABC—had merged with Paramount Theaters to give it a Hollywood link to assist with its programming.

Murdoch's first challenge to major networks came in 1986, when he put comedienne Joan Rivers up against *The Tonight Show Starring Johnny Carson*. Previously Rivers had been a popular fill-in on the Carson show. Although she had been signed to a three-year contract, Rivers was replaced as the regular host less than a year later, after disappointing ratings.

Other Fox shows to challenge the "big three" were *Married ... with Children*, *The Tracey Ullman Show*, *Duel*, *21 Jump Street*, and the tabloid shows *A Current Affair* and *America's Most Wanted*. The new network is also backed by first-run movies from 20th Century-Fox.

Fox was predicting television ratings around 6 percent, compared to the usual 16 or better necessary for the other networks. (A rating is the percentage of 87.4 million television households tuned into a program.) This low projection did not discourage Murdoch because, unlike the big three networks with their billion-dollar overheads, Fox had an overhead of only about 70 salaries.

Although most observers gave the new network little chance for success, Murdoch was prepared to spend nearly $100 million a year for several years on his venture and did not anticipate making a profit until the 1990s.

DEVELOPMENT OF TELEVISION NEWS

Networks began experimenting with news at locally owned stations as early as January 1940, when NBC began airing radio newscaster Lowell Thomas on its New York TV station. CBS's first television news broadcasts began in the spring of 1941. Since early television was unable to broadcast film of news events, newscasters simply read the news aloud to the audience. When President Roosevelt delivered his war message to Congress in December of 1941, for example, CBS's New York station put an American flag in front of the camera and turned on an off-camera fan to make it wave while the station carried the president's voice.

Although World War II produced a number of top-notch radio journalists—such as Edward R. Murrow, William L. Shirer, Eric Sevareid, Walter Cronkite, Charles Collingwood and Howard K. Smith—none of them wanted anything to do with television news after the war because they believed that radio was the more serious medium.

CBS and NBC took the first major steps in network television journalism when they broadcast the Democratic and Republican national conventions in 1948. CBS selected Douglas Edwards as its convention broadcaster; NBC named John Cameron Swayze. Their convention coverage launched both men to television stardom. Edwards soon after went on the air with a nightly 15-minute news show called *The CBS TV News*. Six months later NBC put Swayze on a 15-minute nightly newscast sponsored by Camel cigarettes and called *The Camel News Caravan*. NBC led in the ratings until 1955. In 1956, NBC replaced Swayze with co-anchors Chet Huntley and David Brinkley. In 1960 this news team was able to overtake Edwards in the ratings. Walter Cronkite replaced Edwards at CBS in 1962. A year later the networks doubled the length of the evening news to 30 minutes. It took Cronkite until 1967 before his ratings surpassed those of Huntley and Brinkley. He continued to dominate the ratings until his retirement in 1981.

ABC did not launch a news show until the 1950s, when it put radio actor John Charles Daly on the air as its newscaster. ABC news did not become a ratings contender until the late 1970s when Roone Arledge, the producer of ABC's *Wide World of Sports,* was appointed head of the news division. With the help of newsmen like Frank Reynolds, Peter Jennings and Ted Koppel, Arledge was able to make ABC news popular.

Technical Limitations. Early-day television news could not begin to compare with radio news. Radio could go to the scene of events and broadcast live. TV news required motion-picture cameras, and the film had to be processed after it was shot. Some early network newscasts relied on motion-picture newsreel photographers to provide footage, but often this material was not available until several days after the event. In the meantime, the networks often used still photos, which the newscasters held up in front of them. However, by the 1960s portable cameras and videotape recorders had made television a much more credible news medium because viewers saw pictures of the news events on the day they occurred. Eventually TV provided more people with their news than newspapers and radio combined.

Communist Scare. TV news was not confined to the evening news summaries. In the early 1950s, well-known CBS radio newsman Edward R. Murrow made the switch from radio to television by converting his popular radio show *Hear It Now* to a weekly TV program, *See It Now.* He set a standard for television journalism that has guided the industry ever since. He also was one of the first to show that television could be a powerful force in the culture by tackling some controversial topics, including U.S. Senator Joseph McCarthy.

Senator Joseph McCarthy confers with a colleague during the televised Army-McCarthy hearings in 1954. (AP/Wide World Photos)

House and Senate committees that investigated the alleged infiltration of Communists into the movie industry (see p. 158) also scrutinized television. Their search was greatly aided in June 1950 by the publication of *Red Channels*, which listed the names of 151 radio- and television-industry personnel who were accused of being either sympathetic to or associated with the communist movement. Many people on the list found themselves suddenly out of work and their careers destroyed as a fearful industry took the easy way out to avoid controversy. Some of the better-known names cited were actors Orson Welles, Howard Duff and Edward G. Robinson; musicians Leonard Bernstein, Burl Ives, Judy Holliday and Lena Horne; and radio-television newsmen William L. Shirer and Howard K. Smith. Smith was listed because a communist newspaper had praised his reporting of a particular news event.[2]

Despite the fear that gripped the broadcasting industry, Murrow challenged Senator McCarthy and his scare tactics openly on *See It Now*. On March 9, 1954, Murrow told the nation that the senator was giving "comfort to our enemies" by violating the civil rights of the people he had accused; although McCarthy had not created the atmosphere of fear, he had "certainly exploited it." This broadcast was the third-lowest-rated *See It Now* program of the 1953–54 season, but it had an impact in starting to turn public opinion against the senator. Ironically, McCarthy's response, which was aired on *See It Now* in April, was the program's highest-rated show.[3]

Shortly afterward, McCarthy found himself in a controversy with the army. He was accused of abusing a general during an investigative hearing into the promotion of an army dentist who McCarthy called a "Fifth Amendment Communist." A Senate investigative committee looked into the charges against McCarthy and the 36-day hearing was televised to 20 million Americans. Now the American people could see McCarthy's ruthless and arbitrary tactics firsthand. The senator's popularity began to decline and McCarthyism and the climate of fear subsided. TV had demonstrated that it could be a powerful social force.

Kennedy Assassination. The most profound demonstration of the power of television in bringing news to our popular culture came in November 1963, when President John F. Kennedy was assassinated in Dallas. The three networks provided continuous 24-hour-a-day coverage from Friday through Monday, canceling all commercials at significant cost.

TV cameras at the Dallas jail also captured live the murder of Lee Harvey Oswald, Kennedy's suspected killer, as he was about to be transferred from the Dallas jail to another location.

For four days Americans sat in front of their TV sets watching reruns of both assassinations, historical film of the Kennedy presidency and the emotional burial of the president in Arlington National Cemetery. Television's ability to unite the entire nation in one common emotion demonstrated without doubt just how socially powerful this new mass-communication medium had become.

Vietnam War. As the nation's involvement in the Vietnam war escalated during the 1960s, television was there to bring the war into America's living rooms every night. For the first time in history, Americans could watch ordinary people being killed on foreign battlefields. People could no longer ignore the unpleasantness of war, and soon our involvement in Vietnam began to be questioned. Many blamed television news for turning the Vietnam war into an unpopular one.

The Debate over TV's Newsmaking Role. Television news is profoundly different from newspaper journalism. As TV newsman John Chancellor put it, readers of the print media can be their own editors, selecting what they wanted to read. With television, people have only two choices—leave the TV on or turn it off—and most people choose to leave their sets on.

Eventually some critics started wondering whether television wasn't shaping the news rather than merely reporting it. In the summer of 1968—after the assassinations of Martin Luther King, Jr., and Senator Robert F. Kennedy, widespread riots in urban ghettos and a battle between Chicago police and antiwar demonstrators outside the Democratic national convention—many Americans became convinced that TV news was the cause of the nation's troubles.

The newly elected Republican vice-president Spiro Agnew articulated this concern in 1969:

> *The members of Congress or the Senate who follow their principles and philosophy quietly in a spirit of compromise are unknown to many Americans—while the loudest and most extreme dissenters on every issue are known to every man in the street.*
>
> *How many marchers and demonstrators would we have if the marchers did not know that the ever-faithful TV cameras would be there to record their antics for the next TV show? . . . By way of conclusion, let me say that every elected leader in the United States depends on these men in the media. Whether what I have said tonight will be heard and seen at all by the nation is not my decision; it's not your decision; it's their decision.*[4]

TV Covers the Space Race. Television demonstrated what it could do best in July 1969, when it took the world live to the scene of *Apollo XI's* landing on the moon. Hundreds of millions of people saw the first human steps on the moon. The American dream of space conquest had been achieved and television brought the event into the world's homes—live.

TV's coverage of the space program again impacted the popular culture in January 1986 when the space shuttle *Challenger*, carrying the first teacher into space, exploded on live TV seconds after liftoff. The nation was plunged into mourning. Many people interviewed at the time indicated that they had not felt such an emotional loss since the assassination of President Kennedy 23 years earlier.

Watergate. Although the Watergate scandal was first exposed by newspaper reporters (see p. 133), TV played a crucial role in bringing the story to the masses. Millions of Americans were glued to their television sets as Congress conducted investigative hearings in 1973–74. As a parade of top Nixon administration officials revealed the web of lies, burglaries, money laundering, and obstruction of justice committed on the president's behalf, a growing sentiment for impeachment developed. On August 8, 1974, these same Americans saw their president go on television to announce his resignation.

Iran-Contra Hearings. Some 33 years after TV news demonstrated its influence on the culture by televising the Army-McCarthy hearings, it again set the national news agenda by broadcasting live congressional hearings into the Reagan administration's sale of arms to Iran and the diversion of profits to the Contra "freedom fighters" in Nicaragua.

Whereas TV had earlier transformed Senator McCarthy from a hero to a villain, during the televised Iran-Contra hearings Lt. Col. Oliver North, who had been fired by President Reagan for his illegal activities in the Iran-Contra scandal, was transformed into a folk hero with a cultlike following. Wearing his Marine Corps uniform decorated with ribbons, North—who had been one of President Reagan's National Security advisers—convinced many Americans that he was a young, patriotic officer who was "just following orders from his superiors." North had previously been cast by the press as a villain, or at best a scapegoat. Within days the American consumer culture was selling "Ollie North for President" bumper stickers and T-shirts.

News vs. Entertainment. Over the past four decades, television news has been constantly evolving. Improvements in equipment enabled the first changes to occur. These were followed by changes in style, prompted by the desire for TV news to be "entertaining" in order to attract large audiences and generate higher commercial fees.

Local television news has adopted the "eyewitness" news and "friendly newscaster" approaches. Jokes and friendly chitchat between stories have become standard, and human interest stories and feature reports (movie reviews, sports) take up more and more air time.

A department store employee in Miami takes time out to watch Lt. Col. Oliver North's testimony to the congressional committees investigating the Iran-Contra affair in 1987. Soon afterward, "Ollie for President" T-shirts found their way into pop culture. *(UPI/Bettmann Newsphotos)*

Some newscasters are selected for their appearances and personalities rather than their news judgment, and weathermen and -women are often used to provide comic relief or sex appeal. (This problem was highlighted in the movie *Broadcast News*.) These popular local news "talents" draw large salaries as long as they keep the ratings up. Research on why people watched one newscast instead of another has found that most people prefer programs where the newscasters joke with one another.

One of the latest developments in improving the entertainment value of TV news came in the fall of 1988 when *USA Today* launched *USA Today: The Television Show* in 118 cities. The show featured four anchors and a fast-paced format that delivered up to 40 stories in a half hour. Like the newspaper, it used sophisticated graphics and an occasional in-depth "cover-story."

TV News Sexism. Women, more than men, were finding that an attractive appearance was essential for employment as a television anchorperson. In 1983 a jury awarded Christine Craft, a former Kansas City TV anchor, $500,000 in damages in a sex-discrimination suit. She had been fired from KMBC-TV because a consulting firm had found that she was "too old, too unattractive, and not deferential enough to men." Although a United States District judge threw out the verdict, a new jury awarded her $325,000 in a retrial in 1984. But that award was also overturned, and the Supreme Court refused to hear her final appeal.

The search for the perfect anchor continues, however. One Los Angeles television station faced with declining ratings used galvanic skin response (GSR) tests on randomly selected viewers to determine which anchors to keep and which to fire.

TV News Dominance. Today more Americans claim they get their news from television than from any other source. Since TV cannot begin to provide the variety of stories or the in-depth coverage that newspapers do, this has serious implications for a democracy that needs a well-informed citizenry to function properly.

Although network TV news seems more serious and sophisticated, it too is dependent on ratings and its share of the audience. Often those ratings are dependent on the local news because in most cities, local news immediately precedes network news, and most viewers will watch their favorite local news show and stay tuned to whichever network news follows. The second and third reason people watch one network news show over another, according to William Wheatley, executive producer of *NBC Nightly News*, are the popularity of the anchor and the content.[5]

Also affecting network news since the 1980s has been the entrepreneurial activities of cable TV tycoon Ted Turner, who started Cable News Network (CNN), which provides news around the clock, 24 hours a day. For the first time, the American people were able to watch worldwide TV news whenever they wanted to, rather than when the networks told them they could watch it. This type of independence from the network news "clock" found a niche among many people who were ready to break away from old habits and find new leisure pursuits.

Local vs. Network News. Recent studies have shown that most people identify with their local news more than with network news. A 1986 NBC survey found that when viewers were asked which they would watch—network or local news if they could watch only one—the margin in favor of local news was 52 percent to 45 percent.

New technology was partially responsible for the increase in popularity of local news by the late 1980s. Networks had dominated TV news since 1948 because their larger and more global news-gathering forces were able to deliver the major worldwide and national news stories of the day. However, the new satellite technology of the 1980s made these stories available to stations in advance of the network newscast. Stations were able to purchase satellite news from a variety of sources, including CNN, CONUS Communication (a consortium of stations with specially equipped trucks with dishes that can send and receive television signals via satellites) and Group W's NEWS FEED network.

THE CULTURAL IMPACT OF TELEVISION

Television's impact on our society has been profound. It has changed the life styles of most Americans and become a major influence in our culture. Unlike printing, which took hundreds of years to influence the culture, TV's impact was almost instantaneous.

During television's breakthrough year there were fewer than 20 television stations on the air. According to the A. C. Nielsen Co., this figure grew to 439 by 1955 and totaled 1,220 by the mid-1980s.[6]

The number of television sets in homes also grew rapidly. From 172,000 sets in 1948, the sale of television sets increased at a rate of a quarter million a month for the next two years. The sales figures climbed to five million sets a year during the 1950s, and by 1962, over 90 percent of all households had at least one television set and 13 percent had more than one set. By the mid-1980s there were 125 million television sets in homes, representing nearly 98 percent of American households (a greater percentage than had indoor toilets).[7]

Nielsen reports that most American families today own a minimum of two television sets (1.83 is the national average) and most of these sets (77.7 million) are color. These sets are located in vital living areas, such as the living room, family room, bedroom and kitchen. Because they own multiple sets, many families no longer watch television together and parents often do not know what their children are viewing.[8] TV's dominance as a household communication medium often reduces the level of communication among family members, and as a result much of the culture being disseminated to youngsters today comes from the tube rather than the family.

Nielsen also reports that the average person in the United States today watches more than seven hours of television per day, which translates to more than 2,500 hours per year—the most time-consuming activity except sleeping. Television viewing ranks as the top pastime for children, with the average child viewing more than 18,000 hours by the time he or she is 15. This compares with 11,000 hours of schooling and 3,000 hours of church attendance.[9]

The rich and middle classes were not the only ones to rush to purchase television sets shortly after the medium entered the popular culture. Many lower-class households went into debt to own this luxury item. However, to most Americans, television was not a luxury but rather a psychological necessity; it provided comfort to a lonely mass culture whose inhabitants sought both entertainment and solitude in their homes. Sociologists were puzzled as to how something previously nonexistent could become a psychological necessity the moment it arrived in the culture. The answer seemed to be that television found a niche by bringing the world to individuals isolated from the dominant culture. However, by bringing the world into the home, many cherished activities, such as after-dinner conversations among family members and parents reading bedtime stories to the children, were replaced by TV sitcoms, variety shows and action/adventures.

The new mass medium also provided an opportunity to expand the consumer culture, which had been prevalent since the Industrial Revolution, into the mass culture by providing a new outlet for selling American products. Television became a major medium for advertising, and TV producers devised programming that would deliver audiences for advertisers. The larger the audience watching a show, the more networks could charge for commercials on the show. Television developed into a major business enterprise to sell American goods and services, and at the same time it became a powerful force in transmitting the American culture.

Reflecting Cultural Changes. Television programming has played an important role in reflecting for the masses the cultural changes that have been occurring in American society. When the civil rights movement calling for equality for Americans gained momentum in the 1960s, TV started reflecting these changes. Women and blacks began to be portrayed in other than stereotyped roles for the first time. Sitcoms like *That Girl,* starring Marlo Thomas—who portrayed a young woman making it on her own in the world—and *Julia,* featuring Diahann Carroll as a black nurse and mother, became popular. Prior to that, singer Nat "King" Cole had been the only black to host a network variety show (in the 1950s) and Bill Cosby had been the only black to have a costarring role in a weekly drama series, *I Spy*, in the 1960s. (By the late 1980s Cosby was still going strong on television and starred in one of the top-rated shows—a black sitcom that promoted the nuclear family much like the white versions had done in the 1950s.)

These trends were significant in that they demonstrated that TV was culturally responsive. Besides merely reflecting these cultural changes, television helped transmit them to the masses and by doing so accelerated their acceptance into the mainstream popular culture.

The action/adventure genre also began reflecting these changing times. Women began playing previously male-only roles of cops, detectives and lawyers. Shows such as *Police Woman*, *Charlie's Angels*, *Cagney & Lacey*, *Moonlighting* and *L.A. Law* all showed women in professional rather than subservient roles. However, early versions, like *Charlie's Angels*, were highly criticized for making the females stars more sexy than professional.

As rock music began dominating television with satellite stations like MTV, the action/adventure genre began picking up on the rock-music theme. By the mid-1980s NBC had successfully used the theme of "MTV cops" to produce a hit action/adventure show called *Miami Vice*. The show featured rock-music background sounds, contemporary clothing styles and rapid-paced story lines characteristic of MTV videos. Its star, Don Johnson, soon was enjoying success as both a TV superstar and a rock-recording artist.

Resistance to TV's Cultural Takeover. Despite television's rapid takeover in the American popular culture, it did meet some resistance. In the early years many academics and urban intellectuals resisted TV and viewed it as a "low cultural form" unworthy of serious attention from the "refined and thinking" members of our society.

At first it was a status symbol among the "cultured" *not* to own a television set because the new medium appealed to low cultural interests aimed at delivering the largest audiences. But quality live-drama productions of the 1950s—such as *Playhouse 90*—and important news presentations such as the Army-McCarthy hearings made it difficult for intellectuals to resist this new mass medium. It wasn't long before people in intellectual circles could be heard saying rather sheepishly that "We own one, but we never turn it on."

In 1964—only 16 years after television first started to make inroads into the popular culture—a survey of the 1939 graduating class of Harvard University revealed that 92.5 percent owned at least one TV set and that 13 percent had three or more sets in their home. By the 1960s television had become nearly everyone's mass medium.

Despite this universal acceptance, criticism of television continued, with critics regularly expressing alarm that TV content was aimed at the masses and had little if any educational value. Many were calling television an "electronic mind pacifier" that had a narcotic effect on our culture. This was the theme of Paddy Chayevsky's movie *Network* in the mid-1970s. (Ironically, the movie ended up being the movie of the week on network television.) When one of the film's characters, Howard Beale—a

TV newsman suffering a nervous breakdown—preached the following lines on his "news-entertainment hour," many TV network executives cringed:

> *Television is not the truth. . . . We lie like hell. . . . We deal in illusions, man. None of it is true. But you people sit there day after day, night after night. . . . We're all you know. You're beginning to believe the illusions we're spinning here. You're beginning to think that the tube is reality and that your own lives are like the tube, you eat like the tube, you raise your children like the tube. This is mass madness, you maniacs. In God's name, you people are the real thing: we're the illusions!*[10]

Even in the 1980s, after an entire generation had grown up with the pacifying effects of television and the medium was firmly entrenched in the culture, critics were still making satirical social commentary about its shortcomings. Picking up on the theme that TV was turning people into mental vegetables was a California group that called themselves the Couch Potatoes. Their goal was to bring to the attention of the masses their belief that television is a passive, antiintellectual medium. When asked by a reporter to comment on a two-way cable TV system that allowed viewers to participate in quiz shows and electronic polling by talking back to their TV sets, a Couch Potato spokesperson said: "Why watch TV if you have to think and respond? As far as I'm concerned, the main point of watching TV is that it lets you avoid having to do that. To put it another way, if you're going to have to respond to your TV, you might as well go out and cultivate friendships or read a book or something."[11]

The cultural impact of TV during that last half of the twentieth century has generated a great deal of discussion and concern in several specific areas: the effects of violence on TV, television's influence on children, and the use of the medium to "sell" religion to the masses.

Television and Violence. The question of violence on TV has been around nearly as long as the medium itself. Many critics claim that TV violence increases violence in our society.

The information-limitation theory, some contend, plays a prominent role in causing bizarre and violent behavior in society. This theory holds that some people (usually mentally unbalanced individuals) observe information and activities in the media and then proceed to imitate what they saw. Several specific cases illustrating this theory have received a great deal of discussion and have fueled the arguments for eliminating violence on TV.

The movie *Fuzz*, which first appeared as a book written by Evan Hunter under the pseudonym Ed McBain, was made into a movie starring Burt Reynolds and Raquel Welch. No public outcry developed over the book or the movie. However, when the movie was shown on television, it generated a great deal of concern. Some groups attempted to prevent the movie from being shown by a major network. They objected to a scene in the film in which a group of juvenile delinquents poured gasoline over a skid row vagrant and set him on fire.

The night after the movie was shown on national television, a woman—who had run out of gas in Boston and was carrying a can of fuel back to her car from a corner service station—was accosted by a gang of juveniles. The gasoline was poured over her and she was set on fire. Several nights later, a tramp sleeping along railroad tracks in Florida was doused with gasoline by a gang of youths and set on fire.

When the motion picture *Deer Hunter*, which featured numerous scenes of people playing "Russian roulette," was shown on TV, more than 20 suicides from people playing the deadly game were reported.

Following an NBC-TV network showing of the movie *Born Innocent*, which contained a prison scene in which a female inmate, played by Linda Blair, was raped with a broomstick, a San Francisco girl was raped with a Coke bottle by several other girls who said they had gotten the idea while watching the TV movie. The victim's mother sued NBC and the local TV station, but the court ruled that television could not be held responsible for how some people reacted to scenes in an entertainment program.

Several years later Ronnie Zamora, a Florida teenager, was on trial for murder. His defense attorney, Ellis Rubin, claimed that the youngster was driven to commit the act by watching so much violence on television. The courts found Zamora—not the TV industry—guilty of the murder.

These and other instances of the information-imitation theory are often cited as reasons television violence should be eliminated.

A number of researchers have linked aggressive behavior and television viewing. In a 1982 study the National Institute of Mental Health concluded that "the scientific support for the causal relationship [between violence on TV and aggressive behavior] derives from the convergence of findings from many studies, the great majority of which demonstrate a positive relationship between televised violence and later aggressive behavior."[12]

Over the years television has responded to these concerns by reducing the level of violence. The violent Westerns of the 1950s and 1960s have vanished. Detective shows such as *Starsky and Hutch* were taken off the air for being too violent. They were replaced, however, by action/adventure shows, such as *The A-Team*, that used "make-believe" violence. Some psychiatrists and psychologists charged that shows such as *The A-Team* created a false view of violence by showing the use of automatic rifles, hand grenades and other weapons without ever injuring or killing anyone.

Saturday morning cartoon shows continue to be one of the main targets for anti-violence advocates. A report by the National Coalition on Television Violence reported that by the mid-1980s, there was a "deluge of high-action, violent cartoon shows" aimed at children. Dr. Thomas Radecki, head of the coalition and a psychiatrist, said, "We can only pump so much violence into our people before we explode."[13]

Television and Children. Parents and other groups were not concerned only with TV violence aimed at children. By the mid-1980s the recognition that commercial enterprises were exploiting children by reaching into actual program content to sell children their products was evoking new worries.

The new concern developed after the FCC began deregulating the television industry in the 1980s. This hands-off policy toward TV encouraged toy makers to begin producing their own programs, a practice that had been abandoned after the quiz-show scandal of 1959. Such toy manufacturers as Hasbro Bradley, Mattel, Coleco, Kenner, Tomy, Tonka, Selchow & Righter and even CBS Toys joined forces with

Violence on television and its influence, especially on children, has been a concern since the medium entered the popular culture. This concern has increased in recent years as more and more "latch-key" children turn to the television set as their main after-school companion. *(Charles Gatewood/The Image Works)*

animation houses to produce children's shows that featured planned and existing toys. These product-oriented entertainment shows were in reality 30-minute commercials.

Early program-length commercials featured such lovable dolls as Strawberry Short-cakes and the Smurfs, but by 1985 they included such aggression-oriented products as He-Man and the Masters of the Universe, G.I. Joe: A Real American Hero, Trans-formers, She-Ra: Princess of Power, M.A.S.K. (Medical Armored Strike Command), Thunder Cats, Voltron and Rambo.

Children, who at early ages have difficulty distinguishing between commercials and programs, now found that there was no difference (see Box 9.6). Efforts by Peggy Charren, founder and president of Action for Children's Television (ACT), to get the FCC to enforce its own regulations, which require sponsors to be identified, fell on deaf ears. The FCC philosophy of the 1980s was that the marketplace, not govern-ment regulations, should determine what was in the public interest. In any case, by the end of the 1987–88 season, ratings for the animated superhero shows began to decline, as children tuned in to new live action game shows, like cable network Nick-elodeon's *Double Dare* and Lorimar's *Fun House*, or watched their own video-cassettes.

Concerns about children's TV programming did not start with the product-ori-ented children's shows, however. They are as old as the medium itself. Early concerns centered around physiological effects (will staring at a picture tube ruin a child's eye-sight?) as well as on emotional or psychological effects. Numerous studies have been

BOX 9.6

TOY MAKERS INVADE EUROPE VIA TV SATELLITES

Toy makers have had a captive children's audience on television in the United States for many years. By the mid-1980s they were producing 30-minute-long TV programs featuring their toys. However, many European countries have laws forbidding advertising directed at children.

New mass-media technology in the late 1980s—satellite-to-cable children's programming—began offering toy makers a way around these European laws.

A European Economic Community agreement regarding programs received on cable via satellite held that the programs would be governed by the rules of the country of origin. This ruling was good news for toy makers and a British Children's Channel available on cable in the United Kingdom.

Since the U.K. allows advertising directed at children, the satellite-to-cable Children's Channel became very popular with toy marketers because the signal could be beamed to countries that forbid such advertising.

In December 1986 Scandinavia, which bans children's ads, began receiving the Children's Channel from the U.K. In 1987 the channel was extended to Belgium, the Netherlands and Luxembourg.

Critics of children's television were sickened by the new development. Peggy Charren, president of ACT, said, "It makes me sick that we're using technology to bring a country 'Buy, buy, buy' messages, especially in countries where the government did not think it is appropriate. It's like airwave child abuse."*

*Sean Milmo and Julie Hill, "New Global Expansion: Kid's TV Takes Off," *Advertising Age*, January 12, 1987, p. 46.

conducted over the years to examine TV's effects on children. Early research by the National Television and Radio Center in the late 1950s and early 1960s concluded: "For some children, under some conditions, some television is harmful. For other children, under the same conditions, it may be beneficial. For most children, under most conditions, most television is probably neither harmful nor particularly beneficial."[14]

Most research seems to indicate that children do learn behavior and that television does play a role in teaching that behavior. In her book *Mind and Media*, Patricia Greenfield says that children often take well-known TV characters as examples to be imitated. She points out that the day after "Fonzie" took out a library card on *Happy Days*, there was a fivefold increase in the number of children applying for library cards in the United States. She contends that TV can be a very positive force in the lives of children if it is used constructively and if parents actively see to it that their children interact with the programs' content through discussions and parental explanations.[15]

Such parental involvement is not always possible, however. Recent changes in our culture regarding the traditional nuclear family are creating new problems. The traditional family where the father works and the mother stays home has been replaced with situations where either both parents are working or the household consists of a single parent raising the children. Both of these conditions have created a new kind of child in the United States—the "latchkey kid." Millions of American children today go home from school to fend for themselves.

Many observers of this new trend contend that today's American child no longer obtains his or her cultural values from the traditional family structure, but instead gets them from the mass media. And some critics say that what they are getting is a popular culture filled with sex and violence.

However, some research studies have shown that TV has a positive impact on children's learning. These studies have found that vocabulary levels and general cultural awareness of youngsters starting school seems to be much higher than television-deprived children of the same age. Some TV programs for children, such as *Sesame Street* and *The Electric Company* (both on PBS), are designed to teach youthful viewers.

Another concern over the impact of television on children came from the explosion of the space shuttle *Challenger*. Millions of children were watching the shuttle's take-off in their classrooms because it was carrying the first teacher, Christa McAuliffe, into outer space. McAuliffe was to have given some lessons to the nation's school children from space. Concern was expressed that the explosion may have inflicted some long-lasting psychological damage on many of the young viewers.

Follow-up observations, however, have so far shown that some forgot about the incident within days, while others still remember it. Children with stable home lives and family relationships were less likely to remember the incident than single-parent children, who related to it as a case of other children losing parents.

Child psychiatrist Robert Coles says that what children do with television depends on the nature of their own lives. He points out that if a child has an unstable family life, he or she may be more vulnerable to the emotional and moral power of TV, while a child with a stable home life will not "likely be sucked into the moral wasteland that one finds while watching certain programs." What matters, he says, "is not only the quality of television programming for our young people (or for us, their parents) but the quality of American family life."[16]

Television and Religion. In the late 1980s controversy erupted over another kind of programming—religious broadcasting. Fundamentalist Protestant revivalism has been part of American culture since the religious movement known as the Great Awakening swept the 13 colonies in the 1730s and '40s. Preaching to mass rallies in the open air (and later in tents), ministers from Jonathan Edwards to Billy Graham urged listeners to repent and start a new life.

In the 1950s, as tent revival audiences started to dwindle due to the competition from television, evangelists like Oral Roberts started taking their messages to the home via the TV set. *Televangelism* was born. Television stations began selling air time to evangelical preachers and, since the 1970s, the electronic church has been a successful part of TV programming.

As the cost of air time climbed and the new technology of cable became available, religious broadcasters started turning their attention to this new delivery system. The Christian Broadcasting Network (CBN) built up a cable network that supplemented its own three TV stations. TBN (Trinity Broadcasting Network) and PTL (Praise the Lord or People That Love) followed with their own religious cable networks. Of course, it still costs money to produce cable telecasts, so pitches for donations are a regular feature of many of these networks' shows.

According to a 1984 survey by the University of Pennsylvania's Annenberg School of Communications—done for the National Council of Churches and the National Religious Broadcasters—an estimated 13.3 million people watched at least 15 minutes of religious programming a week. Most of these viewers were female and nonwhite and were less well educated, older, and poorer than the average American. However, they tended to respond to the various calls for contributions to keep the ministries on the air. The Annenberg study found that many viewers contributed regularly to three or more programs.

A 1985 Nielsen survey found an even larger audience for religious programs: 61 million people, representing more than 40 percent of the nation's households, watched one or more of the top-10 syndicated religious broadcasts during the February sweeps period. The most popular program was Pat Robertson's *700 Club*, with 28.7 million viewers. The electronic church has become a multibillion-dollar-a-year enterprise and a significant part of TV programming in our popular culture.

In 1987, the nation's attention was riveted by an electronic "Holy War" that broke out when popular TV evangelists Jim and Tammy Bakker were forced to turn over their lucrative ministry—the PTL Club—to the Reverend Jerry Falwell, head of the Liberty Foundation. Bakker stepped down from his electronic pulpit after admitting that he had had an affair with Jessica Hahn, a church secretary.

Falwell, who said he was taking over the $129-million-a-year ministry only temporarily to help out the troubled Bakker, soon was attacked by Bakker, who said that Falwell had tricked him out of his ministry and was refusing to give the ministry back as promised. Falwell countered that he had been misled by Bakker, whose "sins" went far beyond an indiscretion with Hahn and included mismanagement of millions of dollars of ministry funds. (The Bakkers were later indicted for tax fraud.)

ABC's Nightline recorded its largest audiences in history when it ran back-to-back programs featuring Jim Bakker and Falwell supporters.

This was not the only controversy to surround televangelism in the late 1980s. When Pat Robertson, president of the Christian Broadcasting Network and host of the *700 Club*, announced he would run for the 1988 Republican presidential nomination many objected to his attempt to mix church and state. Robertson did stop appearing on the show during the campaign, however, returning only after he had withdrawn from the race.

When evangelist Oral Roberts told his television audience that God was going to "call him home" if he did not raise $8 million for medical scholarships at Oral Roberts University by a specified date, critics charged that he had gone too far. Despite the criticism and a flurry of bumper stickers saying "Save Your Money—Send Oral Home," the money was raised in time. A few months later Roberts was in trouble again over his comment that he had raised the dead. When challenged, he said that maybe the child hadn't been dead, but "he looked dead."

And finally the popular televangelist Jimmy Swaggart, who had been instrumental in exposing the affair of his rival Jim Bakker, was himself defrocked after admitting to encounters with a prostitute. All the networks carried his tearful confession on the evening news.

These controversies triggered a decline in the millions of dollars raised each week by television preachers. The scandal-ridden PTL ministry declared that it was going into Chapter 11 of the Bankruptcy Act to protect itself from creditors. The series of troubles facing TV evangelism in 1987 and 1988 brought to the forefront an area of programming that had long been ignored by most critics despite its tremendous financial success.

TELEVISION SPECIALIZES

Television, like many other mass media, has entered the stage of specialization. A variety of specialized programming is now available to meet particular interests.

Public Broadcasting. A noncommercial form of broadcasting servicing primarily the elite or high culture is provided through the joint efforts of the Corporation for Public Broadcasting and the Public Broadcasting Service (PBS). Efforts to provide noncommercial educational television (ETV) began in the 1950s. These activities were not too successful, but they did lead to the passage of the Public Broadcasting Act of 1967, which provided for the first interconnected network of ETV stations and federal financial assistance.

PBS programming ranges from in-depth news and Wall Street analysis to opera, classical music and sophisticated British Broadcasting Corporation (BBC) drama and comedy productions. Among the BBC shows are a number of successful serials such as *Civilisation, Masterpiece Theater, Upstairs Downstairs* and *Yes Minister.* PBS also broadcasts programs developed by the Children's Television Workshop (CTW), such as *Sesame Street* and *The Electric Company.*

PBS programming is carried on noncommercial television stations and is usually transmitted by satellite. The biggest source of revenue for public broadcasting is corporate sponsorship; the second largest source is local station membership dues, auctions and other fund-raisers; and the rest is made up by revenues from federal funding through the Corporation for Public Broadcasting and other federal agencies, such as the National Endowment for the Arts.

Despite some excellent programming, PBS does not reach a mass audience. In every major market where noncommercial broadcasting is available, its audience totals less than 5 percent.

Cable and Satellite Television. Although cable television began in the 1940s as a way to relay television signals to remote areas, in the 1970s it shifted its focus to providing specialized programming. Through the use of communication satellites, cable companies can pick up and redistribute a wide range of programming.

By the 1980s the big three networks, their affiliate stations and the relatively few independent stations found themselves competing with a number of new cable and satellite networks.

According to *Broadcasting Cablecasting Yearbook 1986,* more than 38.9 million homes subscribed to cable television and some 7,300 cable TV systems serving 19,000 communities were operating by the mid-1980s.

In addition to cable, several million homes were taking their television signals directly from satellites via a reception dish, bypassing local stations and advertisers.[17]

Large satellite receiving dishes bring television signals to remote areas. *(Eric Neurath/Stock, Boston)*

With the advent of these new methods of TV reception has come an expansion of the numbers of channels available, with some satellite-fed homes receiving over 100 channels.

People with cable or satellite reception can now view channels that feature nothing but sports, religion, sitcoms, rock music, country-and-western music, movies, children's shows, X-rated adult shows, news, live congressional sessions and so forth. Many of these programs can be tuned in any time of the day or night.

For example, cable network ESPN provides sports programming 24 hours a day. In 1987 it broke the networks' monopoly on the electronic ballpark by successfully bidding for the rights to Sunday night NFL football games. (See Chapter 14 for a discussion of the major cable networks.)

When the 22-week-long writers' strike delayed the start of the networks' fall 1988 season, many viewers turned to cable for alternative programming.

Teleshopping. In the mid-1980s *teleshopping* developed as another method of selling consumer goods in the American culture. Unlike regular broadcasting commercials that attempt to create an interest in a product or company, teleshopping is designed to stimulate instant sales. Products are shown on the screen with a discount price and viewers are urged to call in their charge-card numbers immediately before the limited number of products are sold. These programs—many of them broadcasting 24 hours a day—sell everything from cubic zirconia diamonds to fur coats and computers. Some viewers admit to watching these marketing channels more than 12 hours a day. All a viewer needs is a TV set, telephone and credit card to make numerous purchases. It was estimated that in 1987 sales figures from these shows exceeded $2 billion. Although teleshopping first began with Home Shopping Network in 1982, by the late 1980s there were over a dozen such operations.

Home shopping networks on satellite and cable TV ushered in the new consumer craze of teleshopping in the 1980s. The 24-hour a day networks sell a variety of items at volume discount prices. *(Home Shopping Network)*

Even major retailers like Sears have discovered teleshopping. Sears, a catalog sales giant for over 100 years, recognized that television's electronic catalog business, which catered to impulse buying, was superior to print catalogs. So Sears began marketing its merchandise on the QVC home shopping network.

TV started out as a mass medium to provide entertaining programming that would deliver large audiences to advertisers. Today, in the stage of specialization, advertising has become some of the programming.

SUMMARY

Originally just a novelty, television has become the most important entertainment medium in American culture. Although TV was invented in the late 1920s, it didn't enter the popular culture until 1948, following a short period serving the elite culture. By the 1960s it was playing a major role in reflecting and shaping the culture.

Television borrowed much of its early programming from radio. It also featured visual comedy, especially slapstick comedians from the days of vaudeville, such as Milton Berle; variety shows, such as Ed Sullivan's *Toast of the Town*; and shows starring puppets like Cecil the Seasick Sea Serpent and Howdy Doody. One of the finest forms of TV entertainment in the late 1950s was the live drama, which presented character studies rather than action and adventure. Quiz shows and prerecorded action/adventure shows rounded out the entertainment schedule in TV's first decade.

Television entertainment has changed during the past 40 years to reflect the ever-changing culture. Sitcoms, talk shows and made-for-TV movies are now dealing with controversial and socially relevant topics.

Television news was primitive in its developmental days, but it soon became a powerful force. Eventually it dominated the news scene, with more people reporting that they got their news from TV than from any other source. In the 1960s, when assassinations and riots received major coverage, people started blaming TV for shaping the news.

Local television news began changing in the 1970s to become more entertaining for the masses. Feature stories and humor were added to the evening newscast, and newscasters began to be hired for their looks and personalities rather than their news judgment. Network news, which has been a major source of news and information since the early days of television, found that new technology was making local news shows more competitive in the late 1980s.

Television's impact on our culture has been staggering. Ninety-eight percent of American homes have at least one TV set. Children spend more hours watching TV than they spend in school. The average American watches more than seven hours of television a day, an activity second only to sleeping.

Despite the widespread acceptance of television as a mass medium, it remains a controversial enterprise. Violence on TV has been a concern since the beginning, with many people citing the information-imitation theory to support their argument. According to research by the National Institute of Mental Health, TV violence does lead to aggressive behavior by children and teenagers.

Another concern about television's effect on children developed more recently: in the 1980s toy manufacturers started producing product-oriented cartoons for children. By the mid-1980s these 30-minute commercials dominated children's television.

Television's impact on the learning environment of children has been a concern since the early 1950s. Research has shown that TV does influence children but that the degree of that influence seems to depend on the level of involvement of the parent and the quality of the child's home life. Given the changes in the nuclear family and the growing number of "latchkey kids," there is new concern about TV's influence.

Also drawing attention in the 1980s as a concern over television programming was the scandal-ridden "electronic churches." Following publicity about scandals that some televangelists became involved in, some felt that all televangelists were going too far to get money and support from television viewers.

By the 1980s television had entered the stage of specialization in the EPS cycle. Public broadcasting was providing noncommercial programming for the high or elite culture, while cable and satellite channels offered a large variety of specialized programs to meet particular interests. And perhaps inevitably, television, which had from the begining been a vehicle to deliver large audiences to advertisers, was now offering teleshopping channels that ran nothing but ads 24 hours a day.

NOTES

1. James H. Myers and William H. Reynolds, *Consumer Behavior and Marketing Management* (Boston: Houghton Mifflin, 1967), p. 239.

2. Counterattack, *Red Channels: The Report of Communists in Radio and Television* (New York: Counterattack, 1950), pp. 1–100.

3. James R. Wilson, "Murrow Versus McCarthy: An Historical Study of Two 1954 *See It Now* Telecasts and Their Impact on the Two Participants, Edward R. Murrow and Joseph R. McCarthy," Master's thesis, California State University, Fresno, 1976, p. 53.

4. Quoted in George McKenna, *Media Voices: Debating Critical Issues in Mass Media* (Guilford, Conn.: Dushkin, 1982), pp. 67–74.

5. David Shaw, "Future of Network News: Is the Signal Weakening?" *Los Angeles Times*, December 29, 1986, p. 17.

6. *Broadcasting Cablecasting Yearbook 1986* (Washington, D.C.: Broadcasting Publications, 1986), p. H-55.

7. John Brooks, "The Sudden Assault," in *The History of Popular Culture*, Norman F. Cantor and Michael S. Werthman, ed. (New York: Macmillan, 1968), p. 714.

8. *International Television Almanac*, 31st ed. (New York: Quigley Publishing, 1986), p. 8.

9. Ibid.

10. *Network*, dir. Paddy Chayevsky, MGM, 1976.

11. B. A. Krier, "Practitioners of the Art of Zen TV Watching," *Los Angeles Times*, June 6, 1982, pp. 1, 14.

12. *Television and Behavior: Ten Years of Scientific Progress and Implications for the Eighties*, vol. 1 (Rockville, Md.: U.S. Department of Health and Human Services, 1982), pp. 89–90.

13. "Why Children's TV Turns Off So Many Parents," *U.S. News & World Report*, February 18, 1985, p. 65.

14. Wilbur Schramm, Jack Lyle and Edwin Parker, *Television in the Lives of Our Children* (Palo Alto, Calif.: Stanford University Press, 1961), p. 13.

15. Patricia Marks Greenfield, *Mind and Media: The Effects of Television, Video Games and Computers* (Cambridge, Mass.: Harvard University Press, 1984), pp. 25–70.

16. Robert Coles, "What Makes Some Kids More Vulnerable to the Worst of TV?" *TV Guide*, June 21–27, 1986, p. 7.

17. *Broadcasting Cablecasting Yearbook 1986*, p. 9.

ADDITIONAL READING

Barnouw, Erik. *Tube of Plenty: The Development of American Television.* New York: Oxford University Press, 1975.

Bower, Robert T. *Television and the Public.* New York: Holt, Rinehart & Winston, 1973.

Cantor, Muriel, and Pingree, Suzanne. *The Soap Opera.* Beverly Hills, Ca.: Sage Publications, 1983.

Cross, Donna Woolfolk. *Media-Speak: How Television Makes Up Your Mind.* New York: Mentor, 1983.

Edmondson, Madeleine, and Rounds, David. *From Mary Noble to Mary Hartman: The Complete Soap Opera Book.* New York: Stein and Day, 1976.

Epstein, Edward J. *The News from Nowhere.* New York: Random House, 1973.

Greenfield, Jeff. *Television: The First Fifty Years.* New York: Crescent, 1977.

Gitlin, Todd. *Inside Prime Time.* New York: Pantheon, 1985.

———. *Watching Television: A Pantheon Guide to Popular Culture.* New York: Pantheon, 1986.

Himmelstein, Hal. *Television Myth and the American Mind*. New York: Praeger, 1984.

Horsfield, Peter G. *Religious Television: The American Experience*. New York: Longman, 1984.

Johnson, Nicholas. *How to Talk Back to Your Television Set*. Boston: Little, Brown, 1970.

Kaminsky, Stuart M., with Mahan, Jeffrey H. *American Television Genres*. Chicago: Nelson-Hall, 1985.

Leonard, Bill. *In the Storm of the Eye: A Lifetime at CBS*. New York: Putnam, 1987.

Liebert, Robert M. *The Early Window: The Effects of Television on Children and Youth*, 2nd ed. New York: Pergamon, 1982.

Marc, David. *Demographic Vistas: Television in American Culture*. Philadelphia: University of Pennsylvania Press, 1984.

McCabe, Peter. *Bad News at Black Rock: The Sell-Out of CBS News*. New York: Arbor House, 1987.

McNeil, Alex. *Total Television: A Comprehensive Guide to Programming from 1948 to the Present*, 2nd ed. New York: Penguin, 1984.

Newcomb, Horace. *TV: The Most Popular Art*. Garden City, N.Y.: Anchor Books, 1974.

Powers, Ron. *The Newscasters*. New York: St. Martin's, 1978.

Vaughn, Robert. *Only Victims: A Study of Show Business Blacklisting*. New York: Putnam, 1972.

Westin, Av. *Newswatch: How Television Gathers and Delivers the News*. New York: Simon & Schuster, 1982.

Williams, Raymond. *Television: Technology and Cultural Form*. New York: Schocken, 1974.

Woolery, George. *Children's Television: The First Thirty-five Years, 1946–1981*. Metuchen, N.J.: Scarecrow Press, 1985.

Chapter 10

Recorded Music:
Powerful and Controversial

I make a living doing things
most people get arrested for.
—*Ozzy Osbourne*

The recording industry is one of the most underrated, misunderstood and socially powerful of all the mass media today. The influence of this industry was probably best demonstrated in 1984–85, when rock stars raised millions of dollars to feed the starving people of the world.

It all began late in 1984, when a number of British rock musicians, led by Irish punk rocker Bob Geldof of The Boomtown Rats, joined together to record "Do They Know It's Christmas?" to benefit famine victims in Ethiopia. A few months later a coalition of 45 American singers united in an all-night session to record Michael Jackson's song "We Are the World," which became a number one record with proceeds going to starving Africans. Soon Canadian, Latin American and other singers followed suit. In April 1985 "We Are the World" was broadcast in London, Los Angeles, Atlanta, Paris, Rome and other cities in a gigantic simultaneous telecast to raise the world's consciousness about hunger and solicit funds to feed the starving.

These efforts continued in July of that year, when rock groups staged the 16-hour Live Aid concert in Philadelphia and London. The concert was televised to a worldwide audience of more than a billion people using 16 communication satellites. The broadcast was available to 78 percent of the world's TV sets in 169 countries. Proceeds went toward feeding the starving.

The Live Aid movement sparked numerous similar musical causes, such as "Farm Aid" concerts and benefit songs for AIDS research and the Greenpeace environmental movement.

At last the global language of music was being harnessed for worthy causes. Never before had any industry voluntarily done so much to tackle the world's problems. Never before had the music industry demonstrated its influence on society so openly.

HOW IT ALL BEGAN

The influence and significance of music in our culture has long been recognized. More than two thousand years ago, Plato called for strict censorship of popular music in *The Republic*, a book about his concept of an ideal society. He feared that citizens might be tempted and corrupted by "weak and voluptuous" music and led to indulge in demoralizing emotions. Over the centuries many philosophers and scientists have expressed this fear of music's power to corrupt. However, it wasn't until the nineteenth century that music began to be mass-communicated and the criticism began to grow in intensity. This criticism of popular music seems to have reached a peak in the 1980s.

Sheet Music. The pervasiveness of recorded music in today's American popular culture sometimes lets us forget that recordings weren't the first form in which music was mass-communicated in our society. In the nineteenth century music was transmitted in print; sheet music was printed and distributed, first in the elite culture and then, in the late nineteenth and early twentieth centuries, in the popular culture. A variety of popular folk songs were widely distributed and people used the sheet music to play pianos or other instruments at family sing-alongs or social gatherings.

The Talking Machine. Although sheet music was popular, it did not have the cultural impact of recorded music. Thus, when Thomas A. Edison first heard his own words "Mary had a little lamb" repeated back to him from his talking machine in 1877, the stage was set for the development of a powerful mass-communication medium. Edison recognized the potential for his invention and by the following year had formed the Edison Speaking Phonograph Company.

Edison's early *phonograph* used a tin-foil cylinder to record and play back the sound. Two technicians working for Alexander Graham Bell improved on Edison's invention by developing the *graphophone*, which used a wax cylinder instead of tin foil for longer wear and better sound. The new talking machines were first played publicly for vaudeville audiences; later they were leased to saloons, where people could "hear them talk" for a nickel.

The American Graphophone Company and the Columbia Phonograph Company began leasing the talking machines to record dictation in offices during this period. Columbia did well because it had the Washington, D.C., franchise to lease the machines to government offices. The former company failed, and Columbia obtained its patent rights and became known as Columbia-Graphophone.

The next improvement on the early talking machines was the *gramophone*. It changed the way the stylus recorded sound and used a disc instead of a cylinder. The

Elitist	Popular	Specialized	CULTURAL HISTORY OF RECORDED MUSIC	
■			1887	Thomas A. Edison invents the "talking machine."
■			1902	Enrico Caruso begins recording opera.
■			1905	Columbia introduces two-sided discs.
	■		1920s	Black music helps recording industry expand its sales.
	■		1920s	Jazz music evokes charges that music is corrupting young people.
	■		1920s	Covering (white musicians playing black music) leads to development of "White Swing."
	■		1925	Electric phonographs replace hand-cranked machines.
	■		1927	Jukebox invented.
	■		1930s	Recording industry declines due to Great Depression and radio's free music.
	■		1930s	Big Band era keeps recording industry alive.
	■		1940s	Frank Sinatra gains fame appealing to a youthful bobbysoxers audience.
		■	1950s	Specialization of radio introduces black rhythm and blues, to white audiences.
		■	1954	Sam Phillips of Sun Records discovers Elvis Presley, who becomes the king of rock-'n'-roll.
		■	1955	The motion-picture industry, reaching out for a youth audience, uses Bill Haley and the Comets' "Rock Around the Clock" as the theme song for *Blackboard Jungle*.
		■	1955–63	Rock-'n'-roll becomes firmly entrenched in new youth subculture.
		■	1960s	Led by the Beatles and the "British invasion," rock music begins carrying less innocent messages that reflect changing American subcultures.
		■	1970s	The Beatles disband.
	■		1970s	Disco palaces invade American culture.
		■	1976	Punk rock emerges in Britain.
		■	1981	Warner-Amex introduces MTV cable channel; popularizes music videos.
		■	1985	We Are the World and Live Aid concerts raise millions for starving in Africa.
		■	1985	U.S. Senate committee holds hearings on rock-music lyrics; suggests a rating system to warn listeners of explicit lyrics.
		■	1986	Michael Jackson pays a reported $40–50 million for the rights to the Beatles' music.

Thomas Edison, with his newly invented "talking machine." *(Culver Pictures)*

inventor of the gramophone, a German immigrant named Emile Berliner, joined forces with a New Jersey machinist, Eldridge Johnson, to found the Victor Talking Machine Company. They were the first to market the gramophones for use in the home.

The world-famous opera star Enrico Caruso gave people something worthwhile to listen to on their gramophones when he began making records in 1902. Other opera stars followed suit, and the recording industry was on its way. Columbia introduced the two-sided disc in 1905. However, the new talking-machine industry was very much a communication medium for the elite, as only wealthier homes could afford a gramophone and records, which cost 65 cents apiece in a day when $5 a week was a good salary.

RECORDED MUSIC ENTERS THE POPULAR CULTURE

American culture has two distinct forms of folk music, both rooted in American sub-cultures—black music and hillbilly music, now better known as country-and-western. Black music was the first to be transmitted throughout the popular culture through sheet and recorded music. Hillbilly music remained primarily in the Southern region of its origin until the second half of the twentieth century.

Black Music. Early black music, spirituals, gospel and blues, reflected the poverty and oppression of slaves in the South. The only thing the slaves were able to bring with them to this country was their culture, and that culture was expressed through their music.

Black music became popular in the nineteenth century after the Civil War as black musicians were hired to play in saloons and brothels along the Mississippi River. A popular form known as ragtime made the transition from these establishments to the popular culture in the late nineteenth century through the distribution of sheet music.

As ragtime's popularity waned in the early twentieth century, a new form of black music known as Dixieland jazz took its place. The 1920s were known as the Roaring '20s or the Jazz Age. This was a decade when prohibition was in effect and illegal drinking was promoted in speakeasies, which played music and allowed people to enjoy themselves by dancing to the Charleston.

Until 1925 most phonographs were mechanical and hand-cranked. In that year the industry started selling electric phonographs, and the recording industry moved rapidly from the elite culture into the popular. In 1927 987,000 phonographs were sold, along with 104 million records.

As jazz entered the popular culture, it provoked a great deal of criticism—similar to what we hear today about popular music—that it was destroying the morals of the youth. The themes of popular music in the 1920s were very similar to the ones in today's recorded music.

As early as the 1920s, blues songs on such labels as Okeh and Bluebird carried a variety of sexually suggestive titles. This music, which reflected the emotions and struggles of the poorer segments of the black community, often referred to the earthy conditions of everyday life, occasionally including four-letter words. This music was criticized by blacks as well as whites, as the following passage from a black leader indicates: "To respectable, middle class, churchgoing Negroes, blues is often considered evil music; the devil's music that beguiles the listeners and leads him to damnation."[1]

Such charges against recorded music were prevalent during the Jazz Age. The culture was changing during this period as new music, new dances, new styles of dress, the entrance of the new automobile into the popular culture and new moral codes

Black music, such as blues and jazz, played a major role in moving recorded music into the popular culture. Legendary trumpet player Louis Armstrong is shown here with King Oliver's Creole Jazz Band. *(Historical Pictures Service)*

began altering people's behavior. Women began smoking and drinking and listening to jazz in speakeasies. They wore short "flapper" dresses and did the Charleston and other "shimmy dances." Men and women were displaying a new carefree attitude in a culture that had previously been guided by Victorian morality. Even Cole Porter wrote a song about "getting a kick from cocaine" during this period, while Billie Holiday sang about "Love for Sale."

Leaders of such groups as the National Education Association, the Federation of Women's Clubs and various religious organizations took up the anti-jazz cry. The following article in William Randolph Hearst's *New York American* reflected a common view:

Jazz Ruining Girls, Declares Reformer

Chicago, Jan. 21—Moral disaster is coming to hundreds of American girls through the pathological, nerve irritating, sex-exciting music of jazz orchestras, according to the Illinois Vigilance Association.

In Chicago alone the association's representatives have traced the fall of 1,000 girls in the last two years to jazz music.

Girls in small towns, as well as the big cities, in poor homes and rich homes, are victims of the weird, insidious, neurotic music that accompanies modern dancing.

The degrading music is common not only to disorderly places, but often to high-school affairs, to expensive hotels and so-called society circles, declares Rev. Richard Yarrow, superintendent of the Vigilance Association.

The report says that the vigilance society has no desire to abolish dancing, but seeks to awaken the public conscience to the present danger and future consequences of jazz music.[2]

Despite this and similar criticism, the popularity of jazz continued to grow.

Covering. Attempts by the recording industry to sell blues and jazz to the popular culture ran into some difficulties, however. In particular, many whites were reluctant to buy records by black artists. To overcome this, the process of *covering* was developed: white artists were hired to record black music.

White Swing. Benny Goodman, for example, rode to fame playing the music of black songwriter Fletcher Henderson. From blues and jazz came white swing. Swing was a milder, watered-down version of black music that did not reflect the raw emotions of the black experience. Swing became a popular style of music that mainstream tastes could accept.

Jukeboxes and Sales. The recording industry grew and flourished during the last half of the 1920s. The jukebox was invented in 1927 and added another market for the sales of records as well as being a new promotional device for home sales of records (see Box 10.1).

BOX 10.1.

THE CHANGING WORLD OF THE JUKEBOX

A mechanical device that would play a phonograph record for a nickel helped popularize the recording industry when it was introduced in 1927. Known as the jukebox, the device had mechanical arms that would select the correct record and place it on a turntable after someone inserted a coin and pushed a selection button. The records in those days were heavy discs (about 12 inches in diameter) that spun at 78 revolutions per minute.

Just as popular music has changed over the years, so has the jukebox. In the 1940s when much smaller and lighter phonograph records, known as 45s (because they spun at 45 revolutions per minute), replaced 78s in the singles market, jukeboxes had to be redesigned.

Then in the 1980s, the jukebox industry found itself facing another crisis. The 45s were being phased out of the music industry, and by 1986 they accounted for only 5 percent of the records and tapes made.

In 1987 the old 45-playing jukeboxes were replaced with new machines that played compact discs. The king of the jukebox industry, Seeburg, was the first to develop a CD jukebox that would play 3 songs for $1 or 18 songs for $5. Not only did the new jukebox have better sound quality—thanks to the CDs—they contained more selections—700 to 1,000, compared to around 200 in the old 45 jukeboxes.

Adding to the new CD jukeboxes' popularity was the release on CD of a number of popular rock albums by the Rolling Stones and the Beatles. Other old favorites released on CD during 1987 were recordings by Nat King Cole, Judy Garland, Pink Floyd, Kenny Rogers, Bob Seger and Frank Sinatra.

Other music dispensers developed in the 1980s included jukeboxes with large 25-inch color screens that played laser video discs. Produced by Laser Video Music and Rowe International, these music videos cost 50 cents a selection—10 times the amount of the original jukebox.

Since its invention in 1927, the jukebox has played an important role in making popular music an integral part of our culture. *(Historical Picture Service)*

In the 1930s, however, the industry nearly collapsed because the Great Depression seriously curtailed people's ability to spend money on leisure pursuits and because radio was now offering music free. The end of prohibition in 1933 helped record sales, though, by bringing back taverns, which all had jukeboxes playing the latest records.

Radio and Sales. Radio networks also began to see a future in the recording industry, and in 1938 CBS purchased the Columbia Phonograph Company and started promoting its recording stars on network radio. People were encouraged to go out and buy their records.

In the late 1930s a young singer by the name of Francis Albert Sinatra was discovered. Backed by the popular Harry James and Tommy Dorsey band, he became the idol of many young "bobbysoxers" throughout the country. Teenage girls would scream and faint when they saw him in concert or heard his voice on records or radio. Many other popular vocalists, some like Peggy Lee who were from the big band era of the 1930s, became successful as recording artists during the 1940s and early 1950s. Among them were Frankie Laine, Vaughn Monroe, Mel Torme, Perry Como, Vic Damone, Dinah Shore and Doris Day.

During this period radio was forced to find a new niche as a specialized medium because of the entrance of television into the popular culture. As a result, numerous radio stations began to feature specialized types of music.

Rhythm-and-Blues. One of the more popular sounds among young people was coming from the black rhythm-and-blues stations that were broadcasting in metropolitan areas. It started to dawn on recording-industry executives that if they could find white performers to sing rhythm-and-blues, they might capitalize on the expanding audience of young people for this new sound.

In 1951 Cleveland disc jockey Alan Freed, who later coined the term rock-'n'-roll, started mixing black rhythm-and-blues records with records by white artists and aimed his programming at a white radio audience.

Rock-'n'-Roll. Sam Phillips, a Memphis, Tennessee, record promoter—who formed Sun Records in the early 1950s—combed the South for a white country singer who could handle the beat of rhythm-and-blues. "What I need," he said unabashedly, "is a white boy who can sing colored."[3]

In 1954 he found country-and-western singer Elvis Presley and turned him into the "king" of rock-'n'-roll. By 1956 Presley had five songs at the top of the charts. After a hitch in the army he became a motion-picture star as well. Although his recording career faded in the 1970s he was a living legend for many years until his death in 1977.

Rock-'n'-roll was a new form of American music that evolved from a blend of rhythm-and-blues and country-and-western. The motion-picture industry, which was attempting to recover from the television-caused box-office slump by focusing on the youth audience, helped promote rock-'n'-roll in some of its movies. For example, Bill Haley and his Comets' rock-'n'-roll song "Rock Around the Clock" was the theme for *Blackboard Jungle*, a film about juvenile delinquency in the schools. The song became one of the best-selling records of 1955. Television featured rock-'n'-roll shows too, most notably Dick Clark's *American Bandstand*, which played the latest songs each day. The program showed rock stars lip-syncing their hits and teenagers dancing to the music.

The American youth of the 1950s were forming their own subculture with its own fads, clothing styles and music. The early period of rock-'n'-roll—from 1955 to 1963— was an innocent era when a number of teenagers became overnight rock-'n'-roll stars. Recording stars such as Ricky Nelson, Frankie Avalon, Fabian, Paul Anka, Bobby Darin and Bobby Rydell became teen idols. They sang largely about teenage romances. Also popular were female singers and groups such as Lesley Gore, the Shangri-Las, the Ronettes, the Marvelettes and the Crystals.

Not all rock-'n'-roll stars were white, however. As the beat of rock-'n'-roll swept through the youth culture, the music industry began featuring black artists to keep up with the demand for this new sound. Indeed, rock-'n'-roll was instrumental in breaking down the color barrier in music once and for all. The young were less prejudiced than their parents and enjoyed the music without caring about its ethnic origins. Many black entertainers became popular with white as well as black audiences. Among them were Chuck Berry, Fats Domino, Little Richard, Chubby Checkers, Bo Diddley, the Platters, the Shirelles, and the Coasters.

The merging of country-and-western music with rhythm-and-blues also helped move country music into our mainstream popular culture. Many of the early rock-'n'- roll singers were former country stars, and this trend of *crossing over* from country to popular music helped spark country music's acceptance in the popular culture. The 1970s saw the emergence of such popular country-and-western crossover artists as Kenny Rogers, Dolly Parton, Johnny Cash and Willie Nelson.

ROCK MUSIC CHANGES

Rock-'n'-roll was fun, innocent music for the young, a new genre that adults did not accept. Parents complained that the new music sounded awful and described it as a clattering of pots and pans. To keep it out of earshot, they sent their children to their rooms to listen to it. This helped set the stage for what was termed the generation gap between parents and adolescents in the late 1960s.

Cultural Changes. Following the assassination of President Kennedy in 1963, rock- 'n'-roll music became more sophisticated, and its lyrics reflected the troubled and changing times. The counterculture, with its "flower children," "hippies" and psychedelic drug users, had arrived. The slogan of the day was "Make Love, Not War," as the counterculture preached free sex and opposition to U.S. involvement in the Vietnam war. This agenda was expressed in the rock music of the mid- and late 1960s. Songs like the Rolling Stones' "I Can't Get No Satisfaction" and Bob Dylan's "Blowin' in the Wind," "A Hard Rain's Gonna Fall" and "Talkin' World War III Blues" presented ideas and viewpoints far removed from those of mainstream middle-class America.

Many parents were shocked to find that their children were developing values different from their own. They started to blame the schools for teaching such things to their children, unaware that much of the education was going on at home—by the music they had banished to their children's rooms.

The Beatles. One of the most popular recording groups of all times was the Beatles, an English quartet that had a profound impact on American popular culture and middle-class culture worldwide during the 1960s. Although the group disbanded in 1970, their cultural influence was so strong that their popularity continues into the 1990s.

The Beatles, from Liverpool, England, consisted of John Lennon, Paul McCartney, George Harrison and Ringo Starr. In 1964 they led the "British invasion" of rock stars who became household names in the American popular culture. These British performers had grown up with America's Elvis Presley and had adapted his style to create a uniquely British sound. The Beatles and other British groups also triggered a youth fashion revolution in the United States, which consisted of long hair and "Beatle" boots for boys and miniskirts and straight long hair for girls.

The Beatles' early hits were simple and innocent songs such as "I Want to Hold Your Hand" and "She Loves You." Their music changed with the times, however, and began to rely on advanced recording techniques. In 1967 the Beatles released *Sgt. Pepper's Lonely Hearts Club Band.* The album took more than 400 hours to record and was highly sophisticated with many hidden messages and meanings in the lyrics, sound track and album cover. Some claimed four-letter words and other messages were imbedded at a level where they could only be heard by the subconscious mind.

The Beatles synthesized several different types of popular music to achieve their distinctive sound. Although they split up in 1970, their music remains popular today. Rerelease of their music on compact discs in 1987 demonstrated how much life was left in the "Beatles industry." (*Culver Pictures*)

One song in particular—"Lucy in the Sky with Diamonds"—was believed by some observers to be about the use of LSD. They pointed out that the key words in the title start with the letters of this hallucinogenic drug and that the lyrics describe a psychedelic acid trip with such phrases as "tangerine trees and marmalade skies." The Beatles, of course, denied any connection. *Sgt. Pepper* was so successful that 20 years later, in 1987, it was voted by rock critics around the world as the greatest rock album of all time[4] (see Table 10.1).

Some people also zeroed in on the Beatles' top-selling single "Hey Jude" (1968), and said that it too was about the use of drugs. The word "her" was said to refer to heroin in such lyrics as "let her into your heart" and "the minute you let her under your skin/ then you begin to make it better." Beatle John Lennon was reportedly hooked on heroin at the time he wrote the song.[5] However, Beatle business associate and biographer Peter Brown says that Lennon wrote "Hey Jude" to ease the pain for his young son, Julian, while Lennon was divorcing his first wife, Cynthia, and becoming involved with Yoko Ono.[6]

Brown does confirm that the group was one of many who did get heavily involved in drugs. Although the Beatles had been taking amphetamines to help them through concerts since their early days of performing in Hamburg, West Germany, it was not until their first American tour in 1964 that they were turned on to marijuana. According to Brown, "On August 28 a small but auspicious event occurred at the Delmonico Hotel in New York that would grow to affect the consciousness of the world: Bob Dylan turned the Beatles on to marijuana for the first time in their lives."[7] Brown also confirms the Beatles' experimentation with LSD and admits that John Lennon became dependent on heroin.[8]

The change in the Beatles and their music was what kept them so popular. They led the British invasion with a new sound that the youth of America seemed to be waiting for, as Beatlemania swept over the United States in 1964. In April of 1964 the top five singles in this country were all recordings by the Beatles. Other British groups—Herman's Hermits, the Dave Clark Five and Peter and Gordon—had top-10 hits that year, but only the Beatles became a cultural legend because they were willing to change as rock music "grew up" in the troubled decade of the 1960s (see Box 10.2).

Even though the Beatles broke up in 1970, their impact on our popular culture remains profound. Paul, George and Ringo are still performing. When John Lennon was murdered outside his New York apartment in December 1980, the event became one of the biggest news stories of the year. Hundreds of radio and TV stations throughout the United States honored his wife Yoko Ono's request for 10 minutes of silence. Magazines and newspapers ran extensive stories on the shooting and ordinary people's reaction to his death. In 1986 singer Michael Jackson paid between $40 and $50 million to purchase the rights to almost all of the songs written by the Beatles. And in the late 1980s many radio stations were still regularly playing the Beatles' music.

Second Wave of the British Invasion. The second wave of the British invasion brought the Rolling Stones, a group that sang about alienation and social discontent. Reflecting the hostility of the times, the Stones challenged the Beatles as the most popular group in the United States. However, feminist groups greatly criticized the

Table 10.1
The Top 100 Rock-'n'-Roll Albums of All Time

1. *Sgt. Pepper's Lonely Hearts Club Band*, the Beatles
2. *Born to Run*, Bruce Springsteen
3. *Blonde on Blonde*, Bob Dylan
4. *What's Going On*, Marvin Gaye
5. *Born in the U.S.A.*, Bruce Springsteen
6. *The Sun Collection*, Elvis Presley
7. *The Velvet Underground and Nico*, the Velvet Underground and Nico
8. *Pet Sounds*, the Beach Boys
9. *Astral Weeks*, Van Morrison
10. *The Beatles (The White Album)*, the Beatles
11. *Exile on Main Street*, the Rolling Stones
12. *Let it Bleed*, the Rolling Stones
13. *Abbey Road*, the Beatles
14. *Songs in the Key of Life*, Stevie Wonder
15. *Dark Side of the Moon*, Pink Floyd
16. *Live at the Apollo, Vol. 1*, James Brown
17. *Revolver*, the Beatles
18. *Highway 61 Revisited*, Bob Dylan
19. *Never Mind the Bollocks Here's the Sex Pistols*, Sex Pistols
20. *Who's Next*, the Who
21. *Rubber Soul*, the Beatles
22. *Otis Blue*, Otis Redding
23. *Thriller*, Michael Jackson
24. *The Band*, the Band
25. *Blood on the Tracks*, Bob Dylan
26. *Rumours*, Fleetwood Mac
27. *Avalon*, Roxy Music
28. *My Aim Is True*, Elvis Costello
29. *With the Beatles*, the Beatles
30. *Tapestry*, Carole King
31. *The Clash*, the Clash
32. *Bringing It All Back Home*, Bob Dylan
33. *Beggars Banquet*, the Rolling Stones
34. *Forever Changes*, Love
35. *I Want to See the Bright Lights Tonight*, Richard and Linda Thompson
36. *Live!*, Bob Marley and the Wailers
37. *Court and Spark*, Joni Mitchell
38. *Innervisions*, Stevie Wonder
39. *Get Happy!!*, Elvis Costello
40. *London Calling*, the Clash
41. *Entertainment*, Gang of Four
42. *Bridge Over Troubled Water*, Simon and Garfunkel
43. *Squeezing Out Sparks*, Graham Parker and the Rumour

44. *Grievous Angel*, Gram Parsons
45. *Synchronicity*, the Police
46. *Kate and Anna McGarrigle*, Kate and Anna McGarrigle
47. *The Unforgettable Fire*, U2
48. *Hotel California*, the Eagles
49. *Starsailor*, Tim Buckley
50. *Electric Ladyland*, the Jimi Hendrix Experience
51. *Private Dancer*, Tina Turner
52. *Moondance*, Van Morrison
53. *It's Too Late to Stop Now*, Van Morrison
54. *Green River*, Creedence Clearwater Revival
55. *The Stranger*, Billy Joel
56. *Building the Perfect Beast*, Don Henley
57. *Paris 1919*, John Cale
58. *Hunky Dory*, David Bowie
59. *Darkness on the Edge of Town*, Bruce Springsteen
60. *This Year's Model*, Elvis Costello
61. *For Your Pleasure*, Roxy Music
62. *The Pretenders*, the Pretenders
63. *Dreamer*, Bobbie Bland
64. *Music From Big Pink*, the Band
65. *Here's Little Richard*, Little Richard
66. *Who Sell Out*, the Who
67. *Blue*, Joni Mitchell
68. *Aftermath*, the Rolling Stones
69. *Can't Slow Down*, Lionel Ritchie
70. *Stand!*, Sly and the Family Stone
71. *Beatles for Sale*, the Beatles
72. *Young Americans*, David Bowie
 * *Sports*, Huey Lewis and the News
74. *Talking Book*, Stevie Wonder
75. *King Creole*, Elvis Presley
 * *The Notorious Byrd Brothers*, The Byrds
 * *Stranded*, Roxy Music
78. *The 'Chirping' Crickets*, the Crickets
 * *John Wesley Harding*, Bob Dylan
 * *Radio City*, Big Star
81. *Trout Mask Replica*, Captain Beefheart and his Magic Band
 * *The Velvet Underground*, the Velvet Underground
 * *Off the Wall*, Michael Jackson
 * *Let's Get It On*, Marvin Gaye
85. *Imagine*, John Lennon
86. *Amazing Grace*, Aretha Franklin
87. *Horses*, Patti Smith
 * *Making Movies*, Dire Straits
 * *Swordfishtrombones*, Tom Waits
90. *Purple Rain*, Prince and the Revolution

  * *The Rise and Fall of Ziggy Stardust and the Spiders from Mars*, David Bowie
 92. *L.A. Woman*, the Doors
  * *Layla*, Derek and the Dominos
 94. *A Christmas Gift for You*, Phil Spector and Artists
 95. *Going to a Go-Go*, the Miracles
  * *The Last Waltz*, the Band
 97. *Are You Experienced*, the Jimi Hendrix Experience
  * *Pearl*, Janis Joplin
  * *Sweet Dreams*, Eurythmics
100. *Transformer*, Lou Reed

* Indicates a tie.
Reprinted by permission from Paul Gambaccini, *The Top 100 Rock 'n' Roll Albums of All Time* (London: Harmony Books, 1987).

BOX 10.2.

IS PAUL DEAD? SOME IN THE 1960S THOUGHT SO

In 1969 a rumor started that one of the Beatles, Paul McCartney, had been decapitated in an automobile accident and replaced by a look-alike named William Campbell. The rumor swept through the American popular culture and the world.

Fans started finding clues that Paul was dead subliminally imbedded in the Beatles' music and in their album covers. If one listened carefully to the end of "Strawberry Fields Forever" (1967), one was supposed to hear John muttering "I buried Paul." Other clues were found by spinning the Beatles *The White Album* (1968) backward. In the tune "Revolution 9," the phrase "number nine, number nine" sounded like "turn me on dead man, turn me on dead man" when played counterclockwise. By listening carefully to the gibberish sandwiched between "I'm So Tired" and "Blackbird" on that album clue seekers could find the message "Paul is dead man, miss him, miss him."

The cover of *Abbey Road* (1969) offered additional clues. The Beatles were pictured leaving a cemetery with John Lennon dressed in white, Ringo Starr dressed as an undertaker and George Harrison dressed as a gravedigger. McCartney was the only one out of step with the others. He was barefoot, as British corpses are often buried, and had a cigarette in his right hand, supposedly confirming that this was an imposter for the left-handed Paul. The license plate on a Volkswagen parked on the street was "28 IF," which, clue seekers noted, would have been McCartney's age had he lived.

All the Beatles denied not only the rumor but the existence of the "clues." Nevertheless the rumor developed into a genuine folk tale created and spread by the mass media. Sociologist Barbara Suczek claims it was a twentieth-century version of the ancient Greek myth in which a beautiful youth dies and is resurrected as a god.

By the 1970s, the entire episode was a joke, and even John Lennon referred to it in the lyrics of one of his songs. The "Paul Is Dead" hoax significantly increased the sale of the Beatles' albums, and it proved that all kinds of messages could be cleverly transmitted in the sound tracks and album covers of popular music.

Stones for the hostility toward women evident in such songs as "Under My Thumb," about a girl who does just as she is told, and "Time Is on My Side," about a dependent woman who keeps running back to her man. In the 1970s feminists protested a bill-board advertisement for the Rolling Stones' album *Black and Blue*. It showed a woman beaten and tied up with a caption reading "I'm black and blue from the Rolling Stones, and I love it."

Other Favorites. Another popular kind of music in the 1960s was the Motown sound, danceable black soul music that originated in Detroit. This music featured the sounds of Diana Ross and the Supremes, the Temptations and Stevie Wonder. By the early 1970s these groups were singing socially conscious songs like "Love Child" and "Ball of Confusion."

Other groups that were reflecting the new age of social protest and the drug culture during this period were the Doors and Jefferson Airplane. In a quieter, more subtle way, Simon and Garfunkel were also singing about social protest and bitterness.

ROCK SPECIALIZES

From its beginnings in the 1950s, rock music has learned to specialize. Over the years a variety of rock forms—such as pop rock, hard rock, acid rock, punk rock, bubblegum rock, glitter rock, reggae, new wave, heavy metal and Christian rock—have evolved (see Box 10.3).

Disco. In the 1970s, as the Vietnam war came to an end and people began to tire of protest music, they began searching for a new sound. The discotheque—a cabaret where patrons could dance to popular music—began to grow in popularity. Disco music, like rock, had its roots in the beat of rhythm-and-blues. It created a new cultural industry of disco palaces, like the celebrity haven Studio 54 in New York. Disco music brought a new group of stars, from soloists like Donna Summer to groups like the Village People, which consisted of six men dressed as a cowboy, construction worker, Indian, policeman, biker and soldier. One of the hottest disco groups, thanks to their songs for the movie *Saturday Night Fever* (1977), was the Bee Gees.

In the late 1970s, the record industry went into a financial slump similar to the one it had experienced in the 1930s. Part of the problem was an increase in record prices due to the rise in petroleum prices (the vinyl used in records is a petroleum by-prod-uct). But some people, like record producer Richard Perry, blamed disco for the decline in record sales: "Everybody spent their money dancing at discos, not on albums. Disco also was limited to . . . 128 beats per minute, which gave it pulse but no solid melody. All disco began to sound alike. It became totally uninspiring to dance to. It got people out of the habit of buying records. It really hurt the whole music industry."[9]

Punk Rock. Also contributing to the decline of record sales was the recording industry itself, which tried to limit the expenses of promotion by restricting the num-

BOX 10.3.

"HEAVENLY METAL MUSIC"

While some have been working toward banning heavy-metal music claiming that much of its lyrics promote Satanism, the heavenly metal band Stryper has been fighting the devil's music on the top-40 charts.

Stryper found success blending born-again Christian lyrics with a heavy-metal sound and seemed to have made it in the music world when their first video, from their ablum *Calling on You,* debuted on MTV in the late 1980s.

Their 1986 album *To Hell With the Devil* found mainstream acceptance among hard-rock fans and gave defenders of heavy metal support for their argument that its the sound—not the lyrics—that turns on audiences.

The Christian rock band consists of lead singer Michael Sweet, guitarist Oz Fox, drummer Robert Sweet (brother of Michael) and bassist Tim Gaines.

Stryper is just one of a number of rock bands that have taken up the Christian theme in their lyrics in an attempt to combat what many fundamentalist Christian ministers called the "moral corruption" of heavy-metal music.

(AP/Wide World Photos)

ber of new rock groups allowed to record during the 1970s. (This was a classic form of gatekeeping.) Rock-'n'-roll had evolved from a youth subcultural movement of the 1950s to become an Establishment medium that was still providing groups from the 1960s, such as the Rolling Stones, Diana Ross and the Who. Establishment control of the recording industry led in 1976 to the *punk rock* rebellion in England. A new youth subculture, known as punks, began developing a new anti-Establishment music. Some of the first punk-rock bands, such as the Sex Pistols and the Clash, denounced the Establishment's control of mass culture and spoke out against our consumer society. The punk movement spread throughout the world, but it did not become the rage in the United States as it was in Britain. Eventually it was watered down and became popular as new-wave music. Punk and new wave both had an impact on American fashion. While some people bought fashionable new-wave clothing promoted by the Establishment consumer culture, others spiked and colored their hair green or purple to imitate the British punk look.

New Wave. Disco's popularity had declined by the 1980s as punk and new-wave music emerged. Among the new groups rising to popularity were the B-52s, Devo,

BOX 10.4.

U2: FROM PUNK LYRICS TO SOCIAL CONSCIOUSNESS

One of the hottest musical groups around in the late 1980s was U2. In 1987 the group started an 18-month world tour that played to sold-out houses wherever it went. The group soon found itself on the cover of *Time* magazine with the headline "Rock's Hottest Ticket." *Joshua Tree*, the group's sixth album, was breaking sales records, and the album's first single, "With or Without You," rapidly climbed into the top 10 on Top-40 radio stations.

Things had not always been so successful for the Irish group, which formed while the members were attending Mount Temple High School in Dublin. They began struggling to make it in the recording business about the time punk was becoming popular on the British-Irish scene. The group consisted of lead singer-writer Bono (Paul Hewson), lead guitarist the Edge (David Evans), bass guitarist Adam Clayton and drummer Larry Mullen, Jr., who at the age of 14 placed the notice on the high-school bulletin board asking if anyone was interested in starting a rock band. According to their manager, Paul McGuinness, during those early days as a punk group "they were very bad." Although realizing that as musicians they weren't all that good, the group believed in themselves and continued to struggle.

U2 found its rock-'n'-roll niche in the late 1980s by reflecting a new mood that seemed to be finding favor among the young in the culture. The group abandoned the anti-Establishment tone of British punk lyrics (while retaining the sound) and started expressing more humanitarian sentiments. Their music reflected the sense of morality, idealism and conscience young people had shown by giving their support to the Live Aid and other benefit concerts.

Rock music continues into the 1990s as a powerful social force capable of reflecting cultural trends and concerns.

(R. Raiman/Sygma)

Blondie, Elvis Costello, the Cars, the Motels, the Talking Heads, the Police, Duran Duran and Boy George and the Culture Club. This new music plus the development of music videos and the debut of MTV in 1981 helped restore the financial health of the recording industry.

From Bruce to Madonna. By the mid-1980s recording artists like Bruce Springsteen, U2, Michael Jackson, Prince and Madonna were leading popularity charts and selling out concerts within hours after tickets went on sale (see Box 10.4). They also were contributing to the consumer culture by selling concert trinkets that ranged from "Madonna" jewelry to T-shirts. Madonna, who had become a movie star in *Desperately Seeking Susan* (1984) to assist her climb to rock stardom, was featured on the cover of three national magazines in 1985, *Time, Playboy* and *Penthouse.*

Second-Generation Rockers. Now that an entire generation has grown up with rock-'n'-roll, the generation gap seems to have disappeared and the music has "aged." Half of the number-one singles on the *Billboard* charts in 1986 were by artists over 35; four singers were over 40. Young and old are now listening to rock-'n'-roll—the younger ones listening to Janet Jackson, George Michael, Bananarama, Beastie Boys, Run-D.M.C. and U2 while the older ones are still enjoying the records of the Rolling Stones. And the British invasion of the 1960s has been firmly reversed (See Box 10.5).

THE MUSIC VIDEO PHENONEMON (MTV)

In 1981 Warner Amex created an album-oriented rock cable television channel that featured videos supplied by record companies. It targeted 12- to 23-year-olds and became television's only 24-hour-a-day rock-music station. It has had a phenomenal impact on the American popular culture. By the mid-1980s surveys showed that virtually every new band was making at least one music video and that 70 percent of rock enthusiasts indicated that MTV was important in determining which records they would buy.

Music Video Expansion. In 1982 another cable network, USA, started broadcasting *Night Flite,* a program devoted to MTV-type videos. Soon HBO and Showtime were playing videos for youngsters to fill the time between movies. Atlanta superstation WTBS developed a music video show called *Night Tracks,* NBC developed *Friday Night Videos* and even ABC and CBS were airing at least an hour of music videos each week by the mid-1980s. In the meantime, a second 24-hour music video channel, VH-1, debuted on cable, featuring soft rock and aimed at an older audience. Country-and-western fans can enjoy video music on cable's Nashville Network.

Impact on Education. Some educators have complained that students are spending too much time watching MTV and not enough on homework. Although many

BOX 10.5.

THE BRITISH INVASION REVERSED

When the Beatles, Rolling Stones and other British rock groups invaded the American popular culture in the 1960s, it was a one-way invasion. British music critics dismissed American rock music as "bland car wash for the sun-kissed deaf."

However, by 1986 eight of the 10 most acclaimed albums listed in British journals were from the United States. Topping the list were Prince, Run-D.M.C., Janet Jackson, Anita Baker and Cameo. The British popular culture had become enamoured with American black music. Most U.S. critics dismissed Prince's *Parade* as far beneath the daring and imagination of his earlier works, but two of Britain's leading music publications declared it the best album of the year. Prince's *Kiss* was prevented from sweeping the best singles competition by Run-D.M.C.'s *Walk This Way*.

The top 10 LPs, according to English music critics, were as follows:

1. Prince, *Parade*
2. Beastie Boys, *Licensed to Ill*
3. The Smiths, *The Queen Is Dead*
4. Janet Jackson, *Control*
5. Anita Baker, *Rapture*
* Cameo, *Word Up*
7. Run-D.M.C., *Raising Hell*
8. Elvis Costello, *Blood and Chocolate*
9. Sonic Youth, *EVOL*
10. Throwing Muses, *Throwing Muses*

The top 10 singles, according to Britain's leading music journals, were:

1. Run-D.M.C., *Walk This Way*
2. Prince, *Kiss*
3. Gwen Guthrie, *Ain't Nothing Going On But the Rent*
4. Cameo, *Word Up*
5. The Real Roxanne & Howie Tee, *Bang Zoom*
6. The Smiths, *Ask*
7. Davis/Pinckney Project, *You Can Dance*
8. Paul Simon, *You Can Call Me Al*
9. Beastie Boys, *She's on It*
10. Oran (Juice) Jones, *The Rain*

Source: Robert Hilburn, "British Critics Turn All Ears to America," *Los Angeles Times,* January 11, 1987, calendar section, p. 65. Top-10 lists copyright, 1987, Los Angeles Times. Reprinted by permission.

teenagers had been studying with rock music in the background since the 1950s, videos required visual as well as audio attention.

Other educators recognized the significance of MTV and are studying it. For example, California State University at Los Angeles offers a course called Music Video 454. Students study the contents of music video, listen to guest speakers from the video industry and visit sets where some of the videos are produced.

Impact on Other Media. The influence of music videos has not been limited to the recording industry. Rock videos' pace, style and sound have influenced such television shows as *Miami Vice* and such motion pictures as *Top Gun* and *True Stories*.

(*Miami Vice* star Don Johnson and Bruce Willis, who plays David Addison on *Moon-lighting*, became rock recording stars as well as TV stars.) When David Byrne of the Talking Heads starred in the rock video–influenced film *True Stories*, it landed him on the cover of *Time* in 1986 as "rock's renaissance man." In 1987 Michael J. Fox shed his kid-next-door image to play a long-haired, earring-wearing rocker in *Light of Day*. Rock videos of sound tracks from these movies were often used on MTV to plug the films.

Decline in Ratings. MTV's ratings, however, peaked in 1984 with a high of 1.2 percent of the potential audience. Although the ratings seem to have leveled off at 0.6 percent, the cable channel still delivers a large number of 12- to 23-year-olds to advertisers.

In the 1950s, 1960s and 1970s youngsters grew up listening to the sounds and messages of rock music. Today they are experiencing visual as well as audio creations of the rock music world.

CONTROVERSIES SURROUNDING ROCK MUSIC

Criticism and controversy has surrounding recorded music ever since its entrance into the popular culture. The major focus of criticism has been the music's lyrics.

Editorial Statements. We usually think of newspapers as the medium in which editorials are most effectively used. However, in reality, the most effective editorial statements are carried in recorded music because the messages are combined with music's ability to interact with our emotions.

Each record or tape contains an editorial statement. It might be an innocent expression of the joys of love or a socially powerful statement about the need to feed starving people. Instrumental music contains melodies or beats that stir up some type of emotion, whether it be sadness, joy, relaxation or an impulse to dance. Whatever type of music it is, it is directing some form of persuasion toward the listener.

Subliminal Messages? A great deal of criticism has been leveled against the recording industry for releasing music with hidden messages designed to appeal to the subconscious, rather than the conscious, mind. Two types of hidden messages have been singled out in particular: subliminal imbeds and backmasking.

Retail stores have used *subliminal imbeds* for some time. Many department stores and supermarkets now play music that includes a voice, just below the level where it can be consciously heard, that continuously repeats messages such as "You are an honest person; you will not steal." Studies indicate that shoplifting has been reduced significantly when this music is played. People can now buy subliminal tapes that claim to program their minds with various messages that will help them lose weight, stop smoking, think positively and so on.

Many rock music critics charge that subliminal messages also are found in popular music—and often the messages imbedded are quite different from the lyrics. For example, the Beatles are said to have dropped four-letter words into their records below the consciously audible level.

Backmasking, sometimes called backward masking, is even more controversial. People debate not only whether it can affect the listener, but whether it exists at all.

Religious leaders have played records backward for congressional leaders to point out what they say are satanic messages. For example, in Led Zeppelin's all-time favorite, "Stairway to Heaven," phrases that sound very much like "I live with Satan" and "Here's to my sweet Satan" can be heard when the recording is played backward.

The recording artists deny that they have implanted any backward messages. Critics of the backmasking theory say that the similarity in sound to actual messages is coincidental and that, even if it were deliberate, it would be ineffective, since hardly anyone listens to the music backward. Theory proponents, however, claim that the subconscious mind, particularly the right brain, can unscramble these messages while they are played forward. No scientific evidence has been produced to support this theory.

Explicit Lyrics and Heavy Metal. Today the criticism of popular music is focused on the lyrics. In the 1980s some rock artists went to extremes in explicit language and antisocial sentiments. Topics discussed in song lyrics included suicide, incest, homosexuality, bisexuality, illegal drug use, murder of family members and explicit sex and bondage. By most cultural standards, the lyrics were raunchy and vulgar.

In 1986 Prince was singing about sexual activities that would make almost anyone blush, and Ozzy Osbourne, was boasting that he made a living doing things most people get arrested for. (Osbourne was sued by the parents of a suicide victim who had been listening to Osbourne's "Suicide Solution" at the time of his death, but a judge threw the suit out of court).

Some heavy-metal groups were singing about satanic worship, and their music was blamed for the increase in satanic cults in a number of communities. Critics were linking bizarre killings, such as those committed by the Night Stalker in California, as well as sexual abuse of preschool children to heavy-metal music. Songs about marijuana and cocaine were also prevalent in the 1980s, a trend that had been around since the Roaring '20s.

Efforts to Ban Popular Music. In recent years the explicit lyrics have led some religious and parent groups to advocate banning popular music from the airwaves. These groups have also advised parents to get rid of their children's recordings.

Many of these critics grew up with rock-'n'-roll and know firsthand how much influence music can have on impressionable young people. Powerful lobbies have been formed in attempts to get Congress to impose some sort of control over popular music.

Rating System. One of the most powerful of the lobbying groups was the Parents' Music Resource Center (PMRC), a Washington-based organization formed by Tip-

Frank Zappa testifying before a Senate subcommittee considering warning labels for records that contain explicit references to drugs or sexuality. *(UPI/ Bettmann Newsphotos)*

per Gore, wife of Senator Albert Gore of Tennessee, and Susan Baker, wife of Treasury Secretary James Baker. They began pressuring the recording industry to voluntarily label all explicit records so that parents would know what the music contained. They called for either a rating system similar to that used by the motion-picture industry or the printing of lyrics on album covers. Opponents of the PMRC proposal argued that the job of censoring children's listening habits belonged in the home, not with government.

In September 1985 the U.S. Senate held hearings on a plan to protect children from "raunchy lyrics." PMRC presented its rating system proposal to the Senate committee. Testifying against the proposal were such recording artists as Frank Zappa, John Denver and Dee Snider, lead singer of Twisted Sister. The musicians argued that the proposal threatened their First Amendment rights by suggesting censorship of their artistic work. Nevertheless, some senators made it clear that if the industry did not voluntarily "clean up its act," legislation might be passed to do it for them.

A month after the hearings, recording-industry representatives announced that 80 percent of the industry had agreed to start either placing warning labels on records and tapes or printing lyrics on album covers. Although the PMRC had substantially won its battle, critics predicted that the labels and lyrics would *increase* the sale of explicit albums. They also claimed that the attention PMRC had called to such obscure heavy-metal groups as WASP had done more than anything else to promote the sales of their records. One thing seems certain: the voluntary efforts have not hurt record sales.

The Beat, Not the Lyrics. Despite the controversy over explicit lyrics, research in the mid-1980s showed that lyrics about sex, drugs, violence and satanism had little impact on the vast majority of teenagers. In fact, some rock musicians were using their medium and popularity to combat these social ills (see Box 10.6).

At California State University in Fullerton, Lorraine Prinsky, a sociology professor, and Jill Rosenbaum, a criminal justice professor, wanted to know what teenagers thought about rock lyrics. They used a 40-page questionnaire to get teens to describe their favorite songs. They found that only about 7 percent of the teenagers perceived that the 662 songs listed were about sex, violence, drugs or satanism. The study concluded that specific lyrics seem to be of little consequence to most teens, who are far more interested in the beat or overall sound of a recording.

BOX 10.6.

ROCK AGAINST DRUGS

While the Parents' Music Resource Center was calling for voluntary warning labels on rock music and First Lady Nancy Reagan was telling young people to "Just Say No" to drugs—both with limited results—rock musicians were doing their own thing to help young people grapple with the temptations of drug and alcohol abuse.

A series of television commercials aired in the late 1980s—many on MTV—featured rock musicians speaking out against drugs. The project, called Rock Against Drugs (RAD), used a refreshing and effective approach to get the antidrug messages before teenagers. Instead of talking down to the teenage audience and attempting to scare them, the RAD commercials attempted to get the message across without betraying the rebellion and energy of rock-'n'-roll.

Steve Jones—whose colleague, Sid Vicious of the Sex Pistols, died of a heroin overdose—was pictured looking up from his motorcycle snarling "Drugs suck." Vince Neil of Motley Crüe was quoted as saying "I still party with the best of them but now I do it clean."

Although it's impossible to measure the effectiveness of these commercials, letters from fans seemed to indicate some success. One high-school student wrote MTV to say that the commercial by Bon Jovi encouraged him to stop taking drugs. "Those guys were the only people I would listen to," he wrote. "They changed my life around," another fan wrote to rocker Ronnie Dio. "Teachers can preach for hours about how bad drugs are and I still went out and got high. But man, once I heard you say how stupid drugs are, I never touched them again!"[*]

In addition to the antidrug commercials, the rock industry was combating substance abuse in the lyrics of many of its songs. Bob Seger's "American Storm," Huey Lewis's "I Want a New Drug" and Glen Frey's "Smuggler's Blues" all carried antidrug messages. While PMRC and religious groups were condemning KISS for singing satanic messages, one of the group's constant messages for more than 10 years was not to do drugs.

The irony of the decade of the 1980s was that while people were banding together in fear of the evils of rock music, this powerful mass-communication medium was successfully combating one of society's most serious problems—drug abuse.

*Danny Goldberg, "To Reach Teens: Rock Stars Speak Against Drugs," *Los Angeles Times*, June 14, 1987, Opinion section, p. 3.

If the musical themes of the 1980s were really not much different from those of the 1920s, why was such a fuss being made? One answer is that the language used in the 1980s was no longer cute or suggestive; it was completely explicit. Another is that the age of the audience for records has changed. In the 1920s the people who listened to recorded music were mostly in their 20s or at the very youngest, in their late teens. In the 1980s the audience consisted of many impressionable preteenagers who worshipped recording stars like Prince and Madonna with cultlike devotion. In addition, by the 1980s radio, television and home audio and video recorders had made popular music a far more pervasive element in our mass-mediated popular culture than it had been in the 1920s.

Despite the controversies surrounding the recording industry, one thing is certain: it is a multibillion dollar a year enterprise ($4.7 billion in revenue in 1987), which will continue to provide the products the customers will buy (see Box 10.7).

BOX 10.7.

THE BUSINESS OF MUSIC

Popular music is a multibillion-dollar-a-year business that has skyrocketed many to stardom and has kept other talented performers out of the limelight.

How does a musical group make it in the recording industry? The best way is to be discovered by an A & R person—artist-and-repertoire representative. These are the people who discover talent, sign it to the record label they work for, budget the album and then do whatever is necessary to facilitate its production (including finding songs and producers as well as massaging the performers' egos). When the record is pressed, the A & R reps become in-house cheerleaders, pushing the company to mount a campaign to win radio station airplay.

There are fewer than 100 A & R jobs in American record companies. Many such positions are filled by former musicians, record company employees or radio and entertainment managers.

Some A & R reps double as producers, recording the acts they sign and earning royalties on each album, tape or compact disc. A & R rep salaries usually start around $50,000 and go much higher. These reps have liberal expense accounts. Record companies that hire reps look for people with musical expertise and a knowledge of what is current.

What do A & R reps look for when they are seeking new talent? According to John Milward, writing for the *Philadelphia Enquirer*, A & R execs offer the following advice to undiscovered musicians:

- Don't go broke making a slick demo—they're used to hearing things in the raw.

- Don't include more than three or four songs, and make sure the first is a killer.

- Develop as much of a buzz about your live shows as possible, and expand beyond your hometown.

- Don't quit your day job.*

*John Milward, "Giving Their All for the Record," *Philadelphia Enquirer*, January 10, 1988.

OTHER FORMS OF RECORDED MUSIC

Although rock-'n'-roll remains, in its various specialized forms, the undisputed champion of popular music, two other genres of recorded music deserve mention. They are country-and-western and classical.

Country-and-Western. Although Southern folk music has been featured on records and some radio stations for decades, not until recently has country-and-western music climbed to the top of the popular music charts. For example, in 1973 there were about 700 country-music radio stations in the United States; by the 1980s there were almost 1,600.

Hollywood has assisted country-and-western music's move into mainstream America with such movies as *Coal Miner's Daughter* (1980) and *Sweet Dreams* (1985), about the lives of country singers Loretta Lynn and Patsy Cline, respectively. In the late 1970s *Urban Cowboy* with John Travolta popularized country-and-western bars and music.

Country-and-western music has been called many things over the years, including hillbilly music (it originated in the mountains of the South), cowboy music and Okie music (it was brought west by migrants, called Okies, who left the dust-bowl regions around Oklahoma during the Great Depression). In reality, it might best be called white soul music; country songs are about the simpler things in life and about the struggles of rural and small-town working people.

Like rock-'n'-roll, country-and-western has changed over the years. Some of it has adopted the beat of rock—country rock—and the industry is using more sophisticated recording techniques. Efforts to take the "twang" out of country-and-western music also have contributed to its increase in popularity. Today more songs are recorded in the home of country music—Nashville, Tennessee—than in any other American city.

Classical Music. Although classical music was the first successful form of recorded music, with opera stars like Enrico Caruso making records, it has remained primarily in the elite culture. Classical record sales remain steady, but modest. Commercial classical music radio stations have actually declined over the years, from 50 in 1965 to only 25 today. Most fans turn to noncommercial radio and television stations for classical music and other forms of "high cultural" programming.

However, some classical artists, such as opera star Luciano Pavarotti, have gained popular attention due to the mass media informing the popular culture of "high cultural" participants and activities. The lines separating the elite from the popular cultures are not as clearly defined as they once were.

SUMMARY

The power of the recording industry was demonstrated dramatically in the mid-1980s by a series of efforts by popular singers to help the victims of starvation in Africa. Hundreds of millions of dollars were raised by these efforts.

The ability to produce recorded music dates to the invention of the phonograph by Thomas A. Edison in 1877. By the beginning of the twentieth century, opera stars were recording records for home sale in the elite culture.

In the 1920s the recording industry brought black music, such as blues and jazz, into the popular culture. However, the color barrier in our society at the time created the need for white performers to "cover" such music. The color barrier was not eliminated until the recording industry targeted the youth of America as its major market in the 1950s.

The expansion of the youth market led to the development of rock-'n'-roll and contributed to the emergence of the generation gap of the 1960s. Parents refused to listen to the new music, while their children grew up with it. As the editorial statements in this new music changed to reflect the changing culture during the 1960s, only the youth were listening. While these young people were listening to the new rock-'n'-roll, the British invasion, featuring the Beatles and Rolling Stones, was taking place. A new youth subculture developed.

Rock was also instrumental in helping the recording industry move into the specialization stage of media development. A wide variety of forms and style of rock music has evolved through the years.

Recorded music is both powerful and controversial. Each record or tape produced contains an editorial statement that has the ability to persuade. Some of the editorial messages are simple, while others are complex and profound.

Many groups have criticized the lyrics of popular music, and the reported use of subliminal messages and backmasking has generated a great deal of controversy.

Although rock-'n'-roll in its various forms remains the favorite popular music in the American culture, country-and-western and classical music also play an important role in keeping the recording industry healthy.

NOTES

1. Paul Oliver, *The Blues Tradition* (New York: Oak Publications, 1970), p. 23.

2. *New York American*, January 22, 1922.

3. Quoted in Edward Jay Whetmore, *Mediamerica: Form, Content, and Consequences of Mass Communication*, 3rd ed. (Belmont, Calif.: Wadsworth, 1985), p. 129.

4. Paul Gambaccini, *The Top 100 Rock 'n' Roll Albums of All Time* (London: Harmony Books, 1987).

5. Peter Brown and Steven Gaines, *The Love You Make: An Insider's Story of the Beatles* (New York: McGraw-Hill, 1983), pp. 301–303.

6. Ibid.

7. Ibid., p. 155.

8. Ibid., pp. 250–251, 416.

9. Quoted in Don R. Pember, *Mass Media in America*, 4th ed. (Chicago: Science Research Associates, 1983), p. 162.

ADDITIONAL READING

Adorno, Theodor W. *Introduction to the Sociology of Music.* New York: Continuum, 1976.

Belz, Carl. *The Story of Rock,* 2nd ed. New York: Oxford University Press, 1972.

Chapple, S., and Garofalo, R. *Rock 'n' Roll Is Here to Pay.* Chicago: Nelson-Hall, 1977.

Drake-Chenault Enterprises Inc. *History of Rock and Roll.* Canoga Park, Calif.: Drake-Chenault, 1978.

Eberly, Philip K. *Music in the Air: America's Changing Tastes in Popular Music.* New York: Hastings House, 1982.

Frith, Simon. *Sound Effects: Youth, Leisure, and the Politics of Rock 'n' Roll.* New York: Pantheon, 1982.

Gelatt, Roland. *The Fabulous Phonograph: 1877–1977.* 3rd ed. New York: Macmillan, 1977.

Palmer, T. *All You Need Is Love: The Story of Popular Music.* New York: Viking, 1976.

Passman, Arnold. *The Deejays.* New York: Macmillan, 1971.

Pichaske, David. *A Generation in Motion: Popular Music and Culture of the Sixties.* New York: Schirmer Books, 1979.

Read, Oliver, and Welsh, Walter. *From Tin Foil to Stereo: Evolution of the Phonograph.* 2nd ed. Indianapolis, Ind.: Sams, 1976.

Part 4

Media Shapers and Cultural Effects

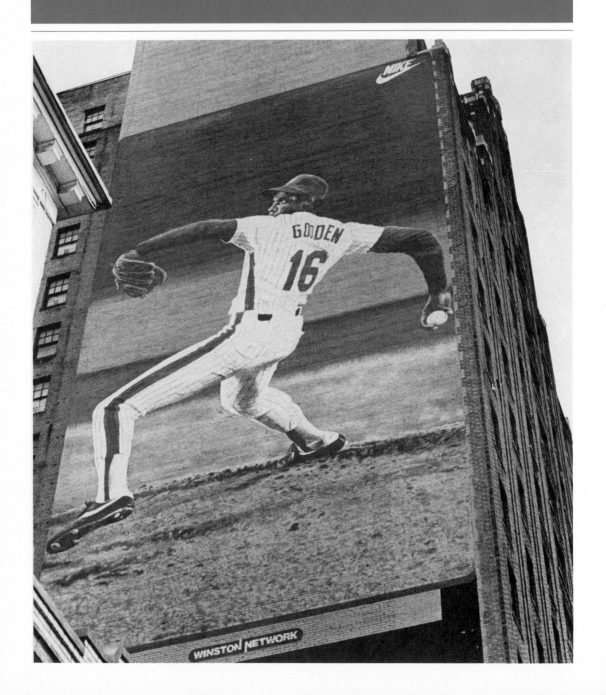

Chapter 11

Advertising: Selling the Message

You can tell the ideals of a
nation by its advertisements.
—*Norman Douglas,* South Wind

One of the basic ingredients of American popular culture is consumption, and it is the advertising industry that makes mass consumption possible. Advertising sells us sexuality, beauty, youth, fashion, happiness, success, status and luxury. When Calvin Klein, for example, advertises blue jeans, he is selling us sex appeal, not jeans. Polo sells us fashion status and Miller beer offers us macho good times.

Research has shown that the average adult can be exposed to 500 advertisements each day from radio, television, newspapers and magazines. (This figure does not include billboards and direct-mail advertisements.)

In 1987 $109 billion was spent on advertising in the United States and these expenditures are growing at a faster rate than the gross national product. Although advertising costs are passed on to consumers, advertising can also save consumers money by delivering more customers to manufacturers, thus making possible mass production and mass consumption, which leads to lower prices. Color television sets, for example, cost $800 to $1,000 when they first went on the market in the late 1950s, but thanks to mass production and consumption, some sets now sell for less than $200.

Advertising is an important element of our culture because it reflects and attempts to change our life styles. New cultural trends and fashions are first transmitted to the mass culture through advertisements.

It is estimated that, by the time a person raised in the United States reaches the age of 21, he or she has been exposed to 1 million to 2 million advertisements.[1] The cumulative effects of this lifelong exposure plays a significant role in shaping our behavior, social beliefs and values. It influences our choice to wear Reebok running shoes, brush our teeth with Crest, and feed our cats Fancy Feast.

Advertising also plays an important role in shaping the kind of mass media we have in this country. Advertising pays the mass media to disseminate its messages and without advertising, our newspapers, magazines and radio and television programming would be far different. We would not have the number or variety of media and programming, and the cost to the consumer would be much higher.

HOW ADVERTISING DEVELOPED

Mass advertising as we know it today is only about a hundred years old. It developed along with industrialization and mass production in the late nineteenth century.

Early Advertising. The concept of advertising dates to early civilization. In 3000 B.C. Babylonian merchants hired barkers to hawk their wares to prospective customers, and placed signs over their doorways to indicate what they sold. This practice continued in ancient Greece and Rome: advertisements were found on walls in the streets of the excavated Roman city of Pompeii. The use of handbills, posters and newspaper advertisements emerged after Gutenberg developed movable type in the fifteenth century.

When Benjamin Franklin established the *Philadelphia Gazette* in 1929, it soon became a favorite medium for advertisers. When the weekly *Pennsylvania Packet and General Advertiser* became a daily in 1784, it featured an entire front page of advertisements for such things as dry goods, food, wine, and tobacco products. When the United States began developing into an industrial nation in the nineteenth century

Early advertisements were posted on walls and other public places. *(The Bettmann Archive)*

and American newspapers and magazines began entering the popular culture, advertising in print media expanded.

First Ad Agency. Credit for organizing the first advertising agency goes to Volney Palmer, who in 1841 started an agency in Philadelphia. On his heels in this new business was another pioneer, John Hooper. These men perceived a need for someone to help publishers sell space to advertisers. (This new industry developed just four years after William Procter and James Gamble joined forces to make soap and candles. Their company—Procter and Gamble—is today the biggest advertiser in the world.) Since they represented publishers rather than advertisers, these early agencies worked quite differently than agencies do today. By the 1870s, however, N. W. Ayer—the nation's oldest ad agency—began representing advertisers, helping them get the best results for their advertising dollars. This is the way agencies all operate today.

Expanding advertising from newspapers to magazines was the brainchild of a young ad man named J. Walter Thompson, who at the turn of the century saw the potential of literary magazines for advertising. He put together the so-called "List of Thirty," important women's and general-interest magazines that would be the best vehicles for advertisers. The list included *Harper's, Ladies Home Journal* and *Cosmopolitan.*[2]

Government Regulations. A lot of early advertising was deceptive and exaggerated. This was the era of patent medicines that claimed to cure everything from cancer to baldness. These heavily advertised products sold to millions, but cured very few. Some of the potions gave relief because their high alcohol content deadened pain; some even contained pain-relieving cocaine and morphine. In 1906 Congress passed the Pure Food and Drug Act to control such advertising, and the Federal Trade Commission (FTC) was formed in 1913 to regulate untruthful claims in advertising. Some states adopted "truth-in-advertising" laws and advertising organizations drew up codes of behavior. Today a number of federal agencies enforce truth in advertising, including the FTC, the Federal Communications Commission (FCC), the Food and Drug Administration (FDA) and the U.S. Postal Service.

Electronic Advertising. Although radio first began to function as a mass-communication medium in 1920, it was not until 1922 that station WEAF in New York began selling air time to advertisers—$100 for 10 minutes. When network broadcasting entered the picture in 1926–27 with the formation of NBC and CBS, the new medium's potential to carry advertisements was fully realized. Ad agencies began producing programs for advertisers. The ad business had become show business. A New York ad agency, Blackett-Sample-Hummert, developed a new type of daytime drama for Procter and Gamble's soap products. The daily serial became known as the soap opera.

Although the first commercial on television was aired by the J. Walter Thompson agency in 1930, it wasn't until 1948 that TV's potential as an advertising medium was realized. Many early programs carried the advertiser's name, such as Milton Berle's popular *Texaco Star Theater* and the *Camel News Caravan.* And soon television became the preferred advertising medium to reach the masses in the United States.

In the 1980s, with the development of cable and satellite TV, a new form of electronic advertising developed—direct-response home shopping services. These cable networks (HSN, CVN, etc.) sell discounted goods directly to consumers, who telephone in their orders to banks of operators. Instead of purchasing air time from cable operators, home shopping networks pay cable operators a percentage of the profits from sales generated.

THEORIES ON ADVERTISING EFFECTIVENESS

Despite the dominant role that advertising plays in American society, people disagree as to whether advertising is as effective as it is thought to be. There seems to be universal agreement that certain types of price advertising (such as supermarket ads in the local newspaper) are effective in generating sales. However, when it comes to national advertising of consumer product images (most ads we see on television and in magazines), the agreement stops.

Minimal Effects Theory. While some believe that advertising makes our mass production-consumption culture possible, others, like sociologist Michael Schudson, contend that advertising does not increase sales. In fact, he says, the opposite is true—an increase in sales simply leads to increases in advertising.[3] This theory was supported by a study conducted by Richard Schmalensee, who found that there was a closer correlation between consumption in a given quarter and advertising in the *next* quarter than between consumption in the given quarter and advertising in the *previous* quarter.[4]

Schudson cites numerous examples to support his contention. He uses the Ford Motor Company's notorious failure with the heavily advertised Edsel to illustrate that advertising expenditures don't always generate sales. The Edsel appeared on the market in 1957 as the most heavily promoted consumer product in history. The company expected to sell 200,000 the first year, but when it took the car off the market two years later, only 109,000 had been sold. The car was ugly, and no amount of advertising was going to get people to buy it. Conversely, he notes that the Hershey Foods Corporation has been a chocolate industry leader since about the turn of the century, even though it didn't start advertising until 1970. Schudson attempts to clinch his argument by pointing out that two large-selling products in the American popular culture today—marijuana and cocaine—are never advertised.[5]

Stephen Fox, in his comprehensive history of American advertising, *The Mirror Makers*, supports the idea that, despite increased advertising expenditures, the industry's influence has declined during the twentieth century.

> From its peak as an independent force in American life in the 1920s,
> advertising has been caught in a tightening vise between two contrary forces.
> Regulation by the government and (finally) by the industry itself has gradually
> limited Madison Avenue's freedom to lie. When restricted, more or less, to
> the truth, advertising lost some of its most powerful, frightening devices. Yet

*even as advertising grew less deceptive, the public grew ever more
sophisticated and skeptical.*[6]

Cutting Edge Theory. Advertising's role in influencing our attitudes, life styles
and culture is beyond dispute. The advertising industry is often on the cutting edge
of new cultural developments and trends in our society.

For example, when cigarette smoking by women started to become fashionable and
suggestive of naughtiness during the Jazz Age of the 1920s, the advertising industry
was there to reflect the new trend. One of the first smoking ads directed toward
women was for Chesterfield cigarettes in 1926. It showed a romantic couple at night,
with the man smoking and the woman sitting next to him. The caption read "Blow
Some My Way." When the women's liberation movement first got rolling, ads began
to depict women in previously stereotypically "male" roles. Often these women were
smoking a "women's cigarette," such as Virginia Slims. When jogging, aerobic exercises and tennis became popular recreations in the 1980s, a glance at magazines
showed much money being spent on advertisements for fashionable clothing for these
activities.

Although some critics blame advertising for creating new cultural trends in order
to sell more goods and services, others argue that the message industry merely reflects
cultural changes.

A-T-R Theory. Getting a person to buy a product involves far more than simply
running an ad in a newspaper or a commercial on television. To best describe the
complexities of advertising, we will use the A-T-R theory, which holds that there are
three main stages in the selling process: awareness, trial, and reinforcement.

Awareness is the easiest step. Through repetition and other advertising techniques,
consumers can be made aware that a product exists. Usually the bigger the advertising
campaign, the more awareness is generated.

Trial, the second step, is much more difficult to induce. Merely advertising a product is not necessarily going to make someone try it. As a result, many companies use
other techniques to get people to try the product, including sending free samples
through the mail or giving them out in stores, giving away discount coupons and offering price reductions.

Reinforcement is the necessary third step to get users to buy the product again.
Studies have shown that after people try a new brand, they usually go back to their
regular brand unless they are constantly reminded about the new brand by effective
advertising. Of course, the new brand must be comparable in quality to the old brand.
If the product does not please the customer, he or she will probably never purchase
it again.

Thus, according to the A-T-R theory, increasing the advertising budget after a
product is established will not necessarily increase *new* sales. However, cutting the
budget will likely reduce repeat sales because some reinforcement will be lost.

Consumers' Information Environment. Advertising is not the only factor in our
decision to make a purchase. As Schudson points out, the normal adult consumer

brings a lifetime of informational resources to any new advertisement. These resources, which he calls the consumer's *informational environment*, include the following:

1. *The consumer's own information from personal experience with the product or related products.*

2. *Word-of-mouth information about the product or related products from family, friends, or acquaintances.*

3. *Information in the media about the product or related products that is not paid advertising. Some of this information will be planted by the public relations efforts of commercial companies and some of it will be independently generated by government reports, consumer groups, journalists, and other noncommercial agencies.*

4. *Information available through formal channels of consumer education, especially the school system, credit institutions, and other agencies.*

5. *Advertisements for rival products and also advertisements for unrelated products, the "clutter" of advertising in general.*

6. *Skepticism about the credibility of the medium in which the ad is placed.*

7. *Skepticism about the credibility of advertising in general.*

8. *Information from nonadvertising channels of marketing.*

9. *Price. This is a special case, and an especially important one, of a nonadvertising channel of marketing.*[7]

Selective Perception. Another factor in determining an advertisement's effectiveness is *selective perception* (see Chapter 1). Advertisers may bombard consumers with television and magazine advertising, sales-promotion discounts and premiums, point-of-purchase displays and other promotional devices, only to find little change in sales figures. Follow-up research will often show that the promotional activities never got through the consumers' *perceptual filters.*[8] In other words, if the public is convinced that the product is worthless, no amount of advertising will change that perception.

Thus it is important to remember that, even though a great deal of money is spent on advertising, the success or failure of these ads to persuade us to buy things is far more complex than one might believe.

PROPAGANDA DEVICES

Although the industry might frown on a discussion of propaganda techniques in a chapter on advertising, there is an important relationship between the two. Webster's defines *propaganda* as "a systematic effort to promote a particular cause or point of view."

Thus, by definition, propaganda is not evil or deceptive. However, over the years, ever since the British used propaganda to solicit U.S. support for the allies' war effort against Germany in World War I, the word has taken on undesirable connotations. But even though the goals of propaganda may not be evil, some of the techniques used are questionable because they appeal primarily to our emotions rather than to our intellect.

Propaganda was probably used most destructively in the 1930s, when Adolf Hitler used it to take control of Germany and neighboring lands. One of Hitler's first acts when he came to power was to name Dr. Joseph Goebbels minister of propaganda. Goebbels immediately took over the German mass media and turned them into propaganda outlets that endorsed Hitler and his reign of terror.

While Hitler waged his propaganda campaign, the rest of the world sat back and watched. Yet years earlier, in 1925, Hitler had spelled out the importance of propaganda and how he planned to use it in his book *Mein Kampf,* which he wrote in prison.

> *The great masses' receptive ability is only very limited, their understanding is small, but their forgetfulness is great. As a consequence of these facts, all effective propaganda has to limit itself only to a very few points and to use them like slogans until even the very last man is able to imagine what is intended by such a word. As soon as one sacrifices this basic principle and tries to become versatile, the effect will fritter away, as the masses are neither able to digest the material offered nor to retain it. Thus the result is weakened and finally eliminated.*[9]

If this philosophy sounds as though it is alive and well in American advertising today, it is because propaganda techniques are still very much in use. But fortunately the American advertising industry is only trying to sell you consumer goods and political candidates, not the bigotry and totalitarianism of Adolf Hitler.

Propaganda is a daily feature of our popular culture. It is a prime ingredient in political rhetoric and is used extensively in advertising campaigns. For these reasons, it is important for all of us to be familiar with the basic propaganda devices so that we can detect them, ward off their emotional appeal and analyze the messages intellectually. The following are some of the more common forms of propaganda devices used today.

Slogans. The slogan is equally effective in advertising and political campaigns. In the latter, it usually takes the form of a chant that can unite large crowds into one common emotion. Examples of political slogans are "Four More Years" used at political conventions; "On strike, shut it down" used by labor and student strikers; "Hey, hey, LBJ, how many babies did you kill today?" used by protesters during the Vietnam War; and "America, love it or leave it," a common bumper sticker during the 1960s. In consumer advertising the list is endless—"Come to Marlboro Country," "You've come a long way baby," "Coke Is It," "Join the Pepsi Generation," "The Uncola," "I Tecate my body," "Light my Lucky," and on and on.

Name Calling. The device of name calling is constantly used in political and ideological battles as well as in commercial advertising campaigns. It tries to make us

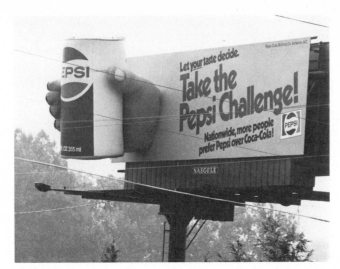

"Take the Pepsi Challenge!" is just one of many slogans used in advertising campaigns. Here an inflatable billboard seems to reach out to passing motorists. *(Nancy Pierce/Photo Researchers)*

form a judgment without examining the evidence on which it should be based. Propagandists appeal to our instincts of hate and fear. They do this by giving "bad names" to those individuals, groups, nations, races or consumer products that they would like us to condemn or reject. Such names as communist, capitalist, imperialist, pervert, egghead and so on are just a few that have been used to discredit the opposition.

Not all name calling is so blatant or direct, however. Often it can work by inference or association. Presidential candidate Al Smith once used indirect name calling against President Franklin D. Roosevelt by stating "There can be only one capital, Washington or Moscow." He was indirectly calling the incumbent president a communist.

Most name calling in advertising uses this indirect approach: "Our painkiller doesn't give you an upset stomach"—implying, of course, that the competition does. Some advertisers actually name a competing brand and charge it with being inferior.

Glittering Generalities. Glittering generalities are broad, accepted ideals and virtuous words that are used to sell a point of view. Like name calling, glittering generalities urge us to accept and approve something without examination. Such expressions as "The American way," "It's in the public interest" and "Taste America's favorite bran flake cereal" are examples. Words like "America," "truth," "freedom," "honor," "liberty," "justice," "loyalty," "progress," "democracy" and "America's favorite" are all common glittering generalities.

Transfer. Some advertisements use symbols of authority, prestige and respect that arouse emotions to sell a cause, candidate or consumer product through the process of subconscious transfer or association. Typical examples are a political candidate photographed next to the American flag ("She's a good American") and cigarette smokers relaxing by a peaceful lake ("Enjoy the natural taste of this brand of cigarette and you too will feel healthy and calm"). Many ads for automobiles feature a sexually attractive person in the passenger seat or at the wheel. The point, of course, is to transfer the sexuality of the person to the brand of vehicle. Designer jeans ads are also effective in transferring sexuality to their product.

Testimonial. An endorsement of a political candidate by celebrities or other well-respected individuals is called a testimonial. When a movie star endorses a particular savings and loan institution, for example, thousands of people may invest there solely on the rationale that, if it is good enough for their idol, it's good enough for them. How many sports fans have selected a certain brand of shaving cream or deodorant because their favorite professional athlete has endorsed it?

Plain Folks. The plain folks device creates the impression that the advertisers or political candidates are just ordinary folks like you and me. In every presidential election, you will see candidates visiting coal mines and factories wearing hard hats. They don't go down into the coal mines, so obviously they don't wear the hard hats for protection. Instead the hats are used to give the impression that they are just ordinary folks like the rest of the workers. Have you ever wondered why laundry detergent ads show "ordinary housewives" rather than attractive models promoting the product?

Card Stacking. Card stacking is the technique by which facts, illustrations and statements are carefully selected to make the maximum impact and sometimes give

"Card-stacking" is a very popular propaganda device in advertisements for medical products. *(Coty, Division of Pfizer, Inc.)*

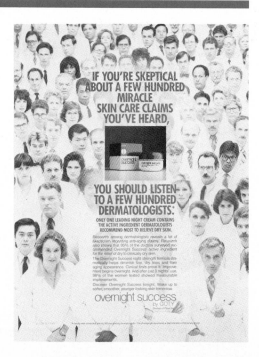

misleading impressions. The cliché that "statistics don't lie, but you can lie with statistics" applies to this technique. A politician may tell his constituents that he votes only for bills that help his district, while neglecting to mention that when special-interest groups have opposed such a bill, he has ducked the issue by not showing up for the vote.

An advertisement claiming that "Four out of five dentists surveyed recommend Chewy chewing gum" will certainly be true, but it could be omitting to say that only five dentists were contacted and that four of them were paid to give an anonymous endorsement.

Bandwagon. The bandwagon device is based on the idea that "if everybody else is doing it, so should you." Jump on the bandwagon, follow the crowd and don't throw your vote away by voting for a loser are clichés associated wtih this device. The psychology behind this technique makes political polling important at election time. The fact that each candidate needs to project the image that he or she is a winner often leads to some conflicting polling results. (Pollsters can skew their results by carefully selecting their samples or by using loaded wording in their questions.) Advertisements telling you to join the Pepsi Generation or to have a good time with the crowd when it's "Miller time" are examples of this type of appeal.

Sex Appeal. We don't ordinarily think of sex as a propaganda device, but it sells products in many ways. In recent years emotional appeals based on sex have been used more and more in product advertising. How about the after-shave-lotion ad that features a sexy female voice saying "Wear English Leather or wear nothing at all"? Or the billboard for Canadian Black Velvet whisky that showed a sexy blonde in a black velvet dress with the words "Feel the Velvet Canadian." And don't forget the Calvin Klein ads of the 1980s that featured partially clad men and women. Sex appeal is used to stimulate emotions and sell consumer products to both sexes.

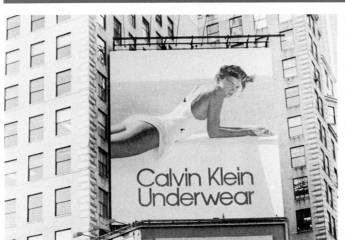

Sex is used to sell just about everything in American culture, from obvious items like underwear to products which would seem to be totally unrelated. (*Barbara Rios/Photo Researchers*)

Music. The last device in our list—music—is also seldom thought of as a propaganda device, yet it is one of the most effective devices in radio and television commercials. Music is an excellent tool for creating specific moods, and it can be used effectively for product identification. Often people will think of a certain product when they hear a tune that has been associated with the product in ads. In politics, music is used to stir the crowds, and the president of the United States uses it effectively to generate a mood of respect when he makes a grand entrance to the strains of "Hail to the Chief."

CONTROVERSIES SURROUNDING ADVERTISING

By its very nature, advertising is controversial. In the early twentieth century people clamored for the regulation of advertising, believing that much of it was exaggerated and untruthful.

As we have seen, government regulations have succeeded in eliminating outright falsehoods from advertising, but many people are still critical. According to Agee, Ault and Emery, most criticism of advertising centers on the following complaints:

1. *Advertising persuades us to buy goods and services we cannot afford.*
2. *Advertising appeals primarily to our emotions, rather than to our intellect.*
3. *Advertising is biased.*
4. *Advertising involves conflicting competitive claims.*
5. *Advertising is unduly repetitious.*
6. *Much advertising is vulgar, obtrusive, irritating.*[10]

The advertising industry has answers for most of these charges. It points out that such criticism merely indicates that advertisers are using natural selling techniques to make customers aware of their products. After all, aren't the above comments true of most types of selling? It is also important to keep in mind that advertising plays a very important role in informing the masses about the many goods and services available.

Subliminal Advertising. However, since the 1950s some criticism has been far more severe. One of the first critics to lash out was Vance Packard, who pointed out in *The Hidden Persuaders* that advertisers were using motivational research and other techniques to sell consumer goods.[11] Packard charged that advertisers were using "depth manipulation," which causes us to do things that are irrational and illogical. Often, he said, ads were filled with messages that were trying to invade the privacy of our minds through hidden subliminal imbeds.

In 1957 a researcher named James Vicary inserted one-frame Coca-Cola and popcorn ads among the 26 frames that are projected on a movie screen every second. Just as the frames around each still photo cannot be perceived by the eye, the advertisements went unnoticed. However, Vicary claimed that peoples' subconscious minds perceived the ads: his research found that Coca-Cola sales increased 18 percent and popcorn sales 57.8 percent after the subliminally imbedded films were shown.[12]

When Vicary was asked to replicate his study under controlled conditions, the new test produced no increase in the sales of either Coke or popcorn.[13] But even though Vicary's claim was invalidated, it had long been known that subliminal stimuli could produce certain behavioral effects under laboratory conditions.[14] What was not known was whether consumers could be motivated to purchase a product by subliminal advertising. In the 1970s Wilson Bryan Key, a mass-communication researcher from Canada, took up Packard's and Vicary's charges. Key advanced the theory that advertisers were using sexually explicit hidden messages, called subliminal imbeds, to sell products. According to Key the messages, primarily in magazine ads, were designed to appeal to our subconscious instincts about sex, death and fear.

By the early 1980s Key had written three popular books on the subject: *Subliminal Seduction*, *Media Sexploitation* and *Clam Plate Orgy*. Key claimed to see such hidden details as castrated penises in Parkay Margarine ads, death masks and skulls in the ice cubes in liquor ads and the word *cancer* in cigarette ads.

Although he couldn't explain how these imbeds worked, Key was convinced that they triggered a subconscious emotional response, ensuring that people would remember the ad and the brand when it came time to buy the product. He has not, however, been able to prove that the ads actually sell more than other ads.

The advertising industry at first ignored Key's charges, claiming that he was nothing more than a "dirty old man" who could see perverted symbols in cloud formations. Some in the industry claimed that the images he saw were mere accidents and were not intended to have any conscious or subconscious effect on consumers.

Finally, in 1984, articles in the industry's trade paper, *Advertising Age*, urged the industry to challenge the lack of evidence for Key's assertions and prove him wrong once and for all. In one article, *Ad Age* reporter Jack Haberstroth published the results of his own survey of 100 randomly selected advertising art directors: of 47 usable responses, only two indicated that they had ever deliberately imbedded a subliminal message.

Nevertheless, some support for Key's contentions has come from other researchers. Warren Breed of the Institute for Scientific Analysis in Berkeley calls imbeds UPOs, or "unidentified printed objects." A study by Breed and James R. DeFoe found hidden images in 45.5 percent of all of the alcoholic-beverage advertisements they examined, a percentage much higher than in ads for other products.[15]

Such discoveries led the Federal Bureau of Alcohol, Tobacco and Firearms to propose rules in 1980 to outlaw subliminal advertising in liquor ads. Although the proposed regulations were distributed for comment and hearings were held, the regulations were never adopted. The executive vice-president of the American Association of Advertising Agencies argued at the hearings that you cannot forbid the use of something that doesn't exist.

The jury is still out on whether there is something to the subliminal imbedding theory. Whatever the outcome, more research needs to be done to determine whether or not the imbeds actually help sell consumer goods.

TELEVISION ADVERTISING

The advent of television dramatically changed American advertising. Today the annual expenditure on TV advertising exceeds $22 billion. These ads are creatively produced and are instrumental in changing American attitudes and life styles as well as in selling products.

What television ads don't do, according to some consumer organizations, is give the viewer much information. Commercials are a slick attempt to get viewers to "feel good" about the product through effective emotional appeals, mostly directed at sexual instincts.

High Cost. Often more money is spent to produce a 30-second commercial than to make the hour-long program in which it is inserted. And the cost of buying TV time is equally high. In 1986 the top-rated television program, NBC's *The Cosby Show,* began charging $400,000 for each 30-second commercial. That was the highest amount ever paid for a commercial in a regular TV series. Only the Super Bowl, which was getting $675,000 for a 30-second spot in 1988, has been able to charge a higher fee.

15-Second Spots. In 1986 all three television networks started running 15-second ads, which allowed them to reduce the cost per ad, double the number of ads run and not reduce revenue. The 15-second advertisements posed a new creative challenge to the industry—packaging a powerful message in half the time and still selling the product to the consumer.

TV Ad Techniques. Many television advertisements have a tripartite structure: the problem, the advice and the resolution. All three messages must be delivered in 15, 30 or 60 seconds. Let's take a mouthwash commercial as an example. First you establish the problem—someone has bad breath. Then you suggest that the person try the advertised mouthwash. This is followed by the person being chased by attractive members of the opposite sex, an obvious resolution of the problem. Quick as a flash the person has gone from disaster to success.

In addition to delivering a message quickly, TV advertising uses imaginative techniques to make the advertised products attractive. For example, food stylists are hired to make advertised food look appealing. According to TV food stylist Lloyd Davis, Elmer's Glue is added to milk in television ads to make it look white and delightful, roasted chickens are spray-painted to look deliciously golden brown and Ivory Soap is added to give coffee a fresh-brewed appearance.[16]

Criticism of TV Ads. Because of its impact on our culture, television advertising has become the focus of considerable criticism in recent years. Probably the longest ongoing controversy concerns advertising directed toward children.

Children's advertising on television is a $200-million-a-year enterprise. According to research findings, the average child sees 20,000 television ads a year—about three hours of commercials a week.

According to psychologist Patricia Greenfield, young children equate all of television except cartoons with reality. Youngsters under the age of seven usually cannot distinguish between a commercial and the program, and they learn a great deal from commercials.[17]

Groups such as Action for Children's Television (ACT) have been campaigning to get regulatory agencies to limit commercials aimed at children. A request for an FCC ban on children's advertising was denied. Opponents of such a ban pointed out that it would have meant the end of commercial television programming for children.

For years, concern has been expressed over the number of ads for sugar-coated breakfast cereals and unrealistic toys. The most recent concern (discussed in Chapter 9) centers around the fact that toy manufacturers are now producing programming for children that stars their products.

Parents have also complained about TV ads that entice children to call 976-prefix telephone numbers to hear such messages as "Santa's Christmas stories." Unlike the toll-free 1-800 numbers, 976 telephone prefixes incur charges. Some parents have been shocked to find hundreds of dollars in 976 charges on their monthly bills. By the mid-1980s revenue from 976 calls placed by children was reported to be in the hundreds of millions of dollars. (In 1987 the California Public Utilities Commission ordered telephone companies to allow customers to block their access to telephone numbers with a 976 prefix. Other states soon followed suit.)

Beer and wine commercials have been the subject of controversy in recent years. Groups such as the National Institute on Alcohol Abuse and Alcoholism (NIAAA), Mothers Against Drunk Drivers (MADD) and Students Against Drunk Drivers (SADD) have pressured Congress to ban beer and wine advertising on television, claiming that it contributes to alcoholism and drunk-driving-related deaths.

The beer, wine and broadcast industries argue that there is no causal relationship between alcohol problems and the commercials. Industry officials say that their ads do not cause people to drink more or entice nondrinkers to drink; they are aimed only at increasing a brand's share of the existing market. Opponents of liquor advertising are skeptical however; they contend that the ads do attempt to attract new drinkers, particularly young people, with their themes of good times, adventure and sex.[18]

It should be pointed out that for years the National Association of Broadcasting has enforced restrictions on liquor advertising. First, no hard liquor can be advertised on

Although ads for cigarettes and hard liquor are banned from American television, these products permeate our culture through other mass media, such as these billboards in New York's Times Square. (Barbara Alper/Stock, Boston)

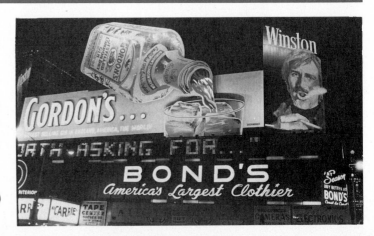

radio or television. Second, broadcasters are prohibited from showing anyone drinking beer or wine in a commercial (glasses can be hoisted, but there is never any sipping). It is all right, however, to show characters in regular programs drinking like fish—alcohol consumption was regulated only in commercials. Third, currently active sports figures are not allowed to appear in beer and wine commercials. This is why all of the Miller Lite commercials featured former athletes. Despite these restrictions, the controversy continues.

Cigarette advertising on television and radio was caught in a similar controversy in the 1960s. The first result of this debate was a requirement that broadcast stations running cigarette advertising had to air counter ads telling of the harmful effects of smoking. These ads began appearing in 1968, and cigarette smoking started to decline. An alarmed tobacco industry then accepted a total ban on cigarette advertising in the electronic media in 1971. When the advertising stopped, so did most of the counter ads, and soon the sales of cigarettes (which could still be advertised in the print media) began to climb.

If the case of cigarette advertising can be used as a guide, banning beer and wine commercials will not help solve this nation's alcohol problem—but counter ads might help.

Zipping and Zapping. The latest headache for television advertisers is new technology that permits viewers to eliminate commercials entirely: the *double Zs*. First of all, viewers can now sit in their easy chairs and change channels during commercials by remote control; this is called zipping in the industry. Second, the VCR (videocassette recorder) allows people to *zap* commercials out of recorded programs by fast-forwarding right through them.

The threats of zipping and zapping can be credited with continual improvements in the quality of TV commercials. The industry must make television ads extremely entertaining and compelling if they are to compete for viewers against the temptations of zipping and zapping. This, unfortunately, largely precludes providing any product information in commercials.

MOTIVATIONAL RESEARCH

Psychological Advertising. From its inception in the nineteenth century, the advertising industry has relied on creative endeavors to sell goods and services. However, by the mid-twentieth century creativity was no longer enough. What was needed were sophisticated techniques that would persuade people to buy more, so that the wheels of our mass-production, mass-consumption economy would keep turning. To develop these techniques, the ad industry turned to consumer research, which could provide insights into the personalities and subconscious desires of the consuming public.

According to Vance Packard, who began writing about this research with alarm in the 1950s, the advertising industry started tailoring its ads to meet the needs of the id. (In Freudian psychology, the id is that part of our mind that generates our most basic animal urges and impulses.)[19]

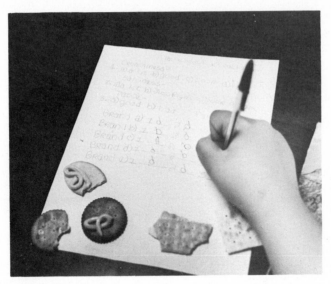

Consumer research plays a crucial role in advertising. It ranges from very simple surveys, like this one sampling cracker preferences among elementary school children, to sophisticated motivational research that uses Freudian psychology to determine why people buy the things they do. *(Miriam Reinhart/Photo Researchers)*

Motivational research, or MR, was the name given to this new area of consumer analysis. Millions of dollars were targeted for MR, and social scientists soon found an industry ready and willing to fund this type of psychological exploration.

MR looked for the hidden "whys" of consumer behavior. It replaced the older statistical research approaches by borrowing from the disciplines of psychology and psychoanalysis. Instead of treating consumers as rational beings who knew what they wanted and why they wanted it, MR examined the subconscious, nonrational levels of motivation and suggested where and how ads should be aimed. The researchers used in-depth interviews, Rorschach (inkblot) tests, stress tests that measured eye-blinking frequencies in stores via hidden cameras, lie detectors, word-association tests and group interviews to compile their data.[20]

One of the leaders in this research was Dr. Ernest Dichter, head of the Institute for Motivational Research. By probing the subconscious, Dichter was able to discover unsuspected areas of tension and guilt that were important to sales psychology. He learned why certain ads had failed in the past and suggested ways to put together advertising campaigns to take advantage of these formerly unknown areas.

Sex sells was an idea that had been around a long time. However, it wasn't until MR research came along that it was discovered just how subtle and complex sexual fantasies are in influencing consumer buying patterns. One study found that men were lured into automobile dealerships by ads and window displays of convertibles because they associated convertibles with youth and adventure and they were symbolic of a mistress. However, men usually ended up buying a sedan; it symbolized the girl they would marry because she would make a good wife and mother. What the industry needed in the 1950s was a new car that had the attractions of both a mistress and a wife. Dichter's organization took credit for suggesting the solution—the hardtop convertible.[21]

Another sexually related discovery was made when an ad agency ordered an in-depth study to find out why a campaign for the Cigar Institute of America had failed.

The ads had shown a smiling woman offering cigars to a group of men. The study revealed that subconsciously men smoke cigars because they know the smell is offensive to women. Thus the smiling woman enticing them to smoke a cigar turned them off.

Conflicts between MR and creativity developed over this new orientation in developing advertising campaigns. Copywriters and art directors regarded advertising as an art, or at least a craft, and resented the new emphasis on psychological research. As Les Pearl of Batten, Barton, Durstine & Osborn put it, "Merchandising men and research men are statistic-ing the creative man to death."[22]

Since earlier consumer research had dealt only with demographics (statistical information on ages, marital status, income, educational levels, etc.) a new name was coined for motivation-oriented research: *psychographics.*

VALS Research. In the 1960s MR and Freudian psychoanalytical theories were challenged by a revival of creative, non–research-oriented ads. However, psychographic research continued. The Stanford Research Institute (now known as SRI International) began working on psychographic research in the 1950s, concentrating on VALS (values and life styles). SRI issued its first report on the interrelationship of social values and consumer buying habits in 1960. The report, called *Consumer Values and Demands,* suggested that a neglected area of market research involved how people's values influence their spending patterns. This report, which was ahead of its time, had very little immediate influence on advertising research at the time.

One of the early pioneers of this research was Arnold Mitchell, a marketing analyst at SRI. Mitchell and his colleagues continued their "values-oriented" research through the 1960s and into the 1970s to determine how the children of the turbulent 1960s would affect the marketplace. What would happen when a generation that seemed to have rejected capitalism came of age? Business needed a marketing strategy to reach these people, and the SRI studies helped advertisers to determine the needs of the "baby boomers."[23]

Nine Life Styles. By the late 1970s SRI had developed a set of nine life styles that it said represented the American popular culture. The nine life styles fell into four larger categories, which were based on people's self-image, aspirations and product use. The four categories are "Need-Driven," "Outer-Directed," "Inner-Directed" and "Integrated." The following is a summary of the nine life styles as originally described by Mitchell[24] (see Figure 11.1).

A. NEED-DRIVEN

1. *Survivors.* Survivors are the poor, the uneducated, and the elderly poor in our culture. They are listed at the bottom of the "Need-Driven" category and represent about 4 percent of the population. They are usually heavy smokers and TV viewers and their buying habits are driven by immediate needs. They feel helplessly trapped by the culture.

Figure 11.1. The nine VALS groups.

2. *Sustainers.* The Sustainers represent about 7 percent of the population. They feel more angry about their status in life than helpless and usually are determined to move up. Many Sustainers find upward mobility through the underground economy. They are usually heavy drinkers and smokers and have impulsive buying habits.

B. OUTER-DIRECTED

3. *Belongers.* Belongers are the largest group, comprising 38 percent of the population. They represent the nation's middle class and are usually conservative, nostalgic, sentimental and conforming. They favor American-made products and enjoy family activities. Although their buying habits center around family and home needs, they do indulge in the latest fads.

4. *Emulators.* Emulators make up 10 percent of the population. They are ambitious, status-conscious, macho individuals who want to make it into the upper levels of society. They bowl, play poker and watch TV while eating dinner. They read magazines, watch TV shows about the rich and famous and drive secondhand luxury cars.

5. *Achievers.* Achievers make up 20 percent of the population and are the movers and shakers of our society. They are the most materialistic, affluent, comfort-loving and successful of the "Outer-Directeds." They own their own homes, use credit cards and do a lot of traveling. They usually prefer participating in sports and attending cultural events to watching television. Their buying preferences are for top-of-the-line luxury items.

C. INNER-DIRECTED

6. *I-Am-Me's.* The transitional stage between Outer-Directed and Inner-Directed is the I-Am-Me stage. Made up mostly of young people who are the children of Achievers, I-Am-Me's represent about 3 percent of the population. They are inven-

tive, impulsive, sometimes exhibitionistic and they usually prefer far-out fads and trendy fashions.

7. *Experientials.* The next Inner-Directed level is called the Experientials. They make up about 5 percent of the population and are attracted to exotic religions, natural foods and spiritual growth. They usually go to movies rather than watch TV and prefer wine to hard liquor. They purchase outdoor sporting equipment and like to ski, hike and camp.

8. *Societally Conscious.* Eleven percent of the population are categorized as Societally Conscious. These Inner-Directeds are usually environmentalists, and they are active in various social causes. They are interested in holistic medicine, jogging and artistic endeavors and they watch more public broadcasting than commercial TV. The best educated of all the VALS types, they rank second to the Achievers in income level. Nevertheless, their buying habits are frugal and simplistic.

D. INTEGRATED

9. *Integrateds.* The last category, making up only 2 percent of the population, combines aspects of Inner- and Outer-Directeds. Integrateds are psychologically mature; they can see many sides of an issue and they enjoy both Inner- and Outer-Directed activities. They have a concern for the needs of others and a world perspective on issues. Because they are so highly individualistic, it is difficult to predict their buying habits.

This ad combines opera and a Rolex watch to sell to a specialized audience of Achievers. *(Rolex)*

The Mission of VALS. In 1978 the VALS project became a separate program at SRI, with a staff of four and 37 clients. By 1984 it had developed into a $2 million operation with 151 clients and a staff of 19.

The VALS program has become more than a market-research project. Its developers see it as a social agent for changing American culture. At its headquarters in Menlo Park, California, the following credo hangs on the wall of each staff member's office:

> *The mission of the VALS program is to exert a positive and creative force in the evolution of the American culture. VALS aims to do this by acquiring, disseminating, and applying insights into how values can aid institutions and individuals to operate in a more humane, productive, and ethical way. Specifically, VALS intends:*
>
> • *To become a significant part of American business thinking.*
>
> • *To enhance public awareness of the role of values in social change.*
>
> • *To contribute to SRI research, remain financially healthy and operate for the enjoyments and personal growth of the staff.[25]*

VALS Users. By the mid-1980s the mass media were using VALS to sell advertising space. *Reader's Digest* used VALS data to persuade reluctant advertisers that its readers were the right type of people to be targeted for the advertisers' products. In 1984 *National Geographic* ran a full-page ad in the *New York Times* telling how they use VALS to help advertisers. The ad was headlined "THE NATIONAL PSYCHO-GRAPHIC." The May/June and July/August 1985 issues of the "Sunset Newsletter" carried articles that told advertisers how they could use VALS data to reach *Sunset's* upscale audience of Achievers and Societally Conscious readers in 18 Western states.

VALS research had come of age. Early doubts about its usefulness had been laid to rest by "The VALS 1980 Field Study," a telephone poll that asked a variety of questions on subjects ranging from attitudes to media habits. The survey yielded a wide variety of information.

Since 1982 Simmons Market Research Bureau and Mediamark Research Inc. have included the new VALS form in their surveys. Each survey polls 20,000 people annually.

Dr. Joseph Plummer, who did early research on life styles in the 1960s and 1970s, summed up the new VALS system as "a classic research model." As executive vice-president for research at Young & Rubicam—one of the largest ad agencies in the world—Plummer said the VALS system is "a whole new dimension for us. Before VALS, we didn't really have a sense of who the consumers out there were. Now we know how they live and what they buy—and why they buy it."[26]

Perhaps the most fundamental use of VALS data lies in market segmentation—different life-style groups tend to buy different products and services, and VALS data will tell you whom to target. Take the automobile, for example. VALS data show that Achievers buy large luxury cars; Belongers tend to purchase "family-size" American-made cars; and the Societally Conscious buy fuel-efficient cars. High-powered perfor-

BOX 11.1.

VALS RESEARCH LEADS TO NEW MAGAZINE GENRE

In 1987 newsstands across the United States started squeezing in a new type of specialized magazine. This magazine genre was reflecting a new interest among the baby boomers, often referred to as the "Yuppie" generation. In a surprise to some observers who had been watching the "Me Generation" Yuppies for a long time, the Yuppies were now focusing on—of all things—the family.

Publications like *Parenting, Father, Child, Children* and *Grandparents* were finding an audience among Yuppies in the late twentieth century. The trend was based on solid market research and was attracting publishing biggies like Time Inc., which had pumped $5 million into *Parenting,* a San Francisco–based publication.

Values and Lifestyles research had shown that members of the Yuppie generation were finally having children and were now focusing their attention on their families. Advertisers, who closely followed VALS research, were readily available to purchase space in these new magazines. *Parenting,* at $5,400 for a full-page ad, sold 200 more ad pages than it had projected during its first 10 issues. *Child,* with full-page ads costing $7,000, also attracted major advertisers, among them Procter & Gamble, Ford, Eastman-Kodak, Saks Fifth Avenue and Sears.

This was just one way that VALS research was paying off for advertisers and media entrepreneurs during the late 1980s.

mance cars are purchased more by Emulators and Experientials, while the Need-Driven support the secondhand car market. (For an example of how publishers have used VALS, see Box 11.1.)

VALS research is also useful in projecting future consumer needs. VALS research has concluded that although the Inner-Directed category represents only 19 percent of the population now, it is growing and is expected to be as large as 33 percent by the 1990s. Products that will appeal to this rapidly expanding category then are on the drawing boards today.

The advertising of consumer goods has become a sophisticated, well-researched industry. The marketing community probably knows at least as much about our American popular culture and its future trends as most sociologists, psychologists and futurists. Whether we like it or not, the advertising industry may know more about us and why we do things than we do ourselves.

SUMMARY

Advertising is a message industry that plays a major role in shaping the content and operation of the mass media. Although advertising has existed since ancient times, mass advertising as we know it today began growing up with the mass media in the late nineteenth century.

Advertising plays an important role in our popular culture because it shapes and reflects our life styles. It is one step ahead of other elements in our culture and is usually the first to reflect social trends. The average adult is exposed to approximately 500 advertisements each day, and more than $109 billion is spent on advertising in the United States each year.

The first ad agency was established in 1841; since then advertising has developed into an important yet controversial message business. Some of the debate deals with whether or not advertising is an effective tool for selling consumer goods. Some contend that advertising does not sell and that its effectiveness cannot be measured because too many other variables are involved. Instead, they believe that advertisers use sales records as indicators of whether or not to increase advertising. If sales go up, so does the amount spent on advertising.

The use of propaganda devices in advertising appeals to our emotions rather than our intellect and is prevalent in American culture. Propaganda devices from slogans to sex appeal are used constantly.

Other advertising controversies include the charge that hidden messages are often subliminally imbedded in advertisements to appeal to our subconscious mind. Hidden appeals to the basic instincts of sex, death and fear are said to be used to sell products. Researchers have found that more of these hidden images can be found in liquor ads than in any other type of product advertising, but evidence that proves whether or not these imbeds have any effect on our buying habits is lacking.

As American industrial society grew in the mid-twentieth century, the production of consumer goods reached a level that required new sophisticated techniques to help mass-distribute the mass-produced goods. In the 1950s the advertising industry turned to motivational research to help stimulate sales.

An outgrowth of motivational research was the study of life styles and how they affect consumer buying patterns. Although it began in the 1950s, life-style research was perfected during the 1960s and 1970s. Today the VALS system is highly regarded in the marketplace. VALS research has divided the American culture into nine distinct life styles: Survivors, Sustainers, Belongers, Emulators, Achievers, I-Am-Me's, Experientials, Societally Conscious and Integrateds.

The VALS studies have led to a wealth of data that are now used on a regular basis to target the appropriate audience for a product; determine what media will best reach the target group; explain why the people in the target audience buy what they do; and help the ad agency develop an effective campaign to sell the product. VALS research is also used to help businesses determine what types of products are going to be marketable in the future.

NOTES

1. Harold Berkman and Christopher Gilson, *Advertising: Concepts and Strategies,* 2nd ed. (New York: Random House, 1987), p. 4.

2. Ibid., p. 34.

3. Michael Schudson, *Advertising, The Uneasy Persuasion: Its Dubious Impact* on *American Society* (New York: Basic Books, 1984), pp. 18–19.

4. Richard Schmalensee, *The Economics of Advertising* (Amsterdam: North-Holland, 1972), p. 43.

5. Schudson, p. 33.

6. Stephen Fox, *The Mirror Makers: A*

History of American Advertising and Its Creators (New York: Morrow, 1984), p. 328.

7. Schudson, pp. 90–91.

8. James H. Myers and William H. Reynolds, *Consumer Behavior and Marketing Management* (Boston: Houghton Mifflin, 1967), p. 138.

9. Adolf Hitler, *Mein Kampf* [English language edition] (New York: Reynal & Hitchcock, 1939), p. 234.

10. Warren K. Agee, Phillip H. Ault and Edwin Emery, *Introduction to Mass Communications*, 9th ed. (New York: Harper & Row, 1988), pp. 360–361.

11. Vance O. Packard, *The Hidden Persuaders* (New York: Pocket Books, 1957).

12. Walter Weir, "Another Look at Subliminal 'Facts,'" *Advertising Age*, October 19, 1984, p. 46.

13. Ibid.

14. R. S. Lazarus and R. A. McCleary, "Autonomic Discrimination Without Awareness: A Study of Subception," *Psychological Review* 58 (1951): 113–122.

15. Warren Breed and James R. DeFoe, "Themes in Magazine Alcohol Advertisements: A Critique," *Journal of Drug Issues* (Fall 1979): 46.

16. *30-Second Seduction*, a *Consumer Reports* special on television advertising, HBO Home Video, 1985.

17. Patricia Marks Greenfield, *Mind and Media: The Effects of Television, Video Games and Computers* (Cambridge, Mass.: Harvard University Press, 1984), pp. 51–53.

18. Michael Jacobson, Robert Atkins and George Hacker, *The Booze Merchants: The Inebriating of America* (Washington, D.C.: Center for Science in the Public Interest, 1983), pp. 44–82, 103–130.

19. Vance Packard, "The Ad and the Id," in *Mass Media and the Popular Arts*, ed. Fredric Rissover and David C. Birch (New York: McGraw-Hill, 1971), p. 9.

20. Ibid., p. 10.

21. Fox, p. 183.

22. Quoted in Fox, p. 182.

23. James Atlas, "Beyond Demographics: How Madison Avenue Knows Who You Are and What You Want," *The Atlantic*, October 1984, p. 51.

24. Arnold Mitchell, *The Nine American Lifestyles* (New York: Macmillan, 1983), pp. 3–37.

25. Atlas, p. 55.

26. Ibid., p. 49.

ADDITIONAL READING

Engel, Jack. *Advertising: The Process and Practice.* New York: McGraw-Hill, 1980.

Foote, N. N. *Consumer Behavior: Household Decision-Making,* vol. 4. New York: New York University Press, 1961.

Key, Wilson Bryan. *Subliminal Seduction.* New York: Signet, 1974.

———. *Media Sexploitation.* New York: New American Library, 1976.

———. *Clam Plate Orgy.* New York: New American Library, 1980.

Myers, James H., and Reynolds, William H. *Consumer Behavior and Marketing Management.* Boston: Houghton Mifflin, 1967.

Riesman, David. *The Lonely Crowd: A Study of Changing American Character.* New Haven, Conn.: Yale University Press, 1950.

Chapter 12

Public Relations: Creating an Image

It is no use putting whipped
cream on the manure pile because
the sun comes out in the morning
and you have the same old manure pile.
—*L. L. L. Golden, public relations consultant*

I n the summer of 1986 Bristol-Myers announced that it was withdrawing all its over-the-counter medications in capsule form as a result of two deaths in the Seattle, Washington, area. (The victims had taken cyanide-tainted capsules of Extra-Strength Excedrin.) The action followed a similar one earlier that year by Johnson & Johnson, which pulled its capsule medications off the market as a result of renewed tampering with its Tylenol products.

In earlier times a company might have ignored negative publicity about deaths attributed to its products and continued with "business as usual." However, this attitude has changed in recent years. Such costly management decisions are the result of modern public relations practice, which tries to foster a positive image for a corporation even during times of crisis and bad publicity.

Public relations (PR), like advertising, is a message business and as such is also controversial. Much of the controversy surrounding PR stems from the facts that this industry is not fully understood and that in the past some PR efforts were nothing more than slick attempts to solve serious problems by issuing flowery press releases. For the most part public relations practices have changed, as the previous examples make clear.

WHAT IS PUBLIC RELATIONS?

The *Random House College Dictionary* defines public relations rather simply: "1. the efforts of a corporation to promote good will between itself and the public. 2. the methods used to promote such good will." In the *Public Relations Handbook* (1971), Philip Lesly expanded on this definition by noting that PR enables institutions and people to learn what others think of them, determine what they must do to earn the good will of others, devise ways to win that good will, and carry on programs designed to secure good will.[1]

Many people confuse PR and advertising. Advertising involves the paid use of time or space in the mass media, usually to sell goods and services. Public relations, on the other hand, uses free space and time in the media to sell corporate images, individuals and good will. However, paid advertising is sometimes used to sell a corporate image or create good will, and it often becomes an important part of the PR practitioner's total campaign.

The term *public relations* means different things to different people. Many people who call themselves public relations practitioners are involved in only a narrow aspect of the field. In the broadest sense, the industry includes such activities as press agentry, promotion, public affairs, publicity and, as previously noted, paid advertising. All of these activities play a major role in shaping the content of the mass media and disseminating cultural information throughout our society. To distinguish among these activities, let's look at each separately.

Public Relations. A PR practitioner is a liaison between an institution and the public. He or she is responsible for setting a public relations policy to represent the corporation or agency to the public and for conducting research to provide adequate feedback from the public to the institution. Usually a PR practitioner works closely with top-level management and is instrumental in influencing management's policy changes. The PR person can be described as a strategist who plans and executes large-scale public relations efforts.

Press Agentry. Public relations had its origins in press agentry, and today some people still think the terms are synonymous. Press agentry consists of planning and staging events that will attract favorable attention to an institution, person, idea or product and placing positive news items in the media about the client. Although early press agents sometimes used fraud and deception to achieve their goals, today's practitioners are more honest and professional.

Promotion. Promotional activities go beyond getting publicity and involve generating support or endorsements for a client. Clients range from churches and charities to political candidates and causes and a variety of social concerns, such as the "Save the Whales" and "Right to Life" movements. Promotional activities often involve fund-raising campaigns.

Public Affairs. The term *public affairs* is misleading because some corporations and government agencies use it to describe their entire PR effort. (Many institutions are now calling their directors of public relations "directors of public affairs," for example.) However, properly speaking the term refers to a narrower public relations activity: direct institutional involvement with community and government relations.

Publicity. Publicity involves placing news and information in the mass media. People who work in this field are skilled in writing publicity in a news format; in government agencies they often carry the title of public information officer. Good public information officers need to have some of the skills and training of professional PR practitioners to handle the occasions when the mass media are seeking unfavorable news and information.

Advertising. Occasionally PR practitioners need to use paid advertising. For example, they may decide to mount an ad campaign to clarify a client's institutional policy or correct an unfavorable image, or to provide assistance with a promotional or press agentry campaign. Public relations personnel who do not have experience in advertising usually call in a professional for assistance. However, many PR agencies today have expanded their operations to include advertising as well.

THE HISTORY OF PUBLIC RELATIONS

Although public relations has been with us in some form through the ages, modern PR traces its roots to early attempts at press agentry in the 1830s, when the metropolitan penny press developed. It was common practice for early press agents to invent stories to promote their clients in these newspapers.

Early Press Agentry. One of the early users of press agentry was P. T. Barnum, who successfully promoted the midget Tom Thumb and Jenny Lind, a singer known as the "Swedish Nightingale"; they became popular sideshow attractions for Barnum's circus. He coined the often-quoted phrase "There's a sucker born every minute."

However, public relations as we now know it developed to help big businesses combat the negative image they had acquired during the Industrial Revolution. By the late nineteenth century it was becoming apparent that many of these industries needed to create a favorable image to offset the public's growing distrust. This need became even more obvious when muckrakers, such as Lincoln Steffens and Upton Sinclair, painted grim pictures of big-business practices around the turn of the century. Stories of huge profits and employee exploitation became common.

Corporate PR. Simple press agentry wasn't enough to overcome suspicions about big business. In fact, the lies and distortions associated with press agentry at the time were the last thing companies needed.

P. T. Barnum used press agentry to promote the midget Tom Thumb, shown here with Barnum. *(UPI/Bettmann Newsphotos)*

One of the first to try to change this negative corporate image was journalist Ivy Ledbetter Lee, considered by many to be the first real PR practitioner. Lee started as a political publicist in 1904, but soon he was working for industrial giants. He began distributing press releases explaining business's side of labor disputes; he told city editors at the local newspapers that he was a "press agent who dealt in the truth."

Government PR. Government became involved in public relations when the United States entered World War I in 1917. President Woodrow Wilson established the Creel Committee, headed by newspaperman George Creel, to promote the sale of Liberty Bonds to finance the war, to censor news about the war and to convince the American people of the necessity of the nation's participation in the war.

A member of the committee, Edward L. Bernays, emerged as a leader in the development of the PR profession after the war. In 1921 he set up his own firm, becoming the first person to call himself a public relations counsel. Two years later he wrote the first book on the subject, *Crystallizing Public Opinion.*[2] He also taught the first course in public relations, at New York University. Bernays eventually earned the title of "father of modern public relations." As his reputation in PR grew, he found himself rejecting an offer by Adolf Hitler to help propagate Nazism.

The U.S. government again turned to public relations for help when it became involved in World War II in 1941. It established the Office of War Information (OWI), headed by radio commentator Elmer Davis. After the war ended, the OWI became the U.S. Information Agency.

This World War I poster for U.S.A. Bonds featured the Boy Scouts of America. World War I saw the first governmental use of public relations campaings to suppor a war effort. *(The Bettmann Archive)*

The Great Depression. The PR industry's road to success as a respected profession was not without setbacks. When the Great Depression hit in 1929, the public was quick to blame big business for the nation's financial woes. A real need existed for corporate public relations people to respond to the critics. However, because businesses were suffering financial hardships and PR was a relatively new field, funds to support institutional public relations were among the first to be cut—at a time when such services were sorely needed.

Post-World War II. After the Great Depression and World War II, however, public relations prospered. Industry and government both began to recognize the need to present their activities favorably to the public.

By the mid-1980s the Department of Labor was reporting that 143,000 people were engaged in PR activities in the United States. In addition to several hundred public relations firms, every sizable organization, whether public or private, had one or more employees working in the field.

Today's public relations professional requires a broad range of skills, including listening, counseling, planning and communicating. Public relations counselors Carl Byoir & Associates describe their business this way:

Analysis—*of policies and objectives of client . . . of relationships with various publics, including employees, customers, dealers, shareholders, the financial community, government and the press. Continuing research keeps the analysis of these relationships up-to-date.*

Planning and programming—of specific undertakings and projects in which public relations techniques can be employed to help attain the objectives through effective communication between the client and its publics.

Implementation—of the programs and projects by maximum and effective use of all avenues of communication, internal and external, to create understanding and stimulate action.[3]

DUTIES OF PR PRACTITIONERS

Employment opportunities for public relations practitioners are numerous. There are some 1,600 PR agencies; corporations employ thousands of PR people, many of them at the top management level; and most government and educational institutions have public relations offices.

PR practitioners are usually college graduates trained in the profession. Formal education is offered at more than 160 colleges and universities in the United States, usually in schools or departments of journalism and mass communication. By the 1980s PR and advertising were the most popular majors in most of these programs.

Diverse Responsibilities. Since the field is so broad, it might be helpful to describe what public relations practitioners actually do. Frank Wylie, a public relations practitioner and an educator, points out that there are major differences between the job duties of an entry-level PR employee and an experienced executive. He says that the average entry-level employees spend 50 percent of their time on techniques, 5 percent on judgment and 45 percent on "running like hell." The experienced executives, on the other hand, spend 10 percent on techniques, 40 percent on administration and 50 percent on analysis and judgment.[4]

Herb Schmertz, vice-president of public affairs for Mobil Oil until his retirement in 1988, described his wide-ranging duties this way:

> *Sometimes I describe myself as a lobbyist who tries to raise certain issues and arguments before the public, the government, and the press. But I am also a publisher—of books, pamphlets, reports, and issue-oriented advertisements. In addition, I am a patron of the arts and culture. I am also a corporate spokesman who explains and defends Mobil's point of view. From time to time, I am an advocate who confronts individuals and institutions whose positions are, in our view, wrong or misinformed. And I am a media critic who refuses to allow inaccurate or damaging stories to go unanswered.*
>
> *In addition to all of this, I am responsible for administering a large department and a hefty budget. As a member of Mobil's board of directors, I participate in corporate investment decisions and other policy issues. When evening rolls around, I often represent the corporation at an art or cultural event, or at a political dinner, or as a guest on a TV interview show.[5]*

Campaign Development. Public relations practitioners use a systematic approach to developing their campaigns. One such approach, developed by Bernays, is called "the engineering of consent" and consists of the following eight steps:

1. *Define goals or objectives.*
2. *Research publics to find whether goals are realistic and attainable, and how.*
3. *Modify goals if research finds them unrealistic.*
4. *Determine strategy to reach goals.*
5. *Plan actions, themes and appeals to publics.*
6. *Plan organization to meet goals.*
7. *Time and plan tactics to meet goals.*
8. *Set up budget.*[6]

As you can see, PR practitioners are skilled professionals who do much more than issue press releases and plant publicity in the media. They are planners who set goals, research needs, establish systematic campaigns and select and work with the media.

EXAMPLES OF PUBLIC RELATIONS ACTIVITIES

Three major types of PR cases dominated the field in the 1980s: behavior modification, combined marketing and PR efforts, and issues and crisis management.

This ad, attempting to curtail drug use by young people, is an example of behavior modification public relations. *(Knoth & Meads Advertising)*

Behavior Modification. Much of the behavior modification PR efforts of the 1980s resulted from an increase in social awareness and concerns. Such campaigns as the need to fasten seat belts, hire the handicapped and not drink and drive received much PR attention during this decade.

Major milk companies and supermarket chains contributed to creating public awareness of missing children at this time by printing pictures of some of these children on milk cartons and shopping bags. One purpose of these PR efforts was to foster the companies' reputations as concerned institutions.

Combined Marketing and PR Efforts. The growth of the combined efforts of marketing and PR also reflects changing cultural attitudes and practices. These activities attempt to expand the marketing efforts of certain institutions, such as museums and hospitals, which until recently saw no need to market themselves.

Museum promotions of traveling exhibits like the Armand Hammer collection of paintings are an example of this successful blend of marketing and PR. Other recent notable examples were the promotion of the 1984 Summer Olympics in Los Angeles, which was privately funded and turned a profit for an activity that had previously been publicly financed, and the refurbishing and celebration of the centennial of the Statue of Liberty in 1986.

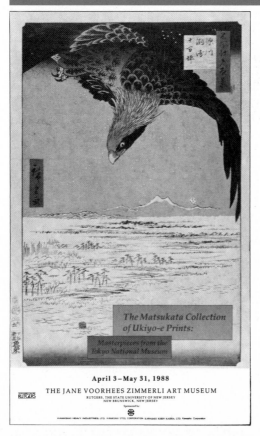

This promotional piece for a recent art exhibit illustrates the new trend toward the use of PR techniques by non-profit institutions. *(The Jane Voorhees Zimmerli Art Museum, Rutgers, The State University of New Jersey)*

Issues and Crisis Management. Issues management attempts to identify and correctly interpret problems before they become a crisis; crisis management attempts to react to crises, such as disasters, in as favorable a climate as possible.

In the 1980s some corporations' issues management began taking on a new and controversial tone. Some firms abandoned their longtime practice of handling the mass media with kid gloves and spoke out forcefully when they felt they had been treated unfairly by the press.

One of the first companies to take this posture was Mobil Oil, which started running full-page ads presenting its position on controversial issues. Companies that have followed Mobil's lead include Chevron, Dow Chemical and W. R. Grace.

Leading Mobil's fight against the media was Herb Schmertz, then its vice-president of public affairs. He challenged biased reporting in major newspapers and the television networks. Although the networks refused to run Mobil's countermedia advertisements, some did appear on independent TV stations and a few network affiliates. Most of the Mobil messages have appeared in newspapers and magazines.

Mobil's counterattacks did not make the company very popular with the media, but Schmertz feels that the ads have made the networks more cautious about airing poorly

Mobil Oil uses paid advertisements to state its position when it feels that the media are distorting a given issue. In this ad, Mobil addresses the issue of acid rain. (*Mobil Corporation*)

Rush to judgment

In recent weeks, the public awareness has been drenched in acid rain.

Prime Minister Mulroney of Canada, at his recent meeting with President Reagan, pressed for a treaty aimed at solving the acid rain problem, which he has called "the litmus test issue" for relations between the two nations. The President has agreed to consider such a bilateral agreement; his action came soon after he pledged to initiate a $2.5-billion, five-year program to demonstrate technologies to reduce sulfur dioxide and nitrogen oxide emissions from coal-burning power plants. These emissions undergo complex chemical reactions in the air to form the acidic precipitation blamed for destroying lakes and forests in the U.S. and Canada alike.

Meanwhile, six states in the northeast, joined by several environmental groups, have announced their intention to sue the federal government to force the Environmental Protection Agency to reduce acid rain by stricter enforcement of the Clean Air Act.

For its part, the EPA has withheld comment on the suit. But EPA has pointed out that the problem is "very complex and difficult," to which we add, "and how."

The complexity is evidenced by scientific analysis. What the scientific community has come up with, basically, is the fact that researchers disagree not only about the causes of acid rain, but also its effects. About the only unanimous conclusion is that acid rain exists. Period.

Here's an example both of the uncertainty and the confusion that surround the issue:

A recent EPA staff study projects that between none and more than 1,000 northeastern lakes might become acidic over the next 50 years if current acidity levels continue. The study was based on the capacity of soils to neutralize acid rain, and the belief that some soils would soon reach the limit of their acid absorption capacity.

But scientists led by Arne Henriksen of the Norwegian Institute for Water Research found no absorption problem, and the EPA is currently reviewing the findings of its staff study. The Henriksen group said that for parts of the northeast in a steady state, no prediction of further acidification could be made.

Other studies provide similar findings. The National Academy of Sciences' National Research Council, in a study published last year, said that a comparison of data dating back to the 1920s showed some lakes in New Hampshire, New York, and Wisconsin became more acidic over time, others became less acidic, and some remained the same. Hundreds of lakes were involved in the survey, and the lack of any clear trend indicates emissions alone can't be the culprit in the cases where acidity increased. Another study, a review of 50 years of data on the alkalinity of lakes in New York and New Hampshire, undertaken at McMaster University in Ontario, found most lakes showed no change since the 1930s. Of the lakes that did change, half became more alkaline, and half, more acidic. And at the State University of New York at Syracuse, researchers have theorized that the decline in Adirondack forests—usually blamed on acid rain—could have been caused by drought and unusually cold winters.

We do not oppose an acid rain cleanup. But, as taxpayers, we should all insist that the government, before it commits $2.5-billion—or any large amounts—establish as quickly as possible both the nature of the acid rain problem and the most efficient means to control it.

Mobil®

© 1987 Mobil Corporation

researched news specials about the oil industry in general and Mobil in particular. On the other hand, Schmertz has cited examples of news reporters going out of their way to "get even" with Mobil.[7] In 1984, after continued run-ins with reporters and editors at the *Wall Street Journal,* Mobil severed all relations with that newspaper. Mobil indicated that it would grant no more interviews, send no more press releases or run advertisements in the *Wall Street Journal.*[8]

Many PR executives, including some in the oil industry, have criticized Mobil's combative approach to issues management. However, two communication researchers studied the new approach and concluded that the news media lost credibility when they attacked firms that responded to the criticism.[9]

The first success in crisis-management public relations is attributed to Ivy Ledbetter Lee, who represented the Pennsylvania Railroad in the early twentieth century. When one of the railroad's trains derailed in 1906, killing and injuring several people, Lee resisted company efforts to hush up the accident (a typical approach to crises at the time). Instead he provided the media with full and accurate accounts of the accident and even ran special trains, at company expense, to take journalists to the scene. He also persuaded the company to conduct a systemwide survey of railroad beds to avoid future derailments and announced that the company would provide financial aid to the families of the killed or injured. As a result, the Pennsylvania Railroad and the railroad industry received their first favorable press coverage in years.[10]

Johnson & Johnson began its first round of crises-management PR in 1981, after seven people in the Chicago area died after taking cyanide-tainted Tylenol capsules. The company immediately took all Tylenol capsules off the market and reissued the product in tamper-resistant containers, spending millions of dollars. Many believed that negative publicity about the Tylenol-related deaths would spell the end of the popular pain reliever, but it rapidly recovered its number-one position in market sales. In March 1983 the Public Relations Society of America's Honors and Awards Committee presented its Silver Anvil Award to Johnson & Johnson and its PR firm, Burson-Marsteller, for their handling of the crisis.

Johnson & Johnson's success was due in part to a company philosophy of social responsibility. Lawrence G. Foster, vice-president of public relations for Johnson & Johnson at the time, described the company's approach: "During the crisis phases of the Tylenol tragedy, virtually every public relations decision was based on sound, socially responsible business principles, which is when public relations is most effective."[11]

Johnson & Johnson used the same management style and philosophy in 1986, when the tamper-resistant containers proved fallible and another woman died from a cyanide Tylenol capsule. This time the company permanently ceased manufacturing all capsule medication.

CONTROVERSIES SURROUNDING PR PRACTICES

The fact that PR practitioners are involved in creating positive images for their clients often causes public concern and criticism. PR efforts determine much of the content of our mass media, and news consumers seldom know the difference between a story written by a news reporter and a public relations news release. When they find out that what they believed to be an unbiased account by a reporter is actually a press release, they become angry.

Wall Street Journal Study. A study of a typical issue of the *Wall Street Journal* found that 53 news stories were based on PR releases and, of these, 32 were reprinted almost verbatim or in paraphrase. Curiously, 20 of these 53 stories—including some taken nearly verbatim from a press release—were identified as having been written by a *Journal* staffer.[12]

These findings are reflective of media content throughout the country. There would be no problem with the fact that PR practitioners generate a large amount of media content if the sources of that content were identified. People could then evaluate the information on the basis of its source, rather than blindly accepting it as unbiased "news."

Positive Aspects of PR News. Public relations practitioners argue that they are actually helping the free flow of information in our society. Our nation has grown very large since its founding more than two hundred years ago. For the concept of a democracy dependent on a well-informed citizenry to work today, journalists must have help in gathering news and information. Public relations assists in this process.

Modern PR may also be an important ingredient in our culture because it provides a broader and sometimes more accurate flow of information. According to Herb Schmertz, most news reporters—particularly television reporters—don't understand business. As a result, they often distort business stories to the detriment of corporations. The job of corporate public relations departments, according to Schmertz, is to reflect accurately for the public the truth about business activities.[13]

"Flacks." Despite the media's dependence on public relations for content and the fact that many PR practitioners have been trained as journalists, a rather cool and distant relationship often exists between journalists working for the media and public relations personnel. Since the early days of press agentry, journalists have called PR people *flacks*. An old edition of the Associated Press Managing Editor's (APME) guidelines, issued in the 1960s, defined a flack as

> a person who makes all or part of his income by obtaining space in newspapers without cost to himself or his clients. Usually a professional . . . they are known formally as public relations men. A flack is a flack. His job is to say kind things about his client. He will not lie very often, but much of the time he tells less than the whole story. You do not owe the PR man anything. The owner of the newspaper, not the flack, pays your salary. Your immediate job is to serve the readers, not the man who would raid your columns.

Lingering Negative Image. Criticism and distrust of public relations linger on, years after the profession has "grown up." This is one of the reasons that some large

BOX 12.1.

DECLARATION OF PRINCIPLES OF
THE PUBLIC RELATIONS SOCIETY OF AMERICA

This declaration serves as a preamble to the Public Relations Society of America's Code of Professional Standards for the Practice of Public Relations.

Members of the Public Relations Society of America base their professional principles on the fundamental value and dignity of the individual, holding that the free exercise of human rights, especially freedom of speech, freedom of assembly and freedom of the press, is essential to the practice of public relations.

In serving the interests of clients and employers, we dedicate ourselves to the goals of better communication, understanding and cooperation among the diverse individuals, groups and institutions of society.

We pledge:

To conduct ourselves professionally, with truth, accuracy, fairness and responsibility to the public;

To improve our individual competence and advance the knowledge and proficiency of the profession through continuing research and education;

And to adhere to the articles of the Code of Professional Standards for the Practice of Public Relations as adopted by the governing Assembly of the Society.

companies have changed the name of their public relations departments to public affairs or communications. Changing the name, however, doesn't necessarily change the image, which, by and large, is caused not by the true PR practitioner but rather by some not-so-professional individuals who call themselves public relations people.

More constructively, many strides have been made to improve the industry's image. The most effective efforts have been made by the Public Relations Society of America (PRSA), which has adopted a stringent code of ethics and mandatory accreditation procedures for all members (see Box 12.1). Today PRSA has more than 12,000 members—a figure that represents less than 10 percent of all the people who claim to be working in public relations. Ironically, although the primary function of the public relations industry is the creation of positive public images, it has failed to create good will for itself.

SUMMARY

Public relations, like advertising, is a message business designed to promote and maintain good will for clients. PR is dependent on the mass media to promote this good will, and the media are dependent on PR practitioners for much of their content.

Public relations now involves a variety of activities, including legitimate press agentry, promotion, working with government agencies (public affairs), publicity campaigns and paid advertising.

The need for PR developed in the late nineteenth century, when big businesses found that they had a very poor public image. Early public relations practitioners, such as Ivy Ledbetter Lee and Edward L. Bernays, helped elevate PR from an activity of merely getting publicity for a client to one that involved a systematic effort to represent the client favorably to the public and research public perceptions adequately.

The federal government got into the public relations business in World War I when it appointed the Creel Committee to present the U.S. war effort to the public in a favorable light.

During the Great Depression of the 1930s businesses curtailed their PR efforts at a time when they needed them most. The U.S. government again cranked up public relations efforts during World War II by creating the Office of War Information. This agency survives today as the U.S. Information Agency.

Today public relations is recognized as an important activity in our society. More than 140,000 people work in this field, and there are several hundred PR firms. In addition, almost all major companies and government agencies have PR personnel on their payroll.

Although most people don't readily recognize public relations activities as such, their impact on our culture is evident. Many of today's PR efforts are directed toward creating behavior modification, assisting in marketing activities and facilitating issues and crisis management.

The mass media rely on public relations practitioners for information to keep the society informed. The public is also served by PR practitioners who accurately interpret the activities of their corporate or government clients.

Although public relations is a respectable profession today, with its own code of ethics, many people who call themselves PR practitioners still do not adhere to the principles of the profession and often use the same dubious tactics as early press agents.

NOTES

1. Philip Lesly, ed., *Public Relations Handbook* (Englewood Cliffs, N.J.: Prentice-Hall, 1971), p. xi.

2. Edward L. Bernays, *Public Relations* (Norman: University of Oklahoma Press, 1952), p. 84.

3. Quoted in Don R. Pember, *Mass Media in America*, 4th ed. (Chicago: Science Research Associates, 1983), p. 292.

4. Frank Wylie, "The New Professionals," speech to the First National Student Conference, Public Relations Student Society of America, Dayton, Ohio, October 24, 1976. (Published by Chrysler Corporation, p. 5.)

5. Herb Schmertz with William Novak, *Good-bye to the Low Profile: The Art of Creative Confrontation* (Boston: Little, Brown, 1986), pp. 16–17.

6. Edward L. Bernays, "The Engineering of Consent," *Industry* 43 (December 1978): 12–13, 36.

7. Schmertz, pp. 66–73.

8. Ibid.

9. David E. Clavier and Frank B. Kalupa, "Corporate Rebuttals to 'Trial by Television,'" *Public Relations Review* 9 (Spring 1983): 24–36.

10. Irwin Ross, *The Image Merchants* (Garden City, N.Y.: Doubleday, 1959), p. 31.

11. Lawrence G. Foster, "The Role of Public Relations in the Tylenol Crisis," *Public Relations Journal* (March 1983): 13.

12. "It's in the Journal. But This is Reporting?" *Columbia Journalism Review* (March/April 1980): 34–36.

13. Schmertz, pp. 82–83.

ADDITIONAL READING

Canfield, Bernard R., and Moore, H. Frazier. *Public Relations: Principles, Cases, and Problems*, 9th ed. Homewood, Ill.: Irwin, 1985.

Center, Allen H., with Walsh, Frank. *Public Relations Practices: Managerial Case Studies*, 3rd ed. Englewood Cliffs, N.J.: Prentice-Hall, 1985.

Creel, George. *How We Advertised America: The First Telling of the Amazing Story of the Committee on Public Information That Carried the Gospel of Americanism to Every Corner of the Globe*. New York: Harper & Row, 1920.

Cutlip, Scott M., and Center, Allen H. *Effective Public Relations*, 6th ed. Englewood Cliffs, N.J.: Prentice-Hall, 1985.

Henry, Kenneth. *Defenders and Shapers of the Corporate Image*. New Haven, Conn.: College and University Press, 1972.

Larson, Keith A. *Public Relations: The Edward L. Bernayses and the American Scene: A Bibliography*. Westwood, Mass.: F. W. Faxon, 1978.

Public Relations Society of America. *Careers in Public Relations*. New York: PRSA, 1983.

Simon, Raymond. *Public Relations: Concepts and Practices*, 3rd ed. New York: Macmillan, 1984.

Sperber, Nathaniel, and Lerbinger, Otto. *Manager's Public Relations Handbook*. Reading, Mass.: Addison-Wesley, 1982.

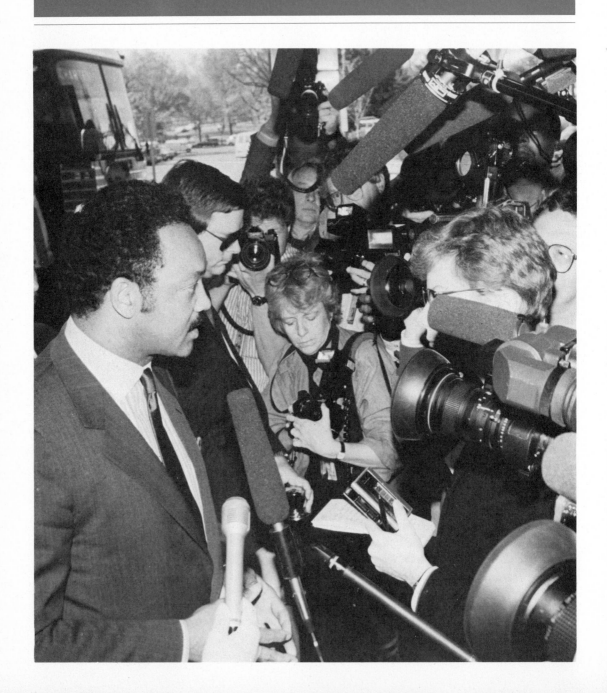

Chapter 13

The Selling of
American Politics

Politics is the gentle art of
getting votes from the poor and
campaign funds from the rich,
by promising to protect each
from the other.
—*Oscar Ameringer, labor organizer and editor*

Flashing strobe lights, electronic thunder and a stirring trumpet rendition of the national anthem burst forth from a videocassette recorder in a New Hampshire living room in 1988. A waving American flag and the Statue of Liberty fade into the background as fireworks explode and hundreds of people cheer presidential candidate Pat Robertson as he walks out of the darkness and begins speaking.

By the late 1980s, slick, professionally produced videos were being used by virtually every American presidential candidate to woo voters. The importance of television images and its newest technology—VCRs—had become an established fact in the American political process.

TV also influenced the types of candidates that were running for office. Robertson, for example, was a former television evangelist and founder of the satellite Christian Broadcasting Network. And he was hoping to succeed two-term Republican President Ronald Reagan who, prior to entering politics, had been a movie and television star.

The importance of television in creating positive images for presidential candidates was first recognized in the 1960s. Live television can transmit an image—be it positive or negative—to millions of Americans instantaneously. Former senator Gary Hart used television to project an image of a bright, articulate political leader who could lead the nation toward new horizons. He soon found himself the front runner for the 1988 Democratic presidential nomination. However, when television reported on his

303

extramarital activities—and showed tape of him lying about it at a press conference—his presidential hopes were shattered.

Since candidates want to project only positive images, political image makers try to minimize live TV and focus on prepackaged videos. The American system of mass communication, which had been given First Amendment protections in 1791 to keep the electorate informed, had changed a great deal from those early days when the media consisted only of partisan public newspapers, relatively few books and a limited number of magazines.

Since the American experiment in democracy is dependent on a well-informed and participating citizenry, an examination of recent trends in mass media coverage of politics and the uses (and abuses?) of the media in political campaign strategies seems appropriate.

OPINION LEADER THEORY

The impact of the mass media on American presidential politics first became a concern to media researchers and political observers in the 1930s. They began to wonder if the new medium of radio, combined with the system of newspapers that was strongly entrenched in American popular culture, might influence voter behavior more powerfully than the traditional political parties.

Lazarsfeld Study. In 1940 a group of researchers headed by Paul Lazarsfeld decided to find out just how much influence the mass media exerted during presidential elections. They examined the media's role in the election between Democratic President Franklin Delano Roosevelt and Republican challenger Wendell Willkie. To gather their data, an extensive test was set up in Erie County, Ohio.[1]

The study's surprising results indicated that neither radio nor print had as much influence on voters as had been suspected. The researchers found that most of the people studied relied more on other people for the information they used to make their voting decisions.

Lazarsfeld then began to study the individuals who were relied on for information, calling them *opinion leaders.* He found that opinion leaders could be just about anyone, from a homemaker next door to a coworker on the assembly line. However, further analysis revealed that these opinion leaders were better informed than the average person and that, in general, they tended to read more newspapers and magazines and listen to more radio news and commentary.

As a result of his findings, Lazarsfeld developed the *two-step flow theory* of communication. This theory advanced the concept that (1) the mass media influence certain individuals and (2) these individuals personally influence others.[2] Subsequent studies of the 1952 and 1956 presidential elections by Campbell, Converge, Miller and Stokes substantiated Lazarsfeld's findings.[3]

Changing Trends. However, research in the 1970s and 1980s seemed to indicate that a number of factors were causing the mass media's indirect or secondary role in determining election outcomes to change. Prevalent among these factors were the advent of the political consultant and the prominent role television had come to play in the American culture.

Political scientist Robert Agranoff described the changing political scene as follows:

The candidate organization, the news event, the computer-generated letter, and most importantly the electronic media are the prevalent means of getting messages across in the modern campaign. The rise of the candidate volunteer and the electronic media has enabled the candidate to bypass the party and appeal directly to electors.[4]

THE RISE OF THE POLITICAL CONSULTANT

The decline in the role of party bosses in helping candidates get elected created a need for someone to take their place. According to Sidney Blumenthal, "Political consultants are the new power within the American political system. The consultants have supplanted the old party bosses as the link to the voters."[5]

Early Pioneers. The pioneers in the political consulting business were a husband-and-wife team in California, Clem Whitaker and Leona Baxter, who founded a public relations firm in 1934. They were instrumental in getting numerous Republicans elected to office until their retirement in 1958. Other successful consultants include Joe Napolitan, Stu Spencer, Bill Roberts, Sandy Weiner, Gerald Rafshoon, Bob Squier, Dick Woodward, Jack McDowell and Hal Evry (see Box 13.1).

Political consultants are professionals with advertising and public relations skills. They also make extensive use of opinion polling in shaping campaigns.

Opinion Polling. Opinion polling can help win elections by finding out what issues are important to voters and what the majority's sentiments are. Candidates can then take a stand on the "right" side of the issues, telling voters what they want to hear. The extensive use of polling to shape campaign rhetoric has come under a great deal of criticism. Before his own campaign for the Senate, Democrat Paul Simon said, "The me-too illness is now compounded by the dramatic rise in public opinion polling and the spectacle of public officials following the implications of the polls, regardless of national need."[6]

In the 1980s President Ronald Reagan hired a firm called Decision/Making/Information to carry out the most extensive (and expensive) poll taking on a continual basis ever conducted for a president. The information from the polls became an important part of White House strategy and sometimes influenced the president's policy decisions.[7]

Creating Images. Political consultants are skillful image makers. Their standard operating procedure is to find out what the voters want and then package the candi-

BOX 13.1.

PROFILE OF A POLITICAL CONSULTANT

In a June 3, 1966, feature article in *Life* magazine, political consultant Hal Evry was quoted as saying he could "elect you to office if you had $60,000, an IQ of at least 120, and could keep your mouth shut." The IQ, Evry noted, was not necessary for being an elected official but was a requirement for having enough sense to understand why it was important to do as he said and not talk to the press or public during the campaign. (Today, he points out that the cost of getting elected is ten times that amount.)

Evry is one of the more colorful and controversial veteran political consultants in America. He started his political consulting business in Los Angeles in 1955 and has been involved in over 500 political campaigns in the United States, Canada and Japan. He boasts a success rate of over 90 percent. He has managed gubernatorial races for George Wallace in Alabama, William Scranton and Raymond Shafer in Pennsylvania, David Hall in Oklahoma and Winthrop Rockefeller in Arkansas, as well as many senatorial and congressional races

and one presidential primary.

The winning formula for election campaigns, according to Evry, consists of "identifying the publics (voters), polling them to learn their opinions, and then communicating with them in such a manner as to win their support" (telling them what they want to hear).

Evry's controversial and unorthodox theories include a strong belief that candidates should not give political speeches. He feels they are a waste of time (usually only people who support a candidate or have already made up their minds on how to vote go to hear politicians speak). Not only that, but the candidate might say something that will offend some of the voters. His advice to candidates is to leave town and let him (Evry) create an image and sell it. (Evry once got a millionaire who wanted to be elected mayor of a California city to vacation in Bermuda during the campaign. When he returned he was the mayor-elect, having won 20 of 21 precincts.)

Many critics of Evry's slick political cam-

date to meet those desires. Journalism educators Shaw and McComb describe this process as follows:

> *The ability of television, newspapers, magazines, movies, radio and a whole host of new communications technologies to mold the public mind and significantly influence the flow of history is a widely ascribed power. In the political arena, candidates spend substantial sums for the services of image-makers—a new kind of mass communication artist and technocrat who presumably works magic on the voter via the mass media.*[8]

Selling Images. The techniques used to sell political candidates have been changing over the years. Instead of debating issues or defending party goals, candidates are now more likely to be packaged and sold to the American public in almost the same way as laundry detergent. As reporter Joe McGinniss put it in 1968, "Style becomes substance. The medium is the massage and the masseur gets the votes."[9]

paigns claim that keeping the candidates away from the public and press degrades the American political system because the whole idea is for the electorate to be well-informed about the candidates' positions on the issues.

Evry is quick to debate this argument by contending that unqualified candidates are elected all the time under the old system and that his method may be bringing in a new caliber of candidate who would not have bothered to run before. He points out that traditional politics attracts only the noisy, boisterous types who love to "press the flesh" and talk at the top of their lungs. Under Evry's system, the refined, introverted type can make it into public office, he says.

Evry also believes very strongly in what he calls his golden rule—"He who has the gold, rules." The more money a candidate spends, the more likely he or she is to win, Evry says. He believes that a person has to be rich to run for political office and tells people planning to run on a limited budget to give their money to the Cancer Society,

where it might do some good. As he points out, "Money does not necessarily guarantee success in a campaign (if an opponent is equally well financed he may run a better campaign). But, while money is no guarantee of success—the lack of money is a guarantee of losing."

Although Evry's attitude toward the American political process seems cynical, he does have some suggestions—equally controversial—for improving the system. He believes that the United States should have standards for political office seekers and qualifications for voters. He argues that we would not let an unqualified person perform brain surgery on us, yet we let anyone run for political office, where they help run the country and influence world affairs. As for voter qualifications, he points out that when the American experiment in democracy was established, the vote in most states was given only to land owners. "Now," he says, "the vote of any vagrant on the street carries as much weight as the richest man in America."

Sources: Personal interviews with Hal Evry; David Chagall, *The New King Makers* (New York: Harcourt Brace Jovanovich, 1981); and Hal Evry, *The Selling of a Candidate: The Winning Formula* (Los Angeles: Western Opinion Research Center, 1977).

But there was more to selling candidates than media advertising. The mass media, which had long set their own news and information agendas (see the discussion of agenda setting in Chapter 1), were now facing competition from the political consultants in the agenda-setting process.

Political consultants often stage *news ploys* (called media events) to get free publicity for their candidates. The news media—fearful they might be scooped by the competition if they refuse to cover these contrived events—dutifully cooperate.

Some successful media events staged by political consultants include a U.S. senatorial candidate in scuba-diving gear swimming to the scene of an oil slick caused by offshore drilling, a California candidate for state treasurer attempting to throw a silver dollar across the Sacramento River on George Washington's birthday and another U.S. senator kicking off his campaign by running in a marathon. All of these events received extraordinary media coverage—far beyond their news value.

On the campaign trail, media events are often contrived photo-opportunities to create a favorable image for the candidate. Here George Bush gingerly holds a pig and Michael Dukakis visits a day-care center during their 1988 campaigns. *(Top: J. L. Atlan/Sygma; bottom: Ira Wyman)*

THE RISE OF POLITICAL ADS AND MEDIA INFLUENCE

The role the mass media play in the political system in the United States has been steadily growing during the twentieth century. Also increasing through the century has been the effective and controversial use of political advertising in the media. Debate over such advertising first emerged in 1916, when both the Republican and Democratic parties hired ad agencies to place advertisements during the presidential election. This activity led Congress in 1917 to consider for the first time regulations on political advertising.[10]

Harding and Coolidge. From then on, advertising and PR people have played important and varied roles in American politics. In the 1920s these roles ranged from paying $20,000 to keep Warren G. Harding's mistress silent during the 1920 campaign to coining the slogan "Keep Cool with Coolidge" to help elect Calvin Coolidge president in 1924.

Roosevelt-Willkie. In 1940 so many high-powered advertising men were supporting Wendell Willkie's campaign against President Franklin D. Roosevelt that the fact
became a campaign issue. Columnist Dorothy Thompson stated on CBS radio,
"These are the boys who have perfected the technique of selling the American people
anything on the shelves." She said that she was supporting Roosevelt because "I am
at long last fed up with the glib copywriters who think you can slug this nation into
an election."[11]

Eisenhower-Stevenson. Although the Republican and Democratic national conventions were first televised in 1948, it wasn't until 1952 that the new medium was
used for advertising during a presidential campaign. General Dwight D. Eisenhower
was the first president to use spot TV commercials. In one day, under the supervision
of ad man Rosser Reeves, he recorded 40 20-second spots, which were broadcast during the last weeks of the campaign. This led George Ball, a staff member of Democratic challenger Adlai Stevenson, to say: "They have invented a new kind of campaign—conceived not by men who want us to face the crucial issues of this crucial
day, but by the high powered hucksters of Madison Avenue."[12]

When Stevenson accepted his party's nomination to challenge Eisenhower again in
1956, he said his opponents would use "shows, slogans and the art of advertising" to
get votes, and that "The idea that you can merchandise candidates for high office like
breakfast cereal—that you can gather votes like box tops—is, I think, the ultimate
indignity to the democratic process."[13] Despite Stevenson's remarks, the convention
where he was appearing and the platform on which he was standing had been orches-
trated and redesigned by an ad agency hired by his party. Advertising agencies were
now firmly entrenched in American presidential politics.

Kennedy-Nixon. Television was not everyone's medium, however. Some people
did not come across well on the TV screen. One of the first politicians to learn this

John F. Kennedy's
ability to project
better during his
televised debates
with Richard Nixon
was critical in his
narrow victory in
1960. This race is
seen as the
dawning of the
media's influence
on electoral
politics. *(UPI/
Bettmann
Newsphotos)*

the hard way was Vice-President Richard M. Nixon, the Republican nominee for the presidency in 1960. Nixon agreed to appear in a series of televised debates with his Democratic challenger, the junior senator from Massachusetts, John F. Kennedy.

The relatively unknown Kennedy came across as youthful, witty, intelligent and appealing. Nixon's TV image was less attractive. Kennedy ended up winning the election by a very narrow margin, and many political observers credited the TV debates for his victory. (It is interesting to note that many people who listened to the debates on radio thought that Nixon had won.)

Kennedy also used television effectively while in office. According to McGinniss, the American people forgave John Kennedy for many mistakes, including a botched-up invasion of Cuba, a perilous confrontation with the Soviet Union over missiles in Cuba and a dangerous bluff in foreign policy in Berlin. McGinniss said: "We forgave, followed, and accepted because we liked the way he looked. And he had a pretty wife. Camelot was fun, even for the peasants, as long as it was televised to their huts."[14]

Johnson-Goldwater. Probably the most controversial political advertisement of all times was aired in 1964 by the Doyle Dane Bernbach advertising agency on behalf of President Lyndon B. Johnson (Johnson had assumed the presidency in November 1963 following the assassination of President Kennedy). Known as the "Daisy" commercial, it showed a three-year-old girl plucking the petals of a daisy while miscounting. The soundtrack then shifted to a Voice of Doom, which completed a countdown from 10 and detonated a nuclear explosion. The commercial suggested that Johnson's Republican challenger Barry Goldwater, with his hawkish stand on national defense, would lead the country to nuclear annihilation.

Although Johnson was able to use television advertising effectively to win his own term as president, he soon found that the new medium was not his "cup of tea." Although he had been a very successful politician in Congress, his TV image was stiff and stilted and lacked the charm that Americans had come to expect from their president during the Kennedy years. In 1968 Johnson, whose image and popularity had reached rock bottom due to his escalation of the war in Vietnam, went on television one more time to announce to the nation that he would not seek reelection.

Nixon-Humphrey. In this same year Richard Nixon made another try at the presidency. This time he hired experts to create a warm, friendly and appealing TV image. A series of commercials showed the "new Nixon" talking with people of all ages and backgrounds. Perhaps not due solely to the new image, Nixon won the presidency in the contest against Johnson's vice-president, Hubert Humphrey.

Raymond K. Price, a former editorial writer for the *New York Herald Tribune* who became a prominent speech writer in Nixon's campaign, was one of the first to suggest that the campaign "attack *personal factors* rather than *historical factors* that were the basis of the low opinion so many people had of Richard Nixon."[15] Feeling there was a problem between the voter and Nixon's image, Price suggested that a new image be created and that the campaign focus on getting a positive response to that image. He said:

The response is to the image, not to the man. . . . It's not what's there that counts, it's what's projected—and carrying it one step further, it's not what he projects but rather what the voter receives. It's not the man we have to change, but rather the received impression. And this impression often depends more on the medium and its use than it does on the candidate himself.[16]

Much of what we know about how Nixon's advisers used television to create a "new Nixon" comes from Joe McGinniss's book *The Selling of the President, 1968.* A newspaper reporter, McGinniss worked on Nixon's advertising and media staff for several months without being detected. The book made it clear that TV images rather than issues had become the new game in American politics.

Nixon-McGovern. Nixon used television effectively again in 1972 to win a landslide victory over Democratic challenger George McGovern. However, when TV began broadcasting the congressional hearings into the Watergate affair in 1973, Nixon's television image began to worsen. Within a year, the man who had won reelection by a landslide was forced to resign from office. Television had made the illegal activities of his administration known to the masses and impeachment was imminent.

Carter-Ford. Gerald R. Ford, who became president following Nixon's resignation, had a difficult time with his television image. Ford's rise to the presidency was the result of a series of unparalleled events. He was a congressman from Michigan when Vice-President Spiro Agnew was forced to resign during a bribery scandal. Nixon appointed Ford vice-president, not expecting that he himself would soon be forced to resign and surrender the presidency to a nonelected vice-president.

At first Ford was treated kindly by the media. Many reporters felt he was a "nice guy" who had become a victim of circumstances. However, when Ford issued a pardon for former President Nixon, the press was outraged. It began scrutinizing his administration and television cameras were there to catch every action. Soon the cameras observed him tumble down the ramp of *Air Force One* in Salzburg, Austria, on his way to a meeting with the Egyptian president, Anwar Sadat. On other occasions he was photographed stumbling, bumping his head and falling while skiing. As the media continued to focus on Ford's apparent lack of coordination, a public image was created of Ford as a stumbler and bumbler.

In 1976 a peanut farmer from Plains, Georgia, challenged Ford for the presidency. James Earl Carter, who wanted people to call him "Jimmy," was a political unknown on the national level, although he had once been governor of Georgia. With the assistance of political consultant Gerald Rafshoon, Carter used television and other media to establish a national identity and win the presidency. TV made Carter's face and voice familiar to millions of voters who had never heard of him, and it established his image as a man of the people, a born-again Christian "who had come to rescue them from the Washington devils."[17]

At first Carter was able to use the media to enhance his image as president. Network news people considered the Carter White House more clever in handling TV than earlier administrations. CBS correspondent Bob Schieffer said, "They know when it's to their advantage to be helpful to us. Like the joint swearing in of an anti-war guy [Sam Brown, director of ACTION] and a disabled Vietnam veteran [Max Cleland, head of the Veterans Administration]. You know you're being had, but you do it exactly the way they want it done because they're right, it's good television."[18]

Reagan-Carter. Television also played a part in Jimmy Carter's downfall. A series of events led to the decline of Carter's public approval ratings from a high of 70 percent to 28 percent in 1979. Among them were scandals involving some of his staff members, the energy crisis, record levels of inflation, his well-publicized and televised flamboyant beer-drinking brother Billy, and finally, on November 4 of that year, the seizure of the American Embassy in Teheran by Iranian students, who captured 63 Americans and held 50 of them hostage for 442 days. As the Americans' captivity continued throughout 1980—an election year—the television networks led each evening's newscast with a count of the number of days Americans had been held (see discussion of agenda setting in Chapter 1).

Jimmy Carter's presidency had faced hard times in a troubled and complex world. His challenger, former California governor Ronald Reagan—who had earlier earned his living performing before movie and TV cameras—developed a television image of a leader who would bring back the glories of the past. According to American mythology, the "good old days" were a time when simple answers solved complex problems and there was no doubt about America's righteousness and superiority. His campaign slogan was "Let's Make America Great Again."

Thanks to his training, Reagan was able to project a relaxed, folksy image as an ordinary man—no politician—during his television debates with Jimmy Carter. Even though Carter was better prepared, Reagan won by appearing to be a calm, confident elder statesman. His now-famous "there you go again" phrase projected an image of a wise and benevolent parent putting down an immature offspring.

After Reagan defeated Jimmy Carter, both Carter and his press secretary, Jody Powell, wrote about what they considered media abuses of power. In his memoirs *The Other Side of the Story*, Powell attacked the country's TV networks and major news-papers. In the *New York Times Book Review*, journalist Lester Bernstein responded:

> The fact is that Jimmy Carter as a national figure was almost invented by the media. He owed more to the engines of publicity for his emergence from obscurity to a Presidential nomination than any politician since Wendell Willkie in 1940. If Mr. Powell takes that as a norm, small wonder that he has felt shortchanged ever since.[19]

After his election, Reagan continued to use television effectively. A master at reading scripts, Reagan used Teleprompters to deliver his speeches. He even took his Teleprompter with him to Germany when he was scheduled to deliver a major televised address. His televised State of the Union addresses before Congress (and the ever-faithful Teleprompters) amazed many Americans who thought he was speaking to them without notes. He also used radio to deliver regular Saturday talks with the nation, much as Franklin Delano Roosevelt had done 50 years earlier.

However, despite his mastery of TV, Reagan experienced the same problems with the press that other presidents had faced. The press began zeroing in on erroneous statements he made during news conferences, and there were numerous leaks to the media from within his administration. He soon limited the number of news conferences to a level far below that of his predecessors and attempted to punish anyone in his administration who leaked information. (Other presidents, like Johnson and Nixon, also attempted to stop leaks and punish offenders.) Those news conferences he did hold were scheduled during television's prime time so that his remarks would be carried live and could not be edited by the networks.

The Reagan administration began to stage news events and set up barriers for press access to news it didn't want covered. When the United States invaded the Caribbean Island of Grenada in 1983, the news media were not told about it until after the event. Because of Reagan's popularity, the media found little support from the public for their protests over the obvious censorship of the invasion.

Reagan-Mondale. When Reagan ran for reelection in 1984, he took full advantage of the media to project his "presidential image" (see Box 13.2). Steven R. Weisman, chief White House correspondent for the *New York Times*, summed up Reagan's use of the media during this election:

> [I]t is increasingly evident that something extraordinary has happened to the relationship between President Reagan and the press. What is now clear is that Mr. Reagan has ignored some of the unstated ground rules under which reporters have traditionally covered the Presidency. As a consequence, he has dramatically altered the kind of information the public receives about him and his administration.
>
> ... He and his aides have ... achieved a new level of control over the mechanics of modern communication—the staging of news events for maximum press coverage, the timing of announcements to hit the largest television audiences. Moreover, the President has displayed his news media artistry at a time when television has become the dominant means by which the public gets its news. From the beginning of his Presidency, Mr. Reagan and his aides have understood and exploited what they acknowledge to be the built-in tendency of television to emphasize appearances and impressions more than information.
>
> Central to the President's overall strategy has been his unusual ability to deal with television and print reporters on his own terms—to decide when, where and how he will engage them. In short, the art of controlled access.[20]

The Reagan presidency ran into more difficulty during its second term, when the press disclosed that the administration had been selling arms to Iran and diverting the profits to rebel forces in Nicaragua. After Congress held televised hearings into the activities, a national poll showed that most people didn't believe Reagan when he said he didn't know about the diversion.

Despite this trouble, two phrases came to characterize the Reagan presidency. Friends as well as critics agreed that he was the *Great Communicator*—probably the

BOX 13.2.

TELEVISION POLITICAL ADVERTISING, REAGAN STYLE

In 1984, after two incumbents seeking a second term had been voted out of office (Gerald Ford in 1976 and Jimmy Carter in 1980), incumbent president Ronald Reagan won reelection by a landslide. He carried every state except his challenger's home state of Minnesota and the District of Columbia.

Assisting Reagan was a cleverly developed advertising campaign that created an image of success, patriotism and a regal presidency. The image was the work of a team of successful Madison Avenue ad executives called the Tuesday Team, Inc. Although these advertising superstars had limited political experience, they had been successful in developing singing feline lyrics for Meow Mix and bandwagon-inducing commercials for Pepsi-Cola. This was considered an asset rather than liability by the Reagan people, who wanted commercials different from the typical ones that attacked the opponent and defended the incumbent's record.

Masterminding the campaign were White House aides Michael Deaver, a former PR account executive who had been assisting Reagan with his image since his campaign for governor of California in 1966, and James Baker, Reagan's chief of staff. They decided to stress broad themes rather than specific issues in order to play up a feeling of patriotism and prosperity. What they didn't want was to spend time defending Reagan's policies from attacks by challenger Walter Mondale.

The Tuesday Team used 16mm film (rather than inferior videotape), lush music, elaborate lighting and the latest in dubbing and editing techniques to create polished television ads. The country was flooded with TV images of President Reagan looking presidential. There were scenes of him in the White House rose garden, picnicking with an Alabama family, talking to assembly-line workers in Michigan and putting on a Smokey the Bear hat in Kentucky—to show his concern for the environment. Some of the ads featured staged campaign rallies with bands playing and clean-cut-looking kids and ordinary folks waving American flags in support of the president. The slogan and voiceover on the commercials said "President Reagan—Leadership That's Working."

In addition, Reagan's political campaign appearances were staged to recreate the images in the ads. People were given flags to wave and "appropriate"-looking people were moved to the front of the crowd. This was done to ensure that the ads would look like actual news events rather than harsh commercial interruptions of the evening's TV entertainment. The ads were designed to blur the line between political commercials and the 6 o'clock news.

Some 40 variations of the ads were developed and aired on network television, at a cost of $25 million. While Reagan's ads were helping build his landslide, Mondale's television campaign was using 20 different commercials featuring the typical "attacking candidate." Mondale's $20 million expenditure for the commercials translated into relatively few votes.

Mondale was well aware of the role television played in his defeat. In a postelection news conference he said: "Modern politics requires television. I think you know I've never really warmed up to television, and in fairness to television, it's never really warmed up to me."

best one ever to hold the office. Critics also called him the *Teflon President*, because—despite the various troubles in his administration—no blame ever seemed to stick to him.

Bush-Dukakis. In the 1988 presidential primaries, media scrutiny or a lack of funds for media advertising eliminated a long list of presidential hopefuls. Months before the Republican National Convention, Vice-President George Bush had sewn up the Republican nomination after swamping challengers Bob Dole, Pete Du Pont, Al Haig, Jack Kemp, and Pat Robertson. Bush made good use of an angry exchange with Dan Rather—broadcast live on the *CBS Evening News*—to counter his earlier media image as a "wimp." He also used extremely negative ads against his most serious rival, Bob Dole, to win the crucial New Hampshire primary.

Governor Michael Dukakis of Massachusetts did not win enough delegates to secure the Democratic nomination until the final primaries in June, although only one other candidate, the Reverend Jesse Jackson, was still in the race by the end. Media fascination with Jackson, the first black man to be a serious contender for a major party nomination, helped him sustain a long primary battle that saw other challengers—Bruce Babbitt, Joe Biden, Dick Gephardt, Al Gore, Gary Hart, and Paul Simon—fall by the wayside.

The high cost of paid media exposure, the failure to project the right media images and the media's magnification of candidates' weaknesses and blunders all took their toll (see Box 13.3).

BOX 13.3.

DEMOCRATS PUT IT TOGETHER FOR TV IN 1988; RATINGS DECLINE

The Democratic National Convention in July of 1988 signaled the beginning of the end of political party conventions as they had been known to television viewers for 40 years.

The convention was a well-organized, made-for-TV event that launched the ticket of Michael Dukakis and Lloyd Bentsen with a demonstration of party unity. The Democrats hired the first-rate Hollywood production team Smith-Hemion to produce the extravaganza for television. The 4,200 convention delegates were outnumbered by over 13,000 news media personnel in Atlanta to cover the event. The number of local television station crews was at an all-time high.

National conventions have been a part of America's political system since 1832. In the early days, state party bosses selected the delegates, nearly always white men, and back-room negotiations usually determined who would be the nominees for president and vice-president. This suspense and intrigue meant that conventions were highly newsworthy events.

The first major news events covered by television when it began entering the popular culture in 1948 were the Democratic and Republican national conventions. The drama of who would emerge as party standard bearers generated public interest and gavel-to-gavel coverage, and conventions became standard network programming every four years.

Inevitably, television coverage began to

change the way conventions were conducted. In 1968, TV cameras showed riots in the streets of Chicago outside the Democratic National Convention, with many demonstrators claiming that they had been shut out of the political system. It became apparent to many that the delegates inside the convention hall were not truly representative of the rank and file, and after the election the party instituted major changes in how delegates would be selected in the future. Of the 4,200 delegates in 1988, 2,050 were women, 1,000 blacks, 300 Hispanics, and 90 Asians.

Party leaders also learned during the years of being under the TV spotlight that infighting and disharmony during the convention hindered their chances of winning in the fall. Although there are more registered Democrats than Republicans, open conflict at Democratic conventions helped the Republicans win six of the nine presidential elections since 1952, when television convention coverage became important in the culture. (In 1960, 1964, and 1976, the years the Republicans lost, the Republican conventions were filled with controversy and bitter infighting.)

By 1988 the Democrats had learned their lesson. They produced the ultimate four-day television commercial, demonstrating harmony, unity and enthusiasm. The fact that the nominees had been predetermined—Dukakis had won the nomination by gathering more than enough delegate votes during primary elections and had selected Bentsen as his running mate before the convention—left only one real newsworthy element to be decided at the convention: would Dukakis's runner-up, Jesse Jackson, fight or support the ticket after Dukakis had passed over the black candidate as a running mate? Jackson's decision to support the ticket was announced on the first day of the convention, before the opening session. Reporters grumbled that there wasn't much news left by the time the convention convened. But the Democrats had what they wanted: national broadcast of strongly partisan speeches by Ann Richards, Edward Kennedy, Jesse Jackson and Dukakis himself gave the ticket an immediate boost in the polls.

However, network television executives suggested that 1988 would be the last year they would provide such extensive coverage. Although the networks had cut their coverage to two hours each night—a far cry from the original gavel-to-gavel coverage—the ratings were at an all-time low, with less than 50 percent of viewers tuning in.

One reason for the low ratings was the lack of suspense. (George Bush gave the Republican convention at least a little suspense by delaying the naming of his running mate, Dan Quayle, until the afternoon of the second day.) Equally important, however, was the fact that viewers were no longer dependent on the networks for their evening's entertainment. Cable channels and independent stations offered a wide range of alternative programming, including gavel-to-gavel coverage of the convention on CNN and C-SPAN for the real political devotees.

ABC News President Roone Arledge was the first to call for reforms in political conventions. Noting that candidates were now preselected in the primaries, he called on the parties to reduce the number of days for conventions. He urged them to join with network executives to come up with something "more appealing" to the American public. He and other network executives made it clear that there would be major changes in how television would cover the conventions in 1992.

Television's influence on the American political system had never been more evident.

EFFECTIVE POLITICAL MEDIA

Although a variety of mass media are used to sell candidates to the public, by the 1980s political consultants had identified three that seemed to work the best. And, as one would expect, the most effective media are the most expensive. This fact has led to an escalation of campaign expenditures in recent years, which in turn has generated numerous proposals for campaign-finance reforms. Many of the suggested reforms, however, are considered violations of First Amendment rights to free speech.

Vote Videos. The newest campaign medium is the vote video, which is distributed to supporters to show friends and other prospective voters in their homes or rented halls. The videos offer razzle-dazzle productions of the candidates shaking hands, flashing smiles, throwing footballs and spitting forth popular slogans for campaign issues. The use of videos in political campaigns has brought a new dimension of political image making into the electoral process. According to some political observers, issues are no longer important in elections and have been replaced with video images.*

*In 1987 a large developer facing a referendum on a city council approval of a billion-dollar hotel-convention center that would transform a small upscale California bedroom community into a convention center on the scale of Las Vegas or Miami spent $50,000 to produce and mail a slick video promoting the virtues of his project to all 1,200 voters in the community. His efforts paid off; the community transformation was approved by a 56–44 percent vote.

Direct mail is widely used in the political arena. Mailings range from campaign brochures to reports from representatives to their constituents, as in this example.

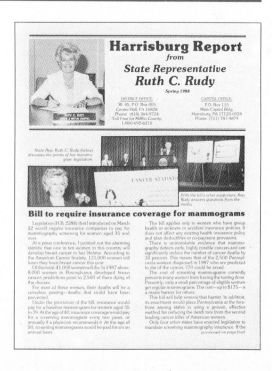

BOX 13.4.

PRETESTING POLITICAL CAMPAIGN ADS

Sophisticated marketing techniques used by the packaged-goods industry are being applied to political advertising campaigns as well. The cynical charge that candidates are being packaged and sold to the public like bars of soap is true to the extent that both use similar test-marketing strategies.

The latest strategy that has been gaining popularity in the 1980s has been pretesting political television ads. According to *Advertising Age* (February 13, 1986), the number of campaigns and candidates pretesting the ads had grown three- to fourfold during the past five years.

Washington-based Democratic pollster Peter Hart says that political ad makers have followed the commercial field because dollars are scarce and the "message must be on target." Political groups are spending some $10,000 to $30,000 to pretest ads before spending hundreds of thousands or millions of dollars on statewide and national campaigns.

Some ads are pretested in studios where the commercial is shown along with other political commercials and television programs. Others are tested over the air in sample markets with follow-up polling. Other times people are shown commercial story boards and asked to select the one that appeals to them the most.

Although pretesting is more expensive, it seems to be producing results at election time.

Direct Mail. Ranking at the top of most political consultants' lists of effective media for a number of years has been direct mail. Computerized equipment can now generate what appear to be personalized letters with the recipient's name throughout and computerized mailing lists can separate groups to receive different messages. A candidate can stress strong support for Social Security in a mailing to older citizens while emphasizing the need for government-funded day care in a mailing to younger voters.

The most effective type of direct mail, according to research by Hal Evry's Western Opinion Research Center in Los Angeles, is a letter from a personal friend or a well-respected community leader.[21] This particular technique applies the opinion-leader phenomenon (discussed earlier) to our modern high-tech mass culture.

Television Advertising. The third effective medium is, of course, television advertising. Like the vote videos, TV commercials sell images rather than discuss issues. These ads are cleverly designed and carefully produced to achieve maximum results. They are often pretested before airing (see Box 13.4).

Author George McKenna, discussing whether we are manipulated by the media, asked, "Who has not seen those 30-second spots showing shirt-sleeved candidates walking through blighted streets looking concerned? Or candidates pledging to get tough on criminals without saying how they would do it? Or a candidate listening sympathetically to *ordinary Americans* telling him their woes, while a voiceover assures us that he cares?"[22]

According to Austin Ranney, former president of the American Political Science Association, television does not necessarily depict reality, but TV's reality has become "the reality in politics." In his book *Channels of Power*, he said that television has reshaped American political culture, weakened political parties, strengthened candidates who have media charisma, weakened the presidency because the president is in the constant glare of TV's cameras and strengthened the government because it can hide from the publicity spotlight.[23]

An Opposing View. Not everyone agrees about TV's power to sell political candidates. Some feel that selective exposure, perception and retention (see Chapter 1) help voters shield themselves from these mediated images.

Two political scientists, Thomas Patterson and Robert McClure, studying the 1972 Nixon–McGovern campaign, found that spot TV commercials do more to educate voters about the issues than manipulate them about the candidates.[24]

They concluded that strong evidence for advertising's ineffectiveness comes from a look at the changes in voters' images of the candidates after presidential ads were aired on television. They conducted a study using a series of George McGovern commercials, showing him in small groups designed to portray him as a man who cared about people. What they found was very little change in public attitudes.[25]

However, the study did determine that people tended to project their own political biases into the candidates' commercials and to see what they wanted to see, rather than what the advertisement intended for them to see.

Here are some of the reactions they received to the McGovern commercials:

He really cares what's happened to disabled vets. They told him how badly they've been treated and he listened. He will help them.
                                        —37-year-old pro-McGovern viewer

McGovern was talking with these disabled vets. He doesn't really care about them. He's just using them to get sympathy.
                                        —33-year-old pro-Nixon viewer

It was honest, down-to-earth. People were talking and he was listening.
                                        —57-year-old pro-McGovern viewer

Those commercials are so phoney. He doesn't care.
                                        —45-year-old pro-Nixon viewer

McGovern had his coat off and his tie was hanging down. It was so relaxed, and he seemed to really be concerned with those workers.
                                        —31-year-old pro-McGovern viewer

He is trying hard to look like one of the boys. You know, roll up the shirt sleeves and loosen the tie. It's just too much for me to take.
                                        —49-year-old pro-Nixon viewer[26]

Should the System Be Changed? Some political observers advocate major changes in the use of television in American elections. Claiming that politics has degenerated into an effort to sell the *prettiest package*, they argue that political advertising should consist only of candidates' *"talking heads."* Under this plan, no skillfully produced commercials designed to sell images rather than issues would be allowed.

In France, for example, political advertising is not allowed on television. Instead, French TV broadcasts five-minute statements by the various candidates following the evening news (a different candidate each evening). Many feel that such a system is preferable, because issues cannot be discussed in 30-second spots, and longer statements are needed for the voter to get a true picture of where candidates stand.

This argument has one flaw: it presumes that people will watch the longer political broadcasts. TV ratings for full-length political programs indicate otherwise. While people usually don't bother to change the channel during a 30-second commercial, they are likely to switch the channel to *Golden Girls* or *Dallas* if faced with a long broadcast by a political talking head.

Such a change would most likely take politics out of the popular culture and limit the dialogue between candidates and voters to an interested elite. Whatever its faults, at least the 30-second spot seems to reach the masses.

NEWS COVERAGE OF ELECTIONS

While most of the criticism of the American political process has been focused on how image makers use the media to sell candidates, news reporters have also been criticized for adding to campaign confusion.

Character Analysis. Following the Watergate affair, when the American people learned that the president of the United States had lied about his knowledge of illegal activities by members of his administration, the press began to pay closer attention to analyzing the character of presidential candidates. In 1987 this heightened scrutiny succeeded in derailing two presidential campaigns. The leading Democratic presidential candidate—Gary Hart—withdrew from the 1988 presidential race after the press published stories about his involvement with actress-model Donna Rice. At a press conference called to announce his decision to quit the race, an angry Hart said:

> We're all going to have to seriously question the system for selecting our national leaders that reduces the press of this nation to hunters and presidential candidates to being hunted, that has reporters in bushes, false and inaccurate stories printed, photographers peeking in our windows, swarms of helicopters hovering over our roof, and my very strong wife close to tears because she can't even get in her own house at night without being harassed. And then, after all that, ponderous pundits wonder in mock seriousness why some of the best people in this country choose not to run for high office.[27]

Several months later Democratic presidential candidate Joseph Biden pulled out of the race because the media had focused on statements he had made that were either

Actress-model Donna Rice and presidential candidate Gary Hart on the cover of the *National Enquirer*, during what the tabloid called "a fun-filled weekend in the Bahamas." This kind of media coverage forced the one-time front-runner out of the race. *(AP/Wide World Photos)*

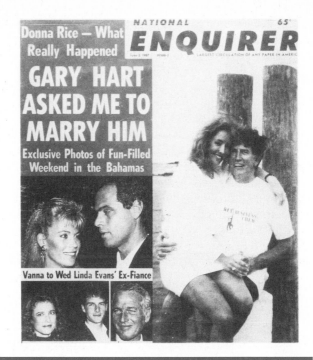

false (he had said that he had graduated near the top of his class in law school when records showed he was nearer to the bottom) or had plagiarized from speeches of others. Not long afterward, Republican candidate Pat Robertson was apologizing for hiding the fact that his marriage took place shortly before the birth of his son, rather than on the day of conception as he had said earlier. "I sowed some wild oats in my youth," he explained.

Some criticized the news media for focusing on personal characteristics rather than issues. Others, however, defended the press by saying that presidential candidates' moral character and judgment was important for voters to know about before an election.

Horse-Race Effect. Another complaint about the press during election campaigns is that reporters tend to focus too much on who is winning the race. This criticism was probably most intense during the 1984 election between incumbent Republican Reagan and Democratic challenger Mondale. Regardless of how hard Mondale and his running mate Geraldine Ferraro tried to talk about the issues, the front-page stories and evening news broadcasts dwelt on who was ahead in the race. This phenomenon has been characterized by some as *the horse-race* mentality of the media.

Projecting Winners. Another election complaint is directed at television news. Ever since TV began projecting the winners of national contests in the 1960s, critics have claimed that the practice was skewing election results. TV networks usually project winners based on computer sampling of polls and surveys conducted as people leave the precincts (known as exit polling). The problem is that in the past the networks have projected winners long before the polls closed in the Western time zones.

In 1980, for example, President Jimmy Carter was televised giving his concession speech before the polls were closed in the West. Some Democratic congressional candidates said they lost their particular elections because many Democrats in these Western states didn't bother to vote after seeing Carter concede.

For two decades Congress and the public tried to persuade the networks to delay projecting winners until all the polls were closed. Network executives responded by saying that they weren't about to withhold information from the American people temporarily. Yet these same network executives regularly delayed broadcasting the 7 o'clock news in the West for three hours each night (the newscast originating in the East at 7 P.M. is actually airing at 4 P.M. Western time). In November 1986 the networks finally agreed not to predict winners in any state until the polls had closed in that state.

Positive Election Coverage.   These trends should not be interpreted as a blanket condemnation of the media in political elections, however. Some newspapers do attempt to cover issues, and the major television networks have made air time available for presidential debates on the issues. Although the ratings for the televised presidential debates seem to be slipping (it was estimated that between 70 and 80 million people watched the Reagan-Mondale debates, down from 120 million in 1980), they do draw large audiences and expose viewers to candidates discussing the issues. Some criticize the debates, however, because they are highly artificial events (ground rules must be approved by both sides before they will agree to debate) and have little resemblance to actual debates.

Television news shows like *Meet the Press* also do an effective job of getting candidates to discuss the issues. The only problem, however, is that these shows' ratings are much lower than those of the evening news, sports and sitcoms.

SUMMARY

The development of a mass culture dominated by the media has made major changes in the American political system, changes some observers feel threaten the very core of American democracy.

In the 1940s the first studies were conducted to determine whether the mass media were changing American voting patterns. The studies showed that opinion leaders, not the media, were directly affecting voter behavior, although the mass media played an indirect role by influencing the opinion leaders. This discovery led to the formulation of the two-step flow theory of political communication: the mass media influence opinion leaders, who in turn influence others.

Follow-up studies in the 1960s and 1970s, however, indicated that the American political system was changing. The long-standing dominance of political parties was waning and political consultants were replacing party bosses. These consultants had advertising, public relations and opinion-polling backgrounds and had moved into the political arena to sell candidates directly to the American people through the mass media, much like others in their professions were selling soap and detergents.

During the twentieth century, the mass media and political advertising began playing significant roles in selling political images. Television, which has become one of the most dominant forms of mass communication in our culture, has emerged as a powerful influence in determining the political destiny of this country. It helped create a winning image for little-known Senator John Kennedy, who narrowly defeated Vice-President Richard Nixon in the 1960 presidential election; led to a decline in popularity of Lyndon B. Johnson; allowed Nixon to win the presidency eight years later by building a more positive television image; and gave national exposure to a little-known peanut farmer and former Georgia governor, Jimmy Carter. By the 1980s the presidency had been turned over to Ronald Reagan, who had made his living communicating in front of the camera. Through his effective use of television, he was soon regarded as one of the most effective communicators ever to hold the office of president.

American political candidates, managed by political consultants, are now using vote videos and direct mail as well as television advertising to get their messages across. Not everyone, however, gives TV so much credit for creating political images. Some studies have indicated that selective exposure, perception and retention play a bigger role in the election process. These studies contend, for example, that people project their own biases into television political commercials and see only what they want to see.

News reporters have been criticized for running stories about candidates' personal lives, downplaying issues and focusing too much on who is winning. Television news has also been criticized for projecting winners on election night before the polls have closed in the West. This has kept many Western voters away from the polls, critics contend. Television has been instrumental in presenting presidential debates to the American public.

NOTES

1. Paul Lazarsfeld, Bernard Berelson and Hazel Gaudet, *The People's Choice* (New York: Columbia University Press, 1968), p. 148.

2. Ibid., p. 151.

3. Angus Campbell, Phillip E. Converge, Warren E. Miller and Donald E. Stokes, *The American Voter* (New York: Wiley, 1960), p. 32.

4. Robert Agranoff, *The New Style in Election Campaigns* (Boston: Holbrook, 1976), p. 6.

5. Sidney Blumenthal, *The Permanent Campaign* (Boston: Beacon Press, 1980), p. 12.

6. Paul Simon, *The Once and Future Democrats: Strategies for Change* (New York: Continuum, 1982), p. 86.

7. John Tebbel and Sarah Miles Watts, *The Press and the Presidency: From George Washington to Ronald Reagan* (New York: Oxford University Press, 1985), p. 541.

8. Donald L. Shaw and Maxwell E. McCombs, *The Emergence of American Political Issues: The Agenda-Setting Function of the Press* (St. Paul, Minn.: West, 1977), p. 3.

9. Quoted in George McKenna, *Media Voices: Debating Critical Issues in*

Mass Media (Guilford, Conn.: Dushkin, 1982), p. 91.

10. Stephen Fox, *The Mirror Makers: A History of American Advertising and Its Creators* (New York: Morrow, 1984), p. 307.

11. Ibid., p. 308.

12. Quoted in Fox, p. 310.

13. Ibid.

14. McKenna, pp. 91–92.

15. Ibid., p. 95.

16. Ibid.

17. Tebbel and Watts, p. 522.

18. Quoted in ibid., p. 526.

19. Lester Bernstein, "The Other Side of the Story, by Jody Powell," *New York Times Book Review*, April 1, 1984, p. 7.

20. Steven H. Weisman, "The President and the Press: The Art of Controlled Access," *New York Times Magazine*, October 14, 1984.

21. Hal Evry, *The Selling of a Candidate: The Winning Formula* (Los Angeles: Western Opinion Research Center, 1977), p. 67.

22. McKenna, p. 97.

23. Austin Ranney, *Channels of Power* (New York: Basic Books, 1983), p. 69.

24. Thomas Patterson and Robert D. McClure, *The Unseeing Eye: The Myth of Television Power in National Politics* (New York: Putnam, 1976).

25. Ibid.

26. Ibid., p. 114.

27. "Hart Statement Text: I'm Not a Beaten Man; I'm an Angry, Defiant Man," *Los Angeles Times*, May 9, 1987, p. 25.

ADDITIONAL READING

Bowers, Thomas A. "Candidate Advertising: The Agenda Is the Message," in Donald Shaw and Maxwell McCombs, *The Emergence of American Political Issues: The Agenda-Setting Function of the Press.* St. Paul, Minn.: West, 1977.

Chagall, David. *The New King Makers.* New York: Harcourt Brace Jovanovich, 1981.

Chester, Edward W. *Radio, Television and American Politics.* New York: Sheed & Ward, 1969.

Edelman, Murray. *The Symbolic Uses of Politics.* Urbana: University of Illinois Press, 1980.

Jacobson, Gary. *The Politics of Congressional Elections.* Boston: Little, Brown, 1983.

Jamieson, Kathleen Hall. *Packaging the Presidency: A History and Criticism of Presidential Campaign Advertising.* New York: Oxford University Press, 1984.

Kelley, Stanley. *Interpreting Elections.* Princeton, N.J.: Princeton University Press, 1983.

Key, V. O. *The Responsible Electorate.* Cambridge, Mass.: Harvard University Press, 1966.

Kraus, Sidney, and Davis, Dennis. *The Effects of Mass Communication on Political Behavior.* University Park: Pennsylvania State University Press, 1976.

Lamm, Richard, and Grossman, Arnold. *1988.* New York: St. Martin's, 1985.

McGinniss, Joe. *The Selling of the President, 1968.* New York: Trident Press, 1969.

Milbrath, Lester, and Goel, M. L. *Political Participation.* Skokie, Ill.: Rand McNally, 1977.

Nimmo, Dan D., and Combs, James E. *Mediated Political Realities.* New York: Longman, 1983.

O'Keefe, Garrett J., and Atwood, L. Edwin. "Communication and Election Campaigns." In *Handbook of Political Communication,* ed. Dan D. Nimmo and Keith R. Sanders. Beverly Hills, Calif.: Sage, 1981.

Patterson, Thomas E. *The Mass Media Election.* New York: Praeger, 1980.

Polsby, Nelson W., and Wildavsky, Aaron. *Presidential Elections.* New York: Scribner's, 1976.

Rivers, William. *The Opinion Makers.* Boston: Beacon Press, 1965.

Scott, Andrew M., and Wallace, Earle. *Politics, U.S.A.: Cases on the American Democratic Process,* 3rd ed. Toronto: Macmillan, 1969.

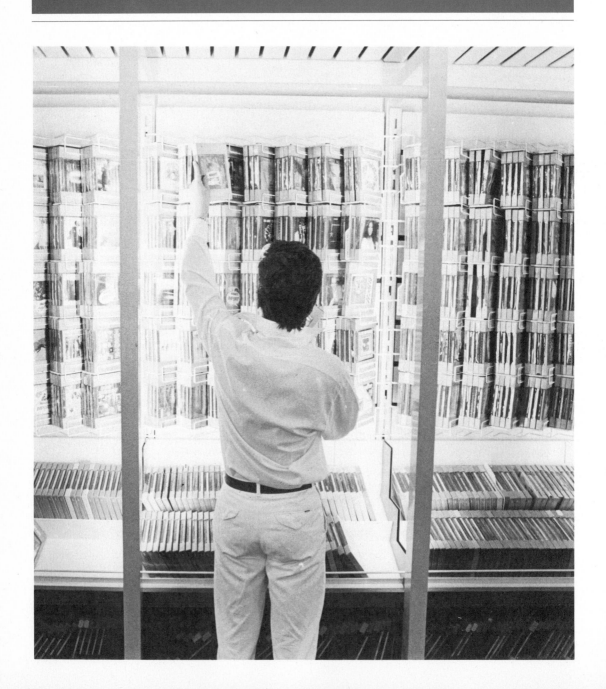

Chapter 14

Changing Trends in Media Technology

The decade of the nineties is
going to be one in which the
traditional newspaper may face
a decline, extinction or at
least complete internal
self-reappraisal.
—*Anthony Smith,* Goodbye Gutenberg

In 1980 Alvin Toffler suggested in his best-selling book *The Third* Wave that civilization was in transition between the second and third great cycles of human history. The first cycle was the agrarian society, which existed until the second cycle, the Industrial Revolution of the late eighteenth and nineteenth centuries. The third cycle, which is now replacing the industrial society, is the information age.

Sociologist Daniel Bell pointed out that by the early 1980s the United States had more people working in the production of information than in manufacturing or agriculture. The information age has been created through the rapid development of such new technologies as coaxial cables, satellite communication, computers, fiber optics, microwave transmission and home video equipment. In the last several decades there has been a complete transformation in the way information is processed in the home and workplace.

PREDICTING THE FUTURE

Not all the predictions of futurists have come true, however. The invention of the transistor by Bell lab engineers in 1947 did lead to the development of the microchip and other technological marvels by the 1960s and early 1970s. Yet, although some futurists predicted that the Unites States would be a *wired nation* by the late 1970s, many of these technological advances have yet to find their place in the American life style.

Some pessimists even envisioned that the events in George Orwell's novel *1984* would become a reality in accordance with the author's time frame. But the year 1984 has come and gone, and Big Brother is not spying on us through television sets hooked up to two-way cable systems—although the technology for such a grim prospect does exist.

Communication Revolution. Still, no one can deny that a communication revolution is under way. What is occurring has been described as follows: "All modes of communication we humans have devised since the beginnings of humanity are coming together into a single electronic system, driven by computers."[1]

Advances in electronic technology, particularly in the fields of telecommunication and computerization, have already affected the ways we receive radio, TV and print communication. And the combination of home computers, satellites, television, telephones and cable systems may soon convert our homes into communication centers. Toffler predicted that by the late 1980s and 1990s many homes would be turned into electronic communication centers—his term was *electronic cottages*—where people would work and study.[2]

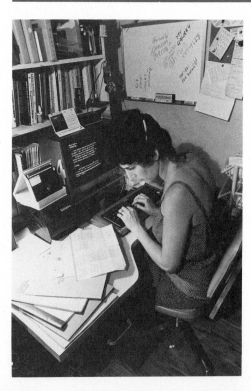

"Telecommuting" is becoming an alternative to fighting busy freeways each day. Many workers involved in information processing, such as the one pictured, can work at home using computer terminals and modems to connect them to their offices. (*John Coletti/Stock, Boston*)

Finding a Niche. How fast the new technologies will become commonplace depends on numerous factors. Just as the mass-media technologies introduced in the nineteenth century had to find a niche in our culture, so too must today's electronic inventions struggle to find their place.

Consumer acceptance of new technologies, however, is just the last step in taking a new technological development from invention to widespread use. First engineers and scientists must invent the item, then venture capitalists and shareholders must be willing to gamble on the product's success and then marketing people must sell the concept to the consumer.

Of all the new mass-communication technologies that have been developed in recent years, cable television, satellite communication, computers and home video equipment have had the most significant impact on our culture. In the next decade we may also see major changes in our culture as a result of teletext, videotext, fiber optics, digital sound, multipoint distribution service, direct broadcast satellites, and high-definition and low-power TV. These innovations may bring about the day when we read our newspapers and magazines on TV screens, watch our favorite TV shows and video movies on larger-than-life silver screens on our living-room walls and do most of our routine banking and shopping from our computerized home information center.

CABLE TELEVISION

Cable television began in the late 1940s as a way to relay television signals to remote communities that could not receive them through the airwaves. However, following the 1975 launching of RCA's communication satellite SATCOM I, the cable industry found a new niche—serving metropolitan areas with expanded TV programming.

As a technology, cable somewhat resembles the telephone, as it involves the wiring of individual homes. Some have said that the cable industry represents the "third wiring of America" (the first and second being the telegraph and the telephone.)[3]

Expanded Programming. Home Box Office (HBO), was the pioneer in expanding programming to the masses via satellite-fed cable service. In 1975 it rented a transponder on SATCOM I and made first-run movies available to cable system operators for a fee.

Cable now provides a wide variety of programming, from standard network broadcasts to a myriad of specialized channels available to cable companies via satellite. Although capable of carrying more than 100 channels, most cable companies still offer only 20 or fewer. However, even this number has greatly altered American television-viewing habits by reducing the big three networks' control over viewers. By 1987, over 44 million households—more than 50 percent of American homes—had cable TV, and these households were watching more cable programs than programs of ABC, CBS and NBC combined.

Viewers hooked up to cable can receive a wide variety of programs, including 24-hour news, arts and entertainment, all sports, all weather, continuous congressional coverage, Christian programming, movies, old TV reruns, children's programming, ethnic programming and soft-core pornography.

Cable News Network (CNN) is one of two all-news networks owned by media entrepreneur Ted Turner. It features continuous news coverage along with a wide variety of features ranging from cooking to life styles. The other news network of Turner Broadcasting System features continuous headline news with fewer features. In addition, Turner owns the Atlanta, Georgia, "superstation" WTBS, which is broadcast by satellite and carried by cable companies throughout the country.

Music Television (MTV) is owned by Warner-Amex and offers—as does VH-1—round-the-clock video rock music, including concerts, video versions of hit records and interviews. In the late 1980s it added game shows like "Remote Control" as well as other long-format programming.

Christian Broadcasting Network (CBN), owned by the Christian Broadcasting Advertising Network, offers family-oriented entertainment stressing positive values, including many 1950s and '60s television family sitcoms. It also broadcasts fundamentalist Christian shows and was instrumental in promoting the presidential candidacy of its founding president, televangelist Pat Robertson.

Entertainment & Sports Programming Network (ESPN) offers in-depth sports coverage and business news. It is owned by Getty Oil Company. In 1987 it started broadcasting Sunday night National Football League games.

Black Entertainment Television (BET) provides black-oriented musical events, political discussions, call-in shows and movies. It is owned by Robert L. Johnson Telecommunications and Taft Broadcasting.

Spanish International Network (SIN), broadcasting in Spanish, offers news, soap operas, sports, musicals, variety shows, movies, specials and live broadcasts from Mexico. It is privately owned by S. A. and Rene Anselmo.

The Silent Network offers original captioned programming for the deaf and hearing-impaired. It carries such programming as game shows, talk shows, aerobics and drama. It is privately owned by Sheldon Altfeld.

Pay-TV. In addition to the above channels, usually available for a basic subscriber fee, cable companies also offer a number of other channels for an extra charge. Sometimes known as *pay TV*, these channels carry prime movies, concerts, sporting events and classic movies. They include HBO, Showtime, Cinemax, the Movie Channel, Select-TV, the Disney Channel and the Playboy Channel.

Public Access. Many cable companies also provide public-access channels that local citizens can use for public-service programming. Schools sometimes use these channels for home education; some communities televise local city council meetings or other programming on local issues.

Two-Way Cable. Although most cable TV operations involve one-way communication, cable is capable of two-way interaction, much like the telephone. One of the first of these installations was the *Qube* system, introduced in 1977 by Warner-Amex in Columbus, Ohio. The system gave viewers an unlimited range of feedback opportunities. They could, for instance, choose the endings to certain dramatic programs and instantly express opinions in polls. The Qube system, however, was not economically successful.

Two-way cable systems also can allow viewers to take part in game shows and can provide home banking and electronic shopping as well as home security-monitoring systems.

While two-way cable uses the same coaxial cable as one-way systems, it also requires bidirectional amplifiers on the cable (two amplifiers in one, capable of sending the signal in two directions), a computer at the headend (the cable system's equipment center, where signals are distributed to the subscribers) and a key pad resembling a hand-held calculator in the home.

Some media critics claim that the two-way cable is potentially dangerous because it is very similar to the monitoring device used by Big Brother in Orwell's *1984*. An Orwellian-style monitoring system has already been used—on volunteers—to observe purchasing trends and advertising effectiveness. The monitors are known as *people meters* (see Box 14.1).

SATELLITE COMMUNICATION

The new telecommunication technology ushered in by the space age has affected the mass media of radio, television and newspapers as well as cable television. The *satellite* is an electronic relay system that operates from outer space. U.S. communication satellites are placed in orbit some 22,300 miles above the equator so that they will rotate at the same speed as the earth (appearing to be stationary) and look down on the continental United States.

How It Works. Satellites are either launched into space by rockets or placed in orbit by space shuttles. They carry transponders that pick up and retransmit signals sent from the ground. Each transponder can carry one television signal or 1,000 telephone messages at a time. Most satellites have 24 transponders, but in the future satellites are expected to carry up to 40. The more transponders, the more complicated and valuable the satellite becomes.

Prior to satellites, TV signals were sent across the nation by microwave relay stations. In many respects, satellite transmission is much like the microwave transmission. Each satellite receives messages on its transponders, amplifies them and transmits them back to earth. However, instead of manipulating microwave signals over and around mountains and into valleys, the satellite avoids ground interference by providing a direct signal into space and back to earth. Satellites are also capable of sending signals many thousands of miles, thus providing a low-cost and long-distance means of telecommunication.

Television Signals. Most of us have seen satellite dishes people have installed to pick up TV signals. The advent of satellite television transmission has made it pos-

BOX 14.1.

"PEOPLE METERS": HIGH-TECH MEDIA MONITORS

Did you know that 27 percent more spaghetti sauce is sold to fans of *Search for Tomorrow* than to fans of *All My Children?* This bit of trivia was very useful to Campbell Soup executives, makers of Prego spaghetti sauce, when they were deciding how to spend their advertising dollars.

This and much more information like it is now available to advertisers through new high-tech research technology. Data about television viewing habits and consumer buying patterns are being monitored in certain parts of the country by new computerized gadgets called *people meters*. These devices consist of a remote-control keyboard that provides data on who is watching TV. When a person turns on the television set, he or she punches a code into the hand-held keyboard. The computer automatically sends each viewer's age, sex and program choice over telephone lines to a computerized data bank.

Some marketing research firms contract with households to provide additional information. People are paid $400 a year to run a hand-held scanner over their grocery shopping receipt so that their purchases can also be fed into a computer. Their buying patterns are then compared to the TV advertisements that they have seen, and the ads' effectiveness is measured.

In 1987, much to the displeasure of the television networks, the A. C. Nielsen Co.— the major TV rating service—began using people meters to determine TV audience sizes. (Prior to people meters, Nielsen used two systems to gather data: First, electronic meters wired to television sets in 1,700 homes recorded the channels that the set was tuned to when it was on. Second, people in 2,600 other homes filled out diaries of their television-viewing habits.) The networks and advertisers have long relied on data gathered by Nielsen to calculate audience sizes for each program, which largely determine the advertising rates charged by the networks.

According to the new people-meter ratings, audiences were some 10 percent smaller than had been determined by the traditional methods. The networks immediately challenged the new technology, claiming that it was biased in favor of people who were comfortable with new technology and against older, more traditional viewers who hadn't yet warmed to computer technology. The technology also exaggerated the impact of cable households, which watch less network programming, network executives claimed. ABC and CBS both notified Nielsen that they were canceling their contracts.

People meters seem to be just the tip of the iceberg when it comes to high-tech's invasion into the area of research on American mass-media consumption patterns. A Seattle, Washington, company has developed a device that senses, through ultrasound waves, how many viewers are in front of the television set and whether any of them leave the room while the TV set is on.

Research also is being done on devices that can identify viewers by their voice and transmit psychological data by analyzing voice stress and other indicators.

Technology is even being developed to monitor print-media consumer patterns. Two New Jersey companies—Pretesting Co. in Englewood and Perception Research Service of Englewood Cliffs—are attempting to interest publishers in glasses that track readers' eye movements (to show what they actually look at on a page) and digital watches that record on a microchip what magazines a person reads.

sible for people living in the most remote regions of the nation or world to join the telecommunications age.

Both local network television affiliates and cable operators can now get their programming signals from space. The first television network to change from microwave to satellite transmission was the Public Broadcasting Service (PBS) in 1978. NBC converted in 1985, and ABC and CBS began making the switch in 1986.

However, this new technology has created new challenges and problems for the industry. The most pressing is who owns these satellite signals and how revenue is collected from them. If networks sell programs to local stations or cable companies and send them via satellite, what is to prevent others from picking up the signals directly and avoiding the locally inserted advertisements and/or monthly cable fees? By 1988 most pay-TV satellite signals were being scrambled to restrict their reception to "authorized" receivers.

Radio Signals. Satellite communication is also used extensively in radio broadcasting. Network and syndicated programming are now available to radio stations throughout the country via satellite receiving dishes. Since computerized signals make it possible for local stations to insert commercials and station identifications, the average listener has no idea that the programming is being beamed simultaneously to radio stations across the country. For example, syndicated programs like "Country Coast-to-Coast," "Stardust" and "Contemporary Top 40," all produced by Satellite Music Network, and Larry King's radio talk show are sent to stations throughout the United States by satellite.

While the new technology has improved the quality of radio programming in rural areas, it has assimilated these rural listeners into the sounds and message of a national mass audience. In many areas, regional cultures are no longer broadcast.

Newspaper Signals. The newspaper industry is also taking advantage of satellite technology to distribute information in printed form. Satellites are used to transmit wire stories for both the Associated Press and United Press International, and Gannett's national newspaper, *USA Today*, is made possible by satellite technology (see Chapter 6). By late 1986 Gannett began publishing an international edition of *USA Today* by beaming its satellite signal to a printing plant in Switzerland.

This speed and efficiency in transmitting news and information, coupled with large chain ownerships of formerly locally owned newspapers, is contributing to the demise of the transmission of local culture in favor of national mass cultural messages.

Other Uses. Satellite technology is also finding wide acceptance in business and personal communication. Worldwide business transactions are being conducted cheaply and efficiently via satellite-fed telephone services, teleconferencing and videoconferencing.

Home telephone users can choose from an array of long-distance carriers, such as Sprint and MCI, that offer service at reduced prices. These carriers use satellite transponders rather than AT&T lines to carry many of their telephone messages.

World-wide business transactions are now conducted cheaply and efficiently
via satellite-fed phone services like teleconferencing and, as shown here,
videoconferencing. *(Courtesy of AT&T)*

Author James Traub has summed up the impact of satellite technology on our culture this way:

> *The capacity of inexpensive, instantaneous nationwide transmission offered by
> the satellite has transformed cable television from a relay station into an
> immense industry; freed broadcast stations from much of their dependence on
> networks; increased the volume and efficiency of long-distance phone service;
> blurred the distinction between print and electronic media and created such
> wholly new technologies as videoconferencing.*[4]

Future Impact. Because satellite dishes are expensive, personal use of satellite TV
remained primarily in the elite culture through most of the 1980s. However, by 1987
there were more than one and a half million satellite dishes installed in America's
backyards. It is predicted that the cost and size of these dishes will soon drop and they
will find their way into the popular culture. Miniature dishes—about the size of an
umbrella—that can fit on a rooftop and cost between $100 and $200 are expected to
be in use by the 1990s, when direct broadcast satellites (DBS) find a niche in the
culture.

When this happens, it may place the American mass culture squarely in the age of
specialization, as each of us will have hundreds of TV channels available for our individual interests.

COMPUTERS

Computer technology has rapidly altered American culture. Not only have personal computers revolutionized many homes, schools and businesses, but they have had a profound impact on mass communication.

Newspaper Uses. Computers started making inroads in the newspaper industry in the 1960s, as a tool to speed up and reduce the costs of typesetting. While this made newspaper publishing much more profitable, it also led to the demise of one of the oldest unions in the United States—the International Typographical Union.

By the 1980s newspaper reporters and editors were using computers to retrieve information, write and edit stories and design pages. Computers were also being used to program the sorting equipment that sent specialized sections of newspapers to particular geographical areas. (Large metropolitan newspapers sell space at reduced rates to advertisers who want to run their ads in copies sold in a specific region.) Newspapers' accounting and recordkeeping procedures were also computerized.

By the mid-1980s laser printers hooked up to inexpensive personal computers were producing graphics for most major newspapers. This inexpensive equipment could also be used for typesetting. Small businesses and printing operations used these computerized *desktop publishing* systems in place of typesetting equipment that cost ten times as much.

Desktop publishing systems may make it possible for newspapers to enter the stage of specialization by allowing individuals with little capital—rather than large companies or chains—to start up small newspapers aimed at a selective market or interest. Computers and laser printers that will not only typeset but perform full pagination (display the layout and design of the entire newspaper page on screen) can be purchased for less than $10,000. This may bring back the era of small individual voices transmitting specialized or regional culture.

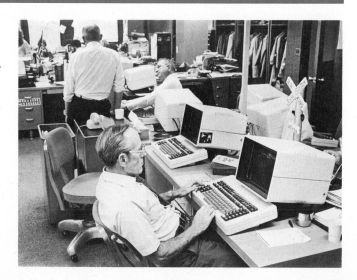

Typewriters, which once dominated newsrooms, have been made all but obsolete by the computer terminal, as this photo of the *Flint* [Michigan] *Journal* newsroom shows. *(Michael Heyman/ Stock, Boston)*

Book Publishing. Computer technology has also made inroads in the book-publishing industry. Some authors compose books on computers and send the floppy disks to their publisher, who uses them first to edit the material and then to typeset it without additional keystroking. By the mid-1980s it was estimated that two-fifths of all published authors were using computers or word processors instead of typewriters, including former president Jimmy Carter, who wrote *Keeping the Faith* on one. The book you are now reading was written on an IBM-PC.

Libraries. Libraries use computers for data retrieval and to reduce storage space. The Library of Congress is putting texts and periodicals on indestructible 12-inch disks, which many people can use at one time. It is predicted that soon all printed material will be stored in computerized memory banks at the time of publication.

The implications of these new storage and retrieval systems on research and the advancement of knowledge in our culture are overwhelming.

Broadcasting. In the 1980s some radio stations started using computers to operate their broadcast studios. The station's entire daily operation could now be programmed into a computer. At the appropriate second the computer could call up a tape cartridge of an announcer's voice giving the time, introducing a record or reading a commercial. The next computer cue would turn on a tape machine to play a preselected song.

As a result, many disc jockeys and radio announcers found themselves replaced by computers. However, some audiences were not ready for this new technology, and a number of stations found that the rather impersonal computers were no substitute for the disc jockey who could respond to telephone requests and had a gift of the gab. By the late 1980s some radio stations had returned to the old way of doing things.

Television stations, cable companies and satellite relay systems were also using the new computer technology in their day-to-day operations in the 1980s.

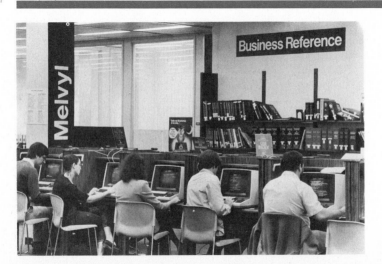

In libraries, computers now play a key part in conducting book searches. *(Spencer Grant/Stock, Boston)*

HOME VIDEO EQUIPMENT

When Ampex introduced the first videotape recorder in 1956, its impact was slight. Although futurists predicted that the new technology would radically alter the way people watched television, only the elite could afford to pay $1,500 for one of the recorders.

Videocassette Recorders. Home video recorders did not enter the popular culture until after 1975, when Sony introduced the Betamax. At first, popular acceptance of the Betamax and a VHS model that followed was slow because of the high cost. However, within 10 years videocassette recorders (VCRs) were selling for less than $300 in some markets, and the impact of this technology could be seen everywhere.

Home video recorders freed the general public from the clutches of the TV networks. People no longer had to schedule their calendars around their favorite shows. Instead, they could tape-record programs and watch them at their convenience. They could also fast forward through commercials.

Home video equipment, which existed in over 44 million American homes by 1988, also provided an alternative to network and cable programming. If someone found nothing of interest on TV, he or she could rent a popular movie.

Video Rentals. By the 1980s, video-rental stores—which rented video movies for as little as 99 cents—could be found in every American community. People could even rent videos at their local supermarket or corner convenience store. The videotape revolution had entered the American popular culture with a vengeance.

The advent of the video-rental business has affected not only the way we watch television but what we watch as well. Although the movie-rental business has hurt motion-picture theaters, it has provided an expanded market for movie producers. By the late 1980s some theaters were getting into the rental business themselves.

By the late 1980s, video stores had sprung up in communities all across America. Some rent tapes for as little as 99 cents. *(Eli Reed/ Magnum)*

Theaters that showed X-rated pornography were the hardest hit by the video-rental business. The ability to watch hard-core films in the privacy of one's home was much more appealing than going to a theater.

The widespread availability of hard-core videos in stores has brought criticism from groups that fear the nation's moral fiber is being threatened. Efforts to ban such videos have failed, although some video store owners have been persuaded to voluntarily locate the adult section discreetly in their stores. However, the anti–adult video movement was continuing its efforts for a total ban in the late 1980s.

The proliferation of hard-core video films has not been limited to the American culture. The British press, for example, has devoted numerous column inches to discussing the problem of "video nasties" in the United Kingdom. Some video store owners in Britain have been jailed on obscenity charges as the authorities try to put an end to the video-porn invasion.

Video Discs. Not all home video equipment has met with success in the marketplace. In 1981 RCA announced that it would start selling videodisc players (VDPs). The discs produced better quality and made it easier to select the starting point on prerecorded material. RCA's idea was to provide inexpensive videodisc machines (the initial price was about $250) and then sell prerecorded discs, thus developing a market for discs sales similar to the one for recorded music.

RCA had a promotional budget of nearly $20 million to launch its new industry. With a new plant to produce VDPs in Bloomington, Indiana, RCA was ready to make a killing. However, at about the same time, videotape recorders were finding their own comfortable niche in the marketplace as the video-rental business began to take off. To meet the demand for rentals, the price of VCRs dropped substantially.

RCA's anticipated sales of the inexpensive disc players did not materialize. Even dropping the price to $150, with discs selling for $20, didn't help. In 1984 RCA announced that it would stop making VDPs. The company closed its Bloomington plant, which had employed 750 people, and wrote off the venture as a $575 million loss.

Other companies involved in the videodisc industry—North American Phillips, MCA and IBM—abandoned their efforts after investing a quarter of a billion dollars. Pioneer remained a lone "pioneer" (pardon the pun) in the videodisc industry. In 1985 it developed a combination audio and video laser disc player, which promoted the perfection of the LaserVision videodisc system. This has given new life to the videodisc technology. Because this system has distinct advantages over videotape players—namely the low cost of reproduction, longer life and easier program selection—business and educational markets are experimenting with videodiscs. They are certain to find their place in our culture soon.

MERGING PRINT AND ELECTRONICS

The computer revolution also ushered in new technology that began to merge print and electronic mass communication. These systems, which provide print text on television screens, are called *videotext* and *teletext*. Both systems were invented in Britain in the early 1970s and to date have been far more successful in Europe than in the United States.

Videotext. The videotext system (sometimes spelled videotex) is a two-way interactive communication system between a home television set and a computer. Users can call up information from the computer's data base—as well as do their shopping and banking without leaving home.

The British Post Office, which runs Britain's telephone system, developed the first successful videotext system, Prestel. The system, which utilizes telephone lines to connect the TV sets and computers, contains thousands of pages of information that are available to subscribers for a monthly charge and a user fee (much like a long-distance telephone service).

Although France, Canada and Japan have also developed videotext systems, the technology has not caught on in the United States. The first major experiment with videotext in the United States was Viewtron, a joint venture in Florida by Knight-Ridder newspapers and AT&T. The experiment, which ran from 1983 to 1986, failed to gain enough subscribers to make it profitable. Other videotext systems were introduced in 1984 by Times Mirror in Orange County, California, and by the *Chicago Sun-Times* and the Honeywell Corporation in the Chicago area. The California operation was called Gateway and the Chicago venture was called Keyfax. Although Gateway claimed that its average subscriber had an income of more than $75,000, it too was soon abandoned.

However many services these systems provided, from news, agribusiness information, weather and travel information to home banking, shopping and security systems, they attracted few subscribers. As a result, none of the systems was profitable, and they remained a novelty for the elite. By the late 1980s videotext was showing little sign of moving into the popular culture.

In addition to its localized experiments with videotext, Time Inc., in conjunction with AT&T, began experimenting with a more limited transactional financial service on a national scale in the late 1980s. Unlike the local ventures, the Time-AT&T operation was not dependent on advertising revenue. It was hoped that the fact that it was national in scope would attract enough users to make the operation profitable.

Teletext. A system that offers one-way interactive viewing of printed text on a television screen is known as teletext. (This system should not be confused with Cabletext, where character generators are used to transmit printed text over available cable channels; Cabletext is not interactive.) In teletext, the viewer uses a hand-held program selector to call up a content listing (menu) and specific pages of information ranging from news to the latest in travel and weather information.

Teletext was invented in the 1960s by British engineers who were working on a way to provide subtitles for the hard of hearing. What emerged in the 1970s was an entirely new mass-communication medium. The British Broadcasting Corporation (BBC) has a version of teletext called Ceefax; the Independent Broadcasting Authority

(IBA) version is called Oracle. The only difference between these two systems is that the IBA version carries advertising while the BBC version does not. The Oracle commercials appear at the bottom of the printed information screen.

Although first introduced in 1974, the teletext system did not receive wide acceptance in Britain until the early 1980s, when TV manufacturers started building teletext converters into their sets. By the mid-1980s more than 2 million British homes could receive teletext information. Teletext technology spread throughout Europe until every Western European and one Eastern European country—Hungary—had a system. The number of teletext users in countries other than Britain remained small, however.

Teletext information is broadcast along with the regular TV signal. In Europe the television signal consists of 625 lines of video information. Twenty-four lines that do not carry picture information are used to transmit the teletext information. (In the United Sates the signal consists of 525 lines, with 21 lines available for teletext information.) The space for teletext information is called the vertical blanking interval (VBI)—the black band on a TV set that appears when the picture is out of adjustment and starts to roll.

Several hundred pages of information can be transmitted in the VBI. (Thousands of pages of information can be transmitted on blank TV channels that carry no picture information.) The teletext information is encoded at the TV station and transmitted over the VBI to the home, where a decoder converts the digitized signal back into readable form.

After a person uses a hand-held keypad to call up the information directory, he or she can then designate the page number desired and the decoder will grab the designated page as it cycles and display it on the screen.

Conflicting Systems. In the United States, teletext, like videotext, is still trying to find a niche. Although a number of companies have experimented with teletext, the FCC has refused to designate a single standard for teletext; as a result there are two separate and incompatible systems in use in this country. One, called World System Teletext (WST), is based on the British teletext system. The other, called the North American Broadcast Teletext Standard (NABTS), is based on the French and Canadian system and is backed by RCA, NBC, Time and AT&T. Although the NABTS system delivers better graphic reproduction, it requires more expensive home decoders, which gives WST an advantage in the marketplace.

NBC began inserting NABTS teletext signals into the VBI sent to affiliates in 1983 but canceled the service in 1985. CBS also began transmitting NABTS signals in 1983, the same year Taft Broadcasting in Cincinnati began broadcasting a WST signal. Ted Turner's cable superstation WTBS carries a national WST signal. The WST teletext system was available free to those who purchased a $250 decoder. Unfortunately, the decoders worked only with a late-model Zenith television receiver. NABTS decoders cost between $800 and $1,000. They too worked only with expensive late-model television sets.

Although some local and national TV outlets are still experimenting with teletext, the technology has not lived up to a 1983 research firm's prediction that by 1990, 20 percent of all U.S. households would be teletext subscribers.

The future of videotext and teletext in the United States remains doubtful at this time. Only if and when it reaches the popular culture is this new technology going to be successful.

OTHER TECHNOLOGICAL ADVANCES

There are a number of other technologies on the horizon that may continue the transformation of American culture.

Fiber Optics. The future for fiber optics seems much brighter than videotext and teletext at the present time. Developed by Western Electric, fiber optics is an engineering breakthrough that makes it possible to carry 100,000 phone calls or more than 100 broadcast signals on a flexible glass strand the size of a human hair. The strand consists of tiny glass fibers that are spliced together by an intricate honeycomb crystal device, which holds them in perfect alignment so that no two are more than one eight-thousandth of an inch out of line.

Unlike wire transmission lines, fiber optics transmit signals on light beams rather than radio waves. These light beams can even go around corners. This new technology is already in use in some international phone services and Sprint has even advertised its use of a nationwide fiber optic system.

The possibilities for use of fiber optics are limitless. Some predict that there will be a fourth wiring of the nation, this time with fiber optics. In the future a single wire may bring telephone, two-way television cable, videotext information and electronic newspapers into a home communication center.

Digital Sound. In May 1983 a jazz-oriented recording company in New York, GRP Records, contracted with a Japanese company to produce the first album manufactured on compact disc (CD). The palm-size, wafer-thin disc of polycarbonate stored music in a numerical system in millions of microscopic pits that could be read by a low-powered laser beam. It was a remarkable new technology that produced extraordinary sounds. Later that year Sony introduced the first compact disc player in the United States. GRP Records had its CD *In the Digital Mood* waiting for the Sony units.

At first it was thought that CDs would remain a novelty for the elite for some time. However, their superior sound reproduction quickly moved them into the popular culture. Because CDs were originally targeted for the elite, most of the early recordings were classical and jazz selections and CD players sold for around $1,000. By 1986, though, CD players were priced at $200 to $300 and such popular recording artists as Bruce Springsteen and Dire Straits were releasing CDs.

By 1986 the sales of GRP Records had risen to more than $10 million, up from less than $1 million in 1984. In 1986 50 million CDs were sold in the United States, up from 800,000 in 1983. The recording industry had not seen such a technological explosion in the marketplace since the development of the long-playing album (LP) some 30 years earlier. Some experts were predicting that CDs would completely replace LPs by 1990.

In 1987, however, Sony introduced a prototype of a new form of technology—digital audio *tape* recorders (DAT). These recorders had the same high-quality sound of laser-read CDs with an added feature: unlike CDs, which could only play prerecorded material, DATs could record digitally as well, thus avoiding the background noise and imprecisions inherent in the analog recordings used on LPs and audiocassettes. Recording companies feared that this superior home recording technology would lead to an increase in pirating (illegal reproduction of music).

In the U.S. Congress legislation was introduced to require DAT manufacturers to insert an anti-copying device in their recorders to protect the American music industry. The issue became moot in 1988, however, when Tandy announced that it would begin selling erasable CDs and CD recorder-players by 1990.

Multichannel, Multipoint Distribution Service (MMDS). Another new technology allows television signals to be delivered by a multipoint distribution service that transmits multiple channels via an omnidirectional high-frequency television signal over the airwaves.

Using a centrally located master transmitter in a community, the MMDS station can relay TV programming using a super-high-frequency microwave signal that can be picked up by customers using a special antenna. The system is capable of providing programming similar to cable systems—but over the airwaves, thus avoiding the expensive installation of cable lines to each home. After a slow start, MMDS was available by 1987 in Cleveland, Washington, D.C., Milwaukee, New York and San Francisco.

Direct Broadcast Satellites (DBS). Another cable industry rival on the horizon is direct broadcast satellites. Unlike current satellite systems, which relay programming primarily to cable systems and broadcast stations, DBS is designed to relay TV programming directly to inexpensive satellite dishes at viewers' homes. The system uses a new generation of high-powered satellites to send the television signals directly to an umbrella-sized receiving dish that can be mounted on a rooftop.

Hughes Communications was expected to launch a 16-channel national DBS system in 1989. Other companies attempting to get into the DBS business in the late 1980s included Dominion Video Satellite, Direct Broadcast Satellite Company, the National Christian Network, Advanced Communications Corporation, Satellite Syndicated Systems and United States Satellite Broadcasting. These systems provide from three to six channels on each satellite.

Whether or not DBS will find its way into the popular culture remains to be seen. To date the technology has raised a number of concerns. The National Association of Broadcasters fears that DBS will provide serious competition to local TV stations and cable companies. Others worry that DBS will enable foreign countries to broadcast signals directly into homes in countries where the government controls the flow of information. This concern prompted the United Nations to pass a resolution in 1982 prohibiting DBS broadcasts across international borders without consent from the receiving nation.

High-Definition Television (HDTV). Most of us have seen giant-screen television sets that are in use in some homes and taverns. Magnified many times its normal size, the TV picture appears to be fuzzy and some of the colors, especially red, lose their detail.

However, the technology is available to make large-screen televisions with quality as clear as a 35-mm motion-picture film. This new high-definition TV may someday do to television what color did to black and white by bringing clear, crisp, larger-than-life images into the home.

HDTV relies on an improvement in the process of sending television signals. At the present time, TV broadcasts consist of a series of dots, called picture elements, arranged in horizontal lines. As noted earlier, the United States uses a system consisting of 525 lines. The TV screen exhibits 30 of these 525-line still pictures every second, giving the illusion of motion. (In many foreign countries and most Western European nations, a 625-line standard is used, which gives a higher-quality picture.) In 1981 a coalition of Japanese companies unveiled an HDTV system that broadcasts a 1,125-line television picture. The system uses a wider screen, has better color reproduction, features stereo sound and provides a dramatic improvement in picture resolution and clarity. Projected onto a large screen, the HDTV system produces a picture with clarity and sharpness similar to that found in a motion-picture theater.

Because of the high cost of converting to the new system, both for TV signal producers and home consumers, the transition from regular TV to HDTV is expected to be gradual. (It took nearly 20 years for color sets to replace black-and-white sets in most American households.) Although the Japanese have already invested millions of dollars in HDTV technology, electronic engineers predicted that the new technology would not begin to enter the U.S. mass market until 1990–1992. The HDTV technology was expected to remain in the elite culture, with sets priced at around $3,000, until at least that time.

The use of this new technology is not limited to larger, better-quality television screens in the home and tavern, however. Cable companies, DBS systems, videotape rental outlets and the motion-picture industry may all eventually get involved with HDTV. The movie industry is expected to cut motion-picture production and distribution costs by transmitting HDTV signals via satellite to theaters around the country. Theaters and video-rental outlets may be the first to get into the HDTV business.

Low-Power Television (LPTV). In 1982 the FCC began issuing licenses for low-power television stations; by 1987 there were 409 LPTV stations on the air. LPTV is a new kind of TV that can transmit for short distances on frequencies that might already be allocated for a high-powered station in a nearby community without interfering with the latter's signal. Because the transmitting distance is short, audiences remain relatively small and the LPTV station must carry a large number of ads (sold at lower cost) to be financially successful.

The fact that low-power TV stations can be put on the air for a fraction of the cost of a high-power station makes the concept attractive to those who want further specialization of television programming to serve minority or cultural interests. The growth of these stations have been slower than expected, however.

IMPLICATIONS FOR THE FUTURE

Only time will tell how fast these new technologies will move into the American popular culture. The potential for our culture to be radically transformed in the near future is limitless.

Two-Way Transacting. If, for example, two-way interactive videotext finds a niche, it may become common practice for us to pay bills, order groceries and concert tickets, do our banking, read the latest news, book airline flights, check weather conditions and so on from our home computers or television sets.

Electronic Print Media. Newspapers and magazines may someday be delivered into the home electronically. The technology is already available and waiting for the cost of manual delivery to become too prohibitive to be continued. When that happens, electronic transmission will take over. This technology will allow a person to produce a hard copy (printout) of any particular story he or she might want to save.

Communication-Work Centers. Complete home communication centers where fiber-optic cables bring in a wide variety of print, radio, television, videotext and other communication services may soon become commonplace. A report commissioned by the National Science Foundation in 1983 speculated that home information systems will have as profound an impact on our culture as the automobile and commercial television had earlier in this century. This will be accomplished by converting our homes into workplaces where people will earn a living working at home computer terminals.

Cultural Transformation. If the home communication-work centers develop as predicted, a spinoff may have a profound impact on our freeway and mass-transit systems, our leisure activities (who will want to watch television at home after a day of staring at a home video display terminal?), our schools, libraries, shopping malls, office buildings, churches and so on.

Alvin Toffler predicts that our current practice of coming home and collapsing in front of the TV set for the evening will be reversed when the home becomes the workplace. He envisions a new trend in which couples who spend the day working together at home will want to go out in the evening. He sees a proliferation of neighborhood restaurants, theaters, pubs and clubs and a revitalization of church and voluntary group activity—all of it involving face-to-face communication.[5]

Megatrends author John Naisbitt describes this as the "high-tech, high-touch" syndrome. As people deal more and more with machines and technology in the workplace, they will want a more personal touch off the job, he says. The rise in computers has already caused the rise in human interaction groups and participatory activities like jogging, tennis, racquetball and Little League, he feels.[6]

One thing seems certain. Our rapidly changing mass-communication technology will have a profound impact on our culture. Although our civilization has changed more during the past one-hundred years than it did in several thousand years before the Industrial Revolution, futurists predict that it will change even more dramatically in the next decade.

SUMMARY

American culture is undergoing a technological revolution that is taking us from the industrial age to an information-based society. The rapid advance of electronic technology since the invention of the transistor in 1947 and the development of the microchip is transforming our society right before our eyes.

The acceptance of technological advances in the field of mass communication has been slower than their development. As was the case in the nineteenth century, the new technology must find a proper niche before it can enter the popular culture.

Among the major developments in mass-media technology in the 1980s were cable television, satellite communication, computers, home video equipment, fiber optics and digital sound recording, as well as experimentation with videotext, teletext, multichannel multipoint distribution services, direct broadcast satellites, high-definition television and low-power television.

Cable television, which originally brought standard TV programming to remote areas, changed in the 1970s to provide expanded and specialized programming for urban consumers.

Communication satellites made worldwide telecommunications possible by providing relay stations in outer space. Satellite transmission has affected the mass media of television, radio and newspapers, and has enabled corporations to conduct their business via teleconferencing and videoconferencing.

Computers have affected every mass-communications medium as well as the way we conduct our business and personal affairs. In the newspaper industry, computers were first used for typesetting. Today they are used to write, edit and typeset stories and to design pages. They are also used to keep books and records and to program machines so that inserts can be added to papers destined for certain geographical areas.

Radio stations use computers to replace disc jockeys, engineers and announcers. Completely computerized stations are commonplace in today's society.

Computers have also led to the development of videotext and teletext technology, which merge print information with television. Although these technologies have not yet become established in the American culture, they have been in use in Europe since the 1970s.

Videotape recorders have transformed the way people watch television and movies and the types of programming they view. Video-rental outlets have sprung up everywhere in the United States. The rapid acceptance of VCRs has temporarily slowed the efforts to market video disc players in our culture, but that seems to be only temporary.

The development of home communication centers that will be used as workplaces as well as recreation and information centers seems imminent. This may dramatically transform our popular culture and life styles.

NOTES

1. John Wicklein, *Electronic Nightmare: The New Communications and Freedom* (New York: Viking, 1981), p. 30.

2. Alvin Toffler, *The Third Wave* (New York: Bantam, 1980), pp. 194–207.

3. Les Brown, "Cable TV: Wiring for Abundance," *Channels* (November/December 1982): 8.

4. James Traub, "Satellites: The Birds That Make It All Fly," *Channels* (November/December 1983): 8.

5. Toffler, p. 372.

6. John Naisbitt, *Megatrends: Ten New Directions Transforming Our Lives* (New York: Warner Books, 1982), pp. 211–229.

ADDITIONAL READING

Baldwin, Thomas F. and McVoy, D. Stevens. *Cable Communication.* Englewood Cliffs, N.J.: Prentice-Hall, 1988.

Bell, Daniel. *The Coming of Post-Industrial Society.* New York: Basic Books, 1976.

Brown, Ronald. *Telecommunications: The Booming Technology.* Garden City, N.Y.: Doubleday, 1970.

Martin, James. *Future Developments in Telecommunications,* 2nd ed. Englewood Cliffs, N.J.: Prentice-Hall, 1977.

Nilles, Jack M. *Exploring the World of the Personal Computer.* Englewood Cliffs, N.J.: Prentice-Hall, 1982.

Singleton, Loy A. *Telecommunications in the Information Age,* 2nd ed. Cambridge, Mass.: Ballinger, 1986.

Smith, Anthony. *Goodbye Gutenberg: The Newspaper Revolution of the 1980s.* Oxford: Oxford University Press, 1980.

Toffler, Alvin. *Future Shock.* New York: Random House, 1970.

Weaver, David H. *Videotex Journalism: Teletext, Viewdata and the News.* Hillsdale, N.J.: Lawrence Erlbaum, 1983.

Williams, Frederick. *The Communications Revolution.* New York: New American Library, 1983.

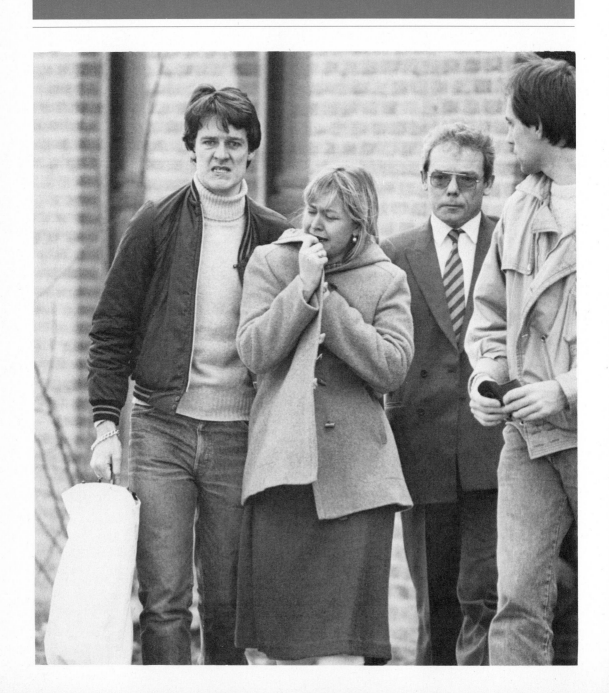

Chapter 15

Media Ethics, Regulations and Cultural Consequences

In my opinion, we are in danger
of developing a cult of the
Common Man, which means a cult
of mediocrity.
—*Herbert Hoover*

On January 22, 1987, 30 reporters and camera technicians gathered in the Pennsylvania state capital of Harrisburg for a news conference that state Treasurer R. Budd Dwyer had called to announce his resignation. He had been convicted the previous month on bribery charges.

The 47-year-old politician appeared nervous and sweaty as he delivered a rambling speech in which he referred to his 22-year political career in the past tense. He told the reporters he was innocent and criticized the prosecutor, judge, governor, justice system and the press—which he said had "feasted" on him during his legal troubles. Then Dwyer pulled a .357 Magnum from a manila envelope, stuck the gun barrel in his mouth and killed himself in front of the horrified onlookers.

What resulted was not just a sensational news story but some serious ethical questions as well. How vividly should the journalists who witnessed the event describe the scene? How much detail should be shown in photographs and television tapes? Some TV stations showed the entire scene in living color while others merely talked about it. Some print journalists reported that Dwyer had shot himself while others described in detail what they had seen. Those who did not spare the grisly details were criticized by many of their fellow journalists and members of the public for going too far. Those criticized defended their actions by stating that as reporters they had a duty to tell and show what happened.

This is just one example of ethical considerations people working in the mass media face in their daily course of actions. Our study of the mass media and their relationship

Pennsylvania State Treasurer R. Budd Dwyer holds a pistol in his hand before shooting himself in front of news cameras. *(AP/ Wide World Photos)*

with American culture would not be complete without a look at such fundamental issues as media ethics, media regulation, and the potential dangers if media content fails to keep pace with rapidly changing media technologies. This chapter will address these issues.

NEWS MEDIA ETHICS

In 1981 Hollywood released *Absense of Malice*, a movie that dealt with news media ethics. In the film a young Catholic woman commits suicide after a newspaperwoman, eager to get an exclusive story about a murder investigation, reports that she has had an abortion. The movie's message is clear: the reporter, played by Sally Field, should not have jeopardized the reputation (and life) of the innocent young woman for the sake of her story.

Absence of Malice was fiction, but the issues it raised were true to life. In 1976, for example, the editors of a Dallas daily newspaper disregarded the threats of a man who said he would commit suicide if the paper printed a story accusing him of being a Soviet spy. The man killed himself the day the story appeared.[1]

Another example of questionable media ethics received a great deal of public attention in 1983. A television news crew in Anniston, Alabama, went to a park and filmed a man setting himself on fire to protest unemployment. The man had telephoned the TV station to tell of his intentions. Although the station did call the police, the news crew made no other effort to stop the man from igniting himself and went to his aid only after he was totally engulfed in flames. Chances are that if the crew had not shown up, the man would not have carried out his threat.

Honesty and Integrity. Not all questions of media ethics involve life-threatening situations. In 1981 Janet Cooke, a *Washington Post* reporter, won the coveted Pulitzer Prize for "Jimmy's World," a story about an eight-year-old heroin addict. After the prize was awarded, Cooke revealed that she had fabricated parts of her story and that Jimmy had never existed. An embarrassed *Washington Post* returned the prize and fired Cooke.

In 1978 the *Chicago Sun-Times* ran a story that exposed a series of payoffs and bribes to city and state inspectors. The newspaper had purchased a bar, called "Mirage," trained several reporters as bartenders, hid photographers behind a ventilation duct and gone into business. Throughout the summer and fall the reporters recorded the activities of inspectors who were willing to accept bribes in exchange for overlooking various fire-, building- and health-code violations. The story was recommended for a Pulitzer Prize by a screening committee, but it was turned down by the foundation's board.

In refusing to consider the story for the prize, Ben Bradlee, board member and executive editor of the *Washington Post,* posed the following question: "How can newspapers fight for honesty and integrity when they themselves are less than honest in getting a story?"[2]

Ethical standards for the media have changed a great deal in recent years. For example, prior to the *Chicago Sun-Times* case, Pulitzer Prizes had been awarded to reporters who had misrepresented their true occupations. The question is whether the good that comes from exposing wrongdoing outweighs questionable or deceptive behavior by the news media. Journalists line up on both sides of this issue.

Accepting Gifts. Another aspect of media ethics that has undergone rethinking in recent years is the acceptance of gifts or "freebies." For many years one of the rewards of being a journalist was the many perquisites *(perks)* that came in the line of duty. Reporters often received free travel, theater passes and athletic event passes in return for stories. Reporters were often treated to lavish parties with free drinks and expensive hors d'oeuvres at the beginning of many annual news and promotional events. Of course, the reporters were expected to write about the activities to which they were invited. Journalists also routinely received free books, record albums and tapes to review.

Around holidays, like Christmas, many newsrooms resembled wedding receptions, piled high with gifts from news sources. A bottle of expensive liquor or a turkey from the mayor to the city desk was commonplace at Christmas.

As discussed in Chapter 8, in 1959 the payola scandal rocked the radio and recording industries, when it was revealed that many disc jockeys had been receiving cash and/or gifts in exchange for promoting records on the air. Journalists who covered the scandal started wondering about their own attitudes toward gifts. How were they supposed to retain their credibility if they were accepting free travel, tickets and gifts from their news sources? Could a reader be expected to believe a rave review about a play, knowing that the critic had been treated to free tickets and a lavish opening-night party by the play's producers?

The Society of Professional Journalists revised its code of ethics to prohibit journalists from accepting gifts. A 1983 survey by the society found that 75 percent of the newspapers and broadcast stations responding to a questionnaire had policies regarding gifts. The policies varied greatly: some news institutions prohibited the acceptance of any gifts, while others set a monetary limit on them. The *Beaver Falls News-Tribune* in Pennsylvania, for example, allowed employees to keep a bottle of liquor but required that a case would have to be returned.

Today some newspapers pay for everything their reporters attend and even the White House now bills journalists for the price of a tourist-class airplane ticket and for meals when reporters travel on *Air Force One* with the president.

Conflicts of Interest. For years journalists have been reporting on the conflicts of interest of other people, particularly politicians. However, journalists are subject to similar conflicts themselves. Can a reporter who is active in the Democratic party, for example, cover political campaigns objectively? Can religion editors objectively report on developments in their own churches? Can a financial reporter write without bias about a company in which he or she owns stock? Or can a news agency—such as a newspaper chain or television network—that has corporate holdings in other business endeavors objectively report about one of its subsidiaries? In 1987 a Kansas congressman called for a congressional order to require General Electric, the nation's second-largest defense contractor, to sell off its NBC network. He asked how NBC could objectively report on such matters as the Strategic Defense Initiative without appearing to have a conflict of interest.[3]

Withholding Information. Another aspect of ethics that plagues journalists is when to withhold information. Not everything that happens in our culture is reported—nor should it be. Deciding what facts should be included in or omitted from a story often is not easy. Should the fact that a person committed suicide or died of AIDS be included in an obituary? Should a reporter write about his discovery that a prominent civic leader is having an affair? If a high-ranking government official is killed in an automobile accident and a number of pornographic magazines are found in the car, should that be reported?

A common practice among journalists is not to reveal the names of rape victims. Sometimes this practice runs into trouble—say, when the rape victim is prominent or the assault occurred during a highly newsworthy crime spree.

Invasion of Privacy. Still another problem for media personnel is the question of invasion of privacy. Often the press intrudes into people's private lives while pursuing a story. Television news crews have received the heaviest criticism in this area. Many viewers become irate when they see a TV reporter shove a microphone into the face of a grief-stricken person and ask how he or she feels about the loss of a loved one.

After the shuttle *Challenger* exploded in 1986, newspapers and television networks showed pictures of Christa McAuliffe's parents watching the explosion. When 241 U.S. servicemen were killed in Lebanon in 1983, journalists flocked to interview the victims' families. Some TV crews even filmed grieving families through the windows of their homes. However, not all journalistic behavior during that incident was inap-

A New Jersey woman is surrounded by reporters at Dulles International Airport, just after she and 50 other passengers and crew members were released from a hijacked airliner. *(UPI/Bettmann Newsphotos)*

propriate. Most families interviewed had agreed to talk to the press, and some indicated that being interviewed helped them deal with their grief. But the question *still* remains: when is intrusion into a person's privacy appropriate and when isn't it? Although the law has specific guidelines as to what constitutes an invasion of privacy and provides victims of such invasion with legal recourse, journalists often must weigh ethical considerations as well.

Double Standards? Although journalists today are more concerned about their ethical behavior than at any time in American history, they are still often criticized for adhering to a double standard. Former Mobil Oil vice-president Herb Schmertz, in his critique of the media, *Good-bye to the Low Profile*, charged that the press is the only institution in the United States that avoids public scrutiny:

> *Whenever those in the news media have been challenged, they have grown righteously indignant. Basking in the glow of Watergate, members of the press have refused to acknowledge that they are ever on the wrong track. Never mind that reputations have been tarnished by untrue stories. Never mind that bad laws have been passed because of zealous crusading that hasn't always portrayed the whole picture. The rush into print or onto the air with ever more sensational scandals and conspiracies was, for a time, all-consuming. In the short run, it sold newspapers and it sold advertising. But in the long run, the public will ultimately be tired of it.*[4]

In 1984, while editorializing on media ethics, *USA Today* asked the following question:

> *Journalism is a high calling. The First Amendment to the Constitution makes the news media free to serve democracy, inform the public, promote debate*

and scrutinize and criticize the conduct of public officials. Some have described these rights and responsibilities of the news media as a "watchdog" role. But who watches the watchdog?[5]

Social Responsibility. As discussed in Chapter 3, to function under the social responsibility theory, the press must report on all aspects of society and it must do so honestly, openly and objectively. It also must allow divergent viewpoints to appear on its editorial pages. In other words, it must serve the entire community.

The press also must be socially responsible for selfish reasons. If it is to remain an important information source in American culture, the press must be a credible source of information. To be credible, it must be socially responsible, and social responsibility includes adherence to strict ethical standards and dedication to disclosing the truth about all institutions, including one's own.

MEDIA ETHICS AND ECONOMICS

Other ethical considerations arise from the fact that the American mass media are businesses designed to make a profit.

Advertiser Influence. One fairly frequent problem occurs when advertisers—who pay the bills and produce the profits for the media—want to control their content. In the South during the civil rights movement of the 1960s, for example, some newspapers sympathetic to the civil rights cause were forced to change their position by economic boycotts instigated by anti–civil rights readers and advertisers.

Another case occurred in Texas in the 1960s, when a newspaper publisher ran several stories about the illegal activities of one of the community's leading citizens. The stories revealed how this individual—a friend and confidant of Lyndon Johnson—had attempted to defraud the government out of millions of dollars in grain subsidies. Community leaders reacted to these stories by starting another newspaper in the town and persuading all the local businesses to boycott the paper that ran the exposé. Even though the stories led to a jail term for the community leader, the crusading publisher was forced out of business.

PR for Advertisers. Not all advertiser influence on media content is as malign as these examples. In small towns, for example, many newspapers run stories that are not really newsworthy but instead are publicity pieces for major advertisers. This type of story is called an *advertorial.* Tom Goldstein, in his book *The News at Any Cost: How Journalists Compromise Their Ethics to Shape the News,* cited several examples of advertorials.

In a 1983 issue of the Reporter, *a weekly in Walton, New York, in a news column adjacent to an advertisement for the Imperial Restaurant, there was an article on the renovations that had been completed at that building. There was a picture of the new entry way with this caption: "From a newly paved parking lot one now may enter Walton's Imperial Restaurant under a new canopy to a new entrance. Foyer includes a large hanging area for coats." A weekly in a neighboring town, the Hancock Herald, ran a picture of the Delaware Land Office in the spring of 1984 with the caption explaining that the real estate firm had a new "outlook" on Hancock as a result of "thermo-pane windows installed on the first floor in the front to replace the old windows that had become leaky." The office is run by a frequent advertiser.*[6]

Such advertiser-controlled hype is not limited to small-town journalism, however. Take a look at the real-estate section of your nearest metropolitan newspaper. Most likely you will find the ads surrounded with *news* stories that report in glowing terms how *wonderful* some of the real-estate developments in the area are and how *wonderfully* they are selling. These stories appear even when the real-estate market is depressed. Such articles often are written not by journalists but by publicists for the developers or by advertising personnel at the newspaper.

Even the *Los Angeles Times*, which is regarded as one of the nation's best newspapers, runs weekly regional real-estate hype sections for such areas as San Diego and the Coachella Valley's communities (both more than a hundred miles away). Although labeled special advertising supplements, these sections look like any other section of the newspaper, and many laymen believe the "news" stories in these supplements (which are actually verbatim press releases) are as legitimate as any others.

Although profitable, such practices raise ethical questions and tend to cloud a newspaper's credibility. Is the reader getting a true picture of real-estate developments in the area? Has media hype influenced people to make bad real-estate investments in second-home markets? Can a reader trust his or her newspaper if certain sections peddle a developer's rosy view of reality as fact?

Television Content. The influence of advertisers on TV content, particularly children's programs, raises serious ethical concerns as well. Is it ethical for toy manufacturers to produce shows that are essentially 30-minute-long commercials for their toy or doll lines? Children, who have a difficult enough time distinguishing between commercials and programs, are now being sold throughout the program by these product-oriented theme shows (see Chapter 9). Is this ethical television programming, or is the industry exploiting its most impressionable audience?

Direct-Response Sales. Another concern emerged when cable systems and satellites started carrying home shopping channels, which consist entirely of direct-response advertising ("Call now for this amazing offer, 1-800-xxx-xxxx"). The hard sell of these programs encourage impulse buying—on credit—and consumers can incur unreasonable and unimaginable debts if they are not careful. What will happen when the TV customer no longer has to get up and go to the telephone to place an order, but simply has to press a button on a hand-held response terminal hooked up to a two-way television?

Chain Ownership. The growing number of newspapers owned by large chains also poses some ethical questions. Do chain-owned media owe their allegiance to the communities they serve, or are they responsible solely to their parent corporation headquartered in another area? In 1977 Panax Corporation told its eight daily and 40 weekly newspapers to run two stories critical of President Jimmy Carter on their front pages. When two editors refused, offering instead to run them as opinions on the editorial page, they were fired for insubordination. Despite community protests, the editors were not reinstated. Panax even refused to run letters to the editor protesting the firings.

When media baron Rupert Murdoch purchased a number of newspapers in the United States, including the *New York Post,* to boost circulation he turned some of them into sensationalizing publications, which demonstrates that he was more interested in making a profit than providing quality journalism.

MEDIA ETHICS AND ENTERTAINMENT

Entertainment in the mass media also generates some serious ethical issues. Some of the more passionately discussed issues of the 1980s included the content of docudramas, which sometimes distort historical events, bizarre distortions of cultural reality and media portrayals of sex and violence.

Cone Effect. One way to understand better how the media influence our perceptions and often distort our view of reality is to examine how we as individuals interact with the media. One of the best diagrams of this process is Edward Jay Whetmore's *cone effect* (see Figure 15.1).[7]

According to Whetmore, all entertainment programming exaggerates and magnifies real life to make it more entertaining and interesting. What results from this process he calls *constructed mediated reality (CMR)*. To be worthy of our attention, CMR is made sexier, funnier, more intense, more violent and more colorful than real life. After all, who would want to read a novel or watch a TV show that was only as interesting as everyday life?

Next the constructed mediated reality is transmitted through a mass medium, such as a book or television set, to an audience. CMR consumers then interpret the messages at a perceptual level. Whetmore calls this *perceived mediated reality (PMR)*. We each interpret the mediated reality differently. A black ghetto child, for example, would interpret an episode of *Family Ties* or *Webster* differently than a middle-class white adult.

After people perceive this mediated reality in their own way, based on their own frames of reference (see Chapter 1), they eventually incorporate it into their own lives. This can lead to distortions if a person perceives media reality—for example, permissive sexuality on soap operas—to be the norm in modern society and changes his or her own behavior accordingly.

With the cone effect in mind, let's look at some of the forms of mass-media entertainment that have provoked the most criticism in recent years.

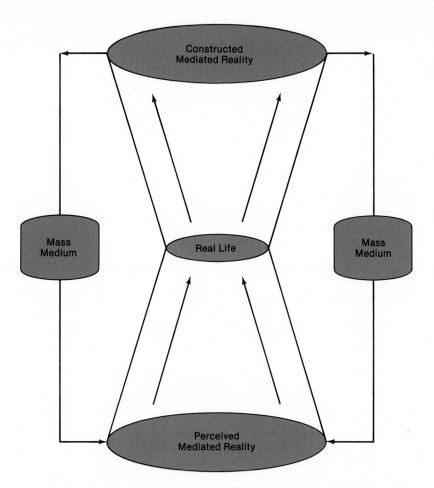

Figure 15.1. The cone effect. *From* Mediamerica, *Third Edition, by Edward Jay Whetmore.* © 1985, 1982 by Wadsworth, Inc. Used by permission of the publisher.

Docudramas. The docudrama, which dramatizes an actual event, sparked considerable controversy in the 1980s. It didn't take long before critics were asking where the facts left off and fiction began.

Among the first critics were historians, who complained about many of the historical docudramas, such as *Liberty* (discussed in Chapter 9). They worried that this distortion of history would deprive the younger generation—which gets most of its information from television—from learning from the mistakes of history.

In addition, the accuracy of several docudramas of the early 1980s was seriously challenged by those who had participated in the real events, such as the investigators and government officials involved in the arrest and conviction of Wayne Williams for a series of murders of black children in Atlanta, Georgia.

The TV docudrama "The Billionaire Boys Club" was aired just months after the club's leader, Joe Hunt, was found guilty of murder. Some charge that these docudramas jeopardize the right to fair trials and appeals. *(Courtesy of NBC)*

In 1987 two television networks aired different docudramas of the same sensational case—making people wonder which was closer to the truth. In January CBS broadcast *At Mother's Request,* a mini-series about a woman who talked her son into killing her wealthy father because he wouldn't give her money. Later that spring, NBC televised its version, *Nutcracker: Money, Madness, Murder,* also as a well-promoted mini-series.

A few months after Billionaire Boys Club leader Joe Hunt was convicted of murder—and only a few days after a judge declared a mistrial in another club associate's murder trial—NBC went on the air in late 1987 with a "fact-based" account of how the charismatic Hunt lured other wealthy young men into a get-rich-quick organization that ended up with the murder of one of their backers. Trials and appeals were still pending.

The ethical problem with docudramas stems from television's dual role as both an information and an entertainment medium. To get high ratings and audience shares (the percentage of TV sets in use that are tuned to a particular program), television has too often been willing to sacrifice information to provide a more entertaining program.

Distortions of Cultural Reality. There is also concern that the media are giving us distorted perceptions of the morals and activities of our own culture. Such charges have been leveled since the novel entered the popular culture in the early days of mass communication. It has progressively intensified, however, as the media's influence has become more pervasive.

Violence in comic books has concerned parents since comics became popular in the 1930s. The focus of this concern shifted to cartoons in the 1950s, when television became the dominant force in our popular culture. *(Barbara Rios/Photo Researchers)*

Comic books came under criticism as early as the 1930s. As the youth culture enthusiastically embraced this new medium, parent groups started calling for a reduction of violence in comic books. Some people predicted that, if action weren't taken, the nation's youth would grow up with a distorted view of reality and a permissive attitude toward violence. The criticism was not totally unfounded. Many youngsters were injured by blows to the head from cap guns and other childhood accidents caused when they reenacted comic-book adventures. The comic-book industry was finally forced to adopt a code of ethics in 1954.

Concern about comic books all but vanished in the 1950s when parents and other advocacy groups turned their attention to the new, more pervasive, medium of television. Children's television entertainment started out with such innocent shows as *Kukla, Fran and Olllie, Howdy Doody, The Mickey Mouse Club,* and *Time for Beany.* But then television started running old movie cartoons on Saturday mornings exclusively for children. Shows that featured the Roadrunner and the Coyote, Popeye, Bugs Bunny and numerous others were now seen for the first time as violence-ridden. People started questioning whether a five-year-old's perception of reality would be distorted when he or she saw the Coyote walk away unharmed after being squashed by boulders and falling off a cliff.

During the 1980s violence-oriented Saturday children's shows continued with such programs as *He-Man and the Masters of the Universe, G.I. Joe: A Real American Hero, Transformers, She-Ra: Princess of Power, M.A.S.K. (Medical Armored Strike Command), Thunder Cats, Voltron* and *Rambo.*

Concern over violence spread to other forms of TV entertainment as well. Westerns, police and detective shows all became targets for critics. The networks, anxious over this new wave of accusations, started toning down violent programs and canceling violence-oriented shows.

Another source of alarm was the distorted picture of American culture painted by both television entertainment and TV news. When sociologists started investigating the causes of riots in American ghettos in the mid-1960s, they started getting answers that pointed a finger at television. Some ghetto residents indicated that they were rebelling against the Establishment because they felt cheated by the system. Their frustrations were traced to hours of watching such television shows as *Father Knows Best, Leave It to Beaver* and *The Adventures of Ozzie and Harriet*, which all showed happy white middle-class families living in comfortable homes with modern furniture, refrigerators and spacious fenced yards.

Soap operas, a mainstay of daytime television from the beginning, have also been the targets of criticism. Do soap operas provide an innocent escape into the troubled lives of others, or do they, as some have charged, distort our view of reality? Do they reflect changes in our culture, or do they cause them? Is the level of permissive sex and adultery in modern soap operas in line with the level that exists in society, or is it an exaggeration? If there are distortions, how do they affect average people when they filter the PMR into real life? Is there a relationship between the tremendous increase in herpes, AIDS, and teenage pregnancies and the escalation of casual sex on television?

Some media critics also worry that the exportation of shows like *Dallas* and *Dynasty* give people in foreign lands a distorted view of Americans. How many foreigners, for example, believe that all Americans are rich, beautiful and successful?

Media Sex and Sexual Violence. The increased depiction of casual sex has not been limited to television. Other media have been reflecting this preoccupation and exploiting themes of sexual violence as well.

Erotic magazines have been portraying more violent sexual practices such as rape, bondage and sadism in recent years. According to a five-year longitudinal study of *Playboy* and *Penthouse* published in 1980, there had been a significant increase in such depictions in these publications.[8] And these publications are tame in comparison to others found in adult bookstores.

According to the 1970 report of the U.S. Commission on Obscenity and Pornography, such a trend should have no harmful effects on our culture. However, the 1986 report of the commission established by Attorney General Edwin Meese concluded that such a trend may cause violence toward women. Although the Meese commission's findings provoked controversy, lawsuits and a minority report from two women commissioners (see Chapter 4), some research studies have indicated that depiction of sexual violence in the media may stimulate violent behavior among some observers.

Studies by Donnerstein and Hallam in 1978[9] and K. A. Baron in 1979[10] indicated that pornography can stimulate violent behavioral tendencies. Other research studies have shown that the highest levels of sexual arousal occur in response to sexually violent pornography[11] and that a substantial number of male students observed in studies on pornography found the idea of rape attractive.[12] However, since all of these studies were conducted on male college student volunteers, care must be taken not to apply the results to sex offenders or any other group without further research.

Still, some researchers are suggesting that sexual violence shown in the media helps to cause it in real life. Research led J. H. Court to conclude that the increase in media sexual violence had caused an increase in sexual attacks on women in the Western world.[13]

Even social scientists who do not support the Meese commission's findings have expressed concern about violent sex in the media. They are worried because the media seldom show pleasant, enjoyable lovemaking in a romantic context. Instead, they note, most of the sex in the media involves some sort of violence or unpleasantness, and media programming often suggests that participants should be punished in some way for their sexual activity. Will this type of depiction eventually change cultural attitudes toward the relationship between sex and love?

Musical lyrics that suggest violence toward women have also become more prevalent in recorded music, some observers charge, particularly since the advent of music videos, which now dominate some TV channels. Some media critics have suggested that the current depiction of sexual violence in the media—particularly in music videos—may erode the progress women have made in their quest to avoid being stereotyped as sex objects.

Coping with the problem of sex and sexual violence in the media is complex. Allowing pressure groups to force governmental censorship might open the door to widespread censorship of any unpopular idea. The answer seems to lie in responses to the following questions: Is there any real harm in the content of media entertainment? And if there is, should the producers of constructed mediated reality exercise more social responsibility in creating this entertainment?

Social responsibility seems to be the key ingredient for all mass-media operations. If our culture is to have high standards, those who shape that culture through the mass media must be extremely careful to adhere to the highest ethical practices.

REGULATING THE MASS MEDIA

One suggestion by those who are concerned about media ethics and practices is that the government play a more active role in keeping the mass media socially responsible. This suggestion, however, alarms those who believe strongly that the press must be free from governmental restraint.

The First Amendment guarantees of protection for free speech and a free press make mass media regulation in the United States different from media regulation in most other countries. Nevertheless, the American mass media are regulated in various ways by government agencies and the courts.

Although the most stringent regulations are imposed by the government on broadcasting media, the print media are subject to some regulation.

Government Regulation of Print Media. Efforts by the government to restrain the print media from publishing objectionable material have been around almost as long as the First Amendment.

The Alien and Sedition Acts represented the first effort by the government to impose restrictions on the press in our new republic. After a decade of partisan press attacks on the Federalists who were in power, these laws were passed in 1798—just seven years after the First Amendment became law—to suppress some critics. Among other things, these acts outlawed false, scandalous and malicious publications against the U.S. government, the president of the United States and Congress. Fifteen people were prosecuted under this law, some for making offhand humorous remarks about President John Adams. When Thomas Jefferson was elected president in 1800, he pardoned everyone convicted under this law, and the acts were allowed to expire.

The Espionage Act of 1917 and the Sedition Act of 1918 enacted similar restrictions in the twentieth century. These laws made it illegal for anyone to openly oppose the nation's involvement in World War I. Some 2,000 people were prosecuted, and major restrictions were placed on ethnic newspapers, particularly German-language newspapers.

In 1971 several newspapers began printing *The Pentagon Papers* in serial form. Based on documents compiled by the Rand Corporation, a California-based think tank, the *Papers* were basically a critical history of the Vietnam war. The Nixon administration obtained a prior restraint order, barring the *New York Times*, *Washington Post* and *Boston Globe* from continuing to print the series until the courts could rule on whether the material would endanger national security.

The case quickly went to the U.S. Supreme Court, which ruled that the government had not proven that anything in the papers would harm the national security. The newspapers won the case and resumed printing the documents. Joining the newspapers was the book-publishing industry, which released instant books carrying the Pentagon Papers report immediately after the Court's decision. Although many people supported the right of the media to print these documents, few bothered to read the newspaper series or books after the court-authorized publication.

The Progressive magazine was restrained by a court in 1979 from printing an article entitled "The H-Bomb Secret: How We Got It and Why We Are Telling It" following action filed by the Carter administration. The article, which had been compiled from nonclassified public documents, accurately told readers how to make a hydrogen bomb. Before the case reached the U.S. Supreme Court, an almost identical article appeared in the *Madison Press Connection*. The government eventually dropped its case against *The Progressive*, which then printed the story. A U.S. Supreme Court showdown between the government and the media as to the *Progressive's* right to publish the article versus the government's right of prior restraint was avoided.

Government Regulation of Broadcasting. In the 1920s, as the new medium of radio spread across the country, some stations tried to get on the air and jammed each other's frequencies with overlapping signals. At that time there were few regulations of radio broadcasting. Previous legislation had dealt only with ship-to-shore types of radio communication. In fact, the only laws on the books required the Secretary of Commerce to grant radio license requests; he did not have the authority to reject any such requests or to assign power and frequencies for radio operations.

Chaos on the airwaves resulted. Many broadcasters, as well as the Secretary of Commerce at the time, Herbert Hoover, became concerned. As a result, Hoover held four radio conferences during the 1920s to allow all interested parties to discuss the problem and suggest possible solutions. These conferences involved educators, legislators, labor officials, businessmen and religious leaders. Each time proposals were made and presented to Congress, but no action was taken—until President Calvin Coolidge finally urged Congress to deal with the problem.

The Radio Act of 1927 established the Federal Radio Commission, a five-member board that was instructed to establish a system for licensing new radio stations and assigning frequencies and power to stations already established. Congress wanted the FRC to complete the project in one year and then disband; future enforcement of broadcast regulations and further licensing action was reserved for the Secretary of Commerce.

But the FRC was still operating seven years later. At that time President Franklin D. Roosevelt asked Congress to update the act by bringing telephone and telegraph operations under the same communications blanket. The result was the Communications Act of 1934, which, in addition to including most of the regulatory legislation of the 1927 act, replaced the "temporary" FRC with a seven-member Federal Communications Commission. This act now covers television as well.

The FCC made it clear from the very beginning that broadcasters would have to operate under the congressional mandate and broadcast in the "public interest, convenience and necessity" if they expected to keep their licenses. The FRC, FCC and Congress have acted on the premise that the airwaves belong to the public, not to private broadcasters. The basis for decisions concerning broadcasters would thus be how responsibly they served the public.

When the commission's right to refuse to renew licenses of stations involved in questionable broadcast practices was first tested, the courts ruled that while the government cannot tell a station in advance not to broadcast something (that would be prior restraint), it can review past performance to determine if a station had been operating in the public interest. If it had not, the government could refuse license renewal.

Although clauses in both the 1927 Radio Act and the 1934 Communication Act stated clearly that "Nothing in this Act shall be understood or construed to give the licensing authority the power of censorship," the U.S. Criminal Code *does* prohibit the broadcasting of anything obscene, indecent or profane. In addition, the FCC established rules regarding fraud and lottery information.

For many years the FCC has required broadcasters to air certain types of program content, noting that news, public affairs, educational, informational and agricultural programs are in the public interest.

Congress included Section 315 in both the 1927 and 1934 legislation to protect candidates for political office. It requires broadcasters to give bona fide political candidates *equal time* and *equal opportunity* on their stations. This requirement—which does not apply to any print medium—means that a station must grant all candidates for a political office the same amount of time if one candidate receives time. This applies not only to free time given to a candidate (in which case all of his or her opponents would receive the same amount of free time on that station) but also to political commercials. If one candidate purchases a certain amount of time for commercials, the station must give all his or her opponents an equal opportunity to purchase advertising time in the same time periods at the same cost.

This equal-opportunity section has been modified to exempt certain types of programs, including newscasts and bona fide news interview programs, such as *Meet the*

Press, Face the Nation and *Nightline*. Candidate debates were also excluded as long as they were sponsored by an outside agency, such as the League of Women Voters, and were covered by radio and television stations as news events. This kept the controls of the debates out of the hands of the candidates and their supporters. However, in 1983 the FCC abolished the sponsorship requirement; broadcasters can now set up and sponsor the debates themselves.

The *Fairness Doctrine* was another important requirement of the FCC up until its abolition in 1987. Not written into the Communications Act, it evolved from commission rulings over the years. The doctrine applied to controversial issues, not politicians.

In the early 1940s the FCC decided that it was not in the public interest for radio stations to air editorials. However, the commission reversed itself in 1949 and encouraged broadcasters to take stands on controversial issues—provided that reasonable time was given to opposing viewpoints. Over the years, this fairness doctrine ruling has required broadcasters to be aware of important community and national issues and to devote broadcasting time to airing all sides of those issues.

The fairness doctrine was applied to advertising content in 1967, when the FCC ruled that because cigarette smoking was a controversial public issue, broadcasters carrying commercials for cigarette companies had to give *free* time to antismoking groups (such as the American Cancer Society and the American Lung Association). This ruling eventually led to congressional legislation banning all cigarette commercials from radio and television as of 1971 (see Chapter 11).

In 1969, in the *Red Lion* decision (named after a personal attack case involving the Red Lion Broadcasting Company in Pennsylvania), the U.S. Supreme Court reaffirmed the fairness doctrine by declaring that the rights of the public, not the broadcaster, are paramount. In that decision the Court ruled that Congress and the FCC were not violating the First Amendment when they required broadcasters to devote air time to replies to personal attacks and editorials.

However, a Federal Court of Appeals challenged this decision in the 1980s when it ordered the FCC to reconsider its position on the fairness doctrine—implying that it might not be constitutional. The case resulted from a suit filed by a Syracuse broadcasting company against an FCC ruling that it had violated the fairness doctrine by not broadcasting anti–nuclear power plant ads after running advertisements in the plant's favor. The broadcaster argued that the rule violated its First Amendment rights.

The FCC did rethink its position, and in 1987 it abandoned the fairness doctrine, saying that it wished to "extend to the electronic media the same First Amendment guarantees that the print media have enjoyed since our country's inception."[14] Anticipating this ruling from a deregulation-oriented FCC, both houses of Congress had passed legislation earlier in the year to codify the fairness doctrine. However, President Reagan vetoed the bill, stating that it was "antagonistic to the freedom of expression."[15]

Deregulation of the broadcasting industry has been a goal of some members of the Congress since 1978 and was a prime objective of the FCC during the Reagan administration. By the mid-1980s radio had experienced major deregulation. Stations were no longer required to devote a certain percentage of their on-air time to news and public affairs programs, to ascertain the needs and interests of their communities through interviews and surveys, or to maintain program logs (although most stations continue to do so for billing purposes). In addition, the requirement that stations could have no more than 18 minutes of commercial time per hour was lifted.

Deregulation of television has proceeded somewhat more slowly. By the mid-1980s, however, the FCC was in the process of recommending to Congress several deregulation provisions that were similar to those enacted for radio. Already abolished was the rule that had prevented television networks from owning cable companies.

FCC censorship of broadcasting stations is technically prohibited by the broadcasting acts of 1927 and 1934. However, the U.S. Supreme Court ruled in 1977 that the commission does have the right to ban the broadcast of indecent speech during hours when children might be in the audience. The case involved a New York radio station that played a George Carlin comedy recording, *Seven Dirty Words You Won't Hear on Television.* Some listeners didn't think they should be heard on afternoon radio either.

Although during the Reagan years the FCC adopted a philosophy of deregulation and believed that the marketplace should determine what was on the airwaves, it was not adverse to attempts at censoring objectionable material. In 1987 the FCC recommended that the Justice Department bring criminal charges against a nonprofit Los Angeles radio station for broadcasting what the FCC claimed was an obscene play about homosexuality and AIDS. The FCC argued that Pacifica Foundation's KPFK-FM had broadcast a play that contained graphic depictions of sex acts between two men and described these activities in a "patently offensive manner." The Justice Department declined to press charges, however.

At the same time, the FCC issued written warnings to a University of California, Santa Barbara, radio station, KCSB-FM, for playing a sexually explicit rock-'n'-roll song, *Makin' Bacon,* and to WYSP-FM in Philadelphia, charging that its morning "shock radio" broadcaster Howard Stern, who mixed humorous sexual innuendos and double entendres with news, music, traffic and weather reports, was "patently offensive as measured by contemporary community standards of the broadcast medium." Floyd Abrams, a leading New York First Amendment attorney, described these FCC actions as "disturbingly insensitive to First Amendment principles."[16]

In addition to the FCC, more than 80 government entities issue regulations that affect broadcasters—including the Federal Aviation Administration, which regulates the placement of lights on broadcasting towers and antennas so that they can be seen by aviators. A major federal agency involved in broadcasting is the Federal Trade Commission (FTC), which monitors advertising on radio and television and in the print media. Of particular concern to the FTC by the mid-1980s was TV advertising directed at children, particularly on the popular Saturday morning shows. The Food and Drug Administration, the U.S. Postal Service and the Alcohol, Tobacco and Firearms Bureau are also involved in regulating and monitoring mass media advertising.

Court Regulation of Media. The judicial branch of government can regulate the mass media by restricting their access and activities via court decisions. For years the press and the courts have clashed over two sometimes conflicting constitutional provisions—the First Amendment right of a free press and the Sixth Amendment guarantee of a fair trial.

Controversy continues to rage around the increased media coverage of sensational trials such as that of convicted "preppy murderer" Robert Chambers, seen here with his lawyer. (UPI/Bettmann Newsphotos)

The free press versus fair trial conflict occurs most often when the press attempts to cover sensational or highly publicized trials. In 1954, for example, Dr. Sam Sheppard was tried in Ohio for the murder of his wife. The Cleveland press sensationalized the case and even pronounced Sheppard guilty before the jury did. In 1966 the Supreme Court overturned Sheppard's conviction, citing unfair publicity.

Many judges and attorneys believe that the press's efforts to cover every detail of a case before the trial is concluded prejudices the jury's ability to render an impartial verdict. As a result, many judges have barred the press and the public from pretrial hearings.

In 1986, however, the U.S. Supreme Court overturned a California Supreme Court decision that pretrial hearings could be closed. In the 7-to-2 deicision, the Court found in favor of the *Riverside Press-Enterprise*, ruling that "public access in criminal trials and the selection of jurors is essential to the proper functioning of the criminal justice system. California preliminary hearings are sufficiently like a trial to justify the same conclusion." The Court added, however, that judges may close pretrial proceedings in rare circumstances when there is no other way to protect the defendant's right to a fair trial (*Press-Enterprise* v. *Superior Court of California for Riverside County* [1986]).

Voluntary press-bar guidelines have been set up in some states in an effort to balance the needs of the press, the bar and the public. To date 26 states have adopted such guidelines, which, however, have no legal force and are effective only as long as all involved parties act reasonably and responsibly.

Courts can also restrain the press by issuing gag orders, which limit what attorneys and court officials can say to the press and what the press can print or broadcast. Journalists who have violated gag orders, believing that the restrictions infringe on their First Amendment rights and the public's right to know, have been found in contempt of court by judges.

The refusal to disclose sources or turn over personal materials such as notes, tapes, photographs and film have also led courts to jail journalists for contempt of court. Although some states have *shield laws*, which allow journalists to protect the identity of their sources, no such protection exists at the federal level. In a 5-to-4 decision in 1972 the Supreme Court ruled that journalists have no absolute privilege to protect sources of information if they are subpoenaed to testify in court proceedings.

Other court regulations of press conduct have been relaxed, however, particularly the longstanding rules banning cameras, tape recorders and microphones from the courtroom. By the mid-1980s these rules had been lifted in more than 40 states. In 24 states the ban had been recinded permanently; in the rest it had been eased on an experimental basis.

The rule against cameras was instituted in the 1930s, when loud, popping flashbulbs were used. In 1935 cameras caused a major disturbance at the trial of Bruno Hauptmann, who was accused of kidnapping and murdering the young son of national hero Charles Lindbergh, and many members of the bar felt that they upset courtroom decorum. Two years after Hauptmann was convicted, the American Bar Association called for a complete ban on courtroom photography. In 1952 and 1963 the ban was extended to include radio and television equipment.

Photography and broadcast equipment have become miniaturized and less conspicuous in recent years, and journalists have been fighting to get the ban lifted. As noted above, these efforts have finally achieved results.

Televising trials has also been slowly gaining acceptance. In recent years 39 states have experimented with televised trials. Opponents say the practice turns attorneys and judges into actors and makes a mockery of justice. However, in states where trials have been televised, the conclusion seems to be that the judges and attorneys are more alert and better prepared.

Consumer Regulation of Media. Consumers can regulate the conduct of the mass media by bringing libel and invasion of privacy suits and by instituting consumer boycotts.

Libel laws are designed to protect the public from uncalled-for attacks or careless errors by members of the press. *Libel* is the defamation of a person's character through the print or broadcast media. *Defamation* is any communication that exposes people to hatred, ridicule or contempt; lowers their esteem in the community; causes them to be shunned; or injures their careers.

Any person who believes he or she has been libeled by the mass media may bring a civil libel suit against those responsible and seek payment for damages. Since actual damages are hard to prove in a libel suit, the plaintiff can seek punitive damages, whose purpose is to punish the libeler. Some punitive damages have run into the millions of dollars, especially in cases where actual malice has been proved. Singer Wayne Newton won a $19.3 million libel suit against NBC in 1986, charging that the television network had seriously injured his reputation when it wrongly broadcast that he had Mafia connections.

Another libel case that resulted in a substantial judgment was Carol Burnett's suit against the *National Enquirer*. The *Enquirer* had run a story that Burnett was seen drunk and disorderly in a Washington, D.C., restaurant. Burnett, who had been active in an antidrug campaign, filed a suit charging that the story injured her reputation and was untrue. She won and was awarded $1.6 million in damages by a California court. The damages were lowered by an appeals court to $750,000.

However, the mass media do not have to lose libel suits to lay out large sums of money. In 1985 *Time* and CBS both spent great sums defending themselves against lawsuits. *Time* was sued by Israeli defense minister Ariel Sharon, and CBS was sued by retired U.S. General William Westmoreland.

Although Sharon was able to prove that *Time* had indeed printed false and defamatory information about him, he was unable to collect from the magazine because he couldn't prove malice. (A 1966 U.S. Supreme Court case, *New York Times* v. *Sullivan*, ruled that public officials must prove malice in order to win damages in a libel judgment.) Still, Sharon considered the fact that he had cleared his name a victory in itself.

Westmoreland, who claimed that CBS had inaccurately portrayed him in a 1982 documentary as having tried to deceive his superiors about the size of the enemy forces in Vietnam, withdrew his suit before the trial was concluded. His charges that CBS had deliberately attempted to discredit him by biased editing and interviewing went unanswered.

There are three defenses against libel:

1. *Truth* is an absolute defense against libel. If it can be proven that a report is true, the plaintiff has no case.

2. *Privileged statements*, those made at legislative, judicial and other official proceedings, are immune to libel suits. For example, if a witness makes a false (or libelous) statement at a trial, the news media can report it as long as the judge doesn't order it stricken from the record. If the witness made the same statement in the courthouse hallway, to print it would be libelous and a suit could be filed.

3. *Fair comment and criticism* is the defense that it is permissible to publish defamatory comments as long as they consist of opinion, rather than fact, about issues of public interest. This defense protects writers of editorials and critics of plays, books, movies, records, sporting events and so on, as long as they are expressing opinions about the public performances of the people involved rather than their private lives.

Invasion of privacy suits are a relatively new form of consumer mass-media regulation. Citizens can recover damages from the media for any of the following reasons: (1) intrusion into a person's physicial solitude; (2) public disclosure of embarrassing private facts; (3) placing the person before the public in a false light; and (4) commercial exploitation of a person's name or likeness.

The two basic defenses for the mass media in an invasion of privacy case are newsworthiness (or public interest) and consent. Any legitimate news story will qualify in the newsworthy category. Consent, however, usually takes proof of a contractual agreement, such as a signed model release (a standard form permitting one's likeness to be published).

Truth is not always a defense for the media in invasion of privacy cases, even though it is in libel suits. Newsworthiness, on the other hand, is not necessarily a libel defense. Something that is perfectly non-libelous may be an invasion of privacy, and vice versa.

Boycotts are another way consumers can try to regulate the mass media. Newspapers and magazines that sell stay in business. Broadcast programs that do not attract large audiences go off the air. Thus the mass media must be sensitive to the demands of consumers.

However, as the mass media grow in size and influence, individual voices get weaker. So people with similar interests have begun to join together to protest media content. Regligious, ethnic, consumer and political groups have all protested media content in recent years, as have women's groups and gay rights organizations. Other groups, such as Action for Children's Television and Parents' Music Resource Center have been instrumental in bringing about governmental scrutiny of mass-media content, but fortunately for the mass media they have not as yet mounted any large-scale boycotts.

CULTURAL CONSEQUENCES

Throughout this book we have attempted to show how our culture is shaped and changed by the mass media. Western civilization remained relatively unchanged until the invention of the printing press in the fifteenth century. After the forces of industrialization, democratization and public education emerged in the nineteenth century, the expansion of the old and development of new mass media accelerated rapidly. As a result, our popular culture was radically transformed.

During the past 20 years the development of new communication technologies has been analogous to a giant snowball gathering speed and size as it rolls down a steep mountain, and it is safe to assume that this phenomenon is only beginning to gain momentum. As these new technologies find their niche in our culture, we are going to see dramatic changes in our life styles. Whether these changes will have a positive or negative impact on our culture remains to be seen.

Form Versus Content. All technological change affects the *form*—the "hardware"—of the mass media. From our discussion of media ethics, we might conclude that the *content* of the mass media—the all-important "software"—has not kept pace.

What will happen if the same media content—more interest in who is winning the political race than in the issues of the campaign, distortions of reality through exaggerated entertainment programs and more casual sex and sexual violence—is disseminated through larger and better television sets and home information centers? Will the transfer of newspaper and magazine material from print to electronic screens mean anything if the information is not any more socially responsible than it is today? Will the availability of hundreds of TV channels transmitted into our homes by satellites or fiber optics advance our culture if the focus remains on entertainment rather than education and we continue to see the same old reruns?

If the content of our culture is to keep pace with its form, major changes need to be made in the mass media. We have learned that the media shape our culture. Perhaps it's time that we in the culture take a more active role in shaping the media.

Before we do this, however, we must keep in mind the importance of the media in our free society and make sure that we maintain the delicate system of checks and balances among the judicial, legislative and executive branches of government that our nation's founders set up. Helping to protect this system is the check and balance that was added by the Bill of Rights—a free press.

Despite the various regulations that are placed on the American mass media, the press in this country still remains one of the freest in the world. This must continue to be the case if American democracy is to survive.

Importance of a Free Press. The concept that a free press is an integral part of a free society was based on the philosophies of John Milton, Andrew Hamilton, James Madison, Thomas Jefferson and others. As Hamilton said in his closing arguments of the John Peter Zenger trial in 1735, "a free press is a cause of liberty—the liberty both of exposing and opposing arbitrary power . . . by speaking and writing the truth."[17]

Our democracy depends on a free press to keep us informed. The temptation of government leaders, the courts and consumers to regulate the media is great. Thus it is important for all of us in American culture to recognize the importance of keeping our mass media free from unreasonable restraints.

Just keeping the media free is not good enough, however. Free yet irresponsible mass media that are insensitive to the needs and desires of their culture are almost as useless as a system of mass media under strict government control.

As a society, we should not tolerate shoddy, arrogant, irresponsible or inadequate performances from any of our mass media. Likewise, society should not let business interests in the media forsake responsibility for financial gains.

Consumer Awareness Needed. It is the obligation of each of us to become aware, concerned, skeptical and demanding. We should be aware of just how well our mass media are or are not performing when it comes to social responsibility and high ethical standards. We should be concerned about inadequate performances. We should be skeptical of any movements to strengthen regulation of the mass media (whether from government, the courts or organized consumer groups). And, most important, we should constantly demand that our mass media perform with the utmost responsibility and concern for the quality of our culture.

The fact that the mass media in the United States are businesses, dependent on making a profit, is important to remember. In any business enterprise the consumer is the most important element in the sales transaction. Without the consumer there is no sale. Television shows must be watched, news articles must be read, magazines and books must be purchased and advertised products must sell if the mass media are to stay in business.

If we were more discriminating in our consumption of the mass media, we might influence the media's content. The number of people listening to radio and watching television are closely monitored. When a show's ratings slip, it is canceled. TV ratings, like newspaper and magazine circulations, determine the advertising revenues a medium generates. The mass media pay close attention to what the majority of people in the culture think. We are the ones who determine whether a place in our culture exists for them. If they fail to give us what we want and demand, we have the power to phase them out of existence.

Thus if the content of the mass media remains less than of the highest quality, the fault is partially ours. Television, for example, will continue to give us *Dynasty*-type programming if that is what people are willing to watch. Sex and violence will continue to dominate movies, videos and magazines if that is what continues to sell. Whether or not the quality of mass-media content keeps pace with technological advances depends on each of us.

SUMMARY

The news media have come under fire in recent years for endangering people's lives, using fraud and deception to gather news stories, fabricating news, accepting gifts from news sources, having conflicts of interest and using poor judgment in determining what should and should not be covered.

Although journalists today are more concerned about ethical standards than ever before, they are still severely criticized for operating under a double standard—one that holds other institutions accountable for anything less than high ethical practices while refusing to criticize or examine their own practices.

The media also have been criticized for questionable ethical standards related to their business activities. Advertisers' attempts to control media content is a problem that has plagued the media for years. Those who pay the bills and produce the profits often feel they should have a say in the media's editorial and entertainment content. Sometimes advertisers threaten to boycott the media if they don't get their way.

Not all advertiser influence is so blatant, however. In small towns the media often run advertorials, news items that are publicity pieces for advertisers. Real-estate sections of most newspapers are filled with advertiser hype disguised as news stories. Although these practices are profitable, they raise ethical concerns about the credibility of the news medium.

Some concern has also been raised about television's new home shopping channels and direct-response advertising. It is feared that excessive impulse buying by consumers could result if two-way interaction with the television set were to become commonplace.

The trend toward large chain ownership of most community newspapers also threatens community journalism. Corporate dictates without concern for local community sensitivities could change American journalism.

Many ethical questions are raised by the level of entertainment that the mass media provide. Concern has been focused on the distortions of historical facts that are presented in docudramas, the overall distortions of present-day cultural realities by television entertainment and the distorted ways in which the media portray sex and violence.

All of these ethical concerns about the mass media highlight the point that a successful medium in American popular culture must be a socially responsible one. Some who express concerns call for more regulation of the media, while others who recognize the importance of a free and independent press feel that the current regulations are adequate.

Despite the First Amendment provision that Congress shall make no laws infringing on the freedom of the press, a number of regulations on the American media do exist. These regulations are imposed by the government, the courts and consumers, who are protected from media abuse by civil laws.

Whether socially responsible mass-media content will keep pace with the media's rapidly expanding technology remains to be seen. If our culture is to advance with its technology, Americans must play an active role in demanding responsible content, while at the same time not forgetting the importance of a free and independent system of mass media in the American democracy.

NOTES

1. Clifford G. Christians, Kim B. Rotzoll and Mark Fackler, *Media Ethics* (New York: Longman, 1983), pp. 114–117.

2. Steve Robinson, "Pulitzer: Was the Mirage Deception?" *Columbia Journalism Review* (July–August 1979): 14.

3. Dennis McDougal, "Congress Takes Off the Gloves at TV Hearings," *Los Angeles Times*, April 30, 1987, Calendar section, p. 1.

4. Herb Schmertz with William Novak, *Goodbye to the Low Profile: The Art of Creative Confrontation* (Boston: Little, Brown, 1986), p. 94.

5. "Media Must Be Free to Correct Abuses," *USA Today*, April 5, 1984, p. 10a.

6. Tom Goldstein, *The News at Any Cost: How Journalists Compromise Their Ethics to Shape the News* (New York: Simon & Schuster, 1985), pp. 91–92.

7. Edward Jay Whetmore, *Mediamerica: Form, Content, and Consequences of Mass Communication*, 3rd ed. (Belmont, Calif.: Wadsworth, 1985), pp. 10–12, 170–171.

8. N. M. Malamuth and B. Skinner, "A Longitudinal Content Analysis of Sexual Violence in the Best-Selling Erotica Magazines," *Journal of Sex Research* 16 (1980): 226–237.

9. E. Donnerstein and J. Hallam, "Facilitating Effects of Erotica on Aggression Against Women," *Journal of Personality and Social Psychology* 36 (1978): 1270–1277.

10. R. A. Baron, "Heightened Sexual Arousal and Physical Aggression: An Extension to Females," *Journal of Research in Personality* 13 (1979): 91–102.

11. N. M. Malamuth, M. Heim and S. Feshbach, "Sexual Responsiveness of College Students to Rape Depictions: Inhibitory and Disinhibitory Effects," *Journal of Personality and Social Psychology* 38 (1980): 399–408.

12. N. M. Malamuth, S. Haber and S. Feshbach, "Testing Hypotheses Regarding Rape: Exposure to Sexual Violence, Sex Differences, and the 'Normality' of Rapists," *Journal of Research in Personality* 14 (1980): 121–137.

13. J. H. Court, "Pornography and Sex Crimes: A Reevaluation in the Light of Recent Trends Around the World," *International Journal of Criminality and Penology* 5 (1977): 129–157.

14. Raymond L. Fischer, "The FCC and the Fairness Doctrine," *USA Today*, magazine, May 1988, p. 42.

15. Ibid.

16. David Crook and Penny Pagano, "FCC Cracking Down on Radio 'Indecency'," *Los Angeles Times*, April 17, 1987, part VI, p. 1.

17. Quoted in Warren K. Agee, Phillip H. Ault and Edwin Emery, *Introduction to Mass Communications*, 9th ed. (New York: Harper & Row, 1988), p. 67.

ADDITIONAL READING

Anderson, Kent. *Television Fraud: The History and Implications of the Quiz Show Scandals.* Westport, Conn.: Greenwood Press, 1978.

Barron, Jerome A. *Freedom of the Press for Whom? The Right of Access to Mass Media.* Bloomington: Indiana University Press, 1973.

————, **and Dienes, C. Thomas.** *Handbook of Free Speech and Free Press.* Boston: Little, Brown, 1979.

Cline, V. H., ed. *Where Do You Draw the Line? An Exploration into Media Violence, Pornography, and Censorship.* Provo, Utah: Brigham Young University Press, 1974.

Cole, Barry, and Oettinger, Mal. *Reluctant Regulators: The FCC and the Broadcast Audience.* Reading, Mass.: Addison-Wesley, 1978.

Compaine, Benjamin M., et al. *Who Owns the Media? Concentration of Ownership in the Mass Communication Industry,* 2nd ed. White Plains, N.Y.: 1982.

Goethals, Gregor T. *The TV Ritual—Worship at the Video Altar.* Boston: Beacon Press, 1981.

Goodwin, H. Eugene. *Groping for Ethics in Journalism.* Ames: Iowa State University Press, 1983.

Halloran, J. D. *The Effects of Mass Communication.* Leicester, England: Leicester University Press, 1964.

Large, Martin. *Who's Bringing Them Up?* Gloucester, England: Alan Sutton, 1980.

Merrill, John C., and Odell, S. Jack. *Philosophy and Journalism.* New York: Longman, 1983.

Moody, Kate. *Growing Up on Television.* New York: Times Books, 1980.

Schramm, Wilbur. "What Is TV Doing to Our Children?" *Sight, Sound and Society: Motion Pictures and Television in America.* Boston: Beacon Press, 1968.

Sinclair, Upton. *The Brass Check: A Study of American Journalism.* Pasadena, Calif.: Published by the author, 1920.

Glossary

ABC American Broadcasting Company; founded after NBC was forced to sell one of its two radio networks in 1943.

Advertorial Advertising copy written in the form of a news story. Sometimes placed in "news columns" of special sections of newspapers labeled "advertising supplement."

AFP Agence France-Presse; a Paris-based French news wire service that was organized in 1945.

Agenda setting A process whereby the mass media shape our awareness of people and events.

Alien and Sedition acts Laws passed in 1798 to silence critics of the government. These laws, which lasted only two years, represented the first U.S. government effort to restrict freedom of the press.

AM radio Amplitude modulation; a form of radio transmission in which sound waves modulate the length (or amplitude) of the carrier wave.

AP The Associated Press; the oldest American news wire service, founded in 1848.

A–T–R A model of how advertising works; stands for awareness, trial, and reinforcement.

Authoritarian theory A theory of the press that asserts that the rulers of society should control what is disseminated to the public in the mass media. Authoritarian theory has an offshoot, Soviet Communist theory. See **Libertarian theory.**

Cable TV A system of sending and receiving TV signals by wire. Cable systems usually receive signals by satellite at a central facility and relay them by cable to homes for a monthly fee.

CBS Columbia Broadcasting System; founded in 1927 under the name United Independent Broadcasters/Columbia.

Chain ownership Two or more newspapers published in different communities by the same company.

Channel A term for the way we send a message. In mass communication, any one of the mass media.

Channel noise Anything that externally interferes with a message in the communication process.

Communication A process involving the sorting, selecting, and sharing of symbols in such a way as to help a receiver elicit from his or her own mind a meaning similar to that contained in the mind of the communicator.

Cult A subcultural group or movement that rejects and refuses to conform to mass-cultural activities or attitudes.

Culture Everything that occurs in a society—all the customs and practices handed down from generation to generation.

Demographic breakout A magazine production technique that enables advertisers to insert ads in only a portion of a given issue. Advertisers can target their ads to specific demographic groups, such as doctors, students, executives, or people earning above a specified income.

Desktop publishing The use of a personal computer to write, edit, typeset, design graphics, and lay out pages for a publication.

Digital sound A method of converting sound electronically into a numerical system to achieve better sound reproduction.

Direct Broadcasting Satellites (DBS) A powerful satellite system that sends signals directly to homes with small, relatively inexpensive rooftop receiving dishes.

Direct mail One of the most effective methods of disseminating information on political candidates and issues. Computerized mailings can send different messages to different audiences.

Docudrama   A form of TV dramatic presentations based on current or historical events.

DuMont   A TV network operating in the early days of television. Named after a pioneer in the development of TV receivers, Allen B. DuMont.

Electronic books   A book reproduced, often in abridged form, on audio cassette. By the 1980s, major publishing houses like Simon & Schuster, Random House, and Bantam all had audio book divisions.

Electronic cottages   A term for the homes of telecommuters, people who work at home connected to an office by a computer terminal.

EPS cycle   The three stages most mass media evolve through: the elitist stage, when a medium is restricted to the educated, aristocratic, and wealthy; the popular stage, when a medium is consumed by the masses; and the specialized stage, when a medium caters to a variety of specific groups.

Equal-time provision   A Federal Communications Commission requirement that all bona fide political candidates have equal opportunity to use the airwaves. (Also known as Section 315.)

Fairness Doctrine   A 1949 Federal Communications Commission ruling that required broadcasters to air both sides of controversial issues. In 1987 the FCC abolished the rule, calling it unconstitutional.

Federal Communications Commission (FCC)   A government agency established in 1934 to regulate wire and radio broadcasting; its authority was later expanded to include television. It took over the duties of the Federal Radio Commission.

Federal Radio Commission (FRC)   A government agency established in 1927 to regulate the airwaves and allocate frequencies for broadcasting.

Feedback   Any observable response to a message in the communication process.

Fiber optics   Tiny flexible glass strands capable of carrying 100,000 telephone or 100 broadcast signals on a wire the size of a human hair.

FM radio   Frequency modulation; a form of radio transmission in which sound waves modulate the frequency of the carrier wave.

Fotonovel   A book that is part text, part picture book, and part comic book. Usually a spinoff of a popular movie or television show.

Freebie   A gratuity; usually tickets, passes, records, or books given to journalists by people seeking favorable treatment from the press.

Gag order   Court-imposed restriction on what attorneys and/or court officials may say to the media during a legal proceeding.

Gatekeeping   The process whereby numerous people become involved in determining what news, information, or entertainment will reach a mass audience.

Glasnost   The policy of "openness" established in the 1980s by Communist Party Secretary Mikhail Gorbachev that has made news and information more readily available in the mass media of the Soviet Union.

Hard news   The factual account of significant news events. See **Soft news.**

High-Definition Television (HDTV)   An extremely clear television signal transmitted at 1,125 lines per pictures (as opposed to the current 525 lines per picture of U.S. broadcasts), allowing excellent reception on larger-than-life TV screens. May one day be used to transmit motion pictures to theaters via satellite.

How-to book   A specialized book giving advice on how to do something; how-to books cater to a wide range of interests.

Industrial Revolution   The social and economic upheavals of the eighteenth and nineteenth centuries that transformed America from an agrarian society to a mechanized, production-oriented culture.

Internal specialization A term used to describe a general-interest magazine that carries a variety of articles and allows readers to specialize by selecting articles of interest; an example is *Reader's Digest*. See **Unit specialization.**

Interpretative reporting A reporting style that developed in the 1930s to provide background for complex stories.

Instant book A book produced in only a few weeks, so it can be sold while the news event it describes is still topical.

Invasion of privacy Information published or broadcast that violates a person's right to be left alone.

Inverted pyramid A style of organizing news stories in which the essential material is placed at the beginning and subsequent paragraphs provide information in declining order of importance.

Investigative reporting News reporting that digs below the surface to uncover important information, usually political corruption or other wrongdoing.

Kinetoscope A four-foot-high box used to show motion pictures in the nineteenth century. The device, developed in Thomas Edison's laboratory, allowed one person at a time to view the pictures. It became a penny arcade attraction.

Libel Published or broadcast information that damages an individual's reputation. There are three defenses against a libel suit: truth, privileged information, and fair comment and criticism.

Libertarian theory The theory of the press that holds that the press should serve the governed (people), not the governors. Libertarian theory has an offshoot, Social Responsibility theory. See **Authoritarian theory.**

Low-power television (LPTV) A system that can transmit television signals at lower cost to a small geographic area (usually a 15–20 mile radius). Can be used to provide spe-

cial-interest programming in metropolitan areas.

Mass culture The things in our culture that are mass-produced and/or shared through the mass media. See **Popular culture.**

Mass communication A process whereby professional communicators use technological devices to share messages over some distance to influence large audiences.

Mass-market paperback Usually a romance, Western, or mystery novel that is mass-produced (a million copies or more) and mass-distributed. It is usually smaller in size than other paperbacks and printed on cheaper paper.

Metropolitan newspaper Originally called the penny press, a newspaper with a style of reporting designed for ordinary people in the popular culture.

Mini-series A multipart TV drama that runs for several consecutive nights. A popular TV genre, it is used to disrupt regular viewing habits and allow networks to promote their other programming during commercial breaks.

Motivational research (MR) Advertising research based on Freudian psychology; used to develop advertising strategies.

MTV Music Television; a cable network launched by Warner-Amex in 1981 to bring 24-hour-a-day music videos to 12- to 23-year-olds.

Muckrakers A term coined by President Theodore Roosevelt to describe reporters who specialized in exposing scandal and corruption.

Multipoint Distribution Service (MDS) A pay-TV system that broadcasts via microwave signals to small antennas. It offers an over-the-airwaves alternative to cable TV.

NBC National Broadcasting Company; founded in 1926 as a subsidiary of the Radio Corporation of America (RCA).

News ploys News events staged by public relations practitioners or political consultants to get free publicity for their clients. Sometimes called media events.

Noise See **Channel noise, psychological noise.**

Nonfiction novel Book based on a true story, but written in the style of a novel, often with invented dialogue and made-up scenes.

Novelization A book based on a successful movie; the opposite of a book made into a movie.

Op-ed page The page opposite the editorial page, where guest columns and other opinion materials usually appear.

Opinion leader A person who influences the thinking of others; usually someone who is better informed by the mass media than the average person.

PBS Public Broadcasting System; a noncommercial television system established by the Public Broadcasting Act of 1967.

Penny press Term first used in the 1830s to describe new American newspapers aimed at the popular culture and selling for 1 cent. Also known as **metropolitan newspapers.**

People meters A hand-held remote control device used by TV rating services to measure the size and demographics of a television audience.

Personalized book A book, usually for children, whose text is stored in a computer. When a purchaser supplies specified personal data, the computer prints out a book with these facts included in the plot.

Political consultants People trained in opinion polling, advertising or public relations who package political candidates and/or issues and sell them to the public.

Popular culture The culture of everyone in a society. This culture is so pervasive that we seldom notice it. (Often used interchangeably with **Mass culture.**)

Popular press The popular national tabloid newspapers in the United Kingdom.

Prime time The three viewing hours on television with the biggest audiences; 7–10 p.m.

in the Central and Mountain time zones, 8–11 p.m. in Eastern and Pacific areas.

Product brokers People who arrange for the use of their clients' products in movies and TV shows.

Protestant Reformation The religious revolt against the Catholic church in the sixteenth century that led to the establishment of Protestant churches. This was the first major social movement to use the new invention of mass communication.

Psychographics A kind of advertising research that gathers information on people's interests, needs, values and lifestyles.

Psychological noise Internal factors that can lead to misunderstanding a message: selective exposure, selective perception and selective retention.

Public relations The business of creating favorable images for clients; it includes press agentry, promotion, public affairs, publicity, opinion research and advertising.

Quality press The full-sized, elite-oriented national newspapers in the United Kingdom.

Ratings Percentage of all households having television sets that watch a particular program.

Red Channels A 1950 report on the alleged Communist infiltration of the broadcast industry. Published by a group called Counterattack, it accused 151 radio and television personalities of having Communist leanings. Most of them lost their jobs.

Regional breakouts Copies of a magazine that are circulated only in a designated geographic region. Magazine advertisers can lower their advertising costs by designating that their ads run in certain regional breakouts.

Reuters British news wire service; organized in the 1850s.

Satellite An electronic relay system that orbits 22,300 miles above the equator; it receives signals from earth, recharges them on a transponder and sends them back to earth to be received by anyone with a receiving dish.

Selective exposure A form of psychological noise that causes people to expose themselves to information that reinforces rather than opposes their general beliefs or opinions.

Selective perception A form of psychological noise that causes people to see, hear and believe only what they want to see, hear and believe.

Selective retention A form of psychological noise that causes people to remember things that reinforce their beliefs and opinions better than things that oppose them.

Semantic noise A form of message interference that occurs when the message gets through exactly as sent but is not understood because terms used are unclear in meaning.

Share The number of TV sets turned on at a given time that are tuned to a specific program.

Sitcom Situation comedy, a popular and long-enduring genre of broadcast entertainment. Although it is a major ingredient of today's TV programming, the sitcom originated on radio.

Social Responsibility theory An offshoot of the libertarian theory of the press that contends that the press must be socially responsible to keep a democratic nation well-informed.

Soft news Feature stories or background information about entertaining items of interest. It includes everything from lifestyle articles to personality profiles and Dear Abby–type columns. Sometimes called "fluff journalism," soft news accounts for most of the content in today's newspapers.

Soap opera A broadcasting genre that originated on radio and now provides popular entertainment for both daytime and prime-time television. Named after the original radio sponsors, soap companies.

Soviet Communist theory An offshoot of the authoritarian theory of the press that believes that the mass media should be state-owned and -operated in order to best serve the government.

Subliminal advertising A technique of hiding images in advertisements; these imbeds are supposed to appeal to the emotional instincts of sex, fear and death, triggering a subconscious response that causes the ad to be remembered.

Tabloid Any half-size newspaper; the term is often used to refer to sensational publications like the *National Enquirer.*

Tabloid television Sensational and titillating TV programming of the late 1980s; examples included Fox networks's "America's Most Wanted" and "A Current Affair."

TASS The official Soviet news wire service, Telegrafnoie Agentsvo Sovetskovo Soyuza.

Teleshopping channels Cable-TV channels that sell merchandise to viewers, who telephone their orders and credit card numbers to 800 numbers. Teleshopping channels feature a wide variety of products at volume discounts.

Teletext A system that provides one-way interactive viewing of printed text carried on the unused space of TV signals. A special converter on the TV set is required to receive these signals.

Televangelism Programs on broadcast and cable TV featuring preachers who use the airwaves as an electronic version of old-fashioned tent revivals.

Two-step flow theory A theory developed by Paul Lazarsfeld to describe the opinion leader concept: (1) the mass media influence certain individuals, and (2) these individuals personally influence others.

Underground press Alternative or counter-culture newspapers published in the 1960s and early 1970s to promote the ideas and cultural reflections that were being ignored by the Establishment press. An outgrowth of the youth subculture.

Unit specialization   A term used to describe a magazine that targets a specialized audience; *Surfer* and *Personal Computing* are examples. See **internal specialization.**

UPI   United Press International; a private news service that was formed in 1958 by the merger of United Press (1907) and International News Service (1909).

Urban Western   A term applied to the police, doctor, and detective action/adventure shows that supplanted the Westerns on television in the 1960s.

VALS   Values and Lifestyles; psychographic research by SRI International that categorizes Americans into nine different lifestyles. Advertisers use VALS to determine the target audiences for their products.

Vaudeville   A nineteenth-century entertainment form that developed to meet the new leisure time needs created by the Industrial Revolution. It was live theater, consisting of comedy skits and musical acts. Although no longer around, its influence can still be seen in modern-day television.

Videocassette recorder (VCR)   Video tape recorders that can record TV programs and play prerecorded movies.

Video disc players   A playback unit that uses prerecorded video discs shaped much like phonograph records.

Videotext   A two-way interactive television system; viewers respond to material shown on the screen, and conduct business and other transactions via a computer keyboard. (Sometimes spelled videotex.)

Vote video   A prerecorded videocassette used to promote political candidates and issues.

Yellow journalism   A derogatory term used to describe American journalism during the turn-of-the-century circulation war between William Randolph Hearst and Joseph Pulitzer, when sensational headlines and stunt reporting were common. The name derives from a feud between Hearst and Pulitzer over the use of the "Yellow Kid" comic strip.

Zapping   Using fast-forwarding to eliminate commercials from TV programs recorded on a VCR.

Zipping   Using a remote-control device to flip from one TV channel to another during commercials.

Index

Abrams, Floyd, 365
Absence of Malice, 350
Achee, Randy, 93
acquired immune deficiency syndrome
    (AIDS), 35, 209, 233, 352, 360, 365
acta diurna, 116
Action for Children's Television
    (ACT), 276, 369
Adams, John, 73, 121–22, 362
Adams, Samuel, 121
Addison, Joseph, 96, 119
Adventures of Huckleberry Finn, 86–87
Adventures of Ozzie and Harriet, 203,
    360
advertising
    A-T-R model of, 267
    children's, 275–76
    consumer information environment,
        267–68
    cutting edge theory of, 267
    early examples of, 254–65
    electronic, 265
    first ad agencies, 265
    government regulation of, 265
    minimal effects theory of, 266–67
    motivational research, 277–79
    propaganda devices, 268–73
    subliminal, 273–74
    television, 274–77
    VALS research and, 279–84
    zipping and zapping of, 277
Advertising Age, 274
advertorial, 254
advocacy journalism, 133–34
Advocate, 108
Agee, Warren, 126, 273
agenda setting, 16–17, 20
Agence France-Presse (AFP), 140
Agnew, Spiro, 213, 311
Agranoff, Robert, 305
Alan Weston Communications, 93
Aldrich, Henry, 157

Alger, Horatio, Jr., 75–76
Alien and Sedition Acts, 50, 122–23,
    361–62
Aliens, 163
Allen, Fred, 186
Allen, Gracie, 186, 189, 201
Allen, Woody, 145–46, 159
Allied Artists, 160
All in the Family, 203–4
All the President's Men, 80
Ameche, Don, 186
American Bandstand, 241
American Bar Association, 367
American Broadcasting Co. (ABC), 23,
    181, 197–200, 204, 206, 209, 211,
    224, 329
American Civil Liberties Union
    (ACLU), 85
American Druggist, 110
American Football League (AFL), 33
American Graphophone Co., 234
American Library Association, 86
American Marconi Company, 180
American Magazine, 97
American Minerva, 122
American Newspaper Publishers Assn.,
    135, 182
American Revolution, 121–22
American Society of Newspaper
    Editors, 54, 129
American Telephone & Telegraph
    (AT&T), 180–81, 193, 339
American Weekly Mercury, 119
America's Most Wanted, 209
Amos 'n' Andy, 186, 189, 201
Amsterdam, Jane, 129
Anka, Paul, 241
Annenberg, Walter, 100–1
Apollo XI, 214
Appleton, Dan, 74
Arbuckle, Fatty, 155
Arledge, Roone, 211

Armat, Thomas, 148
Arthur, 37
Articles of Confederation, 122
Associated Film Productions, 37
Associated Press (AP), 55, 63, 126, 129, 137–38, 140, 182
Associated Press Managing Editor's (APME) guidelines, 297
Astaire, Fred, 156
A-Team, The, 220
Atlantic, The, 61, 97
At Mother's Request, 358
Ault, Phillip H., 126, 273
Aurora, 122
authoritarian press theory, 46–48, 63
Autry, Gene, 81
Avatar (Boston), 135
Avalon, Frankie, 241
Ayer, N. W., 265

B-52, 248
Babbitt, Bruce, 315
Bache, Benjamin Franklin, 122
Backpacker, 106
Baker, James, 254
Baker, Ray Stannard, 98
Baker, Susan, 254
Bakker, Jim and Tammy, 224
Ball, Lucille, 201
ballpark, 28–29, 226
Bantam Books, 67, 83
Barbarella, 162
Barnouw, Erik, 189
Barnum, P. T., 289–90
Barrymore, John, 157
Batten, Barton, Durstine & Osborn (BBDO), 279
Baxter, Leona, 305
Bay Psalm Book, 72–73
Beach Blanket Bingo, 161
Beacon Hill, 204
Beadle, Erastus, 74
Beadle, Irwin, 74
Beastie Boys, 250
Beatles, 37, 151, 242–46, 253, 258
Beaver Falls News-Tribune (PA), 352
Bee Gees, 247

Behind the Green Door, 162
Being There, 37
Bell, Alexander Graham, 174, 193
Bell, Daniel, 327
Ben Hur, 160
Bennett, James Gordon, 125
Benny, Jack, 186, 189, 201
Bentsen, Lloyd, 316
Bergen, Edgar, 186–87, 189, 201
Berkeley Barb, 135
Berkeley, Busby, 157
Berkeley, Sir William, 47
Berle, Milton, 189, 200, 265
Berliner, Emile, 236
Bernays, Edward L., 290, 293, 299
Bernstein, Carl, 80
Bernstein, Leonard, 212
Bernstein, Lester, 312
Berry, Chuck, 241
Better Homes and Gardens, 106
Bewitched, 203
Biden, Joe, 315, 320
Billionaire Boys Club, 358
Bill of Rights, 49, 370
Birth of a Nation, 149–50, 168, 186
Blackboard Jungle, 161, 240
Black Entertainment Television (BET), 330
Blackett-Sample-Hummert, 265
blacklisting, 159, 212
black newspapers, 134–35
Black Panther, 135
Black World, 107
Blair, Linda, 220
Bluebird (record label), 237
Blumenthal, Sidney, 305
Boating, 106
Bob and Carol and Ted and Alice, 162
Bochco, Steven, 208
Bogart, Humphrey, 156, 158
Bombeck, Erma, 136
Bonanza, 201–2
Boni & Liveright, 77
Bonnie and Clyde, 162
books
    censorship of, 72, 83–89

current business trends in, 89
early forms of, 68–70
early public libraries, 70
during Middle Ages, 70–71
in Reformation, 71–72
in Renaissance, 71
stages of development of in U.S., 72–83
types of, 79–83
Boomtown Rats, 233
Boorstin, Daniel, 156
Born Innocent, 220
Boston Gazette, 119, 121
Boston Globe, 362
Boston News-Letter, 119
Bow, Clara, 156
Boyer, Paul, 77
Boy's Life, 107
Brackenridge, Hugh Henry, 73
Bradford, Andrew, 97
Bradford, Tom, 119
Bradford, William, 120
Bradlee, Ben, 351
Brady, John, 103
Brando, Marlon, 39
breakouts, demographic and regional, 103–4
Breed, Warren, 274
Breslin, Jimmy, 134
Brian, Earl W., 138
Bringing Up Baby, 157
Bristol-Myers, 287
British Broadcasting Corporation (BBC), 57–58, 198, 204, 225, 339
British Marconi Company, 178–80
British Post Office, 178, 339
Broadcasting Cablecasting Yearbook, 225
Broadcast News, 215
Brooker, William, 119
Brothers Grimm, 33, 160
Brown, Charles Brockden, 73
Brown, James, 74
Brown, Peter, 243
Brown, Sam, 312
Browne, Ray B., 6
Browning, Robert, 75

Bunker, Archie, 12–13, 203
Burnett, Carol, 367–68
Burns, George, 186, 189, 201
Burson-Marsteller, 296
Burton, Richard, 160
Bush, George, 131, 315–16
Butch Cassidy and the Sundance Kid, 162
Byoir, Carl, 291
Byte, 105

Cable News Network (CNN), 216, 330
cable television
expanded programming of, 15, 225–26, 266, 329–30
pay-TV, 330
public access to, 330
two-way, 330–31, 344
Caesar, Sid, 201
Cagney, James, 156
Cagney and Lacey, 218
Caldwell, Erskine, 77
California Public Utilities Commission, 276
California State University, Fresno, 207
California State University, Fullerton, 255
California State University, Los Angeles, 251
California, University of, at Santa Barbara, 365
Calvin, John, 72
Camel News Caravan, The, 211, 265
Campbell, John, 47, 118–19, 121
Canadian Broadcasting Corporation (CBC), 61
Canadian Press, 60
Canadian Radio-Television Commission (CRTC), 61
Cantor, Eddie, 186
Capone, Al, 156
Capote, Truman, 80, 134
Capra, Frank, 157
Carlin, George, 365
Carnal Knowledge, 162
Carney, Art, 201

Carroll, Diahann, 217
Carter, Billy, 312
Carter, Boake, 182
Carter, Jimmy, 17, 311–12, 322–23, 356
Caruso, Enrico, 236, 257
Casablanca, 146
Casey, William J., 89
Cash, Johnny, 241
Cates, Gilbert, 145
Catholic Church, 26, 46, 71–72, 155
Cave, Edward, 96
censorship, 72, 83–89, 163–68
Central Intelligence Agency (CIA), 87–89
Cerf, Bennett, 77
Challenger, 19, 214, 223, 352
Chancellor, John, 213
Chan, Charlie, 157
channel, 9
channel noise, 10–11
chapbooks, 27
Chaplin, Charlie, 151–53, 156, 168
Charlie's Angels, 218
Chayevsky, Paddy, 218
Checker, Chubby, 241
Chernobyl disaster, 56
Chevron, 295
Chicago Tribune, 131
Chicago Sun-Times, 339, 351
Child, 105
Children, 105
Children's Television Workshop (CTW), 225
Christian Broadcasting Network (CBN), 223–24, 303, 330
Christian History, The, 97
Christian Science Monitor, 129
Chusmir, Janet, 129
Cigar Institute of America, 278
CinemaScope, 160
Cinemax, 330
Cinerama, 160
Citizen Kane, 146, 157
City Streets, 156
Civilisation, 225
Civil War, 75, 97, 126–27, 134, 140, 150, 236

Clark, Dick, 241
Clash, The, 248
Cleland, Max, 312
Clemens, Samuel. See Twain, Mark
Cleveland Press, 130
Cline, Patsy, 257
Close Encounters of the Third Kind, 163
Coal Miner's Daughter, 257
Coasters, 241
Cobbett, William, 122
Coca, Imogene, 201
Coca-Cola, 37, 40, 273
Colbert, Claudette, 157
Cole, Nat "King," 218
Coleman, William, 122
Coles, Robert, 223
College Entertainment Guide, 93
College Woman, 93
Collier's, 98, 103
Collingwood, Charles, 211
colorization, 145–48
Color Purple, The, 168
Colt 45, 201
Columbia Broadcasting System (CBS), 23, 34, 181–83, 189, 200, 204, 206, 210–11, 265, 315, 329, 358, 368
Columbia Phonograph Record Company, 181, 234–36, 240
Columbia University, School of Journalism, 131
Comic Magazine Association of America, 81
Commission on Freedom of the Press, 51
communication
  channel in, 9
  channel noise in, 10–11
  channels of mass, 14–15
  defined, 7, 14
  feedback in, 10
  frame of reference in, 8–9
  group, 7
  interpersonal, 7
  intrapersonal, 7
  mass, 14–15, 20
  message in, 8

nonverbal, 9
psychological noise in, 11–13
receiver of, 10
semantic noise in, 11
source in, 8
symbols in, 8, 11
Communications Act of 1934, 181,
    363–65
Como, Perry, 240
compact disc, 341–42
Complete Woman, 107
computers, media uses of, 327–28,
    345
    book publishing, 336
    broadcasting, 336–37
    libraries, 336
    newspapers, 335
Comstock, Anthony, 77
cone effect, 356–57
Conrad, Frank, 180
Conrad, Paul, 12–13
CONUS Communication, 216
Cooke, Janet, 351
Coogan, Jackie, 152–53
Cool Hand Luke, 162
Coolidge, Calvin, 308, 363
Cooper, Gary, 156, 159
Cooper, James Fenimore, 74
Copley, Helen K., 129
corantos, 118
Cornish, Samuel, 134
Correll, Charles, 186
Cosby, Bill, 218, 275
Cosby, William, 120
Cosmopolitan, 98, 110, 130, 265
Courier, 123
Cowles, Gardner, 100
Craft, Christine, 215
Crawford, Joan, 156
Creel Committee, 290, 299
Creel, George, 290
Cronkite, Walter, 211
Crosby, Bing, 186, 189, 201
Crystals, 241
cults, 37–39
cultural consequences, 369–71
cultural niches, importance of, 30–31

culture
    changes in, 25–40, 100
    commercialization of, 35–37
    criticism of, 33–34
    current complaints about, 34
    definition of, 4, 6
    elite, 5, 20
    industries, 39–40
    mass, 20
    popular, 3, 4–7, 24, 28, 97–98, 116,
        123
    specialized, 7
Cuomo, Mario, 191
Current Affair, A, 209

Daily Courant, 118
Daley, John Charles, 211
Dallas, 36, 157, 187, 320, 360
Dalton, B., 67
Daly, John Charles, 211
Damone, Vic, 240
Dante, Joe, 146
Darin, Bobby, 241
Dave Clark Five, 243
Davis, Elmer, 290
Davis, Lloyd, 275
Day, Benjamin, 123–25
Day, Doris, 86, 240
Days of Our Lives, 35
Days of Wine and Roses, 201
Dean, James, 161
Deep Throat, 162
Deer Hunter, 220
Defenders, The, 203
Defoe, Daniel, 96
DeFoe, James R., 274
De Forest, Lee, 153, 179, 194
Dell, 89
demassification, 7
Denver, John, 254
deregulation, of broadcasting, 364–65
desktop publishing, 335
Detective Comics, 81
Devil in Miss Jones, The, 162
Devo, 248
Diamond Sutra, 70
Diary of Anne Frank, The, 86

Dichter, Ernest, 278
Dickens, Charles, 27, 74
Dickey, Jeffrey, 93
Dickinson, John, 121
Dickson, William Kennedy, 148, 152
Diddley, Bo, 241
Digital, 341–42, 345
Direct Broadcast Satellites (DBS), 334, 342, 345
direct mail, 318
Directors Guild of America, 145
Dire Straits, 341
Dirty Dozen, The, 162
Dirty Harry, 163
Disney Channel, 174, 330
Disney, Walt, 163
docudrama, 206–9, 357
Dole, Bob, 315
Domino, Fats, 241
Donahue, Phil, 205
Doors, 247
Dorm, 94
Dorsey, Tommy, 240
Dos Passos, John, 77
Doubleday, 87, 89
Douglass, Frederick, 134
Dow Chemical, 295
Downey, Morton, Jr., 209
Doyle Dane Bernbach, 310
Dragnet, 203
Dreiser, Theodore, 77
Duck Soup, 157
Duff, Howard, 212
Dukakis, Michael, 131, 315–16
DuMont (television network), 200
Du Pont, Pete, 315
Dürer, Albrecht, 25
Dutton, E. P., 74, 89
Dwyer, R. Budd, 349–50
Dylan, Bob, 241, 243
Dynasty, 157, 187, 206–7, 360, 371

East Village Other, 135
Eastwood, Clint, 163
Easy Rider, 162
Easyrider (magazine), 108
Earthquake, 163

Ebony, 100, 107
Eddy, Nelson, 186
Edison, Thomas A., 148–49, 152, 234–36, 258
Edwards, Douglas, 211
Edwards, Jonathan, 223
Eisenhower, Dwight D., 309
Electric Company, The, 223, 225
elite culture. *See* culture
Emerson, Ralph Waldo, 74
Emery, Edwin, 126, 273
Empire Strikes Back, The, 37, 163
Enquirer, 123
Enlightenment, Age of, 48
EPS cycle, 5–7, 20, 72–83, 134, 150, 161, 189, 225, 228
Espionage Act of 1917, 362
ESPN cable network, 226, 330
Essanay Co., 151
Essence, 107
E.T., 37, 151, 163
ethics, media
    advertiser influences on, 354–55, 371
    chain ownership conflicts and, 136, 356, 371
    conflicts of interest and, 352
    distortions of cultural reality and, 358–60, 371
    docudramas and, 357
    double standards and, 353–54
    gifts and, 351–52
    invasion of privacy and, 352–53
    sex and violence and, 360–61, 371
    social responsibility and, 354, 371
    withholding information and, 352
Everybody's, 98
Evry, Hal, 305–6, 318

Fabian, 241
Face the Nation, 364
Fairbanks, Douglas, 156
Fairness Doctrine, 364
Falcon Crest, 187, 206–7
Falwell, Jerry, 34, 87, 224
Fanning, Katharine, 129
Fanny Hill, 77

Farnsworth, Philo, 198
Farrow, Mia, 206
Father Knows Best, 203, 360
Fathers, 105
Federal Aviation Administration (FAA), 365
Federal Bureau of Alcohol, Tobacco and Firearms, 274, 365
Federal Communications Commission (FCC), 54, 61, 181, 188, 190, 198–200, 265, 276, 340, 363–65
Federal Trade Commission (FTC), 265, 365
Federalist Papers, 122
Federal Radio Commission (FRC), 181, 363
Federation of Women's Clubs, 238
feedback, 10
Fenno, John, 122
Ferraro, Geraldine, 321
Fessenden, Reginald A., 179
fiber optics, 327, 341, 345
Field & Stream, 106
Field, Sally, 350
Fields, W. C., 156
Fifth Estate, 49
First Amendment, 45, 49, 122, 353, 361, 364–66, 371
Flash Gordon, 157
Fleming, J. Ambrose, 179
Fly, The, 163
Flying, 106
Flynn, Errol, 87
Food and Drug Administration (FDA), 265, 365
Footlight Parade, 157
Ford, Gerald, 311
Ford Motor Company, 266
Formula, The, 37
Forsyte Saga, 204
Forty-second Street, 157
Foster, Lawrence G., 296
Fourth Estate, 49
Fox, Michael J., 61, 252
Fox Broadcasting Co., 209–10
Frank, Anne, 86, 88
Franklin, Ann Smith, 129

Franklin, Benjamin, 48, 73, 97, 119–22, 264
Franklin, James, 119
Freed, Alan, 240
Freedom's Journal, 134
Freneau, Philip, 122
Fresno Bee, 129
Friday the 13th, 163
Front, The, 159
Fuzz, 219

Gable, Clark, 36, 155–57
Gaines, William, 103
Gale Directory of Publications, 105
Gannett, 115, 136
Garland, Judy, 156
gatekeeping, 17–20
gazetta, 118
Gazette of the United States, 122
Geldof, Bob, 233
General Electric, 179–80, 193, 198, 352
General Magazine, 97, 119
Genius of Universal Emancipation, The, 97
Gentlemen's Magazine, 96
Gentlemen's Quarterly, 106
Gephardt, Dick, 315
Glamour, 106
glasnost, 51, 56
Gleason, Jackie, 200
Go Ask Alice, 86
Godey's Lady's Book, 98
Goebbels, Joseph, 269
Godfrey, Arthur, 201
God's Little Acre, 77
Gold Diggers of 1933, 157
Golden Girls, The, 320
Goldstein, Tom, 137, 354
Goldwater, Barry, 310
Gone With the Wind, 155, 157, 161
Goodbye, Columbus, 162
Good Housekeeping, 107, 110, 130
Goodman, Benny, 238
Gorbachev, Mikhail, 50
Gore, Al, 254, 315
Gore, Lesley, 241
Gore, Tipper, 253–54

Gosden, Freeman, 186
Graber, Doris, 19
Grace, W. R., 295
Graduate, The, 162
Graham, Billy, 223
Graham, Katherine, 87, 129
Grandparents, 105
Grant, Cary, 157
Great Awakening, 223
Great Depression, 30, 156, 182, 187, 194, 238, 257, 291, 299
Great Library in Alexandria, 70
Great Train Robbery, The, 149, 156, 168
Greeley, Horace, 54, 125–26
Greenfield, Patricia, 222, 275
Green Hornet, The, 81, 186
Grenada, 313
Griffith, D. W., 149–50, 152, 168, 186
Group W, 216
Guardian, 119
Guiding Light, The, 187
Gun & Ammo, 106
Gunsmoke, 201
Gutenberg, Johannes, 24, 46, 71, 89

Haberstroth, Jack, 274
Hadden, Britton, 100
Haig, Al, 315
Haley, Alex, 204
Haley, Bill, 240
Halloween, 163
Hamilton, Alexander, 122
Hamilton, Andrew, 120–21, 370
Hammer, Armand, 294
Happy Days, 204, 222
Harding, Warren G., 308
Hardy, Andy, 157
Hardy, Oliver, 151, 153, 168
Harley-Davidson, 39–40
Harlow, Jean, 156
Harper, James and John, 74
Harper & Row, 78, 89
Harper's, 61, 97, 265
Harper's Bazaar, 110, 130
Harper's Weekly, 98
Harris, Benjamin, 118, 121

Harrison, George, 242–43, 246
Hart, Gary, 132–33, 303, 315, 320–21
Harvard's *Lampoon*, 128
Harvard University, 150
Have Gun, Will Travel, 201
Hauptmann, Bruno, 367
Hawthorne, Nathaniel, 74
Hays Office, 155
Hays, Will H., 155
Hayworth, Rita, 156
Hearst, Patty, 80
Hearst, William Randolph, 31, 54, 127–31, 238
Hearst Corporation, 110, 138
Hearst newspapers, 159
Heatter, Gabriel, 182
Hefner, Hugh, 103
Hemingway, Ernest, 77, 87
Henderson, Fletcher, 238
Henry, Barbara, 129
Henry II (King of France), 26, 72
Henry VIII (King of England), 72
Hepburn, Katharine, 156–57
Herman's Hermits, 243
Hersh, Seymour, 132
Hershey Foods Co., 37, 266
Hertz, Heinrich, 178
High-Definition Television (HDTV), 343, 345
High Noon, 159
High Times, 108
Highway Patrol, 203
Hill, Edwin C., 182
Hill Street Blues, 206
Hispanic newspapers, 135
Hitler, Adolf, 182, 188, 269, 290
Holliday, Judy, 212
Hollywood, 148, 152, 154, 157, 159–60, 169
Hollywood 10, 158–59
Holt, Henry, 89
Home Box Office (HBO), 250, 329–30
Home Shopping Network (HSN), 226
home video equipment
    videocassette recorders, 337, 345
    video discs, 338
    video rentals, 337–38

Honeymooners, 200
Hooper, John, 265
Hoover, Herbert, 362
Hope, Bob, 186
Hopscotch, 37
Horne, Lena, 212
Hot Rod (magazine), 94
Howdy Doody, 201, 227, 359
Howell, Deborah, 129
How the West Was Won, 160
How to Stuff a Wild Bikini, 161
Houghton, Henry Oscar, 74
House Beautiful, 110
House Committee on Un-American
    Activities, 158
Humphrey, Hubert, 310
Hunt, Joe, 358
Hunter, Evan, 219
Hustler, 105
Hutchins, Robert Maynard, 51

iconoscope, 198
Identity, 107
I Dream of Jeannie, 203
I Led Three Lives, 159
I Love Lucy, 203
I Married a Communist, 159
In Cold Blood, 80
Independent Broadcasting Authority
    (IBA), 58, 61, 340
*Indiana Jones and the Temple of
    Doom*, 163
Industrial Revolution, 6, 27, 35, 39, 41,
    74–77, 109, 126
information-limitation theory, 219–20
information processing
  by consumer, 19–20
  by media, 15–20
In God's Name, 80
International News Service (INS), 129
International Typographical Union,
    335
interpretative reporting, 131–32
Intolerance, 150
invasion of privacy, 352–53, 368–69
inverted pyramid, 126
investigative reporting, 132–33

Iran–Contra hearings, 67, 214
Irving, Washington, 73
I Spy, 218
It Happened One Night, 156–57
It's a Wonderful Life, 157
Ives, Burl, 212
I Was a Communist for the FBI, 159
I Was a Teenage Frankenstein, 161
I Was a Teenage Werewolf, 161
Izvestia, 55

Jackson, Janet, 250
Jackson, Jesse, 302, 315
Jackson, Michael, 233, 250
James, Harry, 240
Jaws, 163
Jazz Singer, The, 153–54, 168
Jefferson Airplane, 247
Jefferson, Thomas, 49, 73, 121–23, 362,
    370
Jenkins, Francis, 148
Jennings, Peter, 211
Johnson, Don, 218, 252
Johnson & Johnson, 287, 296
Johnson, Lyndon B., 310, 313, 354
Johnson, Samuel, 96
Jolson, Al, 153, 168
Jones, Jim, 37
Journal of Commerce, 123
Joyce, James, 77
Joy Ride, 161
Jungle, The, 76
Juvenile Prison, 161

Kaltenborn, H. V., 182
KCSB-FM, 365
KDKA (radio), 180–81
Keaton, Buster, 151, 168
Kees, Beverly, 129
Kefauver Crime Committee, 81
Keillor, Garrison, 173–74, 176–77
Kemp, Jack, 315
Kennedy, John F., 87, 213–14, 241,
    309–10, 323
Kennedy, Robert F., 213
Keystone Film Co., 150–51
Key, Wilson Bryan, 274

Khrushchev, Nikita, 50
Kid, The, 152–53
kinetoscope, 148
King Features Syndicate, 129
King, Larry, 190
King, Martin Luther, Jr., 213
King, Stephen, 5
Kipling, Rudyard, 75
Klein, Calvin, 263, 272
Klopfer, Donald S., 77
KMBC-TV, 215
Knight-Ridder, 136, 339
Knots Landing, 187, 206–7
Koppel, Ted, 211
KPFK-FM, 365
Kress, Harold, 160
Ku Klux Klan, 12, 150

Ladies Home Journal, 98, 265
L.A. Law, 206, 218
Laine, Frankie, 240
Laugh-In, 203
Laurel, Stan, 151, 168
Laurie, Piper, 201
Lazarsfeld, Paul F., 99, 304
League of Women Voters, 364
Lear, Norman, 12, 203
Leave It to Beaver, 203, 360
Led Zeppelin, 253
Lee, Ivy Ledbetter, 296, 299
Lee, Richard Henry, 121
Legion of Decency, 155
Lennon, John, 242–43
Lennon, Julian, 243
Lesly, Philip, 288
Letterman, David, 203
Lewin, Kurt, 17
Lewis, Sinclair, 77
libel, 137, 367–68
Liberty Foundation, 34, 224. *See also*
    Moral Majority
Life (magazine), 100, 104
Lincoln, Abraham, 75
Lindbergh, Charles, 367
Lineup, The, 203
Linkletter, Art, 201
Little Caesar, 156

Little, Charles, 74
Little Richard, 241
Live Aid, 15, 233
Lloyd, Harold, 151, 168
Locke, John, 48
Lombard, Carole, 156–57
London Gazette, 118–19
London Plan, 123
Lone Ranger, The, 81, 186
Look (magazine), 100, 103
Los Angeles Free Press, 135
Los Angeles Times, 355
Lorimar, 221
Lowenstein, Ralph, 5, 94
Low-Power Television (LPTV), 343,
    345
Lucas, George, 163
Luce, Henry B., 100
Lumière, Auguste and Louis, 148
Luther, Martin, 26, 46, 71–72
Lux Radio Theater, 187
Lynn, Loretta, 257

Make Room for Daddy, 203
Martin, Dick, 203
Marvelettes, 241
Mason, Perry, 203
Masterpiece Theater, 225
McAuliffe, Christa, 223, 352
McCall's, 98, 107
McCarthy, Charlie, 186–87, 189, 201
McCarthy, Joseph, 211–12
McCarthyism, 159, 211–12, 218
McCartney, Paul, 242–43, 246
McClure, Robert, 319
McClure, Samuel S., 98, 126
McClure's, 98, 126
McCombs, Maxwell, 16, 306
MacDonald, Dwight, 34
McDonald's, 5, 40
McDowell, Jack, 305
McGee, Fibber and Molly, 186
McGinniss, Joe, 306, 310–11
McGovern, George, 311, 319
McKenna, George, 318
McLuhan, Marshall, 12, 26
MacWorld, 105

Mad (magazine), 103
Madonna, 250, 256
Madison, James, 49, 123, 370
magazines
  breakouts, demographic and
    regional, 103
  early American, 97
  early British, 96
  entering popular culture, 97–99
  muckrakers, 98–99
  specialization of, 109–10
  types of, 105–9
Mailer, Norman, 134
Maisel, Richard, 109
Man from U.N.C.L.E., The, 203
Marconi, Guglielmo, 178–80, 194
Marx Brothers, 156–57
Massachusetts Spy, 121
mass communication
  channels of, 14–15
  defined, 14
mass media, early forms
  chapbooks as, 27
  pictorial prints as, 25
  See also individual media
mass movement, first, 26–27, 71–72
Maxwell, James Clerk, 178
Mediamark Research, Inc., 282
Meese, Edwin, 85, 360
Meet the Press, 322, 363–64
Mein Kampf, 269
Méliès, Georges, 149
Melville, Herman, 74
Mercury Theater on the Air, 187
Mergenthaler, Ottmar, 74
Merrill, John, 5, 94
Metalious, Grace, 205
Metro-Goldwyn-Mayer (MGM), 145–
  46, 155, 159–60
metropolitan newspapers, 28, 123
Miami Herald, 129
Miami Vice, 206, 218, 251–52
Michael, George, 250
Middle Ages, 70–71
Midnight Cowboy, 162
Mifflin, George Harrison, 74
Mill, John Stuart, 49

Miller v. California, 84
Milton, John, 48, 370
Minnesota Public Radio, 173, 193
Missing, 37
Mission: Impossible, 203
Mitchell, Arnold, 279
Mitchell, Gwen Davis, 87
Mobil Oil Co., 292, 295–96, 353
Moby-Dick, 74
Modern Bride, 107
Mondale, Walter, 313, 321–22
Monogram (motion-picture studio), 160
Monroe, Marilyn, 103
Monroe, Vaughn, 240
Moonlighting, 218
Moral Majority, 34. *See also* Liberty
  Foundation
Morse, Samuel F., 126, 174, 194
Mothers Against Drunk Drivers
  (MADD), 276
Motion Picture Producers and
  Distributors of America
  (MPPDA), 155
motion pictures
  anti-trust and, 159
  big studio era of, 155–57
  business of, 164–67
  censorship of, 155, 163
  colorization of, 145–48
  comedy, rise of, 150–51
  cultural changes in, 154–55
  disaster films, 162–63
  early history of, 148–55
  genres of, 156–57
  Red scare and, 158–59
  sex and violence in, 162–63
  sound in, 152–54
  special effects in, 160, 163
  television's impact on, 159–60
  videocassettes, 168
  youth films, 161–62
Motor, 110
Motor Boating, 110
Mouseketeer, 151
Movie Channel, 330
Moving Up, 93
Mr. Deeds Goes to Town, 157

Mr. Smith Goes to Washington, 157
Ms., 104
muckrakers, 98
Muhammad Speaks, 135
Multichannel, Multipoint Distribution
    Service (MMDS), 342, 345
Munsey, Frank, 98
Munsey's Magazine, 98
Munsters, The, 203
Murdoch, Rupert, 56–57, 78, 89, 101,
    209, 356
Murrow, Edward R., 182–85, 211
Music Television (MTV), 192, 218,
    250–52, 330
My Lai massacre, 132
My Three Sons, 203

Naisbitt, John, 344
Napolitan, Joe, 305
Nation, 98
National Association for the
    Advancement of Colored People
    (NAACP), 150
National Association of Broadcasters,
    276
National Broadcasting Co. (NBC), 23,
    35, 179–81, 189, 198–201, 209–11,
    216, 218, 265, 275, 329, 340, 352,
    358, 367
National Council of Churches, 224
National Education Association (NEA),
    238
National Enquirer, 131–33, 367–68
National Football League (NFL), 31,
    226
National Gazette, 122
National Geographic, 282
National Institute of Alcohol Abuse
    and Alcoholism, 276
National Intelligencer, 122
National Public Radio, 173–74, 193–94
National Religious Broadcasters, 224
National Science Foundation, 344
Nelson, Ricky, 241
Nelson, Willie, 241
New American Library, 89
New England Courant, 119

new morality, age of, 154
Newhouse, Samuel I., 77–78, 136
Newspaper Enterprise Association
    (NEA), 130
newspapers
    advocacy in, 133–34
    Alien and Sedition Acts and, 122–23,
        361–62
    and the American Revolution, 121–
        22
    basic functions of, 138–39
    biases in, 138–40
    business of, 135–37
    chain ownership of, 136, 356, 371
    colonial American press, 118–23, 140
    early origins of, 116–18
    interpretative reporting in, 131–32
    investigative reporting in, 132–33
    jazz journalism and, 131
    libel suits and, 137
    limited specialization of, 134–35
    in the new Republic, 122
    objectivity of, 130
    in penny-press era, 123–26
    social responsibility and, 130–31, 140
    soft news in, 136
    struggle against authority of, 120
    syndicates, 129–30
    in twentieth century, 130–35, 140
    watchdog function of, 139
    wire services and, 137–38, 140
    in yellow journalism era, 126–30, 140
Newsweek, 93, 100
Newton, Isaac, 48
Newton, Wayne, 367
New Woman, 107
New York American, 238
New York Daily News, 131
New York Post, 122, 129, 356
New York Gazette, 120
New York Herald, 125
New York Journal, 31, 54, 128–29
New York Sun, 28, 123–25
New York Times, 126, 130, 282, 312–
    13
New York Times v. Sullivan, 368
New York Tribune, 125

New York Weekly Journal, 120, 129
New York Woman, 107
New York World, 31, 54, 127–29
nickelodeons, 149
Nielsen, A. C., Co., 216–17, 332
Nightline, 224, 364
Nixon, Richard M., 309–11, 313, 319, 323, 362
North American Review, 97
North, Oliver, 13, 214
North Star, 134
novel, 27
Nutcracker: Money, Madness, Murder, 358
Nuthead, Dinah, 129

Ochs, Adolph, 130
O'Connor, Carroll, 203
Office of War Information, 290
Okeh (record label), 237
Oliver!, 163
Olympic games, 197–98, 294
O'Neal, Ryan, 206
Ono, Yoko, 243
opinion leader, 304
Orwell, George, 328, 331
Osbourne, Ozzy, 233, 253
Österreichischer Rundfunk (ORF), 59–60
Oswald, Lee Harvey, 213
Outcault, Richard, 128–29
Oxford Gazette, 118

Packard, Vance, 273, 277
Pacifica Foundation, 365
Paine, Thomas, 73, 121
Paley, William S., 181
Palmer, Volney, 265
Panax Corp., 356
Paramount, 155, 159
Parenting, 105
Parents' Music Resource Center (PMRC), 253–55, 369
Parton, Dolly, 241
Patterson, Joseph Medill, 131
Patterson, Thomas, 319
Pavarotti, Luciano, 257

payola scandal, 189–90
PC Magazine, 105
PC World, 105
Pearl Harbor, 183
Pearl, Les, 279
Pennsylvania Gazette, 119, 264
Pennsylvania Packet and General Advertiser, 264
penny press, 123–25
Pentagon Papers, 362
Penthouse, 34, 105, 250, 360
People (magazine), 104
people meters, 332
People's Republic of China, 48
Perry, Richard, 247
Personal Computing, 94
Peterson, Theodore B., 46
Peyton Place, 205–6
Phillip, David Graham, 98
Phillips, Sam, 240
Phoenix (Boston), 135
Piaget, Jean, 12
Pickford, Mary, 61, 156
pictorial prints, 25
Pilgrim's Progress, 98
Plato, 234
Platters, 241
Playboy, 34, 103, 105, 250, 360
Playboy Channel, 330
Playgirl, 105
Playhouse 90, 218
Plummer, Joseph, 282
Poe, Edgar Allan, 73–74
Police Woman, 218
political advertising
    direct mail, 318
    television, 318–19
    vote videos, 303–4, 317
political coverage, media
    character analysis in, 320
    horse-race effect in, 321
    projecting winners, 321–22
Poltergeist, 163
Poltergeist II, 163
Pompeii, 264
Poor Richard's Almanac, 73, 119
Pope v. Illinois, 84

popular culture. *See* culture
Porcupine's Gazette, 122
Porter, Cole, 238
Porter, Edwin S., 149, 168
Poseidon Adventure, The, 163
Powell, Jody, 312
Prairie Home Companion, A, 173–74,
　176–77
Pravda, 55
Presley, Elvis, 37, 240
Press-Enterprise v. *Superior Court of*
　California for Riverside County,
　366
press, in foreign lands
　Austria, 58–60, 64
　Canada, 60–61, 64
　Mexico, 61–62, 64
　Soviet Union, 45, 50–51, 55–56, 64
　Third World, 62–64
　United Kingdom, 56–58, 64
press theories, 46–54
　authoritarian, 46–48, 63
　libertarian, 46, 48–50, 63, 139
　social responsibility, 46, 51–54, 64,
　　130, 354
　Soviet Communist, 46, 50–51, 63
Price, Raymond K., 310
Prince, 253, 256
Prinsky, Lorraine, 255
prior restraint, 47
Procter & Gamble, 265
Production Code Administration, 155,
　162
Progressive, The, 362
psychological noise, 11–13
PTL ministry, 223–24
Ptolemy, 146
Public Broadcasting Service (PBS), 193,
　225
Public Broadcasting Act of 1967, 193
Public Enemy, The, 156
Publick Occurrences, 118
public relations
　activities of, 292–96
　behavior modification in, 294
　combined marketing and, 294
　controversies in, 296–98

　corporate, 289–90
　defined, 288–89
　examples of, 293–96
　flacks in, 297
　government, 290
　history of, 289–92
　issues and crisis management in, 295
Public Relations Society of America
　(PRSA), 296, 298
Publish, 105
Publishers Weekly, 89
Pulitzer, Joseph, 31, 54, 127–28, 131
Pulitzer Prize, 351
punk rock, 247–48
Pure Food and Drug Act, 99
Putnam, George Palmer, 74

Qube, 330–31

Racing Forum, 101
Racket Squad, 203
Radecki, Thomas, 220
radio
　beginning of networks, 181
　CBS raid on, 189
　development of, 174–79
　early commercial, 180–81
　as electronic vaudeville, 185
　entertainment, 184–88
　FM, 192–93
　government regulation of, 181
　meeting cultural needs, 182
　news, 181–84
　newspaper opposition to, 182
　payola scandal of, 189
　public, 173–74, 193
　sitcoms, 185–87
　soap operas, 187
　specialization of, 188–93
　World War II and, 182–85
Radio Act of 1927, 181, 363, 365
Radio Advertising Bureau, 174
Radio Corporation of America (RCA),
　77, 179–81, 193, 201, 329, 338, 340
Rafshoon, Gerald, 305, 311
Raiders of the Lost Ark, 163

Rambler, 96
Rand Corporation, 362
Ranalli, Douglas, 94
Random House, 37, 60, 67, 77, 83, 288
Ranney, Austin, 319
Rather, Dan, 315
Raymond, Henry J., 54, 126
Reader's Digest, 94, 100–1, 282
Reagan, Ronald, 17, 45, 182, 214, 303,
    305, 312–14, 321–23, 364–65
Rebel Without a Cause, 161
receiver, 10
recordings
    backmasking on, 253
    Beatles and, 37, 151, 242–46, 253,
        258
    black music, 236–38
    British invasion, second wave, 243–
        47
    classical music, 257
    controversies about, 252–55
    country-and-western, 257
    covering, 238
    cultural changes and, 241–42
    development of popular music, 234–
        36
    disco, 247
    editorial statements on, 252
    explicit lyrics in, 253
    heavy metal, 253
    impact on other media, 251–52
    jazz, 237–38
    jukeboxes and, 238–40
    music videos and, 250–52
    new wave, 248–50
    punk rock, 247–48
    radio and sales of, 240
    rhythm-and-blues, 240
    rock-'n'-roll, 240–55, 257
    second generation rockers, 250
    sheet music, 234
    subliminal messages on, 252–53
    as talking machine, 234
    white swing, 238
Red Channels, 212
Red Lion Broadcasting Co., 364
Red Menace, The, 159

Red scare, 158–59
Reebok, 263
Reeves, Rosser, 309
Reformation, Protestant, 26–27, 46, 48,
    71–72, 90
regulation, media
    consumer boycotts as, 367–69
    of broadcasting, 362–65
    by courts, 365–67
    of print, 361–62
Reid, Wallace, 154
Renaissance, 71
Republic (motion-picture studio), 160
Republican National Committee, 155
Requiem for a Heavyweight, 201–2
Return of the Jedi, 37, 163
Reuters, 140
Review, 96
Reynolds, Burt, 219
Reynolds, Frank, 211
Rice, Donna, 320–21
Rich Man, Poor Man, 204
Rifleman, The, 201
Risky Business, 35
Rivera, Geraldo, 205, 209
Riverside Press-Enterprise, 366
RKO, 145–46, 156, 159
Robe, The, 160
Roberts, Bill, 305
Roberts, Oral, 223–24
Robertson, Cliff, 201
Robertson, Pat, 224, 303, 315, 321
Robinson, Edward G., 156, 212
Rochester [N.Y.] *Democrat &
    Chronicle*, 129
Rock Around the Clock, 161, 240
Rockefeller, John D., 98
Rockwell, Norman, 34
Rocky III, 37
Rogers, Ginger, 156
Rogers, Kenny, 241
Rogers, Roy, 81
Rolling Stone, 134–35
Rolling Stones, 241, 243, 247–48, 258
Romance of Helen Trent, The, 187
Romanticism, 33
Ronettes, 241

Roosevelt, Franklin D., 157, 182–83, 270, 304, 309, 312, 363
Roosevelt, Theodore, 98–99
Roots, 204
Rose Bowl, 31
Rosenbaum, Jill, 255
Ross, Diana, 247–48
Roth v. *United States*, 84
Rowan, Dan, 203
Rowe, Sandra Mims, 129
Run-D.M.C., 250
Runner's World, 106
Russwurm, John B., 134
Rydell, Bobby, 241

San Francisco Examiner, 128
Sarnoff, David, 179–80
Sassy, 107
SATCOM I, 329
satellite communication
   in future, 334, 345
   newspaper uses of, 9, 333
   operation of, 327, 331
   other uses of, 333–34
   radio uses of, 333
   TV uses of, 216, 226, 266, 331
Saturday Evening Post, 97–98
Saturday Night Fever, 247
Saturday Night Live, 203
Scarface, 156
Scarlet Letter, The, 74
Schieffer, Bob, 312
Schmalensee, Richard, 266
Schmertz, Herb, 292, 295–96, 353
Schramm, Wilbur, 46, 48
Schudson, Michael, 28, 266–68
Scribner, Charles, 74
Scripps, Edward W., 127, 130, 138
Section 315 (FCC), 363
Sedgwick, Catherine, 74
Sedition Act of 1918, 362
Seed (Chicago), 135
See It Now, 212
selective perception, 12, 268
Select-TV, 330
Self, 107
Selling of the President, The, 311

semantic noise, 11
Sennett, Mack, 150–51, 168
Serling, Rod, 201
Servan-Schreiber, Jean-Louis, 109
Sesame Street, 223, 225
Sevareid, Eric, 211
Seventeen, 101, 107
Seventeenth Amendment, 128
Sex Pistols, 248
Shadow, The, 81, 186
Shangri-Las, 241
Shape, 107
Sharon, Ariel, 368
Shaw, Donald, 16, 306
Shaw, Irwin, 204
Sheppard, Sam, 366
Shirelles, 241
Shirer, William L., 182–83, 211–12
shock radio, 365
Shore, Dinah, 240
Showtime, 330
Siebert, Fred, 46
Sigourney, Lydia, 74
Silent Network, 330
Silverman, Fred, 205
Simmons Market Research Bureau, 282
Simon and Garfunkel, 247
Simon, Paul, 305, 315
Simon & Schuster, 83
Sinatra, Frank, 87, 240
Sinclair, Upton, 76–77, 98
$64,000 Question, 201
Skelton, Red, 201
Skiing, 106
Slaughterhouse Five, 86, 88
Smith, Adam, 48
Smith, Howard K., 211–12
Smith, Samuel Harrison, 122
Smolla, Rodney, 87
Smothers Brothers, 203
Snider, Dee, 254
sob sisters, 130
Society of Professional Journalists, 351
soft news, 136
Sound of Music, The, 163
source, 8
South Africa, 47–48

Soviet Union, 45, 50–51, 55–56
Spanish-American War, 128
Spanish International Network (SIN),330
specialization, stages of, 78–83, 107–10,
    161–63, 188–93
Spectator, 119
Spencer, Stu, 305
Spielberg, Steven, 37, 163, 168
Sports Afield, 110
Sports Illustrated, 106
Springsteen, Bruce, 250, 341
Squier, Bob, 305
SRI-International, 279
Stalin, Joseph, 50
Stamp Act, 121
Standard Periodical Directory, 108–9
Stanford, Leland, 128
Starr, Ringo, 242–43, 246
Star Trek, 80
Star Wars, 37, 151
Steele, Richard, 96
St. Elsewhere, 206
Steffens, Lincoln, 98
St. Louis Post-Dispatch, 127
St. Paul Pioneer Press Dispatch, 129
Stephens, Ann S., 74
Stern, Howard, 365
Stevenson, Adlai, 309
Stewart, Jimmy, 156–57
Stewart, Potter, 87
Stowe, Harriet Beecher, 75, 97
Students Against Drunk Drivers
    (SADD), 276
Sullivan, Ed, 200, 227
Sumerian clay tablets, 70
Summer, Donna, 247
Sunset (magazine), 282
Super Bowl, 3, 33, 275
Surfer, 94
Swayze, John Cameron, 211
Sweet Dreams, 257

Taft, William Howard, 179
Talese, Gay, 134
Tan, 107
Tarbell, Ida, 98
TASS, 55, 63, 140

Tatler, 96
Taylor, William Desmond, 154
Tebbel, John, 87
technologies, mass media, 327–45
telegraph, development of, 126, 174
telephone, development of, 174–78
Teleprompter, 312
teleshopping, 226–27
teletext, 339–41, 345
televangelism, 223–25
television
    cable, 225–26, 266
    children's, 220–23
    Couch Potatoes and, 219
    Communist scare and, 211–12
    cultural impacts of, 216–25
    daytime, 204–5
    docudramas on, 208–9
    early history of, 198–200
    entering popular culture, 200–3
    FCC freeze on, 200
    hybrid, 208
    Iran-Contra hearings on, 17, 214
    Kennedy assassination and, 213
    live drama on, 201
    mini-series on, 204
    news, 210–16
    prime-time, 205–7
    public, 225
    quiz-show scandal on, 201
    religious, 223–25
    satellite, 216, 225–26, 266
    sexism, in news, 215
    sitcoms, 203–4, 227
    soap operas, 187
    space-flight coverage on, 214
    sports on, 204
    tabloid, 209
    technical limitations of, 211
    teleshopping on, 226–27
    urban Westerns, 202–3
    variety shows, 203
    Vietnam war and, 203, 213, 241
    violence on, 219–20
    Watergate and, 132–33, 139, 214,
        311, 353
    Westerns, 201–3

Temple, Shirley, 156
Ten Commandments, The, 160
Texas Chain Saw Massacres, 163
Thin Man, The, 157
Third World, 62–63
Thirty Seconds over Tokyo, 157
thirtysomething, 198
Thomas, Isaiah, 77, 121
Thomas, Lowell, 182, 210
Thomas, Marlo, 217
Thompson, Hunter S., 134
Thompson, J. Walter, 265
Thoreau, Henry David, 74, 83
Three Dimension (3-D) movies, 160
Three Men and a Baby, 37
Three's Company, 204
Time Books, 67
Time (magazine), 45, 94, 100, 250, 368
Times-Mirror, 136, 339
Titanic disaster, 179
Toffler, Alvin, 7, 327, 344
Top Gun, 251
Torme, Mel, 240
Tower Commission, 67
Towering Inferno, The, 163
Town and Country, 110
Townshend Acts, 121
Tracy, Spencer, 156
Tramp, The, 151
Traub, James, 334
Travolta, John, 257
Trekkies, 37, 80
Triangle Publications, 100–1
Trinity Broadcasting Network (TBN),
    223
Trip to the Moon, 149
True Stories, 251
Turner, Ted, 145–46, 216, 340
TV-Cable Week, 104–5
TV Guide, 100–1, 105
TWA hijacking, 139
Twain, Mark, 75
Twentieth Century, 157
20th Century-Fox, 155, 159
Two of a Kind: The Hillside
    Stranglers, 87

Ulysses, 77
Uncle Tom's Cabin, 75, 97
United Artists, 164
United Fruit Company, 180
United Kingdom, 56–58
United Press International (UPI), 55,
    63, 136, 138, 140
UNESCO, 63
United States Football League (USFL),
    33
Urban Cowboy, 36, 257
USA Today, 9, 115–16, 215, 353
Unsolved Mysteries, 209
Upstairs Downstairs, 204, 225
U.S. Commission on Obscenity and
    Pornography, 360
U.S. Constitution, 122
U.S. Criminal Code, 363
U.S. Information Agency, 290
U.S. News & World Report, 100
U.S. Postal Service, 365
U.S. Supreme Court, 84–87, 89, 159,
    168, 362, 365–68
U.S. v. Paramount Pictures, 159
U2, 249–50

Van Gogh, Vincent, 34
Variety, 154
Vasquez Rana, Mario, 138
vaudeville, 28–30, 149, 185–86
vertical blanking interval (VBI),
    340
Vicary, James, 273–74
Victor Talking Machine Co.,
    236
videocassette recorder (VCR), 168,
    276, 303
videotext, 339, 345
Vietnam, 162, 213, 241
Village People, 247
Village Voice, 12, 135
Virginian-Pilot/Ledger-Star, 129
Virginian, The, 201
Vogue, 106
von Bülow, Claus, 87
vote videos, 303, 317

Walden, 83
Wallace, DeWitt and Lila, 100
Wall Street Journal, 115, 131, 296–97
Warner-Amex, 330–31
Warner Brothers, 154–55, 159, 168
War of the Worlds, 187
Washington, George, 45, 307
Washington Post, 80, 351, 362
WASP (heavy-metal group), 254
Watergate, 80, 132–33, 139, 214, 311, 353
Wayne, John, 156
WDY, 180
WEAF, 180, 265
We Are the World, 233
Webster, Noah, 122
Weiner, Sandy, 305
Weisman, Steven R., 313
Welch, Raquel, 219
Welles, Orson, 157, 187–88, 212
Wells, H. G., 77, 187
West, Mae, 156
Western Electric, 180, 341
Westheimer, Ruth, 190, 192
Westinghouse, 180, 193, 198
Westminster Abbey, 23–24
Westmoreland, William, 368
WGY, 180
Wheatley, William, 216
Whetmore, Edward Jay, 356–57
Whitaker, Clem, 305
White, Paul, 182
Whole Booke of Psalmes. See Bay Psalm Book
Wide World of Sports, 204, 211
Wild Bunch, The, 163
Wilder, Billy, 146
Wild One, The, 39
Wiley, John, 74
Williams, Wayne, 357

Willis, Bruce, 252
Willkie, Wendell, 304, 309, 312
Wilson, James, 73
Wilson, James R., 206–7
Wilson, Woodrow, 99, 149, 179, 290
Winfrey, Oprah, 205
Wirth, Louis, 28
Wizard of Oz, The, 161
Wonder, Stevie, 247
Wonder Years, The, 198
Woman, 107
Woman's Day, 107
Woman's Home Companion, 98
Woodward, Bob, 80
Woodward, Dick, 305
Wordsworth, William, 74
World War I, 99, 111, 152–53, 290, 299, 362
World War II, 78, 111, 157–58, 182–85, 290–91, 299
World Series, 31, 198
Writer's Digest, 103
WTBS, 145
Wyatt Earp, 201
Wylie, Frank, 292
WYSP-FM, 365

Yallop, David A., 80
yellow journalism, 128–29
Yellow Kid, 128–29
Yes Minister, 225
You Can't Take It With You, 157
Young Doctor Kildare, 157
Young and Rubicam, 282

Zappa, Frank, 254
Zenger, John Peter, 120–21, 129, 370
Zeta, 61
Zwingli, Huldreich, 72
Zworykin, Vladimir, 198

EVALUATION OPINIONAIRE

We invite your feedback on this book through this incomplete sentence evaluation. Write down your first thought in the space following the stimulus phrase. Please respond with a complete thought. Your comments will be used to improve this book in future editions. Thank you. Please fold this sheet so the Random House address on the back is visible, tape it, and mail.

1. What I liked about this textbook _____

_____

2. What I disliked _____

_____

3. The clarity of writing _____

_____

4. Compared with other textbooks _____

_____

5. The book spent too much time on _____

_____

6. The book didn't spend enough time on _____

_____

7. The pictures, graphs and charts I liked best _____

_____

8. The pictures, graphs and charts I liked least _____

_____

9. What I will remember most about this textbook _____

_____

10. Other comments: _____

_____

BUSINESS REPLY MAIL

First Class   Permit No. 7775   New York, N.Y.

Postage will be paid by addressee

Peter Labella
% The College Department
Random House, Inc.
201 East 50th Street
New York, NY 10022